Ladies
of the South

Ladies of the South

Recollections of the American Civil War by Two Ladies of the Confederacy

Life in Dixie During the War
1861-1865
Mary A. H. Gay

A Virginia Girl in the Civil War
Myrta Lockett Avary

Ladies of the South
Recollections of the American Civil War by Two Ladies of the Confederacy
Life in Dixie During the War 1861-1865
by Mary A. H. Gay
and
A Virginia Girl in the Civil War
by Myrta Lockett Avary

First published under the titles
Life in Dixie During the War 1861-1862-1863-1864-1865.
and
A Virginia Girl in the Civil War

FIRST EDITION

Leonaur is an imprint
of Oakpast Ltd

Copyright in this form © 2013 Oakpast Ltd

ISBN: 978-1-78282-126-7 (hardcover)
ISBN: 978-1-78282-127-4 (softcover)

http://www.leonaur.com

Publisher's Notes
The views expressed in this book are not necessarily those of the publisher.

Contents

Life in Dixie During the War 1861–1865   7
A Virginia Girl in the Civil War   271

Life in Dixie During the War
1861–1865.

Contents

Introduction	11
Preface	13
Introductory Remarks	15
The Magnolia Cadets	21
The War Record of Dekalb County	26
Labours of Love	36
Labours of Love Continued	40
The Third Maryland Artillery	45
A Daring and Unique Chase	49
Coming Home from Camp Chase	53
Some Social Features	63
Thomie's Second Home Coming	67
A Visit to Dalton	79
A Perilous Trust	86
A Scene in an Atlanta Confederate Hospital	89
Concealing Confederate Clothing	93
The Advance Guard of the Yankee Army	100
The Battle of the 22nd of July, 1864	107
Everett's Desertion	114

A Visit to Confederate Lines	120
The Ten Days' Armistice	127
The Return Home	142
On the Verge of Starvation	151
A Second Trip For Supplies	163
News From the Absent Brother	174
An Incident of the War	180
Picking Up Minie Balls Around Atlanta	183
The Decatur Women's Struggle For Bread	186
My Mother's Death	195
A Reminiscence	199
How The Decatur Women Kept Up the Sabbath School	204
Postal Affairs	210
The Tragic Death of Sallie Durham	213
The Death of Melville Clark	218
The Morton Family	220
Hon. Joseph E. Brown's Pikes and Guns	224
The Pursuit and Capture of the Andrews Raiders	228
Appendix	246
Sherman's March to the Sea	254

Introduction

I am asked to write a few words of introduction to these reminiscences of a lady who, in the pleasant afternoon of a life devoted to deeds of mercy and charity, turns fondly and sympathetically to the past. But there is nothing to be said. What word of mine could add to the interest that inheres in this unpretentious record of a troubled and bloody period? The chronicle speaks for itself, especially to those who remember something of those wonderful days of war. It has the charm and the distinction of absolute verity, a quality for which we may look in vain in more elaborate and ambitious publications. Here indeed, is one of the sources from which history must get its supplies, and it is informed with a simplicity which history can never hope to attain.

We have here reproduced in these records, with a faithfulness that is amazing, the spirit of those dark days that are no more. Tragedy shakes hands with what seems to be trivial, and the commonplaces of every-day life seem to move forward with the gray battalions that went forth to war.

It is a gentle, a faithful and a tender hand that guides the pen—a soul nerved to sacrifice that tells the tale. For the rest, let the records speak for themselves.

Joel Chandler Harris.

Preface

By way of preface to *Life in Dixie During the War*, I scarcely know what to say. I have long felt that it was the duty of the South to bequeath to posterity the traditions of that period; for if we do it not ourselves they will be swallowed up in oblivion. Entertaining this opinion, I have essayed the task of an individual effort, and hope that others may follow my example.

No woman who has seen what I have seen, and felt what I have felt, would be apt to write with less asperity; and yet, now that we have come back to the United States, and mean to stay in it, let the provocation to depart be what it may, I would not put into practice an iota of the war-time feeling. In thus expressing myself, I am sure I represent every Christian in my own beautiful Southland.

There was one for whom these sketches would have had a special interest. An inspiring motive for writing them was that they would be read by my nephew, Thomas H. Stokes, of Atlanta, the only child of the brother so often mentioned. But, ere he had had more than a glimpse of them, he was called away by an Inscrutable Providence, in his pure and beautiful young manhood, as we trust to a Land of Peace more in keeping with his noble, true, and tender heart, than earth with its sin and strife. "Blessed are the pure in heart; for they shall see God."

Mary A. H. Gay.

Decatur, Georgia.

Introductory Remarks

The Tocsin of War.

The tocsin of war has resounded from Mason and Dixon's line to the Gulf of Mexico, from the snow-crested billows of the Atlantic to the tranquil waves of the Pacific.

War! War! War! is the battle cry of a people, who, long suffering and patient, but now, goaded to desperation and thoroughly exasperated, are determined, at all hazards, to protect the rights for which their forefathers fought, bled and died; and which their own Thomas Jefferson embodied in an instrument of writing which, for beauty of diction and wisdom of thought, will go sounding down the corridors of time, so long as time itself shall last—unequalled, unparalleled; and which was adopted without a dissenting voice by the ablest convocation of men ever assembled in national councils as their declaration of human rights and liberties.

Thus, under auspices favourable to the happy and speedy development of a new and glorious country, commenced the government of the freest and happiest people on earth, under the administration of George Washington—an administration which caught the eye of the world and called forth its admiration; and which the most censorious never had the temerity to attack; an administration which secured for the country the alluring title, "The land of the free and the home of the brave." And its fame went abroad in story and in song, and every nation on earth sought its blessings and advantages, and it grew to be a mighty country.

Coeval with the settlement of this beautiful continent by the white man, there came, or rather, there was brought, a race of people which needed the fostering care as well as the strong arm of slavery to kindle the latent spark of intellectual fire which had smouldered for centuries, in, as President Cleveland would say, "innocuous desuetude."

This race of people came not as pioneers in the building up of this great nation, but as a menial race, sold into bondage by their own kith and kin, and not to be endowed with elective franchise nor representation in its councils. It was held in bondage alike in Massachusetts and in South Carolina. Under the auspices of slavery, it became a powerful factor in the building up of the staple industries of the country—the Southern portion of it directly, the Northern portion indirectly, and it received in return more than any other people in bondage has ever received—as a usual thing, good wholesome food, comfortable homes and raiment, and tender treatment in sickness. When they failed to receive these benefits, their masters were improvident and careless alike of the comfort of their own wives and children, and they, too, showed hard usage and neglect. This is not said by way of apology for any treatment received at the hands of Southern slaveholders by this vassal race. I repeat that no people held in bondage ever received so many benefits.

Slavery, as all other institutions, had its evils, and those evils were far greater to the slaveholder than to the slaves. Climatic and other considerations rendered the system of slavery unprofitable in the Northern States of this great and growing republic, and the men at the helm of their respective governments agitated the subject of emancipation.

Having given themselves time to bring the greater number of their slaves South and sell them, they nominally freed the others by legislative enactment; and by this great and magnanimous action, there were so few left that to this day, as attested by Northern tourists, a "darkey," or a "coloured person," is an object of curiosity and great interest.

The country, North and South, was too prosperous. The agitators could stand it no longer. Discord and strife took the place of harmony and peace in the halls of congress, and in the senate chamber of the United States. Men who could in no other way acquire prominence, became conspicuous as champions of an "oppressed and down trodden race," and were swift to slander the white people of the South. Our slaves were taught that murder, rapine, arson, and every species of wickedness known in the catalogue of crime which, in any way, could weaken, yea, destroy the South, was service most acceptable.

The country was in the clutches of an organized mob, determined to precipitate it into the jaws of dissolution. By way of confirming this statement the following resolutions are reproduced.

These resolutions were adopted by a large and representative body of men at Worcester, Massachusetts, soon after Fremont's defeat in

1856, and long before Governor Gist of South Carolina, and other Southern leaders, began to take measures for a peaceable separation, rather than to be forcibly expelled:

> *Resolved,* That the meeting of a state disunion convention, attended by men of various parties and affinities, gives occasion for a new statement of principles and a new platform of action.
>
> *Resolved,* That the conflict between this principle of liberty and this fact of slavery has been the whole history of the nation for fifty years, while the only result of this conflict has thus far been to strengthen both parties, and prepare the way of a yet more desperate struggle.
>
> *Resolved,* That in this emergency we can expect little or nothing from the South itself, because it, too, is sinking deeper into barbarism every year. Nor from a supreme court which is always ready to invent new securities for slaveholders. Nor from a president elected almost solely by Southern votes. Nor from a senate which is permanently controlled by the slave power. Nor from a house of representatives which, in spite of our agitation, will be more proslavery than the present one, though the present one has at length granted all which slavery asked. Nor from political action as now conducted. For the Republican leaders and press freely admitted, in public and private, that the election of Fremont was, politically speaking, the last hope of freedom, and even could the North cast a united vote in 1860, the South has before it four years of annexation previous to that time.
>
> *Resolved,* That the fundamental difference between mere political agitation and the action we propose is this, it requires the acquiescence of the slave power, and the other only its opposite.
>
> *Resolved,* That the necessity for disunion is written in the whole existing character and condition of the two sections of the country—in social organizations, education, habits and laws— in the dangers of our white citizens of Kansas and of our coloured ones in Boston, in the wounds of Charles Sumner and the laurels of his assailant—and no government on earth was ever strong enough to hold together such opposing forces.
>
> *Resolved,* That this movement does not seek merely disunion,

but the more perfect union of the free States by the expulsion of the slave States from the confederation in which they have ever been an element of discord, danger and disgrace.

Resolved, That it is not probable that the ultimate severance of the union will be an action of deliberation or discussion, but that a long period of deliberation and discussion must precede it, and this we meet to begin.

Resolved, That henceforward, instead of regarding it as an objection to any system of policy that will lead to the separation of the States, we will proclaim that to be the highest of all recommendations and the grateful proof of statesmanship; and we will support politically and otherwise, such men and measures as appear to tend most to this result.

Resolved, That by the repeated confession of Northern and Southern statesmen, the existence of the union is the chief guarantee of slavery, and that the despots of the whole world and the slaves of the whole world have everything to hope from its destruction and the rise of a free Northern republic.

Resolved, That the sooner the separation takes place the more peaceable it will be; but that peace or war is a mere secondary consideration in view of our present perils. Slavery must be conquered; peaceably if we can, forcibly if we must.

To keep before the people of the United States, North and South, the hostility of the then controlling spirit of the North towards the South, the above resolutions cannot be repeated too often. Nor were they an isolated example of party fanaticism. The stock and staple of the entire republican press was slander of the Southern people; and like noxious weeds it well nigh rooted out all that was elevating to man, and ennobling to woman. The pulpit became a rostrum from which bitter invective of the South flowed in Niagaran torrents; and the beautiful fields of Poesy were made to yield an abundant crop of briar and bramble and deadly Upas.

The burden of every song, of every prayer, of every sermon, was the "poor down-trodden slave" of the South. What wonder that seed thus constantly and malignantly sown sprang up and bore a crop of discontent which nothing short of "separation" from the enemy could appease. We, too, felt that under the existing circumstances peace or war was a mere secondary consideration in view of our perils in the union, and took measures to withdraw from a sectional union of

States that had ceased to respect State sovereignty outside of its own borders.

The insults and taunts and the encroachments of fifty years had welded the people of the South into a compact party organization, animated for all substantial purposes by one sentiment and one glorious principle of patriotism, and never was there a movement in the annals of nations that had a more unanimous support. And when the tocsin of war resounded from one end of the country to the other, and reverberated over hills and through valleys, the sons and sires in the beautiful Sunny South, from the high born and cultured gentleman in whose veins flowed the blue blood of the cavalier, to the humblest tiller of the soil and the shepherd on the mountain sides, buckled on the paraphernalia of warfare and reported for duty. To arms! To arms! was the patriotic appeal of a people who had no other redress; and I repeat with emphasis that never a people responded with more chivalrous alacrity or more earnestness of purpose.

I was too well versed in the politics of the country, too familiar with the underground workings of the enemy, to hesitate. I, too, enlisted in the struggle, and in the glorious efforts to establish "home rule and domestic felicity," not literally in the ranks of the soldier, but in the great army of women who were willing to toil and to suffer, and to die, if need be, for the cause of the South.

I had but one brother, a darling young half brother, Thomas J. Stokes, who had gone to Texas to practice his chosen profession. With all the intensity of my ardent nature I loved this brother, and would have died that he might live; and yet with all the perils involved, it was with a thrill of pride that I read his long letter breathing, pulsing, with the patriotism illustrated by our ancestry in the revolutionary struggle for American Independence. And now this noble brother and myself, though widely separated, enlisted in aid of the same great cause; the perpetuity of constitutional rights. He to serve on the battlefield, and I to care for the sick and wounded soldiers, or to labour in any capacity that would give greatest encouragement to our cause.

Chapter 1

The Magnolia Cadets

Notwithstanding the restful signification of "Alabama," the State bearing that name had passed the ordinance of secession, and mingled her voice with those of other States which had previously taken steps in that direction.

Then followed a call for a convention, having in view the election of a President of a new Republic to take its place among the nations of the earth, and to be known throughout the world as the Southern Confederacy. As an intensely interested spectator I was at that convention; and will remember, to my dying day, that grand spectacle. Yea, that was a grand and solemn occasion—that of issuing a mandate "Let there be another nation, and to all intents and purposes there was another nation." In the course of human events it requires centuries to evolve such moral courage and sublimity of thought and action; and the proceedings of that day will stand out in bold relief as the acme of patriotic greatness.

Ah! that scene at the capitol of the State of Alabama, when Jefferson Davis, the chosen leader of the Southern people, took the oath of office and pledged undying fidelity to the best interests of his own sunny land.

On that momentous occasion not a word was uttered denunciatory of the States we were seeking to leave in their fancied superiority, and the great concourse of people there assembled was too familiar with the history of the times to require recapitulation of the causes of the alienation which led by rapid ascent to the summit of discontent, and determination to no longer submit to the domination of an enemy.

That scene being enacted as a preliminary, a call was made for Alabama's quota of volunteers to defend the principles enunciated and the interests involved.

The Magnolia Cadets, under the leadership of Captain N. H. R. Dawson, of Selma, were among the first to respond. I accompanied my cousins of Alabama to see this company of noble, handsome young men mustered into the military service of their country. It was a beautiful sight! Wealthy, cultured young gentlemen voluntarily turning their backs upon the luxuries and endearments of affluent homes, and accepting in lieu the privations and hardships of warfare; thereby illustrating to the world that the conflict of arms consequent upon the secession was not to be "a rich man's war and a poor man's fight."

I saw them as they stood in line to receive the elegant silken banner, bearing the stars and bars of a new nation, made and presented to them by Miss Ella Todd and her sister, Mrs. Dr. White, of Lexington, Kentucky, who were introduced to the audience by Captain Dawson as the sisters of Mrs. Abraham Lincoln, the wife of the president of the United States.

I was thus made aware that Mrs. Lincoln and her illustrious husband were Southerners. I have since been in the small, mud-chinked log cabin in Elizabethtown, Kentucky, in which he was born, and in which his infancy and little boyhood were domiciled. Mrs. White had married an Alabamian, and as his wife became a citizen of his State. Her sister, Miss Todd, was visiting her at the enactment of the scene described, and under like circumstances, also became a citizen of Alabama. She married the valiant gentleman who introduced her to the public on that memorable occasion.

I have sought and obtained from Mrs. Mary Dawson Jordan, of Chattanooga, Tennessee, a daughter of Captain Jordan, a complete record of the names of the officers and members of this patriotic company of Alabama's noble sons—native and adopted—which I subjoin as an item of history that will be read with interest by all who revere the memory of the Lost Cause and its noble defenders.

Muster Roll of the "Magnolia Cadets."

N. H. R. Dawson, Captain.

(Enrolled for active service at Selma, Ala., on the 26th day of April, 1861. Mustered into service on the 7th day of May, 1861, at Lynchburg, Va.)

Commanded by Col. Ben Alston of the Fourth Alabama Regiment of Volunteers.

1. N. H. R. Dawson, Captain.

1. Shortbridge, Jr., Geo. D., 1st Lieutenant.
2. McCraw, S. Newton, 2nd Lieutenant.
3. Wilson, John R. 3rd Lieutenant.
1. Waddell, Ed. R., 1st Sergeant.
2. Price, Alfred C., 2nd Sergeant.
3. Daniel, Lucian A., 3rd Sergeant.
4. Goldsby, Boykin, 4th Sergeant.
1. Bell, Bush W., 1st Corporal.
2. Garrett, Robert E., 2nd Corporal.
3. Brown, James G., 3rd Corporal.
4. Cohen, Lewis, 4th Corporal.
1. Melton, George F., Musician.
2. Marshall, Jacob, Musician.
  PRIVATES.
1. Adkins, Agrippa
2. Adams, William S.
3. Avery, William C.
4. Byrd, William G.
5. Beattie, Thomas K.
6. Briggs, Charles H.
7. Bohannon, Robert B.
8. Baker, Eli W.
9. Bradley, Hugh C.
10. Cook, Thomas M.
11. Cook, James W.
12. Cook, Benson.
13. Caughtry, Joseph R.
14. Cole, George W.
15. Cleveland, George W.
16. Clevaland, Pulaski.
17. Cunningham, Frank M.
18. Coursey, William W.
19. Daniel, John R.
20. Densler, John E.
21. Donegay, James G.
22. Friday, Hilliard J.
23. Friday, James L.
24. Friday, John C.
25. Ford, Joseph H.
26. Grice, Henry F.

27. Haden, James G.
28. Harrill, Thornton R.
29. Hannon, Wm. H., Sr.
30. Hannon, Wm. H., Jr.
31. Hooks, William A.
32. Hodge, William L.
33. Jones, William.
34. Jordan, James M.
35. Jackson, Felix W.
36. King, William R.
37. Kennedy, Arch.
38. Kennedy, George D.
39. Lamson, Frank R.
40. Lane, William B.
41. Lowry, Uriah.
42. Lowry, William A.
43. Littleton, Thomas B.
44. Luske, John M.
45. Lamar, John H.
46. Mather, Thomas S.
47. Martin, James B.
48. May, Syd M.
49. May, William V.
50. Melton, Thomas J.
51. Miller, Stephen J.
52. Mimms, George A.
53. Moody, William R.
54. Mosely, Andrew B.
55. McNeal, George S.
56. McKerning, John W.
57. Overton, John B.
58. Overton, Thomas W.
59. O'Neal, William.
60. Paisley, Hugh S.
61. Pryor, John W.
62. Pryor, Robert O.
63. Peeples, Frank W.
64. Raiford, William C.
65. Reinhardt, George L.
66. Robbins, John L.

67. Rucker, Lindsay.
68. Rucker, Henry.
69. Shiner, David H.
70. Stokes, William C.
71. Stone, John W.
72. Stewett, Mayor D.
73. Turner, Daniel M.
74. Thomas, Lewis.
75. Tarver, Ben J.
76. Taylor, William E.
77. Terry, Thomas B.
78. Thompson, John S.
79. Thompson, William E.
80. Ursory, Edward G.
81. Vaughn, Turner P.
82. Wrenn, Theodore J.
83. Whallon, Daniel.

Copied from the original Muster Roll of the Magnolia Cadets, owned by Henry R. Dawson, son of N. H. R. Dawson.

CHAPTER 2

The War Record of Dekalb County

DeKalb county, Georgia, of which Decatur is the county site, was among the first to enrol troops for Confederate service. The first volunteers from Decatur were James L. George, Hardy Randall, L. J. Winn and Beattie Wilson, who went with the Atlanta Greys the last of May, 1861.

The first company from DeKalb county was that of Captain John W. Fowler. It was called the DeKalb Light Infantry, and was mustered into service in Atlanta, as part of the 7th Georgia Volunteers, and left for Virginia on the 1st of June, 1861. Those going from DeKalb county in this company were: First Lieutenant, John J. Powell; Second Lieutenant, John M. Hawkins; Third Lieutenant, James L. Wilson; First Sergeant, M. L. Brown; Second Sergeant, D. C. Morgan; Third Sergeant, D. E. Jackson; Fourth Sergeant, John W. Fowler, jr.; Corporals—H. H. Norman, R. F. Davis, C. W. L. Powell; Privates—W. W. Bradbury (afterwards captain), E. M. Chamberlain, W. W. Morgan, W. L. Herron, P. H. Pate, C. E. McCulloch, James W. McCulloch, L. C. Powell, H. G. Woodall, J. S. Woodall, A. W. Mashburn, V. A. Wilson, W. J. Mason, J. V. Austin, W. M. Austin, John Eads, E. A. Davis, Dr. A. S. Mason, John W. Norman, E. L. Morton, Henry Gentry, W. M. Cochran, J. B. Cochran, James Hunter (promoted captain), W. W. Brimm, William Carroll, C. W. McAllister, J. O. McAllister, and many others from the county, making it a full company.

The second company from DeKalb was the Stephens Rifles, captain, L. J. Glenn. They went into Cobb's Legion about August, 1861. Dr. Liddell, Frank Herron, Norman Adams, John McCulloch, John J. McKoy, and some others, went from Decatur in this company.

The third company was the Murphey Guards, captain, John Y. Flowers. They came from the upper part of the county, near Doraville.

This company was named in memory of Hon. Charles Murphey, of DeKalb county, a prominent lawyer and member of Congress, but then recently deceased. The company had been uniformed by the people of the county, a large share being contributed by Mr. and Mrs. Milton A. Candler, and Mr. and Mrs. Ezekiel Mason. Mrs. Candler, whose maiden name was Eliza Murphey, the only child of Charles Murphey, gave the banner, upon which was inscribed, "The God of Jacob is with us."

The Fourth Company was The Bartow Avengers, Captain William Wright, from the lower part of the county about South River. The Fifth Company, Captain Rankin, was from Stone Mountain. These three last mentioned companies went into the 38th Georgia Regiment, in September, 1861, and belonged to the Virginia Army. The Sixth Company, Captain E. L. Morton's, entered service the last of August, 1861, in the 36th Georgia Regiment, and was with the Western Army under Johnston. The Seventh Company, the Fowler Guards, Captain Clay, went into the 42nd Georgia Regiment in the early part of 1862, and was also in the Western Army.

There were several companies, mostly composed of DeKalb County men, that were made up and went from the camp of instruction near Decatur. Moses L. Brown was captain of one, and L. D. Belisle of another. Besides the companies already named, all of which went into the infantry, there were many soldiers from DeKalb that went into the cavalry and artillery service of the regular army.

In the year 1863, when Georgia was threatened by Rosecrans coming into the State on its northern border, special troops were raised for its defence. Major General Howell Cobb commanded the division; General Henry R. Jackson one of the brigades. In Jackson's Brigade, in the 10th Georgia Regiment State Guards (Col. John J. Glenn and Lieutenant-Colonel J. N. Glenn), we find Company A of Cavalry troops. Of this company Milton A. Candler had command. These troops served through 1863 and 1864.

In April, 1863, Paul P. Winn, now a Presbyterian minister, then a mere youth, went into the army in the 45th Georgia Regiment, commanded by Col. Thomas J. Simmons. Other Decatur boys went into the service from other sections where the war found them located. Among these were Dr. James J. Winn, who enlisted at Clayton, Alabama, with the Barker Greys, and was in the battle of Bull Run. After a year or two he received a surgeon's commission, being the youngest surgeon in the army.

John C. Kirkpatrick, just eighteen, went into the service from Augusta with the Oglethorpe Infantry. With him were his cousin, William Dabney (now a Presbyterian minister in Virginia), and his friend, Frank Stone. This was in 1862, and John remained in the service until the close of the war, having been in severe battles (for he was in Cleburne's Division), including that of Jonesboro. In this engagement were other Decatur boys in other commands. Mr. John B. Swanton, but seventeen years old, was in that battle, and says that by his side stood, when mortally wounded, Franklin Williams, the brother of Mr. Hiram J. Williams. Says Mr. Swanton: "He was so near me I could have touched him with my hand." Three sons of Mrs. Martha Morgan, and cousins of DeWitt Morgan, were all in the service, Henry, Daniel, and Joseph Morgan. Jesse Chewning and Samuel Mann were in the 64th Georgia.

Josiah J. Willard, the only son of Mr. Levi Willard, while a sprightly, active youth, was near-sighted. He had a position in the commissary department at Camp Randolph, near Decatur, and went with it to Macon, July 11th, 1864, and remained there until the place surrendered after the fall of Richmond. He, also, is mentioned in other sketches.

There were also several companies of old men and boys who went into the State service when the last call for troops was made by the Confederate government.

Before the DeKalb soldiers go to meet the fortunes of war, let us recall some incidents that preceded their departure. On the northern side of the court-house square there stood a large building, the residence of Mr. Ezekiel Mason. Here, day after day, a band of devoted women met to make the uniforms for the DeKalb Light Infantry. These uniforms had been cut by a tailor, but they were to be made by women's hands. Among the leading and directing spirits in this work were Mrs. Jonathan B. Wilson, Mrs. Jane Morgan, Mrs. Ezekiel Mason, Mrs. Levi Willard, Miss Anna Davis, Mrs. James McCulloch, and Miss Lou Fowler. The most of this sewing was done by hand.

To the DeKalb Light Infantry, the day before its departure, a beautiful silken banner was given. The ladies of the village furnished the material. The address of presentation was made by Miss Mollie G. Brown. In September, of that same year, my sister was invited to present a banner to Captain William Wright's Company. Her modest little address was responded to in behalf of the company by Rev. Mr. Mashburn, of the Methodist Church. In March, 1862, there was another banner presented from the piazza of "the Mason Corner"—this time to the Fowler Guards, by Miss Georgia Hoyle. This banner was made by the fair hands of Miss Anna E. Davis. By this time the spirit of independence of the outside world had begun to show itself in the Southern-made grey jeans of the soldiers, and in the homespun dress of Miss Hoyle.

This banner, so skilfully made by Miss Anna Davis, had a circle of white stars upon a field of blue, and the usual bars of red and white—two broad red bars with a white one between. The banner of this pattern was known as the "stars and bars," and was the first kind used by the Confederate States. In May, 1863, the Confederate Congress adopted a National Flag, which had a crimson field with white stars in a blue-grounded diagonal cross, the remainder of the flag being white. But, when falling limp around the staff, and only the white showing, it could easily be mistaken for a flag of truce; therefore in March, 1865, the final change was made by putting a red bar across the end of the flag.

But what of the fate of these gallant young men, going forth so full of hope and courage, with tender and loving farewells lingering in their hearts?

Soon, ah! so soon, some of them fell upon the crimson fields of Virginia. James L. George ("Jimmie," as his friends lovingly called him) was killed in the first battle of Manassas. "Billy" Morgan died soon after the battle, and was buried with military honours in a private cemetery near Manassas. Two years after, his brother, De Witt Morgan, worn out in the siege of Vicksburg, was buried on an island in Mobile Bay. At the second battle of Manassas, James W. McCulloch and James L. Davis were both killed. Later on W. J. Mason, William Carroll, John M. Eads, H. H. Norman, Billy Wilson, and Norman Adams, were numbered among the slain. Among the wounded were Henry Gentry, Mose Brown, John McCulloch, W. W. Brimm, Dave Chandler, Riley Lawhorn, and Bill Herring.

A volume could easily be written concerning the bravery and the sufferings of the DeKalb county troops; but I must forbear. Concerning Warren Morton, of the 36th Georgia Regiment, who went into the service at the age of fifteen, and suffered so severely, I will refer my readers to a sketch in the latter part of this book. Of William M. Durham, so young, so gallant, who enlisted in Company K., 42nd Georgia Regiment, much of interest will be found in another chapter.

Among the Decatur members of Cobb's Legion was Mr. John J.

McKoy, who went out in the Stephens Rifles when not more than nineteen years old. He was in the battle of Yorktown, Seven Pines, and in the Seven Days Fight around Richmond. Owing to illness, and to business arising from the attainment of his majority, he came home in 1863, and, hiring a substitute when the conscript law was passed, went to work at the Passport Office in Atlanta. In this same year he was married to Miss Laura Williams of Decatur. Having raised Company A., for the 64th Georgia Regiment, Mr. McKoy was with it when it was sent to Florida, and was in the battle of Olustee or Ocean Pond, in February 1864, where General Alfred H. Colquitt won the title of "The Hero of Olustee." Mr. McKoy remembers to have seen on that eventful day, Col. George W. Scott, then of Florida, but now of Decatur. At the Battle of Olustee, Col. Scott was in command of a regiment of cavalry. The banner of the regiment is now in possession of his daughter, Mrs. Thomas Cooper.

The 64th Georgia was then sent to Virginia in General Wright's brigade. A few days after "The Mine Explosion," or undermining of the Confederate works, an engagement occurred at Deep Bottom. Here, General Girardy, of Augusta, was killed, and several hundred of the Confederates were captured, among the number being Mr. McKoy. This was in July, 1864. He was sent to Fort Delaware, where he remained in prison until the close of the war. Here he spent a whole winter without a fire, and was subject to all that Fort Delaware meant. To escape the horrors of that prison, many of the two thousand officers there confined, took the oath not to fight against the United States. But Mr. McKoy and thirty-four others remained in prison, firm and loyal, even after the surrender, believing and hoping, up to July, 1865, that the war would be carried on west of the Mississippi River.

The soldiers who went to Virginia knew from their own experience the scenes of Manassas, Malvern Hill, Fort Harrison, Sharpsburg, Fredericksburg, Gettysburg and the Wilderness. Yet some of them were left to be surrendered by Lee at Appomatox Court House. The companies which were in the Western Army were in the leading battles of that Division, and were equally brave and abiding in their devotion to the cause.

For many of the foregoing facts concerning the troops from DeKalb, I am greatly indebted to Mr. Robert F. Davis, who went with DeKalb's first company, and who, after braving the perils of the war, came off unscathed. He still lives near Decatur, and is an elder in the Presbyterian Church.

I greatly regret my inability, even if I had the space, to give the names of all the soldiers who went from DeKalb, and to tell of their deeds of bravery and endurance. It has not been intentional that many are wholly omitted. It has been my privilege to see but one muster-roll of our county troops—that of Company K, 38th Georgia Regiment, kindly furnished by Mr. F. L. Hudgins, of Clarkston, a brave soldier who was in command of the company when Lee surrendered. This muster-roll shows that out of the 118 names, forty-six were killed (or died), and seventeen were wounded; that its first Captain, William Wright, resigned, and that three other captains by promotion were all killed, *i. e.*, Gustin E. Goodwin, George W. Stubbs and R. H. Fletcher. Indeed, in nearly every instance, promotion in this Company meant death upon the battlefield. And can we wonder that both the commissioned and the non-commissioned fell, when some of the principal battles in which they were engaged bore such names as Cold Harbor, Malvern Hill, Second Manassas, Sharpsburg, Fredericksburg, Chancellorsville, Winchester, Gettysburg, The Wilderness, Spottsylvania Courthouse, Mechanicsville, Fisher's Hill, Cedar Creek, Louise Courthouse and High Bridge?

In memory of the dead, for the sake of the living and for the descendants of all mentioned therein, I copy the muster-roll of this company:

COMPANY K., 38TH GEORGIA REGIMENT:

Captain William Wright—resigned July, 1862.
1st Lieutenant Julius J. Gober—Died July 26th, 1862.
2nd Lieutenant Gustin E. Goodwin—Promoted captain; killed August 28th, 1862.
3rd Lieutenant George W. Stubbs—Promoted captain; killed July 24th, 1864.
1st Sergeant John S. Johnston—Killed June 27th, 1862.
2nd Sergeant W. R. Henry—Promoted to 1st Lieutenant; lost a leg December 13th, 1862.
3rd Sergeant J. A. Maddox—Killed at Wilderness, May 5th, 1864.
4th Sergeant F. L. Hudgins—Promoted 1st Sergeant; wounded at Malvern Hill; shot through the body at Gettysburg.
5th Sergeant E. H. C. Morris—Promoted 3rd Lieutenant; killed at Second Manassas, August, 1862.

1st Corporal F. M. Gassaway—Killed at Second Manassas, August, 1862.
2nd Corporal J. M. Walker—Died in camp.
3rd Corporal W. A. Ward—Died in camp.
4th Corporal James L. Anderson—Wounded at Manassas and Spottsylvania court house.
John H. Akers—Killed at Second Manassas, 1862.
A. W. Allman—Killed at Cedar Creek, October 19th, 1864.
John Adams—Died in camp.
Enos Adams—
Isaac W. Awtry—
W. A. Awtry—
H. V. Bayne—Disabled by gunshot wound. Still living. (1897)
Allen Brown—
Lewis Brown—
Killis Brown—
William M. Brooks—
H. M. Burdett—
J. S. Burdett—
John S. Boyd—
James E. Ball—Killed at Gettysburg, July, 1863.
W. H. Brisendine—
L. R. Bailey—Transferred to Cobb's Legion.
John E. J. Collier—
James Collier—Died at Charlottesville, Va., 1862.
Z. J. Cowan—
J. J. Cowan—
G. G. Cook—
James E. Chandler—Killed at Sharpsburg, Md., September 17th, 1862.
W. B. Chandler—Died in camp, May 31st, 1863.

John W. Chandler—Killed at Second Manassas, August, 1862.
W. A. Childress—A physician in Atlanta.
J. H. Childers—
J. M. Dowis—Killed at Cold Harbor, June 27th, 1862.
W. H. Ellis—

John Eunis—
R. H. Fletcher—Promoted Captain; killed in 1865.
A. M. Gentry—Died at Savannah in 1862.
W. F. Goodwin—Promoted 3rd Lieutenant; killed at Gettysburg in 1863.
C. H. Goodwin—Killed at Cold Harbor.
Joseph Grogan—
J. H. Grogan—
J. D. Grogan—Killed at Sharpsburg, Maryland, September 17th, 1862.
Gideon Grogan—Killed at Sharpsburg, Maryland, September 17th, 1862.
James H. Gasaway—Disabled by gunshot.
William Gasaway—Disabled by gunshot.
John Gasaway—Discharged.
W. L. Goss—
F. L. Guess—Transferred to the 9th Georgia Artillery Battalion.
H. L. Head—
J. L. Henry—Killed at Coal Harbor, June 27th, 1862.
W. B. Heldebrand—Died recently.
H. H. Hornbuckle—Killed at Coal Harbor, June 27th, 1862.
Joshua Hammond—Killed at Sharpsburg, September 17th, 1862.
R. F. Jones—Killed at Coal Harbor.
J. W. Jones—Disabled by gunshot.
C. S. Jones—Killed in Richmond.
R. D. F. Jones—Disabled by gunshot.
J. M. Jones—
J. H. Jones—Disabled by gunshot.
James Jones—
John F. Kelley—
John H. Kelley—
James Kelley—
W. J. Little—Disabled by gunshot.
George Lee—Died in camp.
A. J. Lee—Discharged.
Wiley Manghon—
J. R. Mitchell—Killed December 13th, 1862, at

Fredericksburg.
W. G. Mitchell—Disabled by gunshot.
E. J. Mitchell—
W. R. Maguire—Disabled by gunshot.
W. A. Morgan—
B. S. McClain—Died in camp.
John W. Nash—Killed December 13th, 1862, at Fredericksburg.
David N. Fair—Killed at Coal Harbor, June 27th, 1862.
W. B. Owen—
J. J. Pruett—Discharged.
John W. Phillips—Killed at Coal Harbor, June 27th, 1862.
John B. Thompson—
Will Thompson—
W. M. Richardson—Disabled at Second Manassas.
J. S. Richardson—Killed at Coal Harbor, June 27th, 1862.
D. D. Richardson—Died at Hanover Junction, 1862.
A. W. Stowers—
W. A. Smith—
J. M. Summey—Shot through at Coal Harbor.
S. J. Summey—Killed at Winchester, Va., June 13th, 1863.
James Toney—Musician.
C. W. Toney—Musician.
M. J. Tweedle—Wounded at Winchester, Va., September 19th, 1864.
S. J. Thomas—
R. L. Vaughn—Died at Savannah, Ga.
J. S. Vaughn—Wounded eight times at Coal Harbor.
W. T. Vaughn—Had both hands blown off.
J. C. Wiggins—Promoted Second Lieutenant; killed in June, 1864.
J. M. Wiggins—
R. W. Wiggins—Killed at Petersburg, Va., March 27th, 1865.
E. W. Wiggins—Killed at Sharpsburg, Maryland, September 17th, 1862.
G. W. Wiggins—
M. O. Wiggins—Disabled at Cedar Creek, October 19th, 1864.
G. W. Wade—Musician.

E. D. Wade—
F. M. Wade—
B. L. Wilson—Killed at Marie's Heights, May 4th, 1863.
W. A. Wright—
W. R. Wood—
Amos Wheeler—Killed at Spottsylvania, May 12th, 1864.
J. H. Wilson—Killed at Gettysburg, July 1st, 1863.
Jordan Wilson—Killed at Coal Harbor, June 27th, 1862.

CHAPTER 3

Labours of Love

To a woman who lives and moves and has her being in the past, an invocation to time to "turn backward in its flight," would seem superfluous. The scenes of other years being ever present, it would also seem that time, as a loving father, would linger fondly around her with panaceas for decay, mental and physical; that her heart would never grow old, and her person never lose the attractions of youth; but, in the economy of Him who doeth all things well, such is not the decree regarding aught that is mortal.

And when the ravages incident to one's career have destroyed personal charm, and divested the mind of sparkling gem, the soul yearns for the protection of childhood and the companionship of youth. Scenes of the past, though dyed with "the blood of martyrs," are ever passing in kaleidoscopic beauty before the mind's eye, and tones too sweet for mortal ear are ever thrilling the heart with strange, sweet, expectant pleasure.

This train of reflection, only far more elaborate, seizes for its guiding star, on this occasion, a scene which at the time of its enactment was indelibly impressed upon my mind, and left living, glowing tints, illuming my pathway through subsequent life; a scene in which lovely girlhood, arrayed in pure white robes, lent a helping hand in the important work of supplying our soldiers with comforts, all the more appreciated because of the source from which emanating.

With closed eyes, I see it now and listen to its enchanting melody. To render it more realistic than could be done by any description of mine, I subjoin a copy of the "Programme," the original of which I have preserved:

GRAND MUSICAL ENTERTAINMENT!
RELIEF FUND
FOR OUR SOLDIERS,
THURSDAY, MAY 15, 1862,
AT THE COURTHOUSE.

By the ladies of Decatur, Georgia, assisted by William H. Barnes, Colonel Thomas F. Lowe, Professor Hanlon, W. A. Haynes, R. O. Haynes, Dr. Geutebruck and Dr. Warmouth, of Atlanta.

PROGRAMME.
Part 1.
1. Opening Chorus—Company.
2. Piano Duet—"March from Norma"—Miss Georgia Hoyle and Miss Missouri Stokes.
3. Solo—"Roy Neil"—Mrs. Robert Alston.
4. Quartette—Atlanta Amateurs.
5. "Tell Me, Ye Winged Winds"—Company.
6. "Our Way Across the Sea"—Miss G. Hoyle and Professor Hanlon.
7. March—Piano Duet—Miss Laura Williams and Miss Fredonia Hoyle.
8. Solo—Professor Hanlon.
9. Comic Song—W. H. Barnes.
10. Violin Solo—Colonel Thomas F. Lowe.
11. Solo—Dr. Warmouth.
12. "When Night Comes O'er the Plain"—Miss M. Stokes and Professor Hanlon.
13. "The Mother's Farewell"—Mrs. Maggie Benedict.

Part 2
1. Chorus—"Away to the Prairie"—Company.
2. Piano Solo—Miss G. Hoyle.
3. Song—Atlanta Amateurs.
4. Coquette Polka—Misses Hoyle and Stokes.
5. Chorus—"Let us Live with a Hope"—Company.
6. "Mountain Bugle"—Miss M. Stokes and Company.
7. "*Mazurka des Traineaux*"—Piano Duet—Misses Hoyle and Stokes.
8. Shiloh Retreat—Violin—Colonel Thomas F. Lowe.

Concluding with the Battle Song: "Cheer, Boys, Cheer"—W. H. Barnes.

Tickets, 50c. Children and Servants, half price.

Doors open 7:30 o'clock. Commence at 8:15 o'clock.

Atlanta Intelligencer Power Print.

Labours of Love

Musical—Atlanta.

The citizens of Decatur were always invited to entertainments, social, literary, and musical, in Atlanta, that had in view the interest, pleasure or comfort of our soldiers; therefore the invitation accompanying the following programme received ready response:

TWELFTH MUSICAL SOIREE
—of the—
ATLANTA AMATEURS,
Monday evening, June 24, 1861,
For the Benefit of
ATLANTA VOLUNTEERS,
Captain Woddail
and the
CONFEDERATE CONTINENTALS,
Captain Seago,
Who Are Going to Defend Our Land.

Let all attend and pay a parting tribute to our brave soldiers.

Programme.
Part 1.

1. We Come Again—(Original)—Company.
2. Dreams—(A Reverie)—Miss J. E. Whitney.
3. Violin Solo—(Hash)—Colonel Thomas F. Lowe.
4. "Not for Gold or Precious Stones"—Miss R. J. Hale.
5. Yankee Doodle—According to W. A. Haynes.
6. Dixie Variations—Mrs. W. T. Farrar.
7. "Two Merry Alpine Maids"—Misses M. F. and J. E. Whitney.
8. "When I Saw Sweet Nellie Home"—Misses Sasseen and Judson.
9. "Root Hog or Die"—W. H. Barnes.

Instrumental Trio, "*La Fille du Regiment*"—Messrs. Schoen and Heindl. Vermicelli, (Variations)—W. H. Barnes and Openheimer.

Part 2

1. "Our Southern Land"—C. P. Haynes and Company.
2. "Through Meadows Green"—Miss M. F. Whitney.[1]
3. Solo—Thomas D. Wright.
4. "Home, Sweet Home"—Miss R. J. Hale.
5. Violin Exemplification—Col. Thomas F. Lowe.
6. "Happy Days of Yore"—Mrs. Hibler.
7. Quartette—(original)—Misses Whitney, Messrs. Barnes and Haynes.
8. "Rocked in the Cradle of the Deep"—Prof. Hanlon. Encore—Ballad.
9. "I Come, I Come"—Misses Sasseen, Westmoreland and Sims.

The whole to conclude with the grand original.

TABLEAU,

(In Two Parts).

The Women and Children of Dixie Rejoicing Over the Success of the Confederate Banner.

Scene 1. The Children of Dixie.
Scene 2. The Women—The Soldiers—Our Flag—Brilliant Illumination.

Doors open at half past 7 o'clock. Curtain will rise at half past 8 o'clock.

Tickets, Fifty Cents. Ushers will be on hand to seat audience.

W. H. Barnes, Manager.

---

1. This lady, Miss "Frank" Whitney, is now, (1897), the wife of Mr. Charles W. Hubner, the well-known Atlanta poet.

CHAPTER 4

Labours of Love Continued

A patriotic co-operation between the citizens of Decatur and Atlanta soon sprang up, and in that, as in all things else, a social and friendly interchange of thought and feeling and deed existed; and we were never so pleased as when aiding each other in the preparation of clothing and edibles for "our soldiers," or in some way contributing to their comfort.

Many of us who had never learned to sew became expert handlers of the needle, and vied with each other in producing well-made garments; and I became a veritable knitting machine. Besides the discharge of many duties incident to the times and tending to useful results, I knitted a sock a day, long and large, and not coarse, many days in succession. At the midnight hour the weird click of knitting needles chasing each other round and round in the formation of these useful garments for the nether limbs of "our boys," was no unusual sound; and tears and orisons blended with woof and warp and melancholy sighs. For at that dark hour, when other sounds were shut out, we dared to listen with bated breath to "the still, small voice" that whispered in no unmistakable language suggestions which would have been rebuked in the glare of the noonday sun.

No mother nor sister nor wife nor aunt of a Confederate soldier, need be told what were the depressing suggestions of that "still, small voice" on divers occasions.

When the knitting of a dozen pairs of socks was completed, they were washed, ironed and neatly folded by one of our faithful negro women, and I then resumed the work of preparing them for their destination. Each pair formed a distinct package. Usually a pretty necktie, a pair of gloves, a handkerchief and letter, deposited in one of the socks, enlarged the package. When all was ready, a card bearing the name of the giver, and a request to "inquire within," was tacked on to each package. And then these twelve packages were formed into a bundle, and addressed to an officer in command of some company chosen to be the recipient of the contents.

I will give a glimpse of the interior of my letters to our boys. These letters were written for their spiritual edification, their mental improvement and their amusement.

"Never saw I the righteous forsaken."
"Full many a gem of purest ray serene,
The dark unfathomed caves of ocean bear;
Full many a flower is born to blush unseen,
And waste its sweetness on the desert air."

P. S.—"Apples are good but peaches are better;
If you love me, you will write me a letter."—M.

"Remember now thy Creator in the days of thy youth."

"If in the early morn of life,
You give yourself to God,
He'll stand by you 'mid earthly strife,
And spare the chast'ning rod."—

P. S.—"Roses are red and violets blue,
Sugar is sweet and so are you."—M.

"Love thy neighbour as thyself."

"May every joy that earth can give
Around thee brightly shine;
Remote from sorrow may you live,
And all of heaven be thine."—

P. S.—Remember me when this you see,
Though many miles apart we be.—M

"Love worketh no ill to his neighbour; therefore love is the fulfilment of the law."

"This above all—to thine own self be true,
And it must follow as night the day,
Thou canst not then be false to anyone."

P. S.—"Sure as the vine twines round the stump,
You are my darling sugar lump."—M.

"The night is far spent, the day is at hand; let us, therefore, cast off the works of darkness and let us put on the armour of light."

"*As for my life, it is but short,*
When I shall be no more;
To part with life I am content,
As any heretofore.
Therefore, good people, all take heed,
This warning take by me—
According to the lives you lead,
Rewarded you shall be."

P. S.—*"My pen is bad, my ink is pale,*
My love for you shall never fail."—M.

"Blessed are the peacemakers; for they shall be called the children of God."

"The harp that once through Tara's halls
The soul of music shed,
Now hangs as mute on Tara's wall,
As if that soul were fled.
So sleeps the pride of former days,
So glory's thrill is o'er;
And hearts that once beat high for praise
Now feel that pulse no more.
No more to chiefs and ladies bright
The harp of Tara swells;
The chord alone that breaks at night
Its tale of ruin tells.
Thus Freedom, now so seldom wakes,
The only throb she gives
Is when some heart indignant breaks
To show that still she lives."—

P. S.—*"My love for you will ever flow,*
Like water down a cotton row."—M

"The earth is the Lord's and the fullness thereof; the world and they that dwell therein.

"For He hath founded it upon the seas, and established it upon the floods.

"Who shall ascend into the hill of the Lord, or who shall stand in his holy place?

"He that hath clean hands and a pure heart; who hath not lifted up his soul unto vanity nor sworn deceitfully."

"*Know thyself, presume not God to scan.*

The proper study of mankind is man."

*P. S.—"Round as the ring that has no end,
Is my love for you, my own sweet friend."—M.*

"God is love."

*"Poor soul, the centre of my sinful earth,
Fooled by those rebel powers that there array,
Why dost thou pine within and suffer dearth,
Painting thy outward walls so costly gay?
Why so large cost, having so short a lease,
Dost thou upon thy fading mansion spend?
Shall worms, inheritors of this excess,
Eat up thy charge? Is this thy body's end?"*

*P. S.—"If you love me as I love you,
No knife can cut our love in two."—M.*

"But this I say, He that soweth sparingly shall reap also sparingly; and he which soweth bountifully, shall reap also bountifully. Every man according as he purposeth in his heart, so let him give, not grudgingly, or of necessity; for God loveth a cheerful giver."

*"Before Jehovah's awful throne
Ye nations bow with sacred joy;
Know that the Lord is God alone;
He can create and He destroy."*

*P. S.—"Above, below, in ocean, earth and skies,
Nothing's so pretty as your blue eyes."—M.*

"I am come a light into the world, that whosoever believeth on Me should not abide in darkness."

*"And neither the angels in heaven above,
Nor the demons down under the sea,
Can ever dissever my soul from the soul
Of the beautiful Annabel Lee."*

*P. S.—"Remember me! Remember me!
When this you see—Remember me!"—M.*

"The Lord shall command the blessing upon thee in the storehouses, and in all that thou settest thine hand unto."

*"Lives of great men all remind us,
We can make our lives sublime,
And departing, leave behind us,*

Footprints on the sands of Time."
P. S.—"Remember well and bear in mind,
A pretty girl's not hard to find;
But when you find one nice and Gay
Hold on to her both night and day."—M.

"He that covereth his sins shall not prosper; but whoso confesseth and forsaketh them shall have mercy."

"I'd give my life to know thy art,
Sweet, simple, and divine;
I'd give this world to melt one heart,
As thou hast melted mine."—Mary.
P. S.—"As the earth trots round the sun,
My love for you will ever run."—M.

CHAPTER 5

The Third Maryland Artillery

Some Old Songs

At some time in 1863, it was my privilege to meet a gallant band of men whose faith in the justice of our cause was so strong that they were constrained to turn their faces Southward and imperil their lives in its defence. These men represented the highest type of manhood in Maryland.

Sickness entered their camp, and the good ladies of Decatur insisted upon providing the comforts of home for the sick and wounded. Those to whom it was my privilege to minister belonged to the Third Maryland Artillery, under command of Captain John B. Rowan.[2]

Among them was one whose appreciation of kindness shown him ripened into an undying friendship, Captain W. L. Ritter, a devoted Christian gentleman, and now an elder in Doctor LeFevre's Church, Baltimore.

His fondness for that beautiful Southern song, by James R. Randall, entitled "Maryland, My Maryland!" was truly pathetic.

I subjoin the words to stir up the souls of our people by way of remembrance.

> MARYLAND, MY MARYLAND.
> *The despot's heel is on thy shore,*
> *Maryland, My Maryland!*
> *His touch is on thy temple door,*
> *Maryland, My Maryland.*
> *Avenge the patriotic gore,*
> *That flowed the streets of Baltimore,*
> *And be the battle-queen of yore,*
> *Maryland, My Maryland.*

---
1. This brave officer was killed near Nashville, Tennessee, Dec. 16th, 1864.

Hark to a wand'ring son's appeal,
Maryland, My Maryland!
My mother state, to thee I kneel,
Maryland, My Maryland!
For life and death, for woe and weal,
Thy peerless chivalry reveal,
And gird thy beauteous limbs with steel,
Maryland, My Maryland.

Thou wilt not cower in the dust,
Maryland, My Maryland!
Thy beaming sword shall never rust,
Maryland, My Maryland.
Remember Carroll's sacred trust,
Remember Howard's warlike thrust,
And all thy slumberers with the just,
Maryland, My Maryland.

Come, 'tis the red dawn of the day,
Maryland, My Maryland!
Come with thy panoplied array,
Maryland, My Maryland.
With Ringold's spirit for the fray,
With Watson's blood at Monterey,
With fearless Lowe and dashing May;
Maryland, My Maryland.

Dear Mother! burst thy tyrant's chain,
Maryland, My Maryland!
Virginia should not call in vain,
Maryland, My Maryland.
She meets her sisters on the plain,
"Sic Semper," 'tis the proud refrain
That baffles minions back again,
Maryland, My Maryland.

Come! for thy shield is bright and strong,
Maryland, My Maryland!
Come! for thy dalliance does thee wrong,
Maryland, My Maryland.
Come to thy own heroic throng,
That stalks with liberty along,
And give a new Key to thy song,

Maryland, My Maryland.

I see the blush upon thy cheek,
Maryland, My Maryland!
But thou wast ever bravely meek,
Maryland, My Maryland.
But, lo! there surges forth a shriek,
From hill to hill, from creek to creek,
Potomac calls to Chesapeake,
Maryland, My Maryland.

Thou wilt not yield the vandal toll,
Maryland, My Maryland!
Thou wilt not crook to his control,
Maryland, My Maryland.
Better the fire upon thee roll,
Better the shot, the blade, the bowl,
Than crucifixion of the soul,
Maryland, My Maryland.

I hear the distant thunder hum,
Maryland, My Maryland!
The Old Line bugle, fife and drum,
Maryland, My Maryland.
She is not dead, nor deaf, nor dumb—
Huzza! she spurns the Northern scum;
She breathes! She burns! She'll come, she'll come!
Maryland, My Maryland.

An additional verse as sung by Mrs. Jessie Clark, of Crisp's Co., Friday night, Sept. 12th, 1862.

Hark! 'tis the cannon's deaf'ning roar,
Maryland, My Maryland!
Old Stonewall's on thy hallow'd shore,
Maryland, My Maryland.
Methinks I hear the loud huzza
Ring through the streets of Baltimore—
Slaves no longer—free once more
Maryland, My Maryland.

There were other songs sung in those days. Some of the most popular were "Bonnie Blue Flag," "Dixie," "Bob Roebuck is my Soldier Boy," "Who will Care for Mother Now?" "Her Bright Smile

Haunts me Still," "Let me Kiss Him for his Mother," "All Quiet Along the Potomac To-Night," "Rock me to Sleep, Mother," "When I Saw Sweet Nellie Home," "Just Before the Battle, Mother." In a collection of old music, now never played, there lie before me copies of these songs. They were published in various Southern cities on paper not firm and smooth, but rather thin and coarse, but quite presentable. What memories these songs awake! Where, oh where, are those who sang them over thirty years ago! Who of the singers are now living? How many have gone to the Eternal Shore?

Chapter 6

A Daring and Unique Chase

In the early spring of 1862, there occurred an episode of the war which, up to that date, was the most exciting that had happened in our immediate section. The story has often been told; but instead of relying upon my memory, I will condense from the written statement of Mr. Anthony Murphy, of Atlanta, Georgia, who was one of the principal actors in the chase.

Mr. Murphy begins his narrative by saying:

On Saturday morning, April 12th, 1862, about 4 o'clock, I went aboard a passenger train that started then for Chattanooga, Tennessee. My business that day was to examine an engine that furnished power to cut wood and pump water for the locomotives at Allatoona, a station forty miles from Atlanta. As foreman of machine and motive power, it became my duty to go that morning. This train was in charge of Engineer Jeff Cain, and Conductor W. A. Fuller. It was known as a freight and passenger train. The train arrived in Marietta, twenty miles from Atlanta, shortly after daylight. I stepped from the coach and noticed a number of men getting on the car forward of the one I rode in.

They were dressed like citizens from the country, and I supposed they were volunteers for the army, going to Big Shanty, now known as Kennesaw, a station about eighteen miles from Marietta, where troops were organized and forwarded to the Confederate army in Virginia and other points. At this station the train stopped for breakfast, and, as the engineer, conductor, myself and other passengers went to get our meals, no one was left in charge of the locomotive. I had about finished, when

I heard a noise as if steam were escaping. Looking through a window I saw the cars move, saw the engineer and fireman at the table, and said to them: 'Someone is moving your engine.' By this time I was at the front door, and saw that the train was divided and passing out of sight.

Mr. Murphy, the conductor, and the engineer then held a brief consultation. He asked about the men who got on at Marietta (who afterwards proved to be a Federal raiding party, Andrews and his men), and remarked: "They were the men who took the engine and three cars." At the time he thought they were Confederate deserters, who would run the engine as far as it would have steam to run, and then abandon it. Mr. Murphy and his two comrades concluded that it was their duty to proceed after them. A Mr. Kendrick, connected with the railroad, coming up, they requested him to go on horseback to Marietta, the nearest telegraph station, and communicate with the superintendent at Atlanta, while they "put out on foot after a locomotive under steam." Knowing they would reach a squad of track-hands somewhere on the line, they had some hope, and they did, in a few miles, meet a car and hands near Moon's Station, about two miles from Big Shanty.

They pressed the car, and two hands to propel it, which propelling was done by poles pressed against the ties or ground, and not by a crank. Soon they reached a pile of cross-ties on the track, and found the telegraph wire cut. Clearing off the ties, they pressed on until they reached Acworth Station, six miles from Big Shanty. There they learned that the train they were pursuing had stopped some distance from the depot, and having been carefully examined by its engineer, had moved off at a rapid rate. This satisfied the pursuers that the capturers of the engine "meant something more than deserters would attempt;" and then they "thought of enemies from the Federal army." Says the narrator:

> We moved on to Allatoona. At this place we received two old guns, one for Fuller, and one for the writer. I really did not know how long they had been loaded, nor do I yet, for we never fired them. These were the only arms on our engine during our chase. Two citizens went along from here, which made about seven men on our little pole-car. As we proceeded toward Etowah, we moved rapidly, being down grade, when suddenly we beheld an open place in the track. A piece of rail had

been taken up by the raiders. Having no brake, we could not hold our car in check, and plunged into this gap, turning over with all hands except Fuller and myself, who jumped before the car left the track. The little car was put on again, and the poling man sent back to the next track-gang to have repairs made for following trains.

Arriving at Etowah, the pursuers found the engine "Yonah," used by the Cooper Iron Company, and pressed it into service. They got an open car, and stocked it with rails, spikes and tools, and moved on to Cartersville. Passing on to Rogers' Station, they learned that the raiders had stopped there for wood and water, telling Mr. Rogers that they were under military orders, and that the engine crew proper were coming on behind. At Kingston the raiders had told that they were carrying ammunition to General Beauregard, on the line of the Memphis and Charleston Railroad, near Huntsville, Alabama. At this point the "Yonah" was sent back to Etowah, and the supply car of the pursuers coupled to the engine "New York." But at Kingston the Rome Railroad connects with the Western & Atlantic road, and the Rome engine and train were in the way.

Instead of clearing the track for the "New York," the crowd at the Kingston depot, having learned the news, took possession of the Rome engine and some cars attached, and pulled out for the chase, which compelled Mr. Murphy and his friends to abandon their outfit and run to get on the same train. A few miles were made, when they found a pile of cross-ties on the rails, and the telegraph wires cut. Clearing the track they moved on, when they encountered another gap. Here Messrs. Murphy and Fuller, believing that they would meet the engine "Texas" with a freight train, left the obstructed train and pressed on again on foot, advising the crowd to return, which they did. The pursuers met the "Texas" two miles from Adairsville, and, motioning the engineer to stop, they went aboard and turned him back.

At Adairsville they learned that Andrews had not been long gone. Says the narrator:

> About three miles from Calhoun we came in sight for the first time of the captured engine, and three freight cars. They had stopped to remove another rail, and were in the act of trying to get it out when we came in sight. . . . . As we reached them, they cut loose one car and started again. We coupled this car to

our engine, and moved after them. . . . . . From Resaca to Tilton the road was very crooked, and we had to move cautiously. The distance between us was short. . . . . I feared ambushing by Andrews—reversing the engine and starting it back under an open throttle valve. . . . . To prevent us closing in on them, the end of the box car was broken out, and from this they threw cross-ties on the track to check our speed and probably derail us. . . . . . I had a long bar fastened to the brake wheel of the tender to give power so that four men could use it to help check and stop the engine suddenly. I also stood by the reverse lever to aid the engineer to reverse his engine, which he had to do many times to avoid the cross-ties.

Passing through and beyond Tilton, we again came in sight. At this point the road has a straight stretch of over a mile. A short distance from Tilton and just as we rounded the curve, 'The General' with the raiders was rounding another curve, leaving the straight line, giving us a fine view for some distance across the angle. . . . . . . The fastest run was made at this point. . . . . . I imagine now, as I write this, I see the two great locomotives with their human freight speeding on, one trying to escape, the other endeavouring to overtake, and if such had happened none might have been left to give the particulars of that exciting and daring undertaking. The chances of battle were certainly against us if Andrews had attempted fight.

Just beyond Dalton the pursuers found the telegraph wire cut. On reaching the "tunnel," they were satisfied that Andrews was short of wood, or the tunnel would not have been so clear of smoke. Passing through the tunnel they kept on, and beyond Ringgold, about two miles, the captors left "The General" and made for the woods. The pursuers were in sight of them. Mr. Fuller and others started after the raiders. Mr. Murphy went on the engine to examine the cause of the stop. He found no wood in the furnace, but plenty of water in the boiler. Says Mr. Murphy:

> I took charge of the engine, 'General,' had it placed on the sidetrack, and waited for the first train from Chattanooga to Atlanta. I reached Ringgold about dark. I went aboard, and reaching Dalton, the first telegraph station, I sent the first news of our chase and re-capture of the 'General' to Atlanta.

CHAPTER 7

Coming Home from Camp Chase

"A letter from Marse Thomie," said our mail carrier, Toby, as he got in speaking distance on his return from the post office.

"What makes you think so?" I said, excitedly.

"I know his hand-write, and this is it," selecting a letter from a large package and handing it to me. The very first glimpse of the superscription assured me of his confident assertion.

The letter was addressed to our mother, and bore a United States postage stamp, and the beloved signature of her only son, Thomas J. Stokes. A thrill of gratitude and joy filled our hearts too full for utterance, as we read:

"My Dear Mother: I have learned that the soldiers of the 10th Texas Infantry will be exchanged for the United States troops very soon, perhaps tomorrow; and then, what happiness will be mine! I can scarcely wait its realization. A visit home, a mother's embrace and kiss, the heart-felt manifestations of the love of two sisters, and the joy and glad expression of faithful servants. I may bring several friends with me, whom I know you will welcome, both for my sake and theirs—they are valiant defenders of the cause we love. *Adieu*, dear mother, and sisters, until I see you at home, 'home, sweet home.'"

"Thomie is coming home!" "Thomie Stokes is coming home!" was the glad announcement of mother, sisters, and friends; and the servants took up the intelligence, and told everybody that Marse Thomie was coming home, and was going to bring some soldiers with him.

Another day dawned and love's labour commenced in earnest. Doors were opened, and rooms ventilated: bed-clothing aired and sunned, and dusting brushes and brooms in willing hands removed every particle of that much dreaded material of which man in all his glory, or ignominy, was created. Furniture and picture frames were polished and artistically arranged. And we beheld the work of the first day, and it was good.

When another day dawned we were up with the lark, and his *matin* notes found responsive melody in our hearts, the sweet refrain of which was, "Thomie is coming"—the soldier son and brother. Light bread and rolls, rusks and pies, cakes, etc., etc., were baked, and sweetmeats prepared, and another day's work was ended and pronounced satisfactory.

The third day, for a generous bonus, "Uncle Mack's" services were secured, and a fine pig was slaughtered and prepared for the oven, and also a couple of young hens, and many other luxuries too numerous to mention.

When all was ready for the feast of thanksgiving for the return of the loved one, the waiting seemed interminable. There was pathos in every look, tone, and act of our mother—the lingering look at the calendar, the frequent glance at the clock, told that the days were counted, yea, that the hours were numbered. At length the weary waiting ended, and the joyous meeting came of mother and son, of sisters and brother, after a separation of four years of health and sickness, of joy and anguish, of hope and fear.

As we stood upon the platform of the Decatur depot, and saw him step from the train, which we had been told by telegram would bring him to us, our hearts were filled with consternation and pity, and tears unbidden coursed down our cheeks, as we looked upon the brave and gallant brother, who had now given three years of his early manhood to a cause rendered dear by inheritance and the highest principles of patriotism, and, in doing so, had himself become a physical wreck. He was lean to emaciation, and in his pale face was not a suggestion of the ruddy colour he had carried away. A constant cough, which he tried in vain to repress, betrayed the deep inroads which prison life had made upon his system; and in this respect he represented his friends—in describing his appearance, we leave nothing untold about theirs. In war-worn pants and faded grey coats, they presented a spectacle never to be forgotten.

Joy and grief contended for the supremacy. We did not realize that even a brief period of good nursing and feeding would work a great change in the physical being of men just out of the prison pens of the frigid North, and wept to think that disease, apparently so deeply rooted, could not be cured, and that they were restored to us but to die. Perceiving our grief and divining the cause, our Thomie took us, our mother first, into his arms and kissed us, and said in his old-time way, "I'll be all right soon."

And Toby and Telitha, the house servants, came in for their share of kindly greeting.

Thomie then introduced us to Captain Lauderdale, Captain Formwalt, and Lieutenant McMurray, his Texas friends and comrades in arms. Our cordial, heart-felt welcome was appreciated by this trio of gentlemen, and to this day we receive from them messages of abiding friendship. Captain Lauderdale was one of the most perfect gentlemen I ever saw—tall, graceful, erect, and finely formed. His face, of Grecian mould, was faultless; and his hair, black as a raven's plumage, and interspersed with grey, would have adorned the head of a king. His bearing was dignified and yet affable, and so polished and easy in manner as to invite most friendly intercourse.

Captain Formwalt was also a fine specimen of manhood—free and easy, gay and rollicking. He seemed to think his mission on earth was to bring cheerfulness and glee into every household he entered.

Lieutenant McMurray was unlike either of his friends. Apparently cold, apathetic and reserved, he repelled all advances tending to cordial relations, until well acquainted, after which he was metamorphosed into a kind and genial gentleman.

Thomie, dear Thomie, was a boy again, and while our guests were refreshing themselves preparatory to dinner, he was going all over the house, for every nook and corner was endeared by association. He opened the piano, and running his fingers over the keys with the grace and ease of his boyhood, he played accompaniments to his favourite songs, "Home Again," and "Way Down Upon the Suwanee River," trying to sing, but prevented by the irrepressible coughing. Then, with nervous hand, he essayed "When this Cruel War is Over." Turning away from the piano, he went to the library and handled with tender care the books he had read in boyhood. Shakespeare, Milton, Byron and Moore possessed no interest for him now; and Blackstone and Chitty were equally ignored.

The books his mother and sister read to him in his childhood were, as if by intuition, selected, and fondly conned and handled. His own name was written in them, and his tearful eyes lingered long and lovingly upon these reminders of boyhood's happy hours. With a sigh he left the library, and espying Toby, who kept where he could see as much as possible of "Marse Thomie," he called the boy and held an encouraging little conversation with him.

Dinner being ready, our mother led the way to the dining room. Our guests having taken the seats assigned them, Thomie took his near his mother—his boyhood's seat at table. By request, Captain Lauderdale asked the blessing. And, oh, what a blessing he invoked upon the "dear ones, who, with loving hands, prepared this feast for the son and brother of the household, and for his friends in peace and comrades in war." Pleasant conversation ensued, and all enjoyed the repast. But the gentlemen seemed to us to eat very little, and, in reply to our expression of disappointment, they explained the importance of limiting themselves for several days in this respect.

As there was no trunk to send for, and no valise to carry, we rightly surmised that the clothing of these good men was limited to the apparel in which they were clad, and it was decided by my mother and myself that I should go to Atlanta and get material for a suit of clothes for Thomie, and good warm underclothing for them all. Arrived at Atlanta, I was irresistibly led by that mystic power, which has often controlled for good results the acts of man, to go to Dr. Taylor's drug store. Here I found King, our faithful negro man, as busy as a bee, labelling and packing medicine for shipment. I approached him and said:

"King, Thomie has come."

"Marse Thomie?"

"Yes."

"Thank God," he said, with fervour.

When I was about leaving the store, he said:

"Miss Mary, just wait a minute, please, and I will get something that I want you to take to Marse Thomie, and tell him I don't want him to be hurt with me for sending it to him. I just send it because I love him—me and him was boys together, you know, and I always thought he ought to 'er took me with him to the war."

"What is it, King?"

"Just a little article I got in trade, Miss Mary," was all the satisfaction he vouchsafed.

When he handed it to me, knowing by the sense of touch that it was a package of dry goods, I took it to Mrs. O'Connor's millinery establishment, and asked the privilege of opening it there. Imagine my astonishment and delight, when I beheld a pattern of fine grey cassimere. I felt of it, and held it up between my eyes and the light. There was nothing shoddy about it. It was indeed a piece of fine cassimere, finer and better than anything I could have procured in Atlanta at that time. The circumstance was suggestive of Elijah and the ravens, and I thanked God for the gift so opportune, and lost no time in returning to the drug store, and thanking King, the raven employed by the Lord to clothe one of His little ones. Nor did I lose any time in adding to the package other articles of necessity, flannel and the best Georgia-made homespun I could procure, and was then ready to take the return train to Decatur. Thomie was deeply touched by the opportune gift, and said that King was a great boy, and that he must see him.

After supper I clandestinely left the house, and ran around to Todd McAllister's and begged him to take the job of making the suit. He agreed to cut the coat, vest and pantaloons by measure, and for that purpose went home with me, shears and tape measure in hand. Having finished this important part of the job, he told me he could not make the suit himself, but he thought if I would "talk right pretty to the old lady," she would do it. Next morning I lost no time in "talking pretty" to the old lady, and, having secured her promise to undertake the work, it was soon in her hands. With the help of faithful, efficient women, and I suspect of her husband, too, the job was executed surprisingly soon. In the meantime the making of flannel garments, and homespun shirts with bosoms made of linen pillow-cases, was progressing with remarkable celerity.

When all was finished, and Thomie was arrayed in his new suit, which set admirably well notwithstanding the room allowed for increasing dimensions, which we doubted not under good treatment he would attain—King Solomon, in purple and fine linen, was not looked upon with more admiration than was he by his loving mother and sisters. His cough had in a measure yielded to remedies, and his cheeks bore the tinge of better blood.

Good Mr. Levi Willard, his wife and children, had already been to see Thomie and the strangers within our gates, and many others had sent kind messages and substantial tokens of regard. And the young people of Decatur, young ladies and little boys, were planning to give him a surprise party. And among these loving attentions was a visit from King, the faithful.

The flowers bloomed prettier, the birds sang sweeter, because of their presence; but time waits for no man, and we were admonished by low conversations and suggestive looks that these men, officers in the army of the Confederacy, were planning their departure.

Many amusing incidents, as well as those of a horrible character, were told of their prison life in Camp Chase. To illustrate the patriotism of Southern men, Colonel Deshler, as a prisoner of war, figured conspicuously; and many anecdotes, ludicrous and pathetic, quaint and original, revealed the deep devotion of his love for the South. In one of these word-paintings, he was represented as sitting on his legs, darning the seat of his pantaloons, when a feminine curiosity seeker came along. When she perceived his occupation, she said with a leer that would have done credit to Lucifer:

"You rebels find it pretty hard work to keep your gray duds in order, don't you?"

Without looking at her, he whistled in musical cadence the contempt he felt for her and her ilk; and the imprecations, he would not have expressed in words, were so distinct and well modulated as to leave no doubt as to their meaning.

The time had come for the nature of the low-toned conversations referred to, to be revealed, and Thomie was chosen to make the revelation. Planning to have mother and sisters present, he discussed the duties of patriotism, and the odium men brought upon themselves by not discharging those duties. Making the matter personal, he referred to himself and friends, to the great pleasure and personal benefit derived from a week's sojourn at home; of the love for us that would ever linger in their hearts; of the pleasant memories that would nerve them in future conflicts; and in conclusion told us that tomorrow they would leave us to join their command at Tullahoma, where the decimated regiment was to stay until its numbers were sufficiently recruited for service.

Instead of yielding to grief, we repressed every evidence of it, and spoke only words of encouragement to these noble men who had never shirked a duty, or sought bomb-proof positions in the army of the Confederacy. After this interview, Thomie abandoned himself to cheerfulness, to almost boyish gaiety. He kept very close to his mother. She had grown old so rapidly since the troubles began, that she needed all the support that could be given her in this ordeal. This he perceived without seeming to do so, and left nothing within his power undone for her encouragement. He even discussed with perfect equanimity the probability, yea, the more than probability, of his getting killed in battle; for, said he, "*he that taketh up the sword, by the sword shall he perish.*"

And, he added, "strong, irrepressible convictions constrained me to enter the army in defence of mother, home, and country. My vote was cast for the secession of my state from the union of states which existed only in name, and I would not have accepted any position tendered me which would have secured me from the dangers involved by that step. I was willing to give my life if need be, for the cause which should be dear to every Southern heart."

Every one present responded to these noble sentiments, for were we not soldiers, too, working for the same noble cause, and aiding and abetting those who fought its battles?

Before retiring to our rooms, Captain Lauderdale, as usual, led in prayer, fervent, deep and soul supporting, more for our mother and ourselves than for himself and his comrades in their perilous positions. And dear Thomie, whom I had never heard pray since his cradle invocation,

*"Now I lay me down to sleep,
I pray the Lord my soul to keep,"*

finished in words thrilling and beautiful. The effect was electrical. Tears and sobs were no longer repressed, and all found relief from long pent-up feelings. O, the blessedness of tears!

Morning came, clear as crystal, and cool and exhilarating. The household were up at early dawn. A strong decoction of coffee was prepared, and fresh cream toast and boiled eggs, meat relishes being served cold. Knapsacks—there were knapsacks now—were packed, and blankets rolled and buckled in straps, and our ebony Confederates, Toby and Telitha, stood ready to convey them to the depot. In order to meet the morning train at seven o'clock we started, but the services of Toby and Telitha were not accepted. The gentlemen said it would never do for soldiers to start off to report for service with negroes carrying their knapsacks and blankets. They had no muskets to shoulder, for of these they had been divested at Arkansas Post, months ago, when captured by the enemy.

Lieutenant McMurray, who was in feeble health, announced himself unable to report for duty, and remained with us several weeks longer.

The parting at the depot did not betray the grief, almost without earthly hope, that was rankling in our hearts, and the "goodbye's" and "God bless you's" were uttered with a composure we little thought at our command.

As the time of his departure had drawn near, Thomie had sought opportunities to tell me much of the young girl in Texas, who had healed the lacerations of his youthful heart, and won the admiration of his manhood, and whom he had made his wife. Upon her devotion he dwelt with peculiar pathos and gratitude; and he concluded these conversations with the request that under any and all circumstances I would be a sister to her. On one occasion we were standing near the piano, and, when we ceased to talk, Thomie opened it, and in tones that came from the heart, and that were tremulous with emotion, he sang, "When this Cruel War is Over."

Why sings the swan its sweetest notes,
When life is near its close?

Since writing the foregoing, I have had access to a journal kept during the war by my half sister, Missouri Stokes, in which are the following entries of historic value:

On the 11th of January, 1868, Arkansas Post, the fort where Thomie was stationed, fell into the hands of Yankees. General Churchhill's whole command, numbering about four thousand, were captured, a few being killed and wounded. We knew that Thomie, if alive, must be a prisoner, but could hear no tidings from him. Our suspense continued until the latter part of March, when ma received a letter from our loved one, written at Camp Chase (military prison), Ohio, February 10th. This letter she forwarded to me, and I received it March 21st, with heart-felt emotions of gratitude to Him who had preserved his life. A few weeks afterwards another letter came, saying he expected to be exchanged in a few days, and then for several weeks we heard no more.

From this journal I learn that the date of Thomie's arrival was May 16th, 1863. My sister wrote of him:

He seemed much changed, although only four years and a half had elapsed since we parted. He looked older, thinner, and more careworn, and gray hairs are sprinkled among his dark brown curls. His health had been poor in the army, and then, when he left Camp Chase, he, as well as the other prisoners, was stripped by the Yankees of nearly all his warm clothing. He left the prison in April, and was exchanged at City Point. How strange the dealings of Providence. Truly was he led by a way he knew not. He went out to Texas by way of the West, and returned home from the East. God be thanked for preserving his life, when so many of his comrades have died. He is a miracle of mercy. After their capture, they were put on boats from which Yankee small-pox patients had been taken. Some died of small-pox, but Thomie has had varioloid and so escaped. He was crowded on a boat with twenty-two hundred, and scarcely had standing room. Many died on the passage up the river, one poor fellow with his head in Thomie's lap. May he never go through similar scenes again!

From this same journal I take the following, written after Missouri's return to the school she was teaching in Bartow County:

Sabbath morning, June 14th. Went to Cartersville to church. Some time elapsed before preaching commenced. A soldier came in, sat down rather behind me, then, rising, approached me. *It was Thomie.* I soon found (for we did talk in church) that he had an order to join Kirby Smith, with a recommendation from Bragg that he be allowed to recruit for his regiment. Fortunately there was a vacant seat in the carriage, so he went out home with us. Monday 15th, Thomie left. I rode with him a little beyond the school-house, then took my books and basket, and with one kiss, and, on my part, a tearful goodbye, we parted. As I walked slowly back, I felt so lonely. He had been with me just long enough for me to realize a brother's kind protection, and now he's torn away, and I'm again alone. I turned and looked. He was driving slowly along—he turned a corner and was hidden from my view. Shall I see him no more? Or shall we meet again? God only knows. After a fit of weeping, and one earnest prayer for him, I turned my steps to my little school.

And thus our brother went back to Texas, and gladly, too, for was not his Mary there?

Of Thomie's recall to join his command at Dalton; of his arrival at home the next February, on his way to "the front;" of his participation in the hard-fought battles that contested the way to Atlanta; and of his untimely death at the fatal Battle of Franklin, Tennessee, I may speak hereafter.

Even in the spring and summer of 1863, the shadows began to deepen, and to hearts less sanguine than mine, affairs were assuming a gloomy aspect. I notice in this same journal from which I have quoted the foregoing extracts, the following:

Our fallen braves, how numerous! Among our generals, Zollicoffer, Ben McCulloch, Albert Sidney Johnston, and the saintly, dauntless Stonewall Jackson, are numbered with the dead; while scarcely a household in our land does not mourn the loss of a brave husband and father, son or brother.

Chapter 8

Some Social Features

In the winter of 1864 there seems to have been a lull of hostilities between the armies at "the front." Morgan's men were rendezvousing near Decatur. Their brave and dashing chief had been captured, but had made his escape from the Ohio penitentiary, and was daily expected. Some artillery companies were camping near, among them Waddell's. There was also a conscript camp within a mile or two; so it is not to be wondered at that the young ladies of Decatur availed themselves in a quiet way of the social enjoyment the times afforded, and that there were little gatherings at private houses at which "Morgan's men" and the other soldiers were frequently represented.

Our brother was absent in Texas, where he had been assigned to duty, but my sister was at home, and many an hour's entertainment her music gave that winter to the soldiers and to the young people of Decatur. My mother's hospitality was proverbial, and much of our time these wintry months was spent in entertaining our soldier guests, and in ministering to the sick in the Atlanta hospitals, and in the camps and temporary hospitals about Decatur.

So near were we now to "the front" (about a hundred miles distant), that several of my brother's Texas comrades obtained furloughs and came to see us. Among these were Lieutenants Prendergast and Jewell, Captain Leonard and Lieutenant Collins, Captain Bennett and Lieutenant Donathan. They usually had substantial boots made while here, by Smith, the Decatur boot and shoe maker, which cost less than those they could have bought in Atlanta. We received some very pleasant calls from Morgan's men and Waddell's Artillery. Among the latter we have always remembered a young man from Alabama, James Duncan Calhoun, of remarkable intellectual ability, refreshing candour and refinement of manner. Ever since the war Mr. Calhoun has devoted himself to journalism.

Among the former we recall Lieutenant Adams, Messrs. Gill, Dupries, Clinkinbeard, Steele, Miller, Fortune, Rowland, Baker, and Dr. Lewis. These gentlemen were courteous and intelligent, and evidently came of excellent Kentucky and Tennessee families. One evening several of these gentlemen had taken tea with us, and after supper the number of our guests was augmented by the coming of Dr. Ruth, of Kentucky, and Dr. H. B. Haynie, surgeon of the 14th Tennessee Cavalry. Dr. Haynie was an elderly, gray-haired man, of fine presence, and with the courtly manners of the old school. On being unanimously requested, he sang us a song entitled: "The Wailings at Fort Delaware," which he had composed when an inmate of that wretched prison. As one of the gentlemen remarked, "there is more truth than poetry in it;" yet there are in it some indications of poetic genius, and Dr. Haynie sang it with fine effect.

The Wailings at Fort Delaware.
By B. H. Haynie, Surgeon 14th Tennessee Cavalry
(Morgan's Division).

Oh! here we are confined at Fort Delaware,
With nothing to drink but a little lager beer,
Infested by vermin as much as we can bear;
Oh Jeff, can't you help us to get away from here?

Chorus—
And it's home, dearest home, the place I ought to be,
Home, sweet home, way down in Tennessee,
Where the ash and the oak and the bonny willow tree,
Are all growing green way down in Tennessee.

The Island itself will do well enough,
But the flat-footed Dutch are filthy and rough,
Oh! take us away from the vandal clan,
Down into Dixie among the gentlemen.

Chorus—And its home, dearest home, etc.

Spoiled beef and bad soup is our daily fare,
And to complain is more than any dare;
They will buck us and gag us, and cast us in a cell,
There to bear the anguish and torments of hell.

Chorus—

The den for our eating is anything but clean,

And the filth upon the tables is plainly to be seen,
And the smell of putrefaction rises on the air,
"To fill out the bill" of our daily fare.

Chorus—

"The sick are well treated," [1] as Southern surgeons say,
"And the losses by death are scarcely four per day;"
It's diarrhœa mixture for scurvy and small-pox,
And every other disease of Pandora's box!

Chorus—

Oh! look at the graveyard on the Jersey shore,
At the hundreds and the thousands who'll return no more;
Oh! could they come back to testify
Against the lying devils, and live to see them die!

Chorus—

"Our kindness to prisoners you cannot deny, [1]
For we have the proof at hand upon which you can rely;
It's no Dutch falsehood, nor a Yankee trick,
But from Southern surgeons who daily see the sick."

Chorus—

Our chaplain, whose heart was filled with heavenly joys,
Asked leave to pray and preach to Southern boys;
"Oh, no!" says the General, "you are not the man,
You are a Southern rebel, the vilest of your clan!"

Chorus—

Oh! speak out, young soldier, and let your country hear,
All about your treatment at Fort Delaware;
How they worked you in their wagons when weary and sad,
With only half rations, when plenty they had.

Chorus—

The barracks were crowded to an overflow,
Without a single comfort on the soldier to bestow;
Oh, there they stood shivering in hopeless despair,
With insufficient diet or clothing to wear!

Chorus—

---

1. The fifth and seventh verses are criticisms upon four Southern surgeons, who gave the Federal authorities a certificate that our prisoners were well treated, and our sick well cared for, and that the average loss by death was only four per day.

*The mother stood weeping in sorrows of woe,
Mingling her tears with the waters that flow;
Her son was expiring at Fort Delaware,
Which could have been avoided with prudence and care.*

Chorus—

*Oh! take off my fetters and let me go free,
To roam o'er the mountains of old Tennessee;
To bathe in her waters and breathe her balmy air,
And look upon her daughters so lovely and fair.*

Chorus—

*Then, cheer up, my brave boys, your country will be free,
Your battles will be fought by Generals Bragg and Lee;
And the Yankees will fly with trembling and fear,
And we'll return to our wives and sweethearts so dear.*

Chorus—

*And it's home, dearest home, the place where I ought to be,
Home, sweet home way down in Tennessee,
Where the ash and the oak, and the bonny willow tree,
Are all growing green way down in Tennessee.*

CHAPTER 9

Thomie's Second Home Coming

Early one morning in the February of the winter just referred to (that of 1864), as my sister lay awake, she heard some one step upon the portico and knock. As Toby opened the door, she heard him exclaim: "Why howd'y, Marse Thomie!" Her first thought was, "now he is back just in time to be in the battle!" for a resumption of hostilities was daily looked for near Dalton. We were all greatly surprised at Thomie's arrival on this side of the Mississippi, as only a few days before we had received a letter from him, written, it is true, so long as the November before, saying he had been assigned to duty out in Texas by General Henry McCulloch. But the consolidation of the regiments in Granbury's brigade having been broken up, he had been ordered back to join his old command. He had left Marshall, Texas, the 28th of January, having made the trip in one month, and having walked four hundred miles of the way.

Under the circumstances, we were both glad and sorrowful at his return. After a stay of three days, he left us for "the front." In the early morning of February 29th, we went with him to the depot, the last time we four were ever together. Parting from him was a bitter trial to our mother, who wept silently as we walked back to the desolate home, no longer gladdened by the sunny presence of the only son and brother. Perhaps nothing will give a more graphic impression of some phases of army life at this time, nor a clearer insight into our brother's character, than a few extracts from his letters written at this period to his sister Missouri, and preserved by her to this day:

Dalton, Ga., March 15th, 1864.—..... Our regiment takes its old organisation as the 10th Texas, and Colonel Young has been dispatched to Texas to gather all the balance, under an order from the war department. We are now in Dalton doing provost duty (our regiment), which is a very unpleasant duty. It is my business to examine all papers whenever the cars arrive, and it is very disagreeable to have to arrest persons who haven't proper papers. The regulations about the town are very strict. No one under a brigadier-general can pass without approval papers. My guard arrested General Johnston himself, day before yesterday. Not knowing him they wouldn't take his word for it, but demanded his papers.

The old general, very good-humouredly showed them some orders he had issued himself, and, being satisfied, they let him pass. He took it good-humouredly, while little colonels and majors become very indignant and wrathy under such circumstances. From which we learn, first, the want of good common sense, and, secondly, that a great man is an humble man, and does not look with contempt upon his inferiors in rank, whatsoever that rank may be.

There is a very interesting meeting in progress here. I get to go every other night. I have seen several baptized since I have been here. There are in attendance every evening from six to seven hundred soldiers. There are many who go to the anxious seat. Three made a profession of religion night before last. I am going tonight. There seems to be a deep interest taken, and God grant the good work may go on until the whole army may be made to feel where they stand before their Maker. Write soon.

  Your affectionate brother,

                Tom Stokes.

From another letter we take the following:

Near Dalton, April 5th, 1864.—We have had for some weeks back very unsettled weather, which has rendered it very disagreeable, though we haven't suffered; we have an old tent which affords a good deal of protection from the weather. It has also interfered some with our meetings, though there is preaching nearly every night that there is not rain. Brother Hughes came up and preached for us last Friday night and seemed to give general satisfaction. He was plain and practical, which is the only kind of preaching that does good in the army. He promised to come back again. I like him very much. Another old brother, named Campbell, whom I heard when I was a boy, preached for us on Sabbath evening. There was much feeling, and at the close of the services he invited mourners to the anxious seat, and I shall never forget that blessed half-hour that followed; from every part of that great congregation they came, many with streaming eyes; and, as they gave that old patriarch their hands, asked that God's people would pray for them. Yes, men who never shrank in battle from any responsibility, came forward weeping. Such is the power of the Gospel of Christ when preached in its purity. Oh, that all ministers of Christ could, or would, realize the great responsibility resting upon them as His ambassadors.

Sabbath night we had services again, and also last night, both well attended, and tonight, weather permitting, I will preach. God help me and give me grace from on high, that I may be enabled, as an humble instrument in His hands, to speak the truth as it is in Jesus, for *'none but Jesus can do helpless sinners good.'* I preached last Sabbath was two weeks ago to a large and attentive congregation. There seemed to be much seriousness, and although much embarrassed, yet I tried, under God, to feel that I was but in the discharge of my duty; and may I ever be found battling for my Saviour. Yes, my sister, I had rather be an humble follower of Christ than to wear the crown of a monarch. Remember me at all times at a Throne of Grace, that my life may be spared to become a useful minister of Christ.

Since my return we have established a prayer-meeting in our company, or, rather, a kind of family service, every night after roll call. There is one other company which has prayer every night. Captain F. is very zealous. There are four in our company who pray in public—one sergeant, a private, Captain F. and myself. We take it time about. We have cleared up a space, fixed a stand and seats, and have a regular preaching place. I have never seen such a spirit as there is now in the army. Religion is the theme. Everywhere, you hear around the camp-fires at night the sweet songs of Zion. This spirit pervades the whole army. God is doing a glorious work, and I believe it is but the beautiful prelude to peace. I feel confident that if the enemy should attempt to advance, that God will fight our battles for us, and the boastful foe be scattered and severely rebuked.

I witnessed a scene the other evening, which did my heart good—the baptism of three men in the creek near the encampment. To see those hardy soldiers taking up their cross and following their Master in His ordinance, being buried with Him in baptism, was indeed a beautiful sight. I really believe, Missouri, that there is more religion now in the army than among the thousands of skulkers, exempts and speculators at home. There are but few now but who will talk freely with you upon the subject of their soul's salvation.

What a change, what a change! when one year ago card playing and profane language seemed to be the order of the day. Now, what is the cause of this change? Manifestly the working of God's spirit. He has chastened His people, and this manifestation of His love seems to be an earnest of the good things in store for us in not a far away future. '*Whom the Lord loveth He chasteneth, and scourgeth every son whom He receiveth.*' Let all the people at home now, in unison with the army, humbly bow, acknowledge the afflicting hand of the Almighty, ask Him to remove the curse upon His own terms, and soon we will hear, so far as our Nation is concerned, 'Glory to God in the highest, on earth peace, good will toward men!'

I received the articles ma sent by Brother Hughes, which were much relished on the top of the coarse fare of the army. . . . . Write me often. God bless you in your labours to do good.

Your affectionate brother,

T. J. Stokes.

From another of those time-stained, but precious letters, we cull the following, under the heading of:

In Camp, Near Dalton, Ga., April 18, 1864.—The good work still goes on here. Thirty-one men were baptized at the creek below our brigade yesterday, and I have heard from several other brigades in which the proportion is equally large (though the thirty-one were not all members of this brigade). Taking the proportion in the whole army as heard from (and I have only heard from a part of one corps), there must have been baptized yesterday 150 persons—maybe 200. This revival spirit is not confined to a part only, but pervades the whole army. . .
. . .Brother Hughes was with us the other night, but left again the next morning. The old man seemed to have much more influence in the army than young men. I have preached twice since writing to you, and the Spirit seemed to be with me. The

second sermon was upon the crucifixion of Christ: text in the 53rd chapter of Isaiah: '*He was wounded for our transgressions and bruised for our iniquities.*'

It was the first time in my life, that is, in public speaking, that my feelings got so much the mastery of me as to make me weep like a child. In the conclusion I asked all who felt an interest in the prayers of God's people to come to the anxious seat. Many presented themselves, and I could hear many among them, with sobs and groans, imploring God to have mercy upon them; and I think the Lord did have mercy upon them, for when we opened the door of the church six united with us. Every Sabbath you may see the multitude wending their way to the creek to see the solemn ordinance typical of the death, burial and resurrection of our Saviour. Strange to say that a large number of those joining the pedo-Baptist branches prefer being immersed; though in the preaching you cannot tell to which denomination a man belongs. This is as it should be; Christ and Him crucified should be the theme. It is time enough, I think, after one is converted, to choose his church rule of faith.

If this state of things should continue for any considerable length of time, we will have in the Army of Tennessee an army of believers. Does the history of the world record anywhere the like? Even Cromwell's time sinks into insignificance. A revival so vast in its proportions, and under all the difficulties attending camp life, the bad weather this spring, and innumerable difficulties, is certainly an earnest of better, brighter times not far in the future.

To the believer in Jesus, we feel sure that these extracts concerning this remarkable work of grace, will prove of deep interest; so we make no apologies for quoting in continuation the following from another of those letters of our soldier brother, to whom the conquests of the cross were the sweetest of all themes:

Near Dalton, April 28th, 1864.—My Dear Sister: I should have written sooner but have been very much engaged, and when not engaged have felt more like resting than writing, and, to add to this, Sister Mary very agreeably surprised me by coming up on last Saturday. She left on Tuesday morning for home. While she was at Dalton, I went down on each day and remained until evening. I fear ma and sister are too much concerned about me, and therefore render themselves unhappy. Would that they could trust God calmly for the issue. And I fear, too, that they deny themselves of many comforts, that they may furnish me with what I could do (as many have to do) without.

The great unexampled revival is fast increasing in interest. I have just returned from the creek, where I saw thirty-three buried with Christ in baptism, acknowledging there before two thousand persons that they were not ashamed to follow Jesus in His ordinance. My soul was made happy in witnessing the solemn scene. In that vast audience everything was as quiet and respectful as in a village chapel; and, by the way, I have seen village congregations who might come here and learn to behave. General Lowry baptized about thirteen of them who were from his brigade. He is a Christian, a soldier and a zealous preacher, and his influence is great.

It was truly a beautiful sight to see a general baptizing his men. He preaches for our brigade next Sabbath. I preached for General Polk's brigade night before last, and we had a very interesting meeting. They have just begun there, yet I had a congregation of some 400. At the conclusion of the services, I invited those who desired an interest in our prayers to manifest their desire by coming to the altar. A goodly number presented themselves, and we prayed with them. I shall preach for them again very soon. The revival in our brigade has continued now for four weeks, nearly, and many have found peace with their Saviour. If we could remain stationary a few weeks longer, I believe the greater portion of the army would be converted. This is all the doings of the Lord, and is surely the earnest of the great deliverance in store for us.

It is the belief of many, that this is the *'beginning of the end.'* From all parts of the army the glad tidings comes that a great revival is in progress. I wish I had time to write to you at length. One instance of the power of His spirit: A lieutenant of our regiment, and heretofore very wild, became interested, and for nearly three weeks seemed groaning in agony. The other day he came around to see me, and, with a face beaming with love, told me he had found Christ, and that his only regret now was that he had not been a Christian all his life. It is growing dark. I must close. More *anon*.

    Affectionately,   Your Brother.

We take up the next letter in the order of time. It is numbered 25. The envelope is of brown wrapping paper, but neatly made, and has a blue Confederate 10 cent postage stamp. It is addressed to my sister, who was then teaching at Corinth, Heard county, Georgia. It is dated:

"Near Dalton, May 5th, 1864." After speaking of having to take charge early the next morning of the brigade picket guard, Thomie goes on to say:

> The sun's most down, but I think I can fill these little pages before dark. Captain F., coming in at this time, tells me a dispatch has just been received to the effect that the Yankees are advancing in the direction of Tunnel Hill, but they have made so many feints in that direction lately that we have become used to them, so don't become uneasy.
>
> The great revival is going on with widening and deepening interest. Last Sabbath I saw eighty-three immersed at the creek below our brigade. Four were sprinkled at the stand before going down to the creek, and two down there, making an aggregate within this vicinity of eighty-nine, while the same proportion, I suppose, are turning to God in other parts of the army, making the grand aggregate of many hundreds. Yesterday I saw sixty-five more baptized, forty more who were to have been there failing to come because of an order to be ready to move at any moment. They belong to a more distant brigade. . . . If we do not move before Monday, Sabbath will be a day long to be remembered—'the water will,' indeed, 'be troubled.' Should we remain three weeks longer, the glad tidings may go forth that the Army of Tennessee is the army of the Lord. But He knoweth best what is for our good, and if He sees proper can so order His providence as to keep us here. His will be done.

The next letter is addressed to me, but was sent to my sister at my request, and is dated "Allatoona Mountains, Near Night, May 22nd." He writes:

> Oh, it grieved my very soul when coming through the beautiful Oothcaloga valley, to think of the sad fate which awaited it when the foul invader should occupy that 'vale of beauty.' We formed line of battle at the creek, at the old Eads place; our brigade was to the left as you go up to Mr. Law's old place on the hill, where we stayed once when pa was sick. Right here,

with a thousand dear recollections of by-gone days crowding my mind, in the valley of my boyhood, I felt as if I could hurl a host back. We fought them and whipped them, until, being-flanked, we were compelled to fall back. We fought them again at Cass Station, driving them in our front, but, as before, and for the same reason, we were compelled to retreat.

******

As I am requested to hold prayer-meeting this evening at sunset, I must close.

Thomie's next letter in this collection is addressed to his sister Missouri, who had returned home, and is headed, simply, "Army of Tennessee, May 31st." It is written in a round, legible, but somewhat delicate hand, and gives no evidence of nervousness or hurry. To those fond of war history, it will be of special interest:

> Our brigade, in fact our division, is in a more quiet place now than since the commencement of this campaign. We were ordered from the battlefield on Sunday morning to go and take position in supporting distance of the left wing of the army, where we arrived about the middle of the forenoon, and remained there until yesterday evening, when our division was ordered back in rear of the left centre, where we are now. Contrary to all expectations, we have remained here perfectly quiet, there being no heavy demonstration by the enemy on either wing. We were very tired, and this rest has been a great help to us; for being a reserve and flanking division, we have had to trot from one end of the wing of the army to the other, and support other troops.

******

Well, perhaps you would like to hear something from me of the battle of New Hope Church, on Friday evening, 27th inst. We had been, since the day before, supporting some other troops about the centre of the right wing, when, I suppose about 2 o'clock, we were hurried off to the extreme right to meet a heavy force of the enemy trying to turn our right. A few minutes later the whole army might now have been in the vicinity of Atlanta, but, as it was, we arrived in the nick of time, for before we were properly formed the enemy were firing into us rapidly. We fronted to them, however, and then commenced one of the hottest engagements, so far, of this campaign. We had no support, and just one single line against a whole corps of the enemy, and a lieutenant of the 19th Arkansas, wounded and captured by them, and subsequently retaken by our brigade, stated that another corps of the enemy came up about sundown. The fighting of our men, to those who admire warfare, was magnificent. You could see a pleasant smile playing upon the countenances of many of the men, as they would cry out to the Yankees, 'Come on, we are demoralized!'

One little incident right here, so characteristic of the man. Major Kennard (of whom I have told you often, lately promoted), was, as usual, encouraging the men by his battle-cry of, '*Put your trust in God, men, for He is with us*,' but concluding to talk to the Yankees awhile, sang out to them, 'Come on, we are demoralised,' when the major was pretty severely wounded in the head, though not seriously; raising himself up, he said:

'Boys, I told them a lie, and I believe that is the reason I got shot.'

The fighting was very close and desperate, and lasted until after dark. About 11 o'clock at night, three regiments of our brigade charged the enemy, our regiment among them. We went over ravines, rocks, almost precipices, running the enemy entirely off the field. We captured many prisoners, and all of their dead and many of their wounded fell into our hands. This charge was a desperate and reckless thing, and if the enemy had made any resistance they could have cut us all to pieces. I hurt my leg slightly in falling down a cliff of rocks, and when we started back to our original line of battle I thought I would go back alone and pick my way; so I bore off to the left, got lost, and completely bewildered between two armies. I copy from my journal:

> Here I was, alone in the darkness of midnight, with the wounded, the dying, the dead. What an hour of horror! I hope never again to experience such. I am not superstitious, but the great excitement of seven hours of fierce conflict, ending with a bold, and I might say reckless, charge—for we knew not what was in our front—and then left entirely alone, causes a mental and physical depression that for one to fully appreciate he must be surrounded by the same circumstances. My feelings in battle were nothing to compare to this hour. After go-

ing first one way and then another, and not bettering my case, I heard someone slipping along in the bushes. I commanded him to halt, and inquired what regiment he belonged to, and was answered, '15th Wisconsin,' so I took Mr. Wisconsin in, and ordered him to march before me—a nice pickle for me then, had a prisoner and did not know where to go.

Moved on, however, and finally heard some more men walking, hailed them, for I had become desperate, and was answered, 'Mississippians.' Oh, how glad I was! The moon at this time was just rising, and, casting her pale silvery rays through the dense woods, made every tree and shrub look like a spectre. I saw a tall, muscular Federal lying dead and the moonlight shining in his face. His eyes were open and seemed to be riveted on me. I could not help but shudder. I soon found my regiment, and 'Richard was himself again.

I went out again to see if I could do anything for their wounded. Soon found one with his leg shot through, whom I told we would take care of. Another, shot in the head, was crying out continually; 'Oh, my God! oh, my God!!' I asked him if we could do anything for him, but he replied that it would be of no use. I told him God would have mercy upon him, but his mind seemed to be wandering. I could not have him taken care of that night, and, poor fellow, there he lay all night.

The next morning I had the privilege of walking over the whole ground, and such a scene! Here lay the wounded, the dying, and the dead, hundreds upon hundreds, in every conceivable position; some with contorted features, showing the agony of death, others as if quietly sleeping. I noticed some soft beardless faces which ill comported with the savage warfare in which they had been engaged. Hundreds of letters from mothers, sisters, and friends were found upon them, and ambrotypes, taken singly and in groups. Though they had been my enemies, my heart bled at the sickening scene. The wounded nearly all expressed themselves tired of the war.

For the numbers engaged upon our side, it is said to be the greatest slaughter of the enemy of any recent battle. Captain Hearne, the old adjutant of our regiment, was killed. Eight of our regiment were instantly killed; two mortally wounded, since dead.

I did not think of writing so much when I began, but it is the first opportunity of writing anything like a letter that I have had. Lieutenant McMurray is now in charge of the Texas hospital at Auburn, Alabama.

******

Well, you are now Aunt Missouri. Oh, that I could see my boy! Heaven has protected me thus far and I hope that God will consider me through this dreadful ordeal, and protect me for Christ's sake; not that there is any merit that I can offer, but I do hope to live that I may be an humble instrument in the hands of my God to lead others to Him. I hold prayer in our company nearly every night when circumstances will permit, and the men don't go to sleep before we are quiet. Poor fellows, they are ever willing to join me, but often are so wearied I dislike to interrupt them.

My sister, let our trust be confidently in God. He can save or He can destroy. Let us pray Him for peace. He can give it us; not pray as if we were making an experiment, but pray believing God will answer our prayers, for we have much to pray for.

My sister subsequently copied into her journal the following extract, taken from his, and written soon after the Battle of New Hope Church:

May 31st, 1864.—Here we rest by a little murmuring brook, singing along as if the whole world was at peace. I lay down last night and gazed away up in the peaceful heavens. All was quiet and serene up there, and the stars seemed to vie with each other in brightness and were fulfilling their allotted destiny. My comrades all asleep; nothing breaks the silence. I leave earth for a time, and soar upon 'imagination's wings' far away from this war-accursed land to where bright angels sing their everlasting songs of peace and strike their harps along the golden streets of the New Jerusalem, and the swelling music bursts with sweet accord throughout vast Heaven's eternal space!

******

Again on Sabbath, June 5th, he writes:

No music of church bells is heard today summoning God's people to worship where the gospel is wont to be heard. We are near a large log church called Gilgal. What a different scene is presented to-day from a Sabbath four years ago when the aged minister of God read to a large and attentive congregation: "*The Lord is my shepherd, I shall not want. He maketh me to lie down in green pastures, He leadeth me beside the still waters.*" O, God, wilt thou not interpose Thy strong arm to stop the bloody strife? Wilt Thou not hear the prayers of Thy people who daily say, Lord, give us peace? The Lord will answer, and soon white-robed peace will smile upon our unhappy country. O God, hasten the day, for we are sorely vexed, and thine shall be all the glory.

Ere peace was to dawn upon his beloved country, his own soul was to find it through the portals of death; but ere that time, save a brief interval of enforced rest, weary marchings and heart-breaking scenes and sorrows were to intervene.

Thomie's next letter is dated "In the Field, near Lost Mountain, June 14th," and the next "In the Ditches, June 22nd, 1864." The next, "Near Chattahoochee River, July 6th, 1864," tells of the retreat of the army from Kennesaw Mountain to Smyrna Church, and of his coming off safely from another "small fight" the day before, in which several of his comrades were killed.

Owing to nervous prostration, and other illness, Thomie was soon after sent to the hospital at Macon, transferred from there to Augusta, and from the latter point given leave of absence to visit his sister, who had found refuge with her cousin, Mrs. T. J. Hillsman, a daughter of Rev. Wm. H. Stokes of blessed memory. Here, with his father's kindred, cheered by beautiful hospitality and cousinly affection, our darling brother enjoyed the last sweet rest and quiet earth was e'er to give him before he slept beneath its sod.

Chapter 10

A Visit to Dalton

From Atlanta to Dalton, $7.75. From the 23rd to the 26th of April, 1864, to Mrs. John Reynolds, for board, $20.00. From Dalton to Decatur, $8.00.

The above statement of the expense attending a round trip to Dalton, Georgia, is an excerpt from a book which contains a record of every item of my expenditures for the year 1864.

This trip was taken for the purpose of carrying provisions and articles of clothing to my brother and his comrades in General Joseph E. Johnston's command. In vain had our mother tried to send appetizing baskets of food to her son, whose soldier rations consisted of salty bacon and hard tack; some disaster, real or imaginary, always occurred to prevent them from reaching their destination, and it was, therefore, determined at home that I should carry the next consignment.

After several days' preparation, jugs were filled with good sorghum syrup, and baskets with bread, pies, cakes and other edibles at our command, and sacks of potatoes, onions and peppers were included. My fond and loving mother and I, and our faithful *aide-de-camps* of African descent, conveyed them to the depot. In those days the depot was a favourite resort with the ladies and children of Decatur. There they always heard something from the front—wherever that might be. The obliging agent had a way, all his own, of acquiring information from the army in all its varied commands, and dealt it out galore to the encouragement or discouragement of his auditors, as his prejudices or partialities prompted. On this occasion many had gone there, who, like myself, were going to take the train for Atlanta, and in the interim were eager to hear everything of a hopeful character, even though reason urged that it was hoping against hope.

I was the cynosure of all eyes, as I was going to "the front;" and every mother who had a darling son in that branch of the army hoped that he would be the first to greet me on my arrival there, and give me a message for her. And I am sure, if the love consigned to me for transmission could have assumed tangible form and weight, it would have been more than fourteen tons to the square inch.

Helpful, willing hands deposited with care my well-labelled jugs, baskets, etc., and I deposited myself with equal care in an already well-filled coach on the Georgia Railroad. Arrived in Atlanta I surreptitiously stowed the jugs in the car with me, and then asked the baggage-master to transfer the provisions to a Dalton freight train. Without seeming to do so, I watched his every movement until I saw the last article safely placed in the car, and then I went aboard myself. Surrounded by jugs and packages, I again became an object of interest, and soon found myself on familiar terms with all on board; for were we not friends and kindred bound to each other by the closest ties? Every age and condition of Southern life was represented in that long train of living, anxious freight.

Young wives, with wee bit tots chaperoned by their mothers and sometimes by their grandmothers, were going to see their husbands, for, perhaps, the last time on earth; and mothers, feeling that another fond embrace of their sons would palliate the sting of final separation. The poor man and the rich man, fathers alike of men fighting the same battles in defence of the grandest principle that ever inspired mortal man to combat, on their way to see those men and leave their benedictions with them; and sisters, solitary and alone, going to see their beloved brothers and assure them once more of the purest and most disinterested love that ever found lodgement in the human heart. Many and pleasant were the brief conversations between those dissimilar in manners, habits and conditions in life; the great bond connecting them rendered every other consideration subordinate, and the rich and poor, the educated and ignorant, met and mingled in harmonious intercourse.

Those were days of slow travel in the South. The roads were literally blockaded with chartered cars, which contained the household goods of refugees who had fled from the wrath and vandalism of the enemy, and not unfrequently refugees themselves inhabited cars that seemed in fearful proximity to danger. Ample opportunity of observation on either side was furnished by this slow travel, and never did the fine, arable lands bordering the Western & Atlantic road from the Chattahoochee river to Dalton give greater promise of cereals, and trees in large variety were literally abloom with embryo fruit. Alas! that such a land should be destined to fall into the hands of despoilers.

At Dalton I went immediately to the agent at the depot, whom I found to be my old friend, John Reynolds, for the purpose of getting information regarding boarding houses. He told me his wife was in that line and would accommodate me, and, to render the application more easy, he gave me a note of introduction to her.

A beautiful, well-furnished room was given me, and a luscious supper possessed exhilarating properties.

In the meantime, Mr. Reynolds had, at my request, notified my brother, whom he knew, of my presence in his house, and I awaited his coming anxiously; but I was disappointed. A soldier's time is not his own, even in seasons of tranquillity, and he was on duty and could not come then, but he assured me on a small scrap of paper, torn from his note-book, that he would come as soon as he could get off "tomorrow morning."

The waiting seemed very long, and yet it had its ending. The night was succeeded by a typical April day, replete with sunshine and shower, and the hopes and fears of a people struggling for right over wrong.

At length the cheery voice of him, who always had a pleasant word for everyone, greeted me, and I hastened to meet him. That we might be quiet and undisturbed, I conducted him to my room, and a long and pleasant conversation ensued. I wish I had time and space to recapitulate the conversation; for its every word and intonation are preserved in the archives of memory, and will enter the grand eternities with me as free from discord as when first uttered. Our mother's failing health gave him concern, but his firm reliance in Him who doeth all things well, quieted his sad forebodings and led the way to pleasanter themes.

He loved to dwell upon the quaint and innocent peculiarities of his younger sister, and, as for his older one, it was very evident that he regarded her fully strong enough to "tote her own skillet," and "paddle her own canoe." A rap upon the door indicated that someone wished to see either one or the other of us. I responded, and was met by a negro boy bearing a huge waiter, evidently well-filled, and covered over with a snow-white cloth. The aroma from that waiter would have made a mummy smile. I had it put upon a table, and then I removed the cover, and saw with gratification the squab pie which I had ordered for dear Thomie, and a greater gratification awaited me, *i. e.*, seeing him eat it with a relish. Nor was the pie the only luxury in that waiter. Fresh butter and buttermilk, and a pone of good corn bread, etc., etc., supplemented by baked apples and cream and sugar.

"Come, dear Thomie, and let us eat together once more," was my invitation to that dinner, and radiant with thanks he took the seat I offered him. I did not have the Christian courage to ask him to invoke a blessing upon this excellent food, but I saw that one was asked in silence, nevertheless, and I am sure that an invocation went up from my own heart none the less sincere.

"Sister, I appreciate this compliment," he said.

"I could do nothing that would compliment you, Thomie," I answered, and added, "I hope you will enjoy your dinner as a love offering from me."

We lingered long around that little table, and many topics were touched upon during that period.

After dinner I asked Thomie to lie down and rest awhile. He thanked me, and said that the bed would tempt an anchorite to peaceful slumber, and he could not resist its wooings. A few minutes after he lay down he was sound asleep. He slept as a child—calm and peaceful. That a fly might not disturb him, I improvised a brush—my handkerchief and a tender twig from a tree near by being the component parts. As I sat by him and studied his manly young face, and read its expression of good will to all mankind, I wept to think that God had possibly required him as our sacrifice upon the altar of our country.

The slanting rays of the Western sun fell full and radiant upon his placid face, and awakened him from this long and quiet slumber. With a smile he arose and said:

"This won't do for me."

Hasty goodbyes and a fervent "God bless you" were uttered, and another one of the few partings that remained to be taken took place between the soldier and his sister.

******

The day was bright and exhilarating, in the month of June, 1864. Gay laughing Flora had tripped over woodland and lawn and scattered with prodigal hands flowers of every hue and fragrance, and the balmy atmosphere of early summer was redolent with their sweet perfume; and all nature, animate and inanimate, seemed imbued with the spirit of adoration towards the Giver of these perfect works. Although many hearts had been saddened by the mighty conflict being waged for the supremacy of Constitutional rights, there were yet in Decatur a large number to whom personal sorrow for personal bereavement had not come, and they were in sympathy with this beautiful scene, whose brilliant tints were but the reflection of divine glory, and whose faintest odour was distilled in the alchemy of heaven.

I was contemplating this scene in grateful admiration, and blended with my thoughts came the memory of my brother, who was in the foremost ranks of the contest. He, too, loved the beautiful and the good, and "looked from nature up to nature's God." All unconsciously I found myself plucking his favourite flowers, and arranging a choice bouquet, a spirit offering to him who might even then be hovering over me and preparing my mind for the sad denouement. With these reflections, I ascended the steps of my cottage home, and turned to take another look upon the enchanting scene, when I saw, approaching, one of my mother's faithful servants, who was hired to Dr. Taylor, a well-known druggist of Atlanta.

Ever apprehensive of evil tidings from "the front," and "the front" being the portion of the army that embraced my brother, I was almost paralyzed. I stood as if riveted to the floor, and awaited developments. King, for that was the name of the ebony-hued and faithful servant whose unexpected appearance had caused such a heart-flutter, came nearer and nearer. On his approach I asked in husky voice, "Have you heard anything from your Marse Thomie, King?"

"No, ma'am; have you?"

The light of heaven seemed to dispel the dark clouds which had gathered over and around my horizon, and I remembered my duty to one, who, though in a menial position, had doubtless come on some kind errand.

"Come in, King, and sit down and rest yourself," I said, pointing to an easy chair on the portico.

"I am not tired, Miss Mary, and would rather stand," he replied.

And he did stand, with his hat in his hand; and I thought for the first time in my life, probably, that he evinced a true manhood, worthy of Caucasian lineage; not that there was a drop of Caucasian blood in his veins, for he was a perfect specimen of the African race and as black as Erebus.

The suspense was becoming painful, when it was broken by King asking:

"Miss Mary, is Miss Polly at home?"

"Yes, King, and I will tell her you are here."

"Miss Polly," my mother and King's mistress, soon appeared and gave him a genuine welcome.

King now lost no time in making known the object of his visit, and thus announced it:

"Miss Polly, don't you want to sell me?"

"No; why do you ask?"

"Because, Miss Polly, Mr. Johnson wants to buy me, and he got me to come to see you and ask you if you would sell me."

"Do you want me to sell you, King? Would you rather belong to Mr. Johnson than me?"

"Now, Miss Polly, you come to the point, and I am going to try to answer it. I love you, and you have always been a good mistuss to us all, and I don't think there is one of us that would rather belong to someone else; but I tell you how it is, Miss Polly, and you musn't get mad with me for saying it; when this war is over none of us are going to belong to you. We'll all be free, and I would a great deal rather Mr. Johnson would lose me than you. He is always bragging about what he will do; hear him talk, you would think he was a bigger man than Mr. Lincoln is, and had more to back him; but I think he's a mighty little man myself, and I want him to lose me. He says he'll give you his little old store on Peachtree street for me. It don't mean much, I know, but, much or little, it's going to be more than me after the war."

And thus this unlettered man, who in the ordinary acceptation of the term had never known what it was to be free, argued with his mistress the importance of the exchange of property of which he himself was a part, for her benefit and that of her children.

"Remember, Miss Polly," he said, "that when Marse Thomie comes out of the war, it will be mighty nice for him to have a store of his own to commence business in, and if I was in your place I would take it for me, for I tell you again, Miss Polly, when the war's over we'll all be free."

But the good mistress, who had listened in silence to these arguments, was unmoved. She saw before her a man who had been born a slave in her family, and who had grown to man's estate under the fostering care of slavery, whose high sense of honour and gratitude constrained him to give advice intelligently, which, if followed, would rescue her and her children from impending adversity; but she determined not to take it. She preferred rather to trust their future well-being into the hands of Providence. Her beautiful faith found expression in this consoling passage of Scripture: "*The Lord is my shepherd, I shall not want.*" And this blessed assurance must have determined her to pursue the course she did, else it would have been reckless and improvident. She told King that when our people became convinced that the troubles between the South and North had to be settled by the sword, that she, in common with all good citizens, staked her all upon the issues of the war, and that she would not now, like a coward, flee from them, or seek to avert them by selling a man, or men and women who had endeared themselves to her by service and fidelity.

Chapter 11

A Perilous Trust

"It is most time to go to the post-office, ain't it, Miss Mary? We are going to get a letter from Marse Thomie this morning."

"What makes you so certain of it, Toby?"

"I don't know'm, but I am; and every time I feels this way, I gets one; so I'll just take my two little black calves and trot off to the office and get it;" and suiting the action to the word he struck a pretty brisk gait and was soon around the corner and out of sight.

Then Decatur received but two mails per day—one from an easterly direction and the other from a westerly direction. The northern, northwestern, southern and southwestern, all coming in on the morning's Georgia Railroad train. Therefore ever since Thomie's return to his command, the western mail was the one around which our hopes and fears daily clustered.

General Joseph E. Johnston's army was, at the time of this incident, at Dalton, obstructing the advance of Sherman's "three hundred thousand men" on destruction bent. And though there had been no regular line of battle formed for some time by the Confederate and Federal forces, there were frequent skirmishes, disastrous alike to both sides. Hence the daily alternation of hopes and fears in the hearts of those whose principal occupation was waiting and watching for "news from the front."

The team of which Toby was the proud possessor did its work quickly, and in less time than it takes to tell it he appeared in sight, returning from the post-office—one hand clasping a package of papers and letters, and the other, raised high above his head, holding a letter. I could not wait, and ran to meet him.

"I've got a whole lot of letters, and every one of them is from Dalton, and this one is from Marse Thomie!"

Toby had read the Dalton post-mark, and had made a correct statement. The well-known chirography of my brother had become so familiar to him that he never mistook it for another, and was unerring in his declarations regarding it. On this occasion Thomie's letter thus read:

My Dear Sister:—Those acquainted with army tactics know that General Johnston is on the eve of an important move, or change of base; and that it should be the effort of the men, officers and privates, to be prepared to make the change, whatever it may be, with as little loss of army paraphernalia as possible. As the Confederate army has no repository secure from the approach of the enemy, several of our friends suggest that you might be willing to take care of anything which we might send to you, that would be of future use to us—heavy overcoats, extra blankets, etc., etc. Consider well the proposition before you consent. Should they be found in your possession, by the enemy, then our home might be demolished, and you perhaps imprisoned, or killed upon the spot. Are you willing to take the risk, trusting to your ingenuity and bravery to meet the consequences? Let me know as soon as possible, as war times admit of little delay. General Granbury, Colonel Bob Young, and others may make known to you their wishes by personal correspondence. Love to my mother and sister, and to yourself, brave heart.

    Affectionately, your brother

              T. J. Stokes.

This letter was read aloud to my mother, and the faithful mail carrier was not excluded. She listened and weighed every word of its contents. For several moments a silence reigned, which was broken by her asking me what I was going to do in the matter.

"What would you have me do?" I asked in reply.

"What would they do, Mary, in very cold weather, if they should lose their winter clothing, overcoats and blankets, now that supplies are so difficult to obtain?"

This question, evasive as it was, convinced me that my mother's patriotism was fully adequate to the occasion, and, fraught with peril as it might be, she was willing to bear her part of the consequences of taking care of the soldiers' clothes.

The return mail bore the following letter addressed jointly to

General Granbury, Colonel Robert Young, Captains Lauderdale and Formwalt, Lieutenant Stokes, and Major John Y. Rankin;

> My Dear Brother and Friends:—I thank you for the estimate you have placed upon my character and patriotism, as indicated by your request that I should take care of your overcoats, blankets, etc., until you need them. If I were willing to enjoy the fruits of your valour and sacrifices without also being willing to share your perils, I would be unworthy indeed. Yes, if I knew that for taking care of those things, I would subject myself to real danger, I would essay the duty. Send them on. I will meet them in Atlanta, and see that they continue their journey to Decatur without delay.
>
> Your friend,
>
> M. A. H. G.

Another mail brought intelligence of the shipment of the goods, and I lost no time in going to Atlanta and having them re-shipped to Decatur. There were nine large dry goods boxes, and I went, immediately on their arrival, to Mr. E. Mason's and engaged his two-horse wagon and driver to carry them from the depot to our home. When they were brought, we had them placed in our company dining-room. This room, by a sort of tacit understanding, had become a storeroom for the army before this important lot of goods came, and, as a dining-room, much incongruity of furniture existed, among which was a large, high wardrobe. The blinds were now closed and secured, the sash put down and fastened, the doors shut and locked, and this room given up to the occupancy of Confederate articles; and thus it remained during the eventful period intervening between the departure of General Joseph E. Johnston's army from Dalton, and Sherman's infamous order to the people of Atlanta and vicinity to leave their homes, that they might be destroyed by his vandal hordes.

CHAPTER 12

A Scene in an Atlanta Confederate Hospital

"Well, my boy, our patients are all getting along nicely in the Fair Ground hospital," was the comforting assurance I gave to Toby, who was my faithful co-worker in all that pertained to the comfort of our soldiers. "Suppose we go to the Empire hospital and see what we can do there."

"Yes'm, I have always wanted to go there."

Taking one of the baskets we had brought with us from Decatur, and which contained biscuits, rusk, broiled and fried chicken, ground coffee and blackberry wine, I handed it to him and we wended our way to the hospital. Things were not in as good shape there as at the Fair Ground hospital. I perceived this at a glance, and, upon asking and receiving permission from the superintendent, I soon tidied up things considerably. Toby brought pails of fresh water, and aided in bathing the faces, hands and arms of the convalescing soldiers, while I hunted up the soldier lads who ought to have been at home with their mothers, and bestowed the tender loving service that woman only can give to the sick and suffering.

Entering one of the wards I perceived a youth, or one I took to be a youth, from his slender fragile figure, and his beardless face, lean and swarthy in sickness, but beautiful in its fine texture and the marblelike whiteness of the brow. That he was of French extraction there could be no doubt. Quietly kneeling by the side of his cot, I contemplated his face, his head, his figure—I listened to his breathing, and watched the pulsations of his heart, and knew that his days, yea, his hours were numbered. Taking his hand in mine, I perceived that the little vitality that remained was fast burning up with fever. Putting back the beautiful rings of raven hair that lay in dishevelled clusters over his classic head, and partly concealed his white brow, I thought of his mother, and imprinted upon his forehead a kiss for her sake. The deep slumber induced by anodynes was broken by that touch, and a dazed awakening ensued. "Mother," was his pathetic and only utterance.

"What can I do for you, my dear child?"

There are looks and tones which are never forgotten, and never shall I forget the utter despair in the eyes, lustrous and beautiful enough to look upon the glory of heaven, and the anguish of the voice, musical enough to sing the songs of everlasting bliss, as he said in tremulous tone and broken sentences:

"I want to see a Catholic priest. I have paid several men to go for me. They have gone off and never returned. I have no money with which to pay any one else."

In silence I listened and wept. At length I said:

"My dear young friend, can you not make confession to '*our Father which art in Heaven*,' and ask Him for Christ's sake to absolve you from all sins of which you may think yourself guilty? He will do it without the intervention of a priest, if you will only believe on Him and trust Him. Can you not do this?"

The pencil of Raphael would fail to depict the anguish of his face; all hope left it, and, as he turned his despairing look upon the wall, tear drops glistened in his eyes and filled the sunken hollows beneath them. Again I took his passive hand in mine, and with the other hand upon his white forehead, I told him he should see a priest—that I myself would go for one, and just as soon as he could be found I would return with him. Before leaving, however, I went to the ward where I had left Toby and the basket, and filling a little glass with wine, I brought it to the sinking youth. He could not be induced to taste it. In vain I plead with him, and told him that it would strengthen him for the interview with the priest. "I am going now, and will come back, too, as soon as I can," I said to the dying youth, for to all intents and purposes he was dying then. Seeing the other patients watching my every movement with pathetic interest, I was reminded to give the rejected wine to the weakest looking one of them.

Leaving Toby either to wait on, or amuse the soldiers of the ward first entered (where I found him playing the latter role, much to their delight), with hasty steps I went to the Catholic parsonage on Hunter street. In response to my ring the door was opened by an Irish woman from whom I learned that the priest was not in, and would not be until he came to luncheon at 12 o'clock m. It was then 11 o'clock, and I asked the privilege of waiting in the sitting room until he came. This being granted, I entered the room consecrated to celibacy, and perhaps to holy thoughts, judging from the pictures upon the walls and the other ornaments. These things furnished food for reflection, and the waiting would not have seemed so long but for the thought of the poor suffering one who had given his young life for our cause. Intuitively I knew the sound of clerical footsteps as they entered the hall, and hastening to meet him I asked, "Is this Father O'Riley?" Receiving an affirmative answer, I told him of the youth at the Empire hospital who refused to be comforted other than by a Catholic priest, and of my promise to bring one to him.

Father O'Riley said he had been out since early morning, visiting the sick, and would be obliged to refresh himself, both by food and repose, but that I could say to the young man that he would be there by 3 o'clock. "O, sir, you don't realize the importance of haste. Please let me remain in your sitting room until you have eaten your luncheon, and then I know you will go with me. I, too, have been out ever since early morning engaged in the same Christ-like labors as yourself, and I do not require either food or repose."

My earnestness prevailed, and in a short while we were at our destination. At my request, Father O'Riley waited in the passage-way leading to the ward until I went in to prepare the young man for his coming. I found him in that restless condition, neither awake nor asleep, which often precedes the deep sleep that knows no waking. Wetting my handkerchief with cold water, I bathed his face and hands, and spoke gently to him, and, when he seemed sufficiently aroused to understand me, I told him in cheerful tones that he could not guess who had come to see him. Catching his look of inquiry, I told him it was Father O'Riley, and that I would bring him in.

Opening the door, I motioned to Father O'Riley to follow me. The dying youth and the Catholic priest needed no introduction by me. There was a mystic tie between them that I recognized as sacred, and I left them alone. Telling Father O'Riley that I consigned my charge to him, and that I would come back tomorrow, I bade them goodbye and left.

The contents of the basket had been gratefully received and devoured by those who deserved the best in the land, because they were the land's defenders.

Tomorrow Toby and I, and the basket, were at the Empire hospital in due time, but the poor suffering youth was not there. The emancipated spirit had taken its flight to Heaven, and all that was mortal of that brave young soldier had been consigned by the ceremonies of the church he loved so well to the protecting care of mother earth.

CHAPTER 13

Concealing Confederate Clothing

On the way to the post-office early one morning in the sultry month of July, 1864, to mail a number of letters which I deemed too important to be entrusted to other hands, I was accosted as follows by "Uncle Mack," the good negro blacksmith, whose shop was situated immediately upon the route:

"Did you know, Miss Mary, that the Yankees have crossed the river, and are now this side of the Chattahoochee."

"Why, no!" I said, and added with as much calmness as I could affect, "I do not know why I should be surprised—there is nothing to prevent them from coming into Decatur."

With an imprecation more expressive than elegant, that evil should overtake them before getting here, he resumed hammering at the anvil, and I my walk to the post-office. Nor was Uncle Mack the only one who volunteered the information that "The Yankees are coming—they are this side the river."

The time had come to devise means and methods of concealing the winter clothing and other accoutrements entrusted to my care by our dear soldiers. In order to save them, what should I do with them?—was a question which I found myself unable to answer. An attempt to retain and defend them would be futile indeed. And I have no right to jeopardize my mother's home by a rash effort to accomplish an impossibility. But what shall I do with these precious things, is the question. A happy thought struck me, and I pursued it only to find it delusive. The near approach of Sherman's army developed the astounding fact that Dr. A. Holmes, of Decatur, a Baptist minister of some prominence, claimed to be a Union man, in full sympathy with any means that would soonest quell the rebellion. This I had not heard, and in my dilemma I went to him to impart my plans and ask advice.

He was morose and reticent, and I hesitated; but, driven by desperation, I finally said: "Dr. Holmes, as a minister of the gospel, are you not safe? All civilized nations respect clerical robes, do they not?"

"I think so," he said, and continued by saying, "I have other claims upon the Federal army which will secure me from molestation."

A look of surprise and inquiry being my only answer, he said, "Amid the secession craze, I have never given up my allegiance to the United States."

"Why, Dr. Holmes!" I said, in unfeigned surprise.

"I repeat most emphatically that I have remained unshaken in my allegiance to the United States. I have no respect for a little contemptible Southern Confederacy, whose flag will never be recognized on land or on sea."

This was a sad revelation to me. On more than one occasion I had heard Dr. Holmes pray fervently for the success of the Southern cause, and to hear such changed utterances from him now, pained me exceedingly. Heartsore and discouraged, I turned from him, and was leaving without the usual ceremony, when he said:

"What can I do for you?"

"I came, sir, to ask a great favour of you, but after hearing you express yourself as you have, I deem it useless to make known my wishes. Good morning."

This interview with Dr. Holmes was very brief; it did not consume as much time as it has done to tell it.

I did not walk in those days, but ran, and it required only a few moments to transfer the scene of action from Dr. Holmes' to my mother's residence. A hurried, whispered conversation acquainted her with the situation; and at my request, and upon a plausible pretence, she took Toby to the depot where she remained until I sent for her. My confidence in Toby had not in the least diminished, but, being a boy, I feared that he might have his price, or be intimidated by threats into the betrayal of our secret; hence the management as above related to get him off the place while I consummated a plan, which, if successful, would be a great achievement, but, if a failure, would be fraught with disaster. In those days "the depot" was a place of popular resort—it was the emporium of news; and either from the agent, or from the Confederate scouts that were ever and *anon* dashing through Decatur with cheerful messages and words of hope, the anxious mothers and sisters of the soldiers often wended their way there in hope of hearing something from their loved ones. Therefore no suspicion was aroused by this going to the depot.

Watching the receding form of my mother until she had passed out of the gate, and Toby had closed it after her, I then went to the rear door and motioned to Telitha, who chanced to be in the right place, to come into the house. After seeing that every outside door was thoroughly secure, I took her into the dining room where the boxes were which contained the winter clothing, blankets, etc., already mentioned as having been sent for storage by our soldier friends at Dalton, and told her in pantomime that the Yankees were coming, and if they saw these things they would kill us and burn the house. She fully understood and repeated the pantomime illustrative of possible—yea, probable—coming events, with pathetic effect. I showed her that I wanted a hammer and chisel with which to take off the lids of the boxes, and she brought them. The lids removed, each article was carefully lifted from its repository and placed on chairs.

This important step being taken towards the concealment of the goods, I raised the sash and opened the shutters of the window nearest the cellar, which was unlocked and open, and Telitha, climbing out the window, received the boxes as I handed them to her, and carried them into the cellar. Old and soiled as the boxes were, they were not in a condition to create suspicion of recent use, so from that source we had nothing to fear. Telitha again in the house, shutters closed, and sash down, preparation was resumed for the enactment of a feat dangerous and rash, the thought of which, even at this remote period, almost produces a tremor. The wardrobe mentioned in a former sketch as an incongruity in a dining room, was emptied of its contents, and inch by inch placed as near the centre of the room as possible; then a large table was placed beside it, and a chair upon that; and then with the help of another chair, which served as a step, I got upon the table and then upon the chair that was upon the table.

As I went up, Telitha followed; standing upon the table she grasped the wardrobe with her strong hands and held it securely. I ascended from the chair to the top of it, stood up and steadied myself, and waited, immovable as a statue, until she got down and brought the chisel and hammer and placed them at my feet, and resumed her hold upon the wardrobe. I stooped and picked up the utensils with which I had to work, and straightened and steadied myself again. The chisel touched the plastered ceiling and the hammering began. Very slow work it was at first, as the licks had to be upward instead of downward, and the plastering was very thick. Finally the chisel went through and was withdrawn and moved to another place, and by repeated efforts I secured an aperture large enough to insert my fingers, and a few well-directed licks round and about so cracked and weakened the plastering that I was enabled to pull off some large pieces.

A new difficulty presented itself. The laths were long, much longer than those of the present day, and I not only had to make a large opening in the ceiling, but to take off the plastering without breaking the laths. More than once the wardrobe had to be moved that I might pull off the plastering, and then with the greatest care prize off the laths. At length the feat was accomplished, and I laid the lids of the boxes, which had been reserved for this purpose, across the joists, and made a floor upon which to lay the goods more than once specified in these sketches. When the last article had been laid on this improvised shelf, I gazed upon them in silent anguish and wept. Telitha caught the melancholy inspiration and also wept. Each lath was restored to its place and the perilous work was completed, and how I thanked the Lord for the steady nerve and level head that enabled me to do this service for those who were fighting the battles of my country.

But the debris must be removed. While the doors were yet closed and fastened, we pounded and broke the plastering into very small pieces and filled every vessel and basket in the house. I then went out and walked very leisurely over the yard and lot, and lingered over every lowly flower that sweetened the atmosphere by its fragrance, and when I was fully persuaded that no spy was lurking nigh I re-entered the house and locked the door. Picking up the largest vessel, and motioning Telitha to follow suit, I led the way through a back door to a huge old ash hopper, and emptied the pulverized plastering into it. In this way we soon had every trace of it removed from the floor. The dust that had settled upon everything was not so easily removed, but the frequent use of dusting brushes and flannel cloths disposed of the most of it.

I now wrote a note to my mother, inviting her to come home, and to bring Toby with her. We kept the doors of the dining room closed, as had been our wont for some time, and if Toby ever discovered the change, he never betrayed the knowledge of it by word or look. After a light breakfast, and the excitement of the day, I felt that we ought to have a good, luscious dinner, and, with the help at my command, went to work preparing it, and, as was my custom of late, I did not forget to provide for others who might come in. More than once during the day Confederate scouts had galloped in and spoken a few words of encouragement; and after taking a drink of water from the old oaken bucket, had galloped out again, so I hoped they would come back when the biscuit and tea-cakes were done, that I might fill their pockets.

After the last meal of the day had been eaten, I held another whispered consultation with my mother, and in pursuance of the course agreed upon I emptied several trunks, and with her help filled one with quilts and blankets, and other bedding; another with china and cut glass, well packed; and another with important papers, treasured relics, etc., and locked and strapped them ready for shipment next morning.

A night of unbroken rest and sleep prepared me for another day of surprises and toil, and before dawn I was up, dressed, waiting for daylight enough to justify me in the effort to see Mr. Ezekiel Mason, and beg him to hire me his team and driver to carry the trunks to the depot. After my ready compliance with his terms, he agreed to send them as soon as possible. The delay caused me to go on a freight train to Atlanta, but I congratulated myself upon that privilege, as the trunks and Toby went on the same train. There was unusual commotion and activity about the depot in Atlanta, and a superficial observer would have been impressed with the business-like appearance of the little city at that important locality. Men, women, and children moved about as if they meant business.

Trains came in rapidly, and received their complement of freight, either animate or inanimate, and screamed themselves hoarse and departed, giving place to others that went through with the same routine. Drays and every manner of vehicles blocked the streets, and endangered life, limb, and property of all who could not vie with them in push, vim, and dare-deviltry. In vain did I appeal to scores of draymen, white and black, to carry my trunks to the home of Mr. McArthur, on Pryor street—money was offered with liberality, but to no avail. Despairing of aid, I bade Toby follow me, and went to Mr. McArthur's. He and his good wife were willing to receive the trunks and give them storage room, but could extend no aid in bringing them there.

At length, as a last resort, it was decided that Toby should take their wheelbarrow and bring one trunk at a time. I returned with him to the depot and had the most valuable trunk placed upon the wheelbarrow, and, with my occasional aid, Toby got it to its destination. A second trip was made in like manner, and the third was not a failure, although I saw that Toby was very tired. Thanking my good friends for the favour they were extending, I hurried back to the depot, myself and Toby, to take the first train to Decatur. Imagine our consternation on learning that the Yankees had dashed in and torn up the Georgia Railroad track from Atlanta to Decatur, and were pursuing their destructive work towards Augusta. Neither for love nor money could a seat in any kind of vehicle going in that direction be obtained, nor were I and my attendant the only ones thus cut off from home; and I soon discovered that a spirit of independence pervaded the crowd. Many were the proud possessors of elegant spans of "little white ponies" which they did not deem too good to propel them homeward. Seeking to infuse a little more life and animation into Toby, I said:

"Well, my boy, what do you think of bringing out your little black ponies and running a race with my white ones to Decatur? Do you think you can beat in the race?"

"I don't know'm," he said, without his usual smile, when I essayed a little fun with him, and I evidently heard him sigh. But knowing there was no alternative, I started in a brisk walk towards Decatur, and said to him, "Come on, or I'll get home before you do." He rallied and kept very close to me, and we made pretty good time. The gloaming was upon us, the period of all others auspicious to thought, and to thought I abandoned myself. The strife between the sections of a once glorious country was a prolific theme, and I dwelt upon it in all of its ramifications, and failed to find cause for blame in my peculiar people; and my step became prouder, and my willingness to endure all things for their sakes and mine was more confirmed. In the midst of these inspiring reflections, Toby, who had somewhat lagged behind, came running up to me and said:

"Oh! Miss Mary, just look at the soldiers. And they are ours, too!"

To my dying day I shall never forget the scene to which he called my attention. In the weird stillness it appeared as if the Lord had raised up of the stones a mighty host to fight our battles. Not a sound was heard, nor a word spoken, as those in the van passed opposite me, on and on, and on, in the direction of Decatur, in what seemed to me an interminable line of soldiery. Toby and I kept the track of the destroyed railroad, and were somewhere between General Gartrell's residence and Mr. Pitts', the midway station between Atlanta and Decatur, when the first of these soldiers passed us, and we were at Kirkwood when that spectre-like band had fully gone. Once the moon revealed me so plainly that a cheer, somewhat repressed, but nevertheless hearty, resounded through the woods, and I asked:

"Whose command?"

"Wheeler's Cavalry," was the simultaneous response of many who heard my inquiry.

"Don't you know me? I am the one you gave the best breakfast I ever ate, that morning we dashed into Decatur before sun-up."

"And I'm the one too."

"O, don't mention it," I said. "You are giving your lives for me, and the little I can do for you is nothing in comparison. May God be with you and shield you from harm until this cruel war is over."

I missed Toby, and looking back, saw him sitting down. I hurried to him, saying, "What is it, my boy?"

"O, Miss Mary, I am so sick. I can't go any further. You can go on home, and let me stay here—when I feel better I'll go too."

"No, my boy, I'll not leave you." And sitting by him I told him to rest his head upon my lap, and maybe after awhile he would feel better, and then we would go on. In the course of a half hour he vomited copiously, and soon after he told me he felt better, and would try to go on. More than once his steps were unsteady and he looked dazed; but under my patient guidance and encouraging words he kept up and we pursued our lonely walk until we reached Decatur.

As soon as we entered the town, we perceived that we had overtaken Wheeler's Cavalry. They were lying on the ground, asleep, all over the place; and in most instances their horses were lying by them, sleeping too. And I noticed that the soldiers, even though asleep, never released their hold upon the bridles. At home I found my mother almost frantic. She knew nothing of the causes detaining me, and supposed that some disaster had befallen me individually. A good supper, including a strong cup of tea prepared by her hands, awaited us, and I attested my appreciation of it by eating heartily. Toby drank a cup of tea only, and said he "was very tired and hurt all over."

Chapter 14

The Advance Guard of the Yankee Army

The day clear, bright and beautiful, in July, 1864, and though a midsummer's sun cast its vertical rays upon the richly-carpeted earth, refreshing showers tempered the heat and preserved in freshness and beauty the vernal robes of May and kept the atmosphere pure and delightful. Blossoms of every hue and fragrance decked the landscape, and Ceres and Pomona had been as lavish with their grains and fruits as Flora had been with flowers.

And I, assisted by Toby and Telitha, had gathered from the best of these rich offerings, and prepared a feast for Wheeler's Cavalry. By the way, strive against it as I would, I was more than once disturbed by the mental inquiry: "What has become of Wheeler's Cavalry? I saw it enter Decatur last night, and now there is not a soldier to be seen. It is true a large number of scouts came in this morning, and spoke comforting words to my mother, and reconnoitred around town fearlessly, but what has become of them?" Hope whispered: "Some strategic movement that will culminate in the capture of the entire Yankee army, no doubt is engaging its attention."

Yielding to these delusive reflections, and the seductive influence of earth, air and sky, I became quite exhilarated and hummed little snatches of the songs I used to sing in the happy days of childhood, before a hope had been disappointed or a shadow cast over my pathway.

These scenes and these songs were not in keeping with the impending disasters even then at our portals. Crapen draperies and funeral dirges would have been far more in keeping with the developments of the day.

Distant roar of cannon and sharp report of musketry spoke in language unmistakable the approach of the enemy, and the rapidity of that approach was becoming fearfully alarming. Decatur offered many advantages as headquarters to an invading, devastating foe, "and three hundred thousand men" under the guidance of a merciless foe ought to have entered it long before they did—and would have done so if their bravery had been commensurate with their vandalism.

"Yank! Yank!" exclaimed our deaf negro girl, Telitha, as she stroked her face as if stroking beard, and ran to get a blue garment to indicate the color of their apparel, and this was our first intimation of their appearance in Decatur. If all the evil spirits had been loosed from Hades, and Satan himself had been turned loose upon us, a more terrific, revolting scene could not have been enacted.

Advance guards, composed of every species of criminals ever incarcerated in the prisons of the Northern States of America, swooped down upon us, and every species of deviltry followed in their footsteps. My poor mother, frightened and trembling, and myself, having locked the doors of the house, took our stand with the servants in the yard, and witnessed the grand *entre* of the menagerie. One of the beasts got down upon his all-fours and pawed up the dust and bellowed like an infuriated bull. And another asked me if I did not expect to see them with hoofs and horns. I told him, "No, I had expected to see some gentlemen among them, and was sorry I should be disappointed."

My entire exemption from fear on that occasion must have been our safeguard, as no personal violence was attempted. He who personated a bull must have been the king's fool, and was acting in collusion with the house pillagers sent in advance of the main army to do their dirty work, and to reduce the people to destitution and dependence. While he thought he was entertaining us with his *quadrupedal didos*, a horde of thieves were rummaging the house, and everything of value they could get their hands upon they stole—locks and bolts having proved ineffectual barriers to this nefarious work. By this time the outside marauders had killed every chicken and other fowl upon the place, except one setting-hen. A fine cow, and two calves, and twelve hogs shared a similar fate.

Several hours had passed since the coming of the first instalment of the G. A. R., and a few scattering officers were perambulating the streets, and an occasional cavalryman reconnoitring. Having surveyed the situation, and discovered that only women and children and a few faithful negroes occupied the town, the main army came in like an avalanche. Yea, if an avalanche and a *simoon* had blended their fury and expended it upon that defenceless locality, a greater change could scarcely have been wrought.

The morning's sun had shone upon a scene of luxuriant beauty, and heightened its midsummer loveliness, but the same sun, only a few hours later, witnessed a complete transformation, and blight and desolation reigned supreme. My mother and myself, afraid to go in the house, still maintained our outdoor position, and our two faithful servants clung very close to us, notwithstanding repeated efforts to induce them to leave. Our group had received addition. Emmeline, a negro girl whom we had hired out in Decatur, had been discharged, and had now come home. She was not so faithful as her kith and kin, and was soon on familiar terms with the bummers. Toby complained of being very tired, and when we all came to think about it, we discovered that we, too, were tired, and without being asked took seats upon the capacious lap of mother earth.

As we were not overly particular about the position we assumed, we must have presented quite an aboriginal appearance. But what mattered it—we were only rebels. Notwithstanding the insignia of the conqueror was displayed on every hand, we felt to a certain degree more protected by the presence of commissioned officers, and ventured to go into the house. I will not attempt a description of the change that had taken place since we had locked the door, and, for better protection, had taken our stand in the yard.

Garrard's Cavalry selected our lot, consisting of several acres, for headquarters, and soon what appeared to us to be an immense army train of wagons commenced rolling into it. In less than two hours our barn was demolished and converted into tents, which were occupied by privates and non-commissioned officers, and to the balusters of our portico and other portions of the house were tied a number of large ropes, which, the other ends being secured to trees and shrubbery, answered as a railing to which at short intervals apart a number of smaller ropes were tied, and to these were attached horses and mules, which were eating corn and oats out of troughs improvised for the occasion out of bureau, washstand, and wardrobe drawers.

Men in groups were playing cards on tables of every size and shape; and whisky and profanity held high carnival. Thus surrounded we could but be apprehensive of danger; and, to assure ourselves of as much safety as possible, we barricaded the doors and windows, and arranged to sit up all night, that is, my mother and myself.

Toby complained of being very tired, and "hurting all over," as he expressed it. We assisted him in making the very best pallet that could be made of the material at our command, and he lay down completely prostrated. Telitha was wide awake, and whenever she could secure a listener chattered like a magpie in unintelligible language, accompanied by unmistakable gestures—gestures which an accomplished elocutionist might adopt with effect—and the burden of her heart was for Emmeline. Emmeline having repudiated our protection, had sought shelter, the Lord only knows where. Alas, poor girl!

As we sat on a lounge, every chair having been taken to the camps, we heard the sound of footsteps entering the *piazza*, and in a moment, loud rapping, which meant business. Going to the window nearest the door, I removed the fastenings, raised the sash, and opened the blinds. Perceiving by the light of a brilliant moon that at least a half-dozen men in uniforms were on the *piazza*, I asked:

"Who is there?"

"Gentlemen," was the laconic reply.

"If so, you will not persist in your effort to come into the house. There is only a widow and one of her daughters, and two faithful servants in it," I said.

"We have orders from headquarters to interview Miss Gay. Is she the daughter of whom you speak?"

"She is, and I am she."

"Well, Miss Gay, we demand seeing you, without intervening barriers. Our orders are imperative," said he who seemed to be the spokesman of the delegation.

"Then wait a moment," I amiably responded. Going to my mother I repeated in substance the above colloquy, and asked her if she would go with me out of one of the back doors and around the house into the front yard. Although greatly agitated and trembling, she readily assented, and we noiselessly went out. In a few moments we announced our presence, and our visitors descended the steps and joined us. And those men, occupying a belligerent attitude towards ourselves and all that was dear to us, stood face to face and in silence contemplated each other. When the silence was broken the aforesaid officer introduced himself as Major Campbell, a member of General Schofield's staff. He also introduced the accompanying officers each by name and title. This ceremony over, Major Campbell said:

"Miss Gay, our mission is a painful one, and yet we will have to carry it out unless you satisfactorily explain acts reported to us."

"What is the nature of those acts?"

"We have been told that it is your proudest boast that you are a rebel, and that you are ever on duty to aid and abet in every possible way the would-be destroyers of the United States Government. If this be so, we cannot permit you to remain within our lines. Until Atlanta surrenders, Decatur will be our headquarters, and every consideration of interest to our cause requires that no one inimical to it should remain within our boundaries established by conquest."

In reply to these charges, I said:

"Gentlemen, I have not been misrepresented, so far as the charges you mention are concerned. If I were a man, I should be in the foremost ranks of those who are fighting for rights guaranteed by the Constitution of the United States. The Southern people have never broken that compact, nor infringed upon it in any way. They have never organized mobs to assassinate any portion of the people sharing the privileges granted by that compact. They have constructed no underground railroads to bring into our midst incendiaries and destroyers of the peace, and to carry off stolen property. They have never sought to array the subordinate element of the North in deadly hostility to the controlling element. No class of the women of the South have ever sought positions at the North which secured entrance into good households, and then betrayed the confidence reposed by corrupting the servants and alienating the relations between the master and the servant. No class of the women of the South have ever mounted the rostrum and proclaimed falsehoods against the women of the North—falsehoods which must have crimsoned with shame the very cheeks of Beelzebub.

"No class of the men of the South have ever tramped over the North with humbugs, extorting money either through sympathy or credulity, and engaged at the same time in the nefarious work of exciting the subordinate class to insurrection, arson, rapine and murder. If the South is in rebellion, a well-organized mob at the North has brought it about. Long years of patient endurance accomplished nothing. The party founded on falsehood and hate strengthened and grew to enormous proportions. And, by the way, mark the cunning of that party. Finding that the Abolition party made slow progress and had to work in the dark, it changed its name and took in new issues, and by a systematic course of lying in its institutions of learning, from the lowly school-house to Yale College, and from its pulpits and rostrums, it inculcated lessons of hate towards the Southern people whom it would hurl into the crater of Vesuvius if endowed with the power. What was left us to do but to try to relieve that portion of the country which had permitted this sentiment of hate to predominate, of all connection with us, and of all responsibility for the sins of which it proclaimed us guilty? This effort the South has made, and I have aided and abetted in every possible manner, and will continue to do so just as long as there is an armed man in the Southern ranks. If this be sufficient cause to expel me from my home, I await your orders. I have no favours to ask."

Imagine my astonishment, admiration and gratitude, when that group of Federal officers, with unanimity said:

"I glory in your spunk, and am proud of you as my countrywoman; and so far from banishing you from your home, we will vote for your retention within our lines."

Thus the truth prevailed; but a new phase of the conflict was inaugurated, as proved by subsequent developments.

Turning to my mother, Major Campbell said:

"Mother, how did our advance guards treat you?"

A quivering of the lips, and a tearful effort to speak, was all the response she could make. The aggravation of already extreme nervousness was doing its work.

"Would you like to see?" I said. He indicated rather than expressed an affirmative answer.

I went around and entered the house, and, opening the front door, invited him and his friends to come in. A hindrance to the exhibit I was anxious to make presented itself—we had neither candle nor lamp, and this I told to the officers. Calling to a man in the nearest camp, Major Campbell asked him to bring a light. This being done, I led the way into the front room, and there our distinguished guests were confronted by a huge pallet occupied by a sixteen-year-old negro boy. A thrill of amusement evidently passed through this group of western men, and electrical glances conveyed messages of distrust when I told them of my walk yesterday afternoon, accompanied by this boy, and his exhaustion before we got home, and his complaints of "hurting all over" before he lay down an hour ago.

A low consultation was held, and one of the officers left and soon returned with another who proved to be a physician. He aroused the boy, asked several questions, and examined his pulse and tongue.

"That will do," said he, and turning to the others, he said:

"He is a very sick boy, and needs medical treatment at once. I will prescribe and go for the medicine, which I wish given according to directions."

Having received a statement of the boy's condition from a trusted source, we were evidently re-instated into the good opinion of Major Campbell and his friends. Telitha had retired from them to as great a distance as the boundaries of the room would permit, and every time she caught my eye she looked and acted what she could not express in words—utter aversion for the "Yank."

We now resumed our inspection of the interior of the house. The contents of every drawer were on the floor, every article of value having been abstracted. Crockery scattered all over the room, suggested to the eye that it had been used to pelt the ghosts of the witches burned in Massachusetts a century or two ago. Outrages and indignities too revolting to mention met the eye at every turn. And the state of affairs in the parlour baffled description. Not an article had escaped the destroyer's touch but the piano, and circumstances which followed proved that that was regarded as a trophy and only waited removal.

"Vandals! Vandals!" Major Campbell sorrowfully exclaimed, and all his friends echoed the opinion, and said:

"If the parties who did this work could be identified, we would hang them as high as Haman."

But these parties were never identified. They were important adjuncts in the process of subjugation.

After wishing that the worst was over with us, these gentlemen, who had come in no friendly mood, bade us goodnight and took their leave. Thus the Lord of Hosts, in his infinite mercy, furnished a just tribunal to pass judgment upon my acts as a Southern woman, and that judgment, influenced by facts and surroundings, was just and the verdict humane.

CHAPTER 15

The Battle of the 22nd of July, 1864

The excitement incident to the morning and evening of yesterday left my mother and myself in no frame of mind for repose, and we spent the night in suspense and painful apprehension of trouble yet to come greater and more dreadful than that through which we had passed. The medicine left for Toby by the physician summoned last night was faithfully administered according to direction, and the morning found him better, though able to sit up only for a short while at a time. Measles had developed, and we felt hopeful that it would prove to be a very slight attack; and such it might have been could we have controlled him properly, but the excitement and ever-varying scenes in the yard, and as far as vision extended, were so new and strange to him that, when unobserved, he spent much of his time at a window commanding the best view of the scene, and, thus exposed to a current of air, the disease ceased to appear on the surface and a troublesome cough ensued.

Having been without food since the preceding morning, our thoughts turned to the usual preparation for breakfast, but alas, those preparations had to be dispensed of, as we had nothing to prepare. This state of affairs furnished food for at least serious reflection, and the inquiry, "What are we to do?" found audible expression. The inexorable demands of hunger could not be stifled, and we knew that the sick boy needed hot tea and the nourishment which food alone could give, and yet we had nothing for ourselves or for him—so complete had been the robbery of the "advance guards" of the Grand Army of the Republic that not a thing, animate or inanimate, remained with which to appease our hunger. "What are we to do?" was iterated and reiterated, and no solution of the question presented itself.

Even then appetizing odours from the camp-fires were diffusing themselves upon the air and entering our house, but aliens were preparing the food and we had no part in it. We debated this question, and finally resolved not to expose ourselves to the jeers and insults of the enemy by an act of ours that would seem to ask for food; but that we would go to our Southern citizens in the war-stricken and almost deserted town, and, if they were not completely robbed, ask them to share their supplies with us until we could procure aid from outside of the lines so arbitrarily drawn.

In this dilemma an unexpected relief came to us, and convinced us that there was good even in Nazareth. A large tray, evidently well-filled, and covered with a snow-white cloth, was brought in by an Irishman, who handed a card to my mother containing these words:

"To Mrs. Stokes and daughter, Miss Gay, with compliments of (Major) Campbell.

"Please accept this small testimonial of regard and respectful sympathy."

The latter part of the brief message was the sesame that secured acceptance of this offering, and my mother and myself jointly acknowledged it with sincere thanks, and again we thought of Elijah and the ravens. The contents of the tray—coffee, sugar, and tea, sliced ham and a variety of canned relishes, butter, potatoes, and oatmeal and bread, were removed and the tray returned. That tray on its humane mission, having found its way into our house, more than once opportunely reappeared. We enjoyed the repast thus furnished, although briny tears were mingled with it.

The day passed without any immediate adventure. Great activity prevailed in army ranks. The coming and going of cavalry; the clatter of sabre and spur; the constant booming of cannon and report of musketry, all convinced us that the surrender of Atlanta by the Confederates was quite a matter of time. A few thousand men, however brave and gallant, could not cope successfully with "three hundred thousand" who ignored every usage of civilized warfare, and fought only for conquest.

I cannot say how long this state of affairs lasted before Wheeler's Cavalry, supported by Confederate infantry, stole a march upon the Yankees and put them to flight. Garrard and his staff officers were in our parlour—their parlour *pro tem.*—holding a council; the teamsters and army followers were lounging about promiscuously, cursing and swearing and playing cards, and seeming not to notice the approaching artillery until their attention was called to it, and then they contended that it was their men firing off blank cartridges. I intuitively felt that a conflict was on hand. Ma and I held whispered conversations and went from one window to another, and finally rushed into the yard. Men in the camps observed our excitement and said, "Don't be alarmed, it is only our men firing off their blank cartridges."

The irony of fate was never more signally illustrated than on this occasion. I would have laid down my life, yea, a thousand breathing, pulsing lives of my own, to have witnessed the overthrow of the Yankee army, and yet, I may have been the means of saving a large portion of it on that occasion. Dreading for my mother's sake and for the sake of the deaf girl and the sick boy, an attack upon the forces which covered our grounds, I ran to one of the parlour doors and knocked heavily and excitedly. An officer unlocked the door and opening it said:

"What is it?"

"Our men must be nearly here," I replied.

"Impossible," he said, and yet, with a bound he was in the yard, followed in quick succession by each member of the conclave.

A signal, long, loud, and shrill, awakened the drowsy, and scattered to the four winds of heaven cards, books and papers; and, in a few minutes, horses and mules were hitched to wagons, and the mules, wagons and men were fairly flying from the approach of the Confederates. Women and children came pouring in from every direction, and the house was soon filled. Before Garrard's wagon train was three hundred yards away, our yard was full of our men—our own dear "Johnnie Rebs." Oothcaloga Valley boys, whom I had known from babyhood, kissed, in passing, the hand that waved the handkerchief. An officer, ah, how grand he looked in gray uniform, came dashing up and said:

"Go in your cellar and lie down; the Federals are forming a line of battle, and we, too, will form one that will reach across the grounds, and your house will be between the two lines. Go at once."

My mother ran and got Toby's shoes and put them on for him, and told him to get up and come with her, and as he went out of the house, tottering, I threw a blanket over him, and he and Telitha went with ma to our near neighbour, Mrs. Williams, her cellar being considered safer than ours. I remained in our house for the twofold purpose of taking care of it, if possible, and of protecting, to the best of my ability, the precious women and children who had fled to us for protection. Without thought of myself I got them all into the room that I thought would be safest, and urged them to lie down upon the floor and not to move during the battle. Shot and shell flew in every direction, and the shingles on the roof were following suit, and the leaves, and the limbs, and the bark of the trees were descending in showers so heavy as almost to obscure the view of the contending forces.

The roaring of cannon and the sound of musketry blended in harmony so full and so grand, and the scene was so absorbing, that I thought not of personal danger, and more than once found myself outside of the portals ready to rush into the conflict—for was not I a soldier, enlisted for the war? Nor was I the only restless, intrepid person in the house on that occasion. An old lady, in whose veins flowed the blood of the Washingtons, was there, and it was with the greatest difficulty that I restrained her from going out into the arena of warfare. The traditions of her ancestors were so interwoven with her life, that, at an age bordering on four score years and ten, they could not relax their hold upon her; and she and I might have gone in opposite directions had we fled to the ranks of the contending armies.

Mine was, no doubt, the only feminine eye that witnessed the complete rout of the Federals on that occasion. At first I could not realize what they were doing, and feared some strategic movement; but the "rebel yell" and the flying blue-coats brought me to a full realization of the situation, and I too joined in the loud acclaim of victory. And the women and children, until now panic-stricken and silent as death, joined in the rejoicing. All the discouragement of the past few weeks fled from me, and hope revived, and I was happy, oh, so happy! I had seen a splendidly equipped army, Schofield's division, I think, ignominiously flee from a little band of lean, lank, hungry, poorly-clad Confederate soldiers, and I doubted not an over-ruling Providence would lead us to final victory.

When the smoke of the battle cleared away, my mother and her ebony charge returned home. Toby quickly sought his pallet, and burning fever soon rendered him delirious the greater part of the time. In one of his lucid intervals, he asked me to read the Bible to him, and he told me what he wanted me to read about, and said:

"Miss Missouri used to read it to me, and I thought it was so pretty." And I read to him the story of the cross—of Jesus' dying love, and he listened and believed. I said to him:

"My boy, do you think you are going to die?"

"Yes'm, I think I am."

I bowed my head close to him and wept, oh, how bitterly.

"Miss Mary, don't you think I'll go to heaven?" he anxiously asked.

"Toby, my boy, there is one thing I want to tell you; can you listen to me?"

"Yes'm."

"I have not always been just to you. I have often accused you of doing things that I afterwards found you did not do, and then I was not good enough to acknowledge that I had done wrong. And when you did wrong, I was not forgiving enough; and more than once I have punished you for little sins, when I, with all the light before me, was committing greater ones every day, and going unpunished, save by a guilty conscience. And now, my boy, I ask you to forgive me. Can you do it?"

"Oh, yes'm!"

"Are you certain that you do? Are you sure that there is no unforgiving spirit in you towards your poor Miss Mary, who is sorry for all she has ever done that was wrong towards you."

"Oh, yes'm!"

"Then, my boy, ask the Lord to forgive you for your sins just as I have asked you to forgive me, and He will do it for the sake of Jesus, who died on the cross that sinners might be redeemed from their sins and live with Him in heaven."

I can never forget the ineffable love, and faith, and gratitude, depicted in that poor boy's face, while I live; and as I held his soft black hand in mine, I thought of its willing service to "our boys," and wept to think I could do no more for him, and that his young life was going out before he knew the result of the cruel war that was waged by the Abolitionists! He noticed my grief, and begged me not to feel so badly, and added that he was willing to die.

I arose from my position by his bed and asked him if there was anything in the world I could do for him. In reply he said:

"I would like to have a drink of water from the Floyd spring."

"You shall have it, my boy, just as soon as I can go there and back," and I took a pitcher and ran to the spring and filled and refilled it several times, that it might be perfectly cool, and went back with it as quickly as possible. He drank a goblet full of this delicious water and said it, was "so good," and then added:

"You drink some, too, Miss Mary, and give Miss Polly some."

I did so, and he was pleased. He coughed less and complained less than he had done since the change for the worse, and I deluded myself into the hope that he might yet recover. In a short while he went to sleep, and his breathing became very hard and his temperature indicated a high degree of fever. I urged my mother to lie down, and assured her that if I thought she could do anything for Toby at any time during the night I would call her.

I sat there alone by that dying boy. Not a movement on his part betrayed pain. His breathing was hard and at intervals spasmodic. With tender hands I changed the position of his head, and for a little while he seemed to breathe easier. But it was only for a little while, and then it was evident that soon he would cease to breathe at all. I went to my mother and waked her gently and told her I thought the end was near with Toby, and hurried back to him. I thought him dead even then; but, after an interval, he breathed again and again, and all was over. The life had gone back to the God who gave it, and I doubt not but that it will live with Him forever. The pathos of the scene can never be understood by those who have not witnessed one similar to it in all its details, and I will not attempt to describe it.

No timepiece marked the hour, but it was about midnight, I ween, when death set the spirit of that youthful negro free. Not a kindred being nor a member of his own race was near to lay loving hand upon him, or prepare his little body for burial. We stood and gazed upon him as he lay in death in that desolated house, and thought of his fidelity and loving interest in our cause and its defenders, and of his faithful service in our efforts to save something from vandal hands; and the fountain of tears was broken up and we wept with a peculiar grief over that lifeless form.

My mother was the first to become calm, and she came very near me and said, as if afraid to trust her voice:

"Wouldn't it be well to ask Eliza Williams and others to come and 'lay him out?'"

Before acting on this suggestion I went into another room and waked Telitha and took her into the chamber of death. A dim and glimmering light prevented her from taking in the full import of the scene at first; but I took her near the couch, and, pointing to him, I said:

"Dead!—Dead!"

She repeated interrogatively, and, when she fully realized that such was the case, her cries were pitiable, oh, so pitiable.

I sank down upon the floor and waited for the paroxysm of grief to subside, and then went to her and made her understand that I was going out and that she must stay with her mistress until I returned. An hour later, under the manipulation of good "Eliza Williams"—known throughout Decatur as Mrs. Ammi Williams' faithful servant—and one or two others whom she brought with her, Toby was robed in a nice white suit of clothes prepared for the occasion by the faithful hands of his "Miss Polly," whom he had loved well and who had cared for him in his orphanage.

We had had intimation that the Federals would again occupy Decatur, and as soon as day dawned I went to see Mr. Robert Jones, Sen., and got him to make a coffin for Toby, and I then asked "Uncle Mack," and "Henry"—now known as Decatur's Henry Oliver—to dig the grave. Indeed, these two men agreed to attend to the matter of his burial. After consultation with my mother, it was agreed that that should take place as soon as all things were in readiness. Mr. Jones made a pretty, well-shaped coffin out of good heart pine, and the two faithful negro men already mentioned prepared with care the grave. When all was in readiness, the dead boy was placed in the coffin and borne to the grave by very gentle hands.

Next to the pall-bearers my mother and myself and Telitha fell in line, and then followed the few negroes yet remaining in the town, and that funeral cortege was complete.

At the grave an unexpected and most welcome stranger appeared. "Uncle Mack" told me he was a minister, and would perform the funeral service—and grandly did he do it. The very soul of prayer seemed embodied in this negro preacher's invocation; nor did he forget Toby's "nurses," and every consolation and blessing was besought for them. And thus our Toby received a Christian burial.

Chapter 16
Everett's Desertion

During the early spring of that memorable year, 1864, it was announced to the citizens of Decatur that Judge Hook and family, including his accomplished daughter, Mrs. Whitesides, and her children, from Chattanooga, had arrived at the depot, and were domiciled, *pro tem.*, in cars which had been switched off the main track of the famous old Georgia Railroad. This novel mode of living, even in war times, by people in their monetary condition and social standing, naturally attracted much attention, and brought us to a full realization of approaching danger. That this family, accustomed to all the luxuries of an elegant home, should live in such an abode, with its attendant privations, was convincing proof that the home they had abandoned had become intolerable because of the proximity of the enemy; and it was also fearfully suggestive that that ubiquitous enemy was extending his dominion and bringing the fiery, bloody conflict into the very heart of the "rebellion."

A rebellion, by way of parenthesis, which impartial historians will put on record as the grandest uprising of a long suffering people that was ever known in the annals of nations; "a mutiny" (as that chief of Southern haters, John Lathrop Motley, whose superb egotism impressed him with the idea that his influence could change the political trend of Great Britain towards the South, has seen proper to denominate it) in the camp of American councils brought about by unceasing abuse of the Southern States by political tricksters, whose only hope of survival lay in the hatred for the South thus engendered.

The coming of Judge Hook's family was hailed with pleasure by all good and loyal citizens, and was a ligament connecting more closely states suffering in a common cause; and we all called upon them and soon numbered them with our intimate friends. Mrs. Whitesides and

Miss Hook were effective workers in all that benefited our soldiers or their families.

Judge Hook was superintendent of the Government Iron Works, and literally brought the foundry as well as the operatives with him. Among the latter was a man by the name of Everett, who, with his family, consisting of his wife and five children, occupied an old one-room house near a corner of our home lot. Although a hearty, hale, and rather good-looking man, Everett was very poor, and the first time I ever saw his wife she came to borrow "a little flour." As my mother never turned away from a borrower, Mrs. Everett's vessel was filled to overflowing, and, besides, a pitcher of buttermilk and a plate of butter was given to her, for which she was extremely grateful.

An acquaintance thus begun continued during the spring and early summer months, and there was not a day during that period that my mother did not find it convenient to do something for this family. Mrs. Everett was more than ordinarily intelligent for a person in her position, and the blush which mantled her pretty cheeks when she asked for anything betrayed her sensibility; and her children were pretty and sweet-mannered. I never saw Everett, only as I met him going and coming from his work, and on those occasions he showed the greatest respect for me by taking off his hat as he approached me, and holding it in his hand until he had fully passed.

He seemed to be a steady worker, and if he ever lost a day I never heard of it; and Mrs. Everett was industrious, but much of the time unemployed for lack of material with which to work, and she often begged for something to do. She was anxious to work for our soldiers, and told me that all of her male relatives were in the Confederate army. This circumstance endeared her very much to me; and I made the support of his family very much easier to Everett than it would have been had he lived in a non-appreciative neighbourhood. And when the village girls met at our house to practice for concerts for the benefit of our soldiers, which they did almost weekly, I never forgot that Mrs. Everett's brothers were in our army fighting valiantly, no doubt, for our cause, and I always asked her to come and bring her children to my room and listen with me to the sweet music and patriotic songs.

As time sped, many opportunities for witnessing Mrs. Everett's devotion to her native land presented themselves; and her service to its defenders, though humble and unobtrusive, was valuable. Her children, too, always spoke lovingly of our soldiers, and were never more happy than when doing something for them. At length the time came for another move of the foundry, and quietly, as if by magic, it and its appurtenants, under the judicious management of Judge Hook, got on wheels and ran at the rate of thirty-five miles an hour until it reached Augusta—another haven of rest invested with heavenly beauty. After the departure of this important adjunct to this portion of the Confederacy, it was discovered that Everett and his family remained in Decatur. And a remarkable change came over them. Instead of the free-spoken, unsophisticated woman that she had always appeared to be, Mrs. Everett became reserved and taciturn, and seldom left the enclosure by which her humble dwelling was surrounded. And the children ceased to cheer us by their merry prattle and daily trip for a pitcher of buttermilk, which, under the changed and unexplained circumstances, my mother sent to them.

On the never-to-be-forgotten 19th of July, 1864, when a portion of Sherman's army dashed into Decatur, it obtained a recruit. In an incredibly short time, Everett was arrayed in the uniform of a Yankee private, and was hustling around with the Yankees as if *"to the manner born."*

On the 22nd of July, when the Confederates ran the Yankees out of the little village they had so pompously occupied for a few days, Everett disappeared, and so did his family from the little house on the corner. I supposed they had left Decatur, until I went out in town to see if I could hear anything from the victors—their losses, etc.—when by chance I discovered that they had taken shelter in the old post-office building on the northeast corner of the court-house square.

The morning after the hurried evacuation of Decatur by the Federal troops, I arose, as was my custom, as day was dawning, and, as soon as I thought I could distinguish objects, I opened the front door and stepped out on the portico. As I stood looking upon the ruin and devastation of my war-stricken home, imagine my surprise and consternation when I saw a white handkerchief held by an invisible hand above a scuppernong grape arbour. My first impulse was to seek security within closed doors, but the thought occurred to me that someone might be in distress and needed aid. I therefore determined to investigate the case. In pursuance of this object I went down the steps, and advanced several yards in the direction of the waving signal, and asked:

"Who is there?"

"Come a little nearer, please," was the distinct answer.

"I am near enough to hear you; what can I do for you?" I said, and did go a little nearer.

"Miss Mary, don't be afraid of me; I would die for you and such as you, but I cannot die for a lost cause"—and through an opening in the foliage of the vines, which were more on the ground than on the scaffolding, a head protruded—handsome brown eyes and dark whiskers included—Everett's head, in all the naturalness of innocence.

I thought of his wife and of his children, and of his wife's brother in the Confederate army, and again asked with deliberation:

"What can I do for you?"

"Bless me or curse me," was the startling answer, and he continued:

"Your kindness to my wife and children has nerved me to come to you and ask that you will aid me in seeing them, especially her. Will you do it?"

"Yes, though I despise you for the steps you have taken, I will grant your request. Don't be afraid that I will betray you."

"Where shall I go?" he asked, with a perceptible tremor in his voice.

"While I am out here seeming to prop up these shrubs, make your way to the kitchen and enter its front door, and don't close it after you, but let it remain wide open. But be still until I tell you to start."

As if going for something, I walked hastily around the house and kitchen, and entering the latter brought out an old hoe, and seemed to use it quite industriously in banking up earth around fallen shrubbery. Watching an opportunity—for in those war times all things, animate and inanimate, seemed to have ears—I said:

"When I go into the house, you must go into the kitchen, and be certain to let the doors remain open."

I never knew how Everett made his journey, whether upright as a man, or upon all-fours like a beast.

From sheer exhaustion my poor mother was sleeping still, and Toby's breathing and general appearance as he lay upon his pallet, plainly indicated the presence of deep seated disease. I looked around for Telitha, and not seeing her, went into the dining room where I found her sitting by a window. By unmistakable signs she made me understand that she had witnessed the entire proceeding connected with Everett through the window blinds.

Soon the loud tramping of horses' feet caused me to run again to the front door, and I beheld a number of our scouts approaching.

I went to meet them and shook hands with every one of them. No demonstration, however enthusiastic, could have been an exaggeration of my joy on again seeing our men, our dear Confederate soldiers, and yet I thought of Everett and trembled.

"Have you seen any Billy Yanks this morning?" was asked by several of them; and I replied:

"No, I have not seen any since our men ran them out of Decatur yesterday."

"How did they treat you while they were here?"

"You see the devastation of the place," I replied. "Personally we escaped violence; but I would like you to go into the house and see the condition of affairs there."

Said they:

"It would not be new to us. We have seen the most wanton destruction of property and household goods wherever they have gone."

"Do wait and let me have a pot of coffee made for you. The Yankees gave our negro girl quite a good deal of it, and not using it herself, she gave it to my mother, and I want you to enjoy some of it," I said. They replied.

"Soldiers can't wait for luxuries."

"Goodbye and God bless you," was their parting benediction. And then as if impelled by some strange inspiration they galloped round to the well. I ran into the house and got several tumblers and fairly flew out there with them, as there was no gourd at the well. The kitchen was in close proximity, and the door stood invitingly open. What if a bare suspicion should prompt these brave men to enter? Alas! All would be up with the poor miscreant who had thrown himself upon my mercy, and who was even then lurking there under my direction. But, thank the good Lord, they did not enter, and after again invoking God's blessings upon me, they galloped off in a southerly direction; and never did retreating sounds give more relief.

I went into the house. My mother, thoroughly exhausted, and perhaps discouraged, chose to remain in bed, and as she lay gazing intently upon the wall above her, I doubt if she saw it, so intense was her meditation. As Telitha by this time had a fire made in the dining room, I prepared a pot of good strong coffee, and after partaking of the exhilarating beverage myself, and seeing that each of the household was supplied, I took the remainder with necessary adjuncts to Everett. Never will I forget his appearance as we stood face to face—he a miserable deserter from the cause I loved, and the recipient of favours

I scorned myself for bestowing. I told him I would go at once for his wife, and that after seeing her he must make his way into the enemy's lines as soon as possible.

A few minutes sufficed to carry me to Mrs. Everett's retreat, already mentioned. I sat down on the front doorsteps and drew from my pocket a newspaper, which chanced to be there, and commenced reading aloud. At length I saw that my presence had attracted the notice of the children, and I called them. One by one they came to me, and I shook hands with them and asked them about their mother. Hearing my voice and inquiries, she spoke to me most pleasantly. I asked her to come out and take a seat by me on the steps. She did so, blushingly and timidly. I wrote on the margin of the paper, "Send the children away," and handed it to her. She did so. Assured that they were not in hearing distance, I held the paper before me, and, as if reading, I told her the story of my early interview with her husband; of his earnest desire to see her; of my consent, on her account, to plan a meeting with her; of his secretion in our kitchen; and the necessity of the greatest caution in our movements.

I told her that after walking around a little, and exchanging experiences with the brave ladies of the village, she would see me, by keeping watch, going home, and then she could take a little basket in her hand, as if going for something, and come on to our house. She implicitly followed my directions. My mother received her as if nothing of an unpleasant nature had transpired; and, although it is a very difficult problem, and never solved without the aid of necromancy, I undertook to deduct something from nothing, and so far succeeded that I had several small packages to lay in her basket as she started. Knowing that she knew the way to the kitchen, I gave her a wish that all would end well, and bade her goodbye, never, doubtless, to meet her again on earth.

The tears flowed plenteously down her cheeks, and her tongue refused to speak, but the pressure of her hand attested gratitude, and affection, and farewell. I got a glimpse of her as she went out of the alley gate; but I never knew when he abandoned his hiding place. I heard that about dusk a Federal army wagon, under protection of a company of troops, came and took her and her little children out of Decatur.

CHAPTER 17

A Visit to Confederate Lines

No news from "the front;" no tidings from the loved ones in gray; no friendly spirit whispering words of cheer or consolation. Shut up within a narrow space, and guarded by Federal bayonets! not a ray of friendly light illuminated my environment.

The constant roaring of cannon and rattling of musketry; the thousand, yea, tens of thousands of shots blending into one grand continuous whole, and reverberating in avalanchan volume over the hills of Fulton, and the mountain heights of old DeKalb—told in thunder tones of the fierce contest between Federal and Confederate forces being waged without intermission for the possession of Atlanta.

The haughty, insolent boast of the enemy, now that Joe Johnston was removed from the command of the Army of the Tennessee, that they would make quick work of the rebellion, and of the complete subjugation of the South, had in no way a tendency to mitigate anxiety or to encourage hope. Thus surrounded, I sought and obtained permission to read Federal newspapers. The United States mail brought daily papers to the officers in command of the forces quartered in our yard; and through this medium I kept posted, from a Northern standpoint, concerning the situation of both armies. While there was little in these dispatches gratifying to me, there was much that I thought would be valuable to my people if I could only convey it to them; and I racked my brain day and night, devising ways and means by which to accomplish this feat. But the ways and means decided upon were, upon reflection, invariably abandoned as being impracticable.

In this dilemma, a most opportune circumstance offered an immediate solution of the difficult problem. In the midst of a deep study of the relative positions of the two armies, and of the hopes and fears animating both, a tall, lank, honest-faced Yankee came to the door of the portico and asked "if Miss Gay was in."

I responded that I was she, and he handed me a letter addressed to myself. I hastily tore it open and read the contents. It was written by a reverend gentleman whose wife was a distant relative of my mother, and told that she was very ill. "Indeed," wrote he, "I have but little hope of ever seeing her any better, and I beg you to come to see her, and spend several days."

I showed the letter to my mother, who was sitting nearby, and, like myself, engaged in studying the situation. She strenuously objected to my going, and advanced many good reasons for my not doing so; but my reasons for going counteracted them all in my estimation, and I determined to go.

Taking Telitha with me, I carried the letter to the Provost Marshal, and asked him to read it and grant me the privilege of going. After reading the letter, he asked me how I obtained it, and received my statement. He then asked me if I could refer him to the party who brought it to me. Leaving the letter with him, I ran home and soon returned with the desired individual who had fortunately lingered in the yard in anticipation of usefulness. Convinced that the invitation was genuine, and for a humane purpose, this usually morose marshal granted me "a permit" to visit those poor old sick people, for the husband was almost as feeble as his wife. I told the obliging marshal that there was another favour I should like to ask of him, if he would not think me too presumptuous. "Name it," he said. I replied:

"Will you detail one or more of the soldiers to act as an escort for me? I am afraid to go with only this girl."

To this he also assented, and said it was a wise precaution. He asked when I wished to come home.

"Day after tomorrow afternoon," I told him, and received assurance that an escort would be in waiting for me at that time.

It now became necessary to make some important preparations for the trip. A great deal was involved, and if my plans were successful, important events might accrue. A nice white petticoat was called into requisition, and, when I got done with it, it was literally lined with Northern newspapers. *The Cincinnati Enquirer*, and *The New York Daily Times*; *The Cincinnati Commercial Gazette*, and *The Philadelphia Evening Ledger*, under the manipulation of my fingers, took their places on the inner sides and rear of the skirt, and served as a very stylish "bustle," an article much in vogue in those days. This preparatory work having been accomplished, it required but a few moments to complete my toilet, and, under the auspices of a clear conscience and a mother's blessing, doubtless, I started on a perilous trip. The ever-faithful Telitha was by my side, and the military escort a few feet in advance.

After a walk of a mile and a half, I reached my destination for that day. I found the old lady in question much better than I had expected. Nervous and sick himself, her husband had greatly exaggerated her afflictions. By degrees, and under protest, I communicated to these aged people my intention of carrying information to Hood's headquarters, that might be of use to our army. I knew that these good old people would not betray me, even though they might not approve my course, and I confided to them my every plan. Both were troubled about the possible result if I should be detected; but my plans were laid, and nothing could deter me from pursuing them.

The rising sun of another day saw Telitha and me starting on our way to run the gauntlet, so to speak, of Federal bayonets. These good old people had given me much valuable information regarding the way to Atlanta—information which enabled me to get there without conflict with either Confederate or Federal pickets. Knowing the topography of the country, I took a circuitous route to an old mill; Cobb's, I believe, and from there I sought the McDonough road. I didn't venture to keep that highway to the city, but I kept within sight of it, and under cover of breast-works and other obstructions, managed to evade videttes and pickets of both armies. After walking fourteen or fifteen miles, I entered Atlanta at the beautiful home of Mrs. L. P. Grant, at the southern boundary of the city. That estimable lady never lost an opportunity of doing good.

The lessons of humanity and Christian grace impressed upon her youthful mind, and intensified by the life-long example of her devoted mother, Mrs. Ammi Williams, of Decatur, had called into action all that is ennobling in woman. On this occasion, as upon every other offering an opportunity, she remembered to do good. She ordered an appetizing lunch, including a cup of sure enough coffee, which refreshed and strengthened me after my long walk. Her butler having become a familiar personage on the streets of Atlanta, she sent him as a guide to important places. We entered the city unchallenged, and moved about at will.

The force of habit, probably, led me to Mrs. McArthur's and to Mrs. Craig's on Pryor street; and, by the way, these friends still own the same property, and occupy almost the same homes. The head of neither of these families was willing to accompany me to Confederate headquarters, and without a guide I started to hunt them for myself. What had seemed an easy task now seemed insurmountable. I knew not in what direction to go, and the few whom I asked seemed as ignorant as myself. Starting from Mrs. Craig's, I went towards the depot. I had not proceeded very far before I met Major John Y. Rankin. I could scarcely restrain tears of joy. He was a member of the very same command to which my brother belonged.

From Major Rankin I learned that my brother, utterly prostrated, had been sent to a hospital, either in Augusta or Madison. He told me many other things of interest, which I cannot mention now, unless I was compiling a history instead of a series of personal reminiscences. Preferring not to stand upon the street, I asked Major Rankin to return with me to Mrs. Craig's, which he did, and spent an hour in pleasant conversation. Mrs. Craig was a delightful conversationalist, and while she was entertaining the major with that fine art, I retired to a private apartment, and with the aid of a pair of scissors ripped off the papers from my underskirt and smoothed and folded them nicely, and after re-arranging my toilet, took them into the parlour as a trophy of skill in outwitting the Yankee.

Telitha, too, had a trophy to which she had clung ever since we left home with the tenacity of an eel, and which doubtless she supposed to be an offering to "Marse Tom," and was evidently anxious that he should receive it. Having dismissed Mrs. Grant's butler as no longer necessary to my convenience, Major Rankin, myself and Telitha went direct to the headquarters of his command. The papers seemed to be most acceptable, but I noticed that the gleanings from conversation seemed far more so. The hopefulness and enthusiasm of our soldiers were inspiring. But alas! how little they knew of the situation, and how determined not to be enlightened. Even then they believed that they would hold Atlanta against Herculean odds, and scorned the idea of its surrender. At length the opening of Telitha's package devolved on me. Shirts, socks and soap, towels, gloves, etc., formed a compact bundle that my mother had sent to our soldiers. Many cheery words were said, and goodbyes uttered, and I left them to meet once more under very different circumstances.

I now turned my thoughts to our negroes, who were hired in different parts of the city. Rachel, the mother of King, hired herself and rented a room from Mr. John Silvey, who lived upon the same lot on Marietta street upon which he has since erected his present elegant residence. In order that I might have an interview with Rachel without disturbing Mr. Silvey's family, I went to the side gate and called her. She answered and came immediately. I asked her if she realized the great danger to which she was continually exposed. Even then "shot and shell" were falling in every direction, and the roaring of cannon was an unceasing sound. She replied that she knew the danger, and thought I was doing wrong to be in Atlanta when I had a home to be at. I insisted that she had the same home, and a good vacant house was ready to receive her.

But she was impervious to every argument, and preferred to await the coming of Sherman in her present quarters. Seeing that I had no influence over her, I bade her goodbye and left. Telitha and I had not gone farther than the First Presbyterian church (not a square away) from the gate upon which I had leaned during this interview with Rachel, before a bombshell fell by that gate and burst into a thousand fragments, literally tearing the gate into pieces. Had I remained there one minute longer, my mortal being would have been torn to atoms. After this fearfully impressive adventure, unfortified by any "permit" I struck a bee line to Mrs. Grant's, having promised her that I would go back that way and stop awhile.

An old negro man belonging to Mrs. Williams, who had "come out" on a previous occasion, was there, and wanted to return under my protection to his home within the enemy's lines. Very earnest assurances from Mrs. Grant to that effect convinced me that I had nothing to fear from betrayal by him, and I consented that he should be a member of my company homeward bound. Two large packages were ready for the old man to take charge of, about which Mrs. Grant gave him directions, *sotto voce*. Putting one of them on the end of a walking cane he threw it over his right shoulder, and with his left hand picked up the other bundle. Telitha and I were unencumbered.

With a good deal of trepidation I took the advance position in the line of march, and walked briskly. We had not proceeded very far before we encountered our pickets. No argument was weighty enough to secure for me the privilege of passing the lines without an official permit. Baffled in this effort, I approved the action of the pickets, and we turned and retraced our steps in the direction of Atlanta, until entirely out of sight of them, and then we turned southward and then eastward, verging a little northward. Constant vigilance enabled me to evade the Yankee pickets, and constant walking brought me safely to the home of my aged and afflicted friends, from which I had started early in the morning of that day.

Not being tired, I could have gone home; but the policy of carrying out the original programme is too apparent to need explanation. These friends were conservative in every act and word, and, it may be, leaned a little out of the perpendicular towards that "flaunting lie," the United States flag; therefore they were favourites among the so-called defenders of the Union, and were kept supplied with many palatable articles of food that were entirely out of the reach of rebels who were avowed and "dyed in the wool."

A few minutes sufficed to furnish us with a fine pot of soup (and good bread was not lacking), of which we ate heartily. The old negro man was too anxious to get home to be willing to spend the night so near, just for the privilege of walking into Decatur under Yankee escort, and said he was "going home," and left me.

The next day my escort was promptly on hand, and in due time I was in Decatur, none the worse for having put into practice a favourite aphorism of the Yankees, that "all things are fair in war."

The old man had preceded me, and faithful to the behest of Mrs. Grant, had turned over a valuable package to my mother.

Not many mornings subsequent to the adventure just related, I discovered upon opening the door that the Yankee tents seemed to be vacant. Not a blue-coat was to be seen. What could it mean? Had they given up the contest and ignominiously fled? As if confirmatory of the gratifying suggestion, the booming of cannon in the direction of Atlanta was evidently decreasing. Then again I thought perhaps the wagon train had been sent out to forage upon the country, and as it would now have to go forty-five and fifty miles to get anything, it required an immense military escort to protect it from the dashing, sanguinary attacks of the "rebels."

The latter thought was soon dismissed and the former embraced, and how consoling it was to me. Before the sun had attained its meridian height, a number of our scouts appeared on the abandoned grounds; and what joy their presence gave us! But they left us as suddenly as they came, and on reflection we could not think of a single encouraging word uttered by them during their stay. Suspense became intolerable. With occasional lulls, the roaring of cannon was a continuous blending of ominous sound.

In the midst of this awful suspense, an apparition, glorious and bright, appeared in our presence. It was my brother. He had left Madison a few days before, where he had been allowed to spend a part of his furlough, instead of remaining at the Augusta hospital, and where he received the tender ministrations of his estimable cousin, Mrs. Tom Hillsman, and her pretty young daughters, and the loving care of his sister Missouri, who was also at this time an inmate of her cousin's household. How I wished he could have remained there until restored to health. One less patriotic and conscientious would have done so. His mother's joy at meeting her beloved son, and under such circumstances, was pathetic indeed, and I shall never forget the effort she made to repress the tears and steady the voice as she sought to nerve him for the arduous and perilous duties before him.

Much of his conversation, though hurried, was regarding his Mary, in Texas, and the dear little boy dropped down from heaven, whom he had never seen. The shades of night came on, and darker grew until complete blackness enveloped the face of the earth, and still the low subdued tones of conversation between mother, son and daughter, mingled with unabated interest. Hark! Hark! An explosion! An earthquake? The angry bellowing sound rises in deafening grandeur, and reverberates along the far-off valleys and distant hilltops. What is it? This mighty thunder that never ceases? The earth is ablaze—what can it be? This illumination that reveals minutest objects? With blanched face and tearful eye, the soldier said:

"Atlanta has surrendered to the enemy. The mighty reports are occasioned by the blowing up of the magazines and arsenals."

Dumbfounded we stood, trying to realize the crushing fact. Woman's heart could bear no more in silence, and a wail over departed hopes mingled with the angry sounds without.

Impelled by a stern resolve, and a spirit like to that of martyred saints, our brother said:

"This is no place for me. I must go."

And then he put an arm around each of us, and kissed us with a fervour of love that knew no bounds, and was quenching itself in unfathomable hopeless tenderness. The quiet fortitude and patriotism of his mother gave way in that dread hour, and she cried aloud in agonizing apprehension of never again clasping to her bosom her greatest earthly joy. No pen can describe the scene of that last parting between mother and son, and in sheer impotency I drop the curtain.

As he walked away from his sobbing mother, through the war-illuminated village, I never beheld mortal man so handsome, so heroically grand. His great tender heart, which I had seen heave and sway under less trying circumstances, seemed to have ossified, and not an emotion was apparent.

CHAPTER 18

The Ten Days' Armistice

After every morsel of food had been taken from the people, and every vestige of nutrition extracted from the earth, the following order, in substance, was proclaimed throughout the land held by the right of conquest:

All who cannot support themselves without applying to the United States Commissary for assistance, must go outside of our lines, either north or south, within the period of time mentioned in this order, etc., etc.

And by this order, and by others even more oppressive and diabolical, the Nero of the nineteenth century, alias William Tecumseh Sherman, was put upon record as the born leader of the most ruthless, Godless band of men ever organized in the name of patriotism—a band which, but for a few noble spirits who, by the power of mind over matter, exerted a restraining influence, would not have left a Southerner to tell the tale of fiendishness on its route to the sea.

And now, like Bill Nye, after one of his sententious and doubtless truthful introductions to a Western sketch, I feel easier in my mind, and will proceed with my reminiscences of that unholy period of this country, and tell the truth about it, without favour or prejudice, if it kills me. After this *pronunciamento* had been issued, all was bustle and rapid movement in every household within the boundaries of usurpation.

Under the strong arm of military power, delay was not permitted. Homes were to be abandoned, and household goods and household gods to be left for the enemy, or destroyed; and liberty under our own vine and fig tree was to be a thing of the past, and dependence upon strangers a thing of the future. In preparation for this enforced change, much that should have been done was left undone, but there was no time to correct mistakes—the armistice was only for ten days.

What were we to do, my mother and myself, was a question which presented itself with startling seriousness, and had to be answered without delay. Our farm in Gordon county had already been devastated by the invading army, and every improvement destroyed, and if we should lose our home in Decatur we would be poor indeed. But what were we to do? If we left our home, we knew it would share the fate of all other "abandoned" property, and furnish material for a bonfire for Nero to fiddle by; and if we remained, by grace of better men than he, what assurance had we that by any means within our grasp we could obtain even a scanty subsistence, or be protected from personal abuse and insult by an alien army whose gentlemen were vastly in the minority.

We learned that our neighbours and friends, Mrs. Ammi Williams and her estimable son, Mr. Frederick Williams, (an invalid from paralysis)—whose influence over General Schofield prevented my banishment from Decatur the very first night of its occupancy by the Federal army—and the venerable Mr. and Mrs. Buchanan (the latter a Bostonian and educated in Emerson's celebrated school for young ladies), and other families as true to the South as the needle to the pole, were going to remain and take their chances within the enemy's lines, and we determined to do so too.

The officers in command of the post, especially the provost marshal, interrogated us very closely regarding our plans and expectations during the occupancy of the place by Federal forces. Having satisfied them that our only remaining servant would do washing and ironing at reasonable prices, and that we would do darning and repairing, we were given a written permit to remain within the lines.

I, however, had a work to do, a feat to perform, which for audacity and courage, has seldom been surpassed, which would not admit of my staying at home until I had made a little trip to Dixie.

Knowing the value of his influence, I again went to Mr. Frederick Williams, and confiding my plans to him, asked his assistance in getting permission to go out and return during the armistice. I never knew what argument he employed for the accomplishment of this object. I only know by inference. But I received a letter from General Schofield, adjutant-general, of which the subjoined is an exact transcript:

Decatur, Ga., Sept. 1, 1864.

Miss Gay—It was hard for me to reconcile my conscience to giving the enclosed recommendation to one whose sentiments I cannot approve, but if I have committed an error it has been on the side of mercy, and I hope I'll be forgiven. Hereafter I hope you will not think of Yankees as all being bad, and beyond the pale of redemption.

Tomorrow I leave for my own home in the 'frozen North,' and when I return it will be to fight for my country, and against your friends, so that I suppose I shall not have the pleasure of again meeting you.
Very respectfully,

J. W. Campbell.

And that Major Campbell's gallant act may be fully appreciated, I will add the letter which secured for me the great favour which I had the temerity to ask.

Headquarters, Army of Ohio,
Decatur, Ga., Sept. 14, 1864.

My Dear Colonel—I have the honor to introduce Miss Mary A. H. Gay, of this village, and I recommend her case to your favourable consideration. I do not know exactly what orders are now in force, but if you think you can grant her desires without detriment to the public service, I am confident the indulgence will not be abused.
Very respectfully your obedient servant,

J. W. Campbell.

To Colonel J. C. Parkhurst, Pro. Mar. Gen.,
Army of the Cumberland.

Thus recommended by one high in army ranks, Colonel Parkhurst granted me the privilege of going to see my young sister, then in Augusta, and carrying anything I might have saved from the ravages of the war, "unmolested." Fortified by these letters I went to the Provost Marshal in Decatur and told him I would be ready to go to Atlanta tomorrow morning at 8 o'clock, and I wanted to carry some old bedclothing and other things to my sister, and would be grateful for an ambulance, or an army wagon all to myself, and an Irish driver. He promised that both should be at my service at the time indicated—not, however, without the sarcastic remark that "if the Yankees had been as bad as I had said they were, they would not have left anything for me to carry."

I ran to my mother and imparted to her the glad tidings of success, and in a whispered conversation we soon had definite plans arranged for the consummation of the perilous duty before me. I went to the Federal camp and asked for some crocus sacks such as are used in the transportation of grain, and quite a number were given to me. I shook them thoroughly inside and out, and put them by. A ball of twine and some large needles had found their way into the house. The needles were threaded and placed in convenient proximity to the sacks. Telitha watched every movement with interest and intuitively divined its import. The wardrobe was empty and my very first touch moved it at least one inch in the desired direction, and a helping hand from her soon placed it in favourable position.

This much being accomplished, I took a seat by my mother on the front door-steps and engaged in a pleasant conversation with a group of young Federal soldiers, who seemed much attached to us, and with whom I conversed with unreserved candour, and often expressed regret that they were in hostile array towards a people who had been goaded to desperation by infringement upon constitutional rights by those who had pronounced the only ligament that bound the two sections of the country together, "a league with hell, and a covenant with the devil." This I proved to them by documents published at the North, and by many other things of which they were ignorant.

While thus engaged, Captain Woodbury approached and said: "I learn that you are going out into Dixie, Miss Gay."

"Yes, for a few days," I replied.

"I am prepared to furnish a more pleasant conveyance to Atlanta than the one you have secured," said he, and continued, "I have a handsome new buggy and a fine trotter, and it will take only a few minutes to reach there. Will you accept a seat with me?"

If all the blood within me had overflowed its proper channels, and rushed to the surface, I could not have flushed more. I felt it in the commotion of my hair, and in the nervous twitching of my feet. The indignation and contempt that I felt for the man! That one who was aiding and abetting in the devastation of my country and the spoliation of my home, should ask me to take a seat with him in a buggy which he doubtless had taken, without leave or license, from my countrymen, was presumptuous indeed, and a severe rebuke. But "prudence being the better part of valour," I repressed all that would have been offensive in word and act, and replied with suavity, "Thank you, Captain Woodbury, for the honour you would have conferred upon me, but I cannot accept it." Receiving no reply, I added:

"Let me in candor make a statement to you, and I think you will approve the motive that prompts my decision. I have not sought to conceal the fact that my only brother is in the Confederate army; he is there from motives purely patriotic, and not as a mercenary hireling. He is fighting for the rights guaranteed by the Constitution of the United States, a constitution so sacred that our people have never violated it in any particular, and of which we have shown our highest appreciation by adopting it *verbatim*, as the guiding star of the Southern Confederacy. You are in an army claiming to be fighting for the Union, and yet the government that sent you out on this glorious mission ignores every principle of fraternal relation between the North and the South, and would subvert every fundamental principle of self-government and establish upon the wreck a centralized despotism. Could I, while you and I are so antagonistic, accept your offer and retain your good opinion? I think not, and I prefer to go in the conveyance already stipulated."

Silence, without the slightest manifestation of anger, assured me that my argument against taking a buggy drive with him to Atlanta had not been lost on Captain Woodbury, of Ohio, a member of Garrard's Cavalry.

After this episode we bade our callers "good-evening," went into the house and busied ourselves with the important work before us—a work which probably would not attract attention because of the darkness that would surround the scene of its execution. The table and chair had been placed, as once before, by the wardrobe already mentioned, and a little respite was employed in viewing the situation. The door connecting our room and this dining-room was generally kept shut. At length night came on with its friendly, helpful darkness. The shutters of the windows had been closed for weeks, and secured by nails, and the house had been too often searched and plundered to be suspected of containing valuables.

Therefore, we felt that if no unusual sound attracted notice we would accomplish our object unsuspected. But I was anxious and nervous in view of what was before me, and wanted the perilous work over with. So when the darkness of night fully enshrouded the earth, with no other light than that which found its way from the camp-fires of the enemy through the latticed shutters, I stepped into the chair and thence upon the table, and Telitha followed and drew the chair up after her. Then with her strong dusky hands she seized the wardrobe as if it had been a toy in her hands. I steadied the chair by the wardrobe and stepped into it, and another step landed me on top of the wardrobe. My fingers penetrated the crevice between the slats which I wanted to pull off, and to a slight effort they yielded. Lest the noise occasioned by dropping them might attract notice, I stooped and laid each piece down as I drew it off the joist.

When the aperture thus made was sufficient, I began to draw from their hiding place the precious Confederate overcoats and other winter apparel confided to my keeping (as already related), by soldiers of General Joseph E. Johnston's army, when they were at Dalton. One by one each piece was taken out and dropped down upon the floor. But by a lamentable oversight we afterwards found that one article had been left—a woollen scarf for the neck, knitted for my brother by his loving young wife in Texas.

Carefully I descended, and, with the aid of the girl, placed the chair, the table, and the dear old wardrobe (which deserves to be immortalized in song and story), in less suspicious positions, and then proceeded to pack in the sacks, already mentioned, the precious articles. The thought occurred to me that my mother would like to have a hand in this labour of love, and I opened the door between us. I shall never forget her appearance as she stood as if riveted to the spot, near a window, watching the moving figures without. I approached her and in a cheerful whisper told her that I was now putting the things in the sacks, and I knew she would like to have an interest in the job.

She tried to respond, but she was too nervous to do so. Slowly but surely she was yielding to the pressure upon nerve and brain. As each sack was filled, a threaded needle securely closed the mouth. In a short while a number of these sacks stood in a group, as erect as if on parade, and I verily believe that if the host of profane, godless braggarts (with but few exceptions) who surrounded the house could have seen them at that time and known their contents, they would have evacuated Decatur in mortal fear of the ghosts of "Johnnie Rebs."

This important work having been accomplished without discovery or even a shadow of suspicion, I felt vastly relieved, and thanked the Lord with all my heart for the health, strength, and ingenuity which had enabled me to consummate it. My mother and I lay down upon the same bed, and were soon blessed with the invigorating influence of "tired nature's sweet restorer."

The song of the lark had ceased to be heard in this war-stricken locality; chanticleer had long since furnished a savoury meal for camp followers, and the time-pieces had either been spoiled or stolen; but there was a silent, unerring chronometer within that never deviated, and needed no alarm attachment to arouse me from slumber, and the dawn found me up and preparing for the duties and perhaps the dangers of the day.

Telitha had become quite an attraction to a bevy of men who occupied soldiers' quarters, and wore soldiers' uniforms, and drew pay for doing so, from Uncle Sam's coffers; and as she had been trained to ideas of virtue and morality she often came in frowning and much ruffled in temper by their deportment towards her. Being almost entirely deaf and dumb, her limited vocabulary was inadequate to supply epithets expressive of the righteous indignation and contempt which she evidently felt—she could only say, "Devil Yank, devil," and these words she used with telling effect both to the amusement and chagrin of the Yankees. This state of affairs convinced me that for her protection she would have to be kept within doors, and I therefore assumed the task of drawing the water, and a few other jobs indispensable even in life's rudest state.

On this occasion, when I went to the well for a bucket of water, before preparing our frugal breakfast, I was asked by early marauders why I did not let "that young coloured lady draw the water." I candidly answered them, and told them I was going to ask the officers of the encampment to protect her while I was gone, and I also would ask them to report any misdemeanour toward her, that they might witness, at headquarters.

After a good night's rest my mother's nerves seemed all right again, and by 7 o'clock we had finished our breakfast, which consisted of bread and butter and coffee—the latter luxurious beverage being furnished by one whose heart was in touch with humanity. That the aperture in the ceiling of the dining room might not be discovered until I got the contraband goods out of the house, I had brought the sacks containing them into the adjoining room, and it was therefore the work of a very few minutes to convey them to the wagon, when that vehicle, drawn by a span of fine horses, under the guidance of the Irish driver, drove up to the front door. "Put those sacks into the wagon," I said, pointing to them.

When the last one of them was stored away safely in that moving repository, one of those feelings of relief and security came over me that had more than once given me courage to brave successfully impending danger—and I donned my hat, and bade my mother and the faithful girl an almost cheerful "Goodbye," and took my seat by the driver, *en route* for Dixie. Would I get there? Ah! that was the question that had blanched my mother's cheek when I said "Goodbye." But hope, etc., *"eternal in the human breast,"* whispered "yes," and thus encouraged, I spoke grateful words to the Irish driver, and asked him many questions about the land of the shamrock and sunny blue skies. He was evidently flattered by my favourable knowledge of the Emerald Isle, and would have done anything within his power for me. God bless the Irish forever!

I asked him to drive under my direction to the residence of my estimable friends, Mr. and Mrs. Posey Maddox, the parents of the accomplished and erudite Charles K. Maddox, of Atlanta. To my great joy I saw wagons in the yard, already laden with their household goods, to be carried to the depot and turned over to the Federal authorities, who assumed the transportation of them to Jonesboro and the safe delivery of them to the Confederate authorities, who in turn assumed the transportation and delivery of them to the nearest Confederate station. Mr. Maddox had secured the use of an entire freight car, and gladly consented to take me and my baggage in with theirs. Mrs. Maddox was particularly glad to have me go with them, and to her I confided the character of my baggage, and received in return many words of sympathy and approbation.

Those who have studied mythical lore, and dwelt in imagination upon the attributes of mythical characters, especially those of an evil nature, can perhaps form some idea of the confusion and disquiet of an entire city yielding its possession to an alien army, which now, that success had been achieved by brute force, was bent upon the utter impoverishment of the people, and their extreme humiliation. Curses and imprecations too vile to repeat, and boisterous laughter, and vulgar jests resounded through the streets of Atlanta. Federal wagons followed in the tracks of Confederate wagons, and after a few light articles were placed in the latter for Southern destination, the former unblushingly moved up to receive pianos and other expensive furniture which found its way into every section of the North. And this highway robbery was permitted by William Tecumseh Sherman, the Grand Mogul of the Army of the Republic. Truly had the city of Atlanta been turned into a veritable pandemonium.

At length our time came to move in the worse than death-like processions going southward, and in a short while we were at Jonesboro, our destination, so far as Federal aid extended. As soon as I stepped from the car I wended my way to the Confederate officer of the day, whom I recognized by his regalia, and told him of my success in concealing and bringing out of Federal lines the winter clothing of our soldiers. He listened with polite attention and said it was a wonderfully interesting story, but altogether improbable.

"Go with me and I will prove to you the truthfulness of it," I eagerly said.

As it was a bleak equinoctial day, and drizzling rain, Mr. and Mrs. Maddox had not yet left their car (by way of parenthesis, I would say that the favours shown to these excellent people was in consideration of Mr. Maddox being a very prudent minister of the gospel), and, when we reached it, I asked Mr. Maddox to roll one of my sacks to the door. He did so, and I then asked the officer to examine its contents. A blade of a pen-knife severed the twine with which the edges of the mouth had been sewed together, and the loved familiar gray and brass buttons, and other articles, verified the truth of my statement. He looked amazed, and exhausted his vocabulary of flattering encomiums upon me, and, what was more desirable and to the point, he asked what he could do in the matter, and assured me that there was nothing within the range of his jurisdiction that he would not do. I told him that the object of my coming to him was to ask that he send me and my precious charge to General Granbury's headquarters, as, among other overcoats, I had one of his in charge, as well as many other things belonging to his staff officers. He told me the finest span of Confederate horses and the best ambulance on the ground should be at my service as soon as possible.

During the interim, I opened wide my eyes and took in the situation in all its horrible details. The entire Southern population of Atlanta, with but an occasional exception, and that of many miles in its vicinity, were dumped out upon the cold ground without shelter and without any of the comforts of home, and an autumnal mist or drizzle slowly but surely saturating every article of clothing upon them; and pulmonary diseases in all stages admonishing them of the danger of such exposure. Aged grandmothers tottering upon the verge of the grave, and tender maidens in the first bloom of young womanhood, and little babes not three days old in the arms of sick mothers, driven from their homes, were all out upon the cold charity of the world.

Apropos, I will relate an incident that came under my observation during my brief stay at this station: When one of the long trains from

Atlanta rolled in with its living freight and stopped at the terminus, a queenly girl, tall and lithe in figure and willowy in motion, emerged from one of the cars, and stood, the embodiment of feminine grace, for a moment upon the platform. In less time than it takes to chronicle the impression, her Grecian beauty, classic expression and nobility of manner, had daguerreotyped themselves upon the tablets of my memory never to be effaced by mortal alchemy.

The pretty plain debeige dress, trimmed with Confederate buttons and corresponding ribbon, all conspired to make her appear, even to a casual observer, just what she was—a typical Southern girl who gloried in that honour. She stood only a moment, and then, as if moved by some divine inspiration, she stepped from the car, and falling upon her knees, bent forward and kissed the ground. This silent demonstration of affection for the land of Dixie touched a vibrating chord, and a score or more of beautiful girlish voices blended in sweetest harmony while they told in song their love for Dixie. I listened spellbound, and was not the only one thus enchanted. A United States officer listened and was touched to tears. Approaching me, he asked if I would do him the favour to tell him the name of the young lady who kissed the ground.

"I do not think she would approve of my telling you her name, and I decline to do so," I said in reply. Not in the least daunted by this rebuff he responded: "I shall learn it; and if she has not already become the wife or the affianced of another, I shall offer her the devotion of my life."

The Confederate officer of the day, God forever bless him! came for me. The army wagon was ready and standing by Mr. Posey Maddox's car, waiting to receive its precious freight, and a few minutes sufficed to transfer it from car to wagon, and, after waiting to see the last sack securely placed in the wagon, I, too, got in and took my seat by the driver. A long cold drive was before us, but I was so robust I had no fear of the result.

The driver was a veritable young Jehu, and we got over the ground rapidly; but, owing to a mistake in following directions, it was a long time before we reached our destination, the course of which must have been due west from Jonesboro, and through a dense forest. And oh, the beauty of that forest! It will remain a living, vivid memory, as long as life endures. Its rich and heavy foliage had been but lightly tinged by the frosts of autumn, and it was rendered more beautiful by the constant dripping of rain drops from every leaf and blossom. As the evening came on, dense, impenetrable clouds canopied the earth, and shut out every ray of sunlight, and almost every ray of hope. At length night came on, dark and weird, and silent, and we were still in the woods, without compass or star.

Just as my brave heart was about to succumb to despair, a vision of delight burst upon me—a beacon light, yea, hundreds of beacon lights, appeared before me, and filled my soul with joy. The camp-fires of General Cleburne's brave men beckoned us onward, and gave us friendly greeting. Every revolution of the wagon wheels brought us perceptibly nearer the haven of rest. Sabbath-like quiet reigned throughout the encampment. No boisterous sounds nor profane imprecations broke the stillness. But there was a sound that reached my ear, filling my soul with joy unspeakable. A human voice it was. I had heard it before in the slight wail of infancy; in the merry prattle of childhood; in the melodious songs of youth; in the tender, well-modulated tones of manhood; and now—there was no mistaking it—in the solemn, earnest invocation to the Lord of Hosts for the salvation of the world, for the millennial dawn, and that "peace on earth, and good will to men," which would never again be broken by the clarion of war, or earth's rude alarms. No sweeter voice ever entered the courts of Heaven.

My obliging young driver stopped the horses at a favourable distance, and I heard the greater part of that grand prayer, and wept for joy. When it was finished, we moved on, and were hailed by a sentinel who demanded the countersign, I believe it is called. The driver satisfied him, and calling to a soldier, I asked him if he knew Lieutenant Stokes. "Like a book," he answered. "Please tell him his sister Mary is here," I said. In a moment I was clasped in his arms with the holy pressure of a brother's love.

His first thought on seeing me was that some calamity must have occurred, and he said, "Sister, is Ma or Missouri dead?"

"No, Thomie, but Toby is."

His brave head bowed low and he wept—sobbed audibly. I told him of Toby's loving mention of him, and of the boy's hope of Heaven. After his natural paroxysm of grief had subsided, he looked up, and with an ineffable smile, said:

"Sister, I know you have a secret to tell—what is it?"

"It is this; I have saved all those precious things that were sent to me from Dalton, and I have brought them to deliver to their rightful owners. Help me to do so as quickly as possible, that I may go back to

Jonesboro tonight."

Had a bombshell exploded at his feet, the effect could not have been more electrical. He bounded to General Granbury's tent with the agility of a deer; he told the news to him and the others assembled there; and he came back, and they all came with him; and had I been a magician, I could not have been an object of greater interest. General Granbury protested against my return to Jonesboro through the darkness of the night, and offered his tent for my occupancy, saying he would go in with some of the other officers. Colonel Robert Young, a friend of years' standing, was also earnest in his efforts to keep me from carrying out my purpose to go back, and I gave it up. I knew that I was with friends, and permitted myself to be lifted out of the wagon and conducted to the general's tent. I took a seat upon a camp stool which was placed for me about the centre of the tent. The general and his staff officers sat around, and my dear brother was very near me.

Thus arranged, a conversation was commenced which continued with slight interruptions into the "wee sma' hours" of the night. Colonel Young seemed to have something upon his mind which rendered him indifferent to society, or some duty to perform which required his attention outside the tent. At length, however, he came to the door and asked my brother to come out awhile. In a short time both of them came in together, and Colonel Young, after asking us to excuse the interruption of the conversation, remarked that there was something outside that he would like for us to see. My brother took me by the hand and led me out in front of the tent, and all the officers stood in a group around. Imagine my surprise when I perceived a long line of soldiers before us, and an officer on horseback galloping from one end of the line to the other. I ventured to ask my brother if they were going to have a moonlight drill without the moon? He smiled, and a faint pressure of the hand indicated that there was something on the *tapis* that would please me, but I must wait until it was revealed to others as well.

In much less time than it has taken to record this episode a signal was given, and one of the grandest cheers ever heard by mortal man resounded through the midnight darkness and the dense forest, and was echoed over hill and dale. Another signal and another cheer, and yet another of each, and I broke down completely and cried heartily. What had I done that my name should thus be honoured by men enduring all the hardships of warfare and fighting for my principles; and yet to me it was the most acceptable compliment ever paid to living woman. I often fancy I hear those voices now blending in one grand harmonious shout of praise to the great God of Heaven and earth, who has doubtless given rest to many of those weary ones.

Once more in General Granbury's tent, at the earnest solicitation of all present, I continued the rehearsal of all the Federal army news that I had gleaned from close perusal of the United States newspapers and from careless and unsuspicious talkers. General Granbury was evidently startled when I told him that I had heard Federal officers say "Hood was working to their hand precisely in going back to Tennessee, as Thomas was there with an army that was invincible, and would whip him so bad that there would not be a Johnnie Reb left to tell the tale;" and they criticised severely the "generalship" of giving an invading army unobstructed route to the goal of their ambition, which, in this case, was South Carolina. I was asked by one of my auditors to give my impression of the situation, and I did so.

As I described the magnitude of the Federal army, and its vindictive spirit as I had seen it, and its implacable feeling towards the South, I saw a shade of sadness pass over the noble faces of all present. "Have you lost hope of the ultimate success of our cause?" was a question I was compelled to answer, because anxiously asked. I, however, imitated a Yankee by asking a question in reply, as to what our resources were, and if they were deemed adequate to cope with a foe which had the world to draw from, both for men and means? "But have you lost hope?" was the question I was called upon to answer without equivocation.

Silence and tears which would well up were interpreted to mean what my tongue refused to speak. My brother perceiving this, put his hand on mine as it lay motionless upon my lap, and said, "Cheer up, sister mine; if you could have seen 'Old Pat's' men on drill this afternoon, you would think we are some ourselves."

Colonel Young continued to seem very much engaged outside, and, since the demonstration in my honour, had given us only an occasional glimpse of himself. At length he came to the door and said, "Lieutenant, I should like to speak to you." My brother responded to the call, and soon returned and said: "As there is a hard day's march before us for tomorrow, we must let the general get a little sleep, and this brave sister of mine must need it, too. Come, let me conduct you to your room."

Goodbyes were spoken that night which, in the providence of God, were destined never to be repeated, and Thomie and Colonel

Young led the way to a brand new tent, never used before, and opened the door that I might enter. Thomie said, "My room is next to yours, sister. Pleasant dreams, and refreshing slumbers," and he kissed me goodnight.

"Goodnight, dear brother." "Goodnight, dear friend," said I, as he and Colonel Young left the tent. By the dim light I surveyed the "room" and its furnishings, and wept to think that dear Confederate soldiers had deprived themselves of comforts that I might be comfortable. A handsome buffalo robe lay on the ground; and a coat nicely folded for a pillow, and a gray blanket for a cover, invited me to repose. A small pan of water for morning ablution, and a towel, and a mirror about the size of a silver dollar, and a comb and brush, furnished every needed convenience. I removed the skirt of my dress that it might not be wrinkled in the morning, and my mantle for the same cause, and lay down and slept, oh, how sweetly, under the protecting care of those noble men, until awakened by the sweet familiar voice of my brother, saying, "Get up, sister, or you will not be ready for the roll-call," was his never-to-be-forgotten morning salutation.

"*As a short horse is soon curried*," it required only a few moments to make myself presentable, and just as I was about announcing myself in that condition, Thomie again appeared at the door with a plate containing my breakfast in one hand, and a tin cup containing a decoction, which he called coffee, in the other. "Here is your breakfast, sister;" and he added, "the ambulance is waiting to carry you to Lovejoy's station. Lieutenant Jewell and myself have been detailed to accompany you there."

The army wagons were already falling in line one after another and moving onward in a northwesterly direction; and what remained of the infantry and cavalry of that once magnificent army, which so often had achieved victory under General Joseph E. Johnston, had made their last grand bivouac on Georgia soil, and were moving onward in the line of march to Tennessee, under the command of Hood. They were leaving many a gallant comrade who had bitten the dust and drenched the soil of Georgia with their life-blood, and although they must have feared that the flag they loved so well was now leading them to defeat, yet not one of those true hearts would have deserted it for the wealth of India.

As they marched in a different direction from that I was going to take, and the demand for rapid movement was imperative, I could not follow them long with my eye, but the memory of the little I saw will ever be fresh, and, like an inspiration yet to me, their bayonets glittered in a perfect halo of glory, for the mists and clouds of the preceding day had passed away during the night, and a blue sky and bright sun gladdened the earth.

The two young lieutenants took seats opposite to me in the ambulance. Thus arranged, I caught every movement and look of that dear brother from whom I was so soon to part. He never looked more handsome, or appeared to greater advantage. I was his guest, and he entertained me with a "feast of reason and a flow of soul." At my request he sang some of the songs of "Auld Lang Syne," but he preferred to talk of our mother and our sister. He recalled incidents of his childhood, and laughed heartily over some of them. He spoke of his Mary in Texas and his love for her, and he took from his vest pocket the impression of the foot and hand of his only child, a dear little boy whom he had never seen, and kissed them, then folded them carefully and put them back in his pocket and said:

"I must hurry back to Texas."

But back of all this glee and apparent hopefulness I saw, in characters unmistakable, that he was almost bereft of hope, and sustained only by Christian resignation.

We knew, by the immense crowd of people standing and sitting around on improvised seats, that we were approaching the station. The two soldiers got out of the ambulance with the elasticity of youth and health, and Thomie assisted me out. I stood for a moment, as if uncertain where to go, and Lieutenant Jewell grasped my hand and said:

"Goodbye, dear Miss Mary!" and stepped back into the wagon and resumed his seat.

Seeing a large, square old house, which appeared to be full of people, Thomie and I advanced toward it a few steps. Suddenly, as if admonished that a soldier's duties should have precedence over everything else, he took me in his arms and kissed me fervently once, twice, thrice. I understood for whom they were intended—that trio of kisses. Not a word did he speak, and when he turned his back on me I saw him brush off the silent tears, and more than one step was uneven before his nerves became steady and he ready to report for duty. I felt intuitively that I should never look upon his face again, and I watched him with riveted eyes until I could no longer see him, and then I gazed upon the vehicle containing him until it, too, disappeared forever from my sight. Then, and not till then, I gave way to pent-up sorrow, and cried as one without hope—unreservedly.

CHAPTER 19

The Return Home

Dazed by a full realization that my brother and every male relative and friend were in the octopus arms of war, cruel and relentless, I stood riveted to the spot where my brother had parted from me, until a gentle hand touched my shoulder, and a pleasant voice gave me friendly greeting. Turning I saw Mrs. Anderson, sister of the brave and gallant Robert Alston, whose tragic fate is known to every reader in this country.

"I am glad to see you. I have just seen your brother Robert," I said.

"Where? Where? Do tell me that I may go to him!" cried his devoted sister, laughing and weeping alternately.

Having ascertained that the long train of exiles would not leave the station for several hours, I offered to conduct the tender-hearted woman to the camp-fire of her brother. The route took me over the same ground which only a few moments ago I had travelled with my own dear brother; and along which I had seen so vividly a lean, gaunt, phantom hand pointing at his retreating form. Even the horses' tracks and the ruts made by the wheels could be plainly traced by their freshness and the yet quivering sands; and as I gazed upon them, I fancied they were connecting links between me and him which were binding our souls together, and which I would never grow weary in following.

These reflections were often disturbed by questions about "my dear brother Robert," and by alternate sobs and laughter. The distance seemed much greater, now that I was walking it, but at length we attained our destination, the headquarters of a few of General John Morgan's gallant defenders of Southern homes and firesides. It would require the descriptive power of a Sims or a Paul Hayne to give an adequate idea of the meeting on this occasion of this demonstrative brother and sister. I will not undertake to do so. He, too, was ready to move in that disastrous campaign, which lost to us the *creme de la creme* of the Army of the Tennessee, and which aided, as if planned by the most astute Federal tactician, Sherman, in his "march to the sea."

During the interview between Colonel Alston and his sister, it developed to him that his pretty home had been abandoned to the tender mercies of the enemy by the family in whose care he had left it, and that the Yankees had shipped his wife's elegant European piano, mirrors and furniture, as well as his library, cut glass and Dresden china to the North; and, besides, in the very malignity of envy and sectional hate, had mutilated and desecrated his house in a shameful manner. His imprecations were fearful; and his vows to get even with the accursed Yankees were even more so. The lamb of a few moments ago was transformed into a lion, roaring and fierce. He accompanied his sister and myself on our return to the station; and never will I forget that walk.

The station reached, the scene of separation of brother and sister was again enacted, and he, too, went to battle-fields, sanguinary and relentless, she to peaceful retreats undisturbed by cannon's roar.

Here, as at Jonesboro, the face of the earth was literally covered with rude tents and side-tracked cars, which were occupied by exiles from home—defenceless women and children, and an occasional old man tottering on the verge of the grave, awaiting their turn to be transported by over-taxed railroads farther into the constantly diminishing land of their love. During the afternoon I boarded an already well-filled south-bound train, and moved about among its occupants as if at home. For were we not one people, the mothers, wives and sisters of Confederates? The diversity of mind, disposition and temper of this long train of representative women and children of Atlanta, and many miles contiguous, who were carrying minds and hearts brimful of memories never to be obliterated, but rather to harden into asphalt preservation, was illustrated in various ways.

Some laughed and talked and jested, and infused the light and warmth of their own sunny natures into others less hopeful; some were morose and churlish, and saw no hope in the future and were impatient with those who did see the silver lining beyond the dark cloud suspended over us; and some very plainly indicated that if our cause failed, they would lose all faith in a prayer-answering God; and others saw wisdom and goodness in all His ways and dispensations, and were willing to submit to any chastisement if it only brought them nearer to the Mercy Seat.

After many delays and adventures, not of sufficient importance to relate, I reached Griswoldville. Here I was received with open arms by that good old father and mother in Israel, Rev. Dr. John S. Wilson and his wife, and his excellent family, whom I found residing in an old freight car. But they were living in a palace compared to many of their neighbours and friends, who had scarcely a shelter to protect them from the inclemency of the weather. Every moment of time with these good people was spent in answering questions and receiving blessings. Not long after this pleasant meeting, Stoneman's raiders came into Griswoldville, and the household effects of Dr. Wilson's family were consumed by devouring torches. All their winter clothing, the doctor's library and his manuscript sermons, were burned to ashes. These sermons were the result of the study and experience of forty years. But this grand old soldier of the cross, although on the verge of threescore years and ten, faltered not; for his eye was fixed on the goal of his heavenly inheritance. Wherever he went, he still preached, and died a few years afterwards at his post in Atlanta, having missed but two preaching appointments in all his ministry, one of these on the Sabbath before he died.

By a circuitous route, which I can now scarcely recall, in the course of time I reached Augusta, the beautiful. I wended my way through the crowded thoroughfares to the residence of friends on Green street, where my sister had sojourned for several weeks, far from the distracting confusion of warfare. After all these long and varied years, I never see that Elysian street without feeling as if I would like to kneel and kiss the ground whereon she found surcease of hostile tread and rancorous foe.

I could scarcely approach the house, in exterior beautiful in all that makes a home attractive. I feared that within sorrowful tidings might await me. No word of the absent sister had come through the enemy's lines since they were first established, and now I dreaded to hear. More than once I stood still and tried to nerve myself for the worst tidings that could be communicated. And then I ascended the stone steps and rang the door-bell. When the butler came, I hurriedly asked if Miss Stokes was in. As if apprehending my state of feelings, he answered with a broad African grin: "She is, ma'am."

The pressure of a mountain was removed from my heart, and with a lighter step than I had taken for some time I entered that friendly portal, a welcome guest. A moment sufficed for him to carry the joyous tidings of my presence to my sister, and, as if by magic, she was with me. O, the joy and the sadness of our meeting! To say that each of us was glad beyond our ability to express it, would be a tame statement; and yet neither of us was happy.

There was too much sadness connected with ourselves and our country to admit of happiness; yet the report of our mother's fortitude and usually good health, and the hopeful spirit of our brother, and his numerous messages of love and playful phraseology, cheered my sister so much that she rallied and did all she could to render my brief stay with her as pleasant as possible. And there was a charm in her sweet voice and pleasant words that were soothing to me, and did much to assuage my own grief. Nor were our good friends wanting in efforts of like character. They, too, had drank deep of Marah's bitter waters. Two noble boys, yet in their teens, had been laid upon the sacrificial altar, an oblation to their country. And a fair young girl had gone down into the tomb, as much a sacrifice to Southern rights as if slain on the battle-field. One other girl and her war-stricken parents survived, and they were devoting their lives to the encouragement of those similarly bereaved.

Although I knew it would pain her greatly, I thought it would be wrong to leave without telling my sister about Toby's death, and, therefore, I told her. Like our brother, she wept, but not as one without hope. She had been his spiritual instructor, and thoroughly taught him the great and yet easy plan of salvation; and I have never doubted that he caught on to it, and was supported by the arm of Jesus, as he "*passed through the dark valley and the shadow of death*."

The time for leaving this peaceful retreat came, and was inexorable; nor would I have stayed if I could. There was a widowed mother, whose head was whitened, not so much by the frost of winters as by sorrow and care, grief and bereavement, awaiting my coming—oh, so anxiously! Waiting to hear from the soldier son, who, even for her sake, and that of his gentle young wife and baby boy in Texas, would listen to no plan of escape from the dangers involved by his first presidential vote. Waiting to hear from the fair young daughter, whom she preferred to banish from home rather than have her exposed to the rude chances of war. That she might not be kept in painful suspense, I determined not to linger on the way.

I, therefore, took the morning train on the good old reliable Georgia Railroad for Social Circle. The parting from my sister pained me exceedingly; but I knew she had put her trust in the Lord, and He would take care of her. It may be asked why I did not have the same faith regarding the preservation of my brother. He, too, was a Christian. "He *that taketh the sword shall perish by the sword*," is a divine assertion, and it was constantly repeating itself in my ears; yea, I had heard him repeat it with emphasis.

The trip from Augusta to Social Circle was replete with melancholy interest, and differed very materially from the trip from Atlanta to Jonesboro. Here those who had the courage to do so were returning to their homes, and were on the *qui vive* for every item of news obtainable from within the enemy's lines; but nothing satisfactory encouraged their hope of better treatment. One marked difference appeared in the character of those who were venturing homeward. There was scarcely any young persons—not a single young lady. The good old mother railroad was very deliberate in her movements, and gave her patrons time to get acquainted and chat a little on the way, and this we did without restraint.

We discussed the situation, and narrated our diversified experiences, and this interchange of thought and feeling brought us very near together, and made us wondrous kind to one another. At one of the stations at which the train stopped, and had to wait a long while, I saw several of the young soldiers from Decatur. Among them was Ryland Holmes, and, I think, Mose Brown.

About a dozen ladies were going within the enemy's lines and would there separate for their respective homes. We agreed to hire a wagon team and driver at Social Circle, that we might take it "turn about" in riding to Stone Mountain. As I was the only one going beyond that point, I determined to take my chance from there for getting to Decatur, and go on foot if need be. Our plan was successful, as, after much effort, we obtained an old rickety wagon, which had doubtless done good service in its day, and a yoke of mis-mated oxen, and a negro driver. For this equipage we paid an enormous sum, and, thinking we ought to have the full benefit of it, we all got into the wagon to take a ride.

Compassion for the oxen, however, caused first one and then another to descend to the ground, and march in the direction of home, sometimes two abreast and sometimes in single file. Night overtook us at a house only a short distance from the Circle, and in a body we appealed for shelter beneath its roof. The man of the family was at home, under what circumstances I have never heard, and to him we appealed, and from him we received an ungracious "permit" to stay in his house. Seeing no inviting prospects for rest and repose, I established myself in a corner and took out of my reticule some nice German wool that had been given to me by my friends in Augusta, and cast on the stitches for a throat-warmer, or, in the parlance of that day, "a comforter." Mine host watched the process with much interest.

When the pattern developed, he admired it, and expressed a wish to have one like it. Glad of the privilege to liquidate my indebtedness for the prospective night's shelter, I told him if he would furnish the material I would knit him one just like it. The material seemed to be in waiting, and was brought forward, soft, pretty lambs' wool thread, and I put it in my already well-filled hand satchel to await future manipulation. The accommodation in the way of bedding was inadequate, and more than one of our party passed a sleepless night; but what mattered it? Were we not Confederate soldiers, or very near akin to them?

As the first sunbeams were darting about among the tree tops, I donned my bonnet and bade *adieu* to our entertainers, and started on my journey homeward, walking. Being in the very vigour of womanhood, and in perfect health, I never experienced the sensation of fatigue, and I verily believe I could have walked to my desolated home sooner than the most of the resources within our means could have carried me; and I was impatient under the restraint and hindrance of slow teams. Hence my start in advance of the other ladies. And I wanted to be alone. The pent-up tears were constantly oozing out of my eyes and trickling down my face, and I wanted to open the flood-gates and let them flow unrestrainedly. I wanted to cry aloud like a baby. I plunged into the woods, for the seldom travelled road was scarcely a barrier to perfect solitude. I walked rapidly, and closed my eyes to all the attractions of nature lest they divert my mind, and appease my hungry heart.

I wanted to cry, and was even then doing so, before I got ready for it. At length I came to a rivulet of crystal water, as pure as the dew drops of Arcadia. I sat down beside it and mingled the anguished tears of my very soul with its sparkling, ever-changing, nectarian waters. I bathed my hot face and hands in the pellucid stream, and still the lachrymal fountain flowed on. I thought of my lonely mother, surrounded by those who were seeking the subversion of all that her heart held dear, and I cried. I thought of my brother—of his toilsome marches and weary limbs, and of his consecrated life—and I cried. I thought of the fair young sister, still hopeful in early womanhood, and I refused to be comforted, and wept bitterly.

In this disconsolate frame of mind, I was ready to give up all hope and yield to direful despair. At this fearful crisis a still, small voice whispered, "Peace, be still!" The glamour of love invested sky and earth with supernal glory. The fountain of tears ceased to flow, and I looked around upon the handiwork of the Great Supreme Being in whose creation I was but an atom, and wondered that He should have been mindful of me—that He should have given surcease of agony to my sorrowing soul. All nature changed as if by magic, and the witchery of the scene was indescribable. The pretty wildwood flowers, as I bent my admiring gaze upon them, seemed to say in beautiful silent language, "Look aloft." The birds, as they trilled their morning roundelay, said in musical numbers, "Look aloft;" and the merry rivulet at my feet affected seriousness, and whispered, "Look aloft." Thus admonished, "in that moment of darkness, with scarce hope in my heart," I looked aloft—looked aloft.

By and by the ladies came in sight, some walking and others riding in the wagon; and I pitied most those who were in the wagon. As soon as they were within speaking distance, one of the ladies said: "You should have stayed for breakfast. It was quite appetizing." Reminded of what I had lost, I was led to compare it with what I had gained, and I would not have exchanged loss and gain for anything in the world. I had to admit, however, that there was a vacuum that needed replenishing; but I was inured to hunger, and, save a passing thought, I banished all desire for food, and thought only of the loved ones, so near and yet so far, and in spite of myself the fountain of tears was again running over.

The long tramp to Stone Mountain was very lonely. Not a living thing overtook or passed us, and we soon crossed over the line and entered a war-stricken section of country where stood chimneys only, where lately were pretty homes and prosperity, now departed. Ah, those chimneys standing amid smouldering ruins! No wonder they were called "Sherman's sentinels," as they seemed to be keeping guard over those scenes of desolation. The very birds of the air and beasts of the field had fled to other sections. By constant and unflagging locomotion we reached Stone Mountain sometime during the night. We went to the hotel and asked shelter and protection, and received both, but not where to lay our heads, as those who had preceded us had filled every available place. I had friends in the village, but I had no assurance that they had remained at home and weathered the cyclone of war.

Therefore, early in the morning, hungry and footsore, I started all alone walking to Decatur. The solitude was terrific, and the feeling of awe was so intense that I was startled by the breaking of a twig, or the gruesome sound of my own footsteps. Constantly reminded by ruined homes, I realized that I was indeed within the arbitrary lines of a cruel, merciless foe, and but for my lonely mother, anxiously awaiting my return, I should have turned and run for dear life until again within the boundaries of Dixie.

I must have walked very rapidly, for, before I was aware of it, I found myself approaching Judge Bryce's once beautiful but now dilapidated home. He and his good wife gave me affectionate greeting and something to inflate a certain vacuum which had become painfully clamorous. And they also gave me that which was even more acceptable—a large yam potato and a piece of sausage to take to my mother.

I begged Judge Bryce to go with me at least part of the way to Decatur, but he was afraid to leave his wife. His experience with the Yankees had not been an exceptional case. They had robbed him of everything of value, silver, gold, etc., and what they could not carry away they had destroyed, and he denied most emphatically that there was a single gentleman in the Federal army. In vain did I tell him that we owed the preservation of our lives to the protection extended us by the few gentlemen who were in it.

After a brief rest, I resumed my way homeward, and oh, with what heart-sickening forebodings I approached that sacred though desolate abode! Anon the little town appeared in the distance, and upon its very limits I met several of Colonel Garrard's cavalry officers. Among them a diversity of temper was displayed. Some of them appeared very glad to see me, and, to anxious inquires regarding my mother, they replied that they had taken good care of her in my absence, and that I ought to have rewarded them for having done so by bringing "my pretty young sister" home with me. A

lthough I did not entertain one iota of respect for the Federal army as a whole, I knew there were a few in its ranks who were incapable of the miserable conduct of the majority, and my heart went out in very tender gratitude to them, especially those who had sought to lessen the anguish of my mother. These men threw the reins into the hands of out-riders, and got off their horses and walked with me to the door of my home. Their headquarters were still in the yard and had been ever since first established there, with the exception of a very few days. My return was truly a memorable occasion. Manifestations assured me that the highest as well as the lowest in that command was glad to see me, and in their hearts welcomed me home. To good Mr. Fred Williams I was indebted, in a large measure, for kindly feeling and uniform respect from that portion of the Federal army with which I came in contact.

My mother had seen me coming and had retreated into as secluded a place as she could find, to compose herself for the meeting, but the effort was in vain. She trembled like an aspen leaf, her lips quivered and her tongue could not articulate the words she would have spoken. Alas! the tension was more than she could bear. I dwelt upon the fact that Thomie and Missouri were well and had sent her a world of love. I tried to infuse hope and cheerfulness into everything I told her, but she could not see it, and her poor over-taxed heart could bear up no longer, and she cried as Rachel weeping for her children, long and piteously. No purer tears were ever borne by heaven-commissioned Peri into the presence of a compassionate Saviour, than those shed by that patriotic though sorrowing mother.

Chapter 20

On the Verge of Starvation

"What is it, Ma? Has anything happened?"

"No, only Maggie Benedict has been here crying as if her heart would break, and saying that her children are begging for bread, and she has none to give them. Give me a little of the meal or hominy that you have, that we may not starve until we can get something else to eat, and then take the remainder to her that she may cook it as quickly as possible for her suffering children."

We had spent the preceding day in picking out grains of corn from cracks and crevices in bureau drawers, and other improvised troughs for Federal horses, as well as gathering up what was scattered upon the ground. In this way by diligent and persevering work, about a half bushel was obtained from the now deserted camping ground of Garrard's cavalry, and this corn was thoroughly washed and dried, and carried by me and Telitha to a poor little mill (which had escaped conflagration, because too humble to attract attention), and ground into coarse meal. Returning from this mill, and carrying, myself, a portion of the meal, I saw in the distance my mother coming to meet me. Apprehensive of evil, I ran to meet her and asked:

"What is it, Ma? Has anything happened?"

With flushed face and tear-toned voice she replied as already stated. My heart was touched and a division was soon made. Before starting on this errand, I thought of the probable delay that inexperience and perhaps the want of cooking utensils and fuel might occasion, and suggested that it would hasten the relief to the children to cook some bread and mush and carry it to them already for use. A boiling pot, left on the camping-ground, was soon on the fire ready to receive the well-prepared batter, which was to be converted into nutritious mush or porridge. Nor was the bread forgotten. While the mush was cooking the hoe-cakes were baking in good old plantation style. These were arranged one upon another, and tied up in a snow-white cloth; and a tin bucket, also a trophy from the company, was filled with hot mush. I took the bread, and Telitha the bucket, and walked rapidly to Doctor Holmes' residence, where Maggie Benedict, whose husband was away in the Confederate army, had rooms for herself and her children. The Rev. Doctor and his wife had refugeed, leaving this young mother and her children alone and unprotected.

The scene which I witnessed will never be obliterated from my memory. On the doorsteps sat the young mother, beautiful in desolation, with a baby in her arms, and on either side of her a little one, piteously crying for something to eat. "Oh, mama, I want something to eat, so bad." "Oh, mama, I am so hungry—give me something to eat." Thus the children were begging for what the mother had not to give. She could only give them soothing words. But relief was at hand. Have you ever enjoyed the satisfaction of appeasing the hunger of children who had been without food until on the verge of starvation? If not, one of the keenest enjoyments of life has been denied you. O, the thankfulness of such a privilege! And oh, the joy, melancholy though it be, of hearing blessings invoked upon you and yours by the mother of those children!

While this needful food was being eaten with a zest known only to the hungry, I was taking in the situation, and devising in my own mind means by which to render more enduring relief. The meal we had on hand would soon be exhausted, and, though more might be procured in the same way, it would be hazardous to depend upon that way only. "*God helps those who help themselves,*" is a good old reliable proverb that cannot be too deeply impressed upon the mind of every child. To leave this young mother in a state of absolute helplessness, and her innocent little ones dependent upon the precarious support which might be gleaned from a devastated country, would be cruel indeed; but how to obviate this state of affairs was a serious question.

The railroad having been torn up in every direction communicating with Decatur, there seemed to be but one alternative—to walk—and that was not practicable with several small children.

"Maggie, this state of affairs cannot be kept up; have you no friend to whom you can go?"

"Yes," she replied. "Mr. Benedict has a sister near Madison, who has wanted me and the children to go and stay with her ever since he has been in the army, but I was too independent to do it."

"Absurd! Well, the time has come that you must go. Get the children ready, and I will call for you soon," and without any positive or defined plan of procedure, I took leave of Maggie and her children. I was working by faith, and the Lord directed my footsteps. On my way home I hunted up "Uncle Mack," a faithful old negro man, who preferred freedom in the midst of privation with his own white people, to following the Federal army around on "Uncle Sam's" pay-roll, and got from him a promise that he would construct a wagon out of odds and ends left upon the streets of Decatur. The next thing to be done was to provide a horse, and not being a magician, nor possessed of Aladdin's lamp, this undertaking must have seemed chimerical to those who had not known how often and how singularly these scarcely formulated plans had developed into success. This day had been one of constant and active service, and was only one of the many that furnished from sixteen to eighteen working hours. No wonder, then, that exhausted nature succumbed to sleep that knew no waking until the dawn of another day.

Next morning, before the sun rose, accompanied by the Morton girls, I was on my way to "the cane-brakes." I had seen many horses, whose places had been taken by others captured from farmers, abandoned and sent out to the cane-brake to recuperate or to die, the latter being the more probable. Without any definite knowledge of the locality, but guided by an over-ruling providence, I went direct to the cane-brake, and there soon made a selection of a horse, which, from the assortment at hand, could not have been improved upon. By a dextrous throw of a lasso, constructed and managed by the young friends already mentioned, he was soon captured and on his way to Decatur to enter "rebel" service. His most conspicuous feature was a pair of as fine eyes as ever illuminated a horse's head, large, brown and lustrous.

There were other conspicuous things about him, too; for instance, branded upon each of his sides were the tell-tale letters, "U. S.," and on his back was an immense sore which also told tales. By twelve o'clock, noon, Uncle Mack appeared upon the scene, pulling something which he had improvised which baffled description, and which, for the sake of the faithful service I obtained from it, I will not attempt to describe, though it might provoke the risibilities of the readers. Suffice it to say that as it carried living freight in safety over many a bridge, in honour of this I will call it a wagon. Uncle Mack soon had the horse secured to this vehicle by ropes and pieces of crocus sack, for harness was as scarce a commodity as wagons and horses. I surveyed the equipage from centre to circumference, with emotions pathetic and amusing. It was awfully suggestive.

And as I viewed it in all its grotesqueness my imagination pictured a collapse, and my return home from no very distant point upon my all-fours, with one of the fours dragging after me in a dilapidated condition. I distinctly heard the derisive gibberish and laughter of old Momus, and thought I should explode in the effort to keep from joining in his mirthfulness. As I turned my head to take a sly glance at my mother, our eyes met, and all restraint was removed. With both of us laughter and sobs contended for the mastery, and merriment and tears literally blended. Thus equipped, and with a benediction from my mother, expressed more by looks and acts than by words, I gathered the ropes and started like Bayard Taylor to take "Views Afoot," and at the same time accomplish an errand of mercy which would lead me, as I led the horse, over a portion of country that in dreariness and utter desolation baffles description—enough to know that Sherman's foraging trains had been over it. Leading the horse, which was already christened "Yankee," to Dr. Holmes' door, I called Maggie to come on with her children.

"I can't bring my things out, Miss Mary. Somebody must come to carry them and put them in the wagon."

"I can," I said, and suiting the action to the word, ran into the house where, to my amazement, three large trunks confronted me. What was to be done? If they could be got into the wagon, what guarantee was there that poor Yankee could haul them in that tumblesome vehicle? However, I went for Uncle Mack to put the trunks in the wagon, and in front of them, in close proximity to the horse's heels, was placed a chair in which Maggie seated herself and took her baby in her lap, the other children nestling on rugs at her feet.

Poor Yankee seemed to feel the importance of his mission, and jogged along at a pretty fair speed, and I, who walked by his side and held the ropes, found myself more than once obliged to strike a trot in order to maintain control of him. Paradoxical as it may seem, I enjoyed this new phase in my service to the Confederacy—none but a patriot could render it, and the whole thing seemed invested with the glamour of romance, the sequel of which would be redemption from all connection with a people who could thus afflict another people of equal rights. While Maggie hummed a sweet little lullaby to her children, I contemplated the devastation and ruin on every side. Not a vestige of anything remained to mark the sites of the pretty homes which had dotted this fair country before the destroyer came, except, perhaps, a standing chimney now and then.

And all this struck me as the willing sacrifice of a peerless people for a great principle, and looking through the dark *vista* I saw light ahead—I saw white-robed peace proclaiming that the end of carnage had come. Even then, as I jogged along at a snail's pace (for be it known Yankee was not uniform in his gait, and as his mistress had relaxed the tension of the ropes, he had relaxed the speed of his steps) up a pretty little hill from whose summit I had often gazed with rapturous admiration upon the beautiful mountain of granite nearby, I had so completely materialized the Queen of Peace that I saw her on the mountain's crest, scattering with lavish hand blessings and treasures as a recompense for the destruction so wantonly inflicted. Thus my hopeful temperament furnished consolation to me, even under darkest circumstances.

Maggie and the children became restive in their pent-up limits, and the latter clamoured for something to eat, but there was nothing to give them. Night was upon us, and we had come only about eight miles, and not an animate thing had we seen since we left Decatur, not even a bird, and the silence was unbroken save by the sound of the horse's feet as he trod upon the rocks, and the soft, sweet humming of the young mother to her dear little ones. Step by step we seemed to descend into the caverns of darkness, and my brave heart began to falter. The children, awestruck, had ceased their appeal for bread, and nestled closer to their mother, and that they might all the more feel her protecting presence, she kept up a constant crooning sound, pathetic and sad. Step by step we penetrated the darkness of night—a night without a moon, starless and murky. The unerring instinct of an animal was all we had to guide us in the beaten road, which had ceased to be visible to human ken.

A faint glimmer of light, at apparently no very great distance, gave hope that our day's journey was almost ended. Yankee also caught the inspiration and walked a little faster. Though the time seemed long, the cabin, for such it proved to be, was finally reached, and I dropped the ropes, and, guided by the glimmer of light through the cracks, went to the door and knocked, at the same time announcing my name. The door was quickly opened. Imagine my surprise when recognized and cordially welcomed by a sweet friend, whose most humble plantation cabin was a pretty residence in comparison with the one she now occupied. Maggie, too, as the daughter of a well-known physician, received cordial welcome for herself and children. And thus a kind Providence provided a safe lodging place for the night.

Nature again asserted itself, and the children asked for something to eat. The good lady of the house kissed them, and told them that supper would soon be ready. The larger one of her little sons drew from a bed of ashes, which had been covered by glowing coals, some large yam potatoes which he took to a table and peeled. He then went outside the cabin and drew from a keg an earthen-ware pitcher full of sparkling persimmon beer, which he dispensed to us in cups, and then handed around the potatoes. And how much this repast was enjoyed! Good sweet yams thoroughly cooked, and the zestful persimmon beer! And I thought of the lonely mother at a desolated home, whose only supper had been made of coarse meal, ground from corn which her own hands had helped to pick from crevices and cracks in improvised troughs, where Garrard's cavalry had fed their horses.

After awhile the sweet womanly spirit that presided over this little group, got a quilt and a shawl or two, and made a pallet for the children. The boys put more wood upon the fire, and some in the jambs of the fireplace, to be used during the night; and then they went behind us and lay down upon the floor, with seed cotton for pillows, and the roof for covering. Our kind hostess placed additional wraps over the shoulders of Maggie and myself, and we three sat up in our chairs and slept until the dawn.

Accustomed to looking after outdoor interests, I went to see how Yankee was coming on, and found him none the worse for the preceding day's toil. Everything indicated that he had fared as sumptuously as we had—a partly-eaten pumpkin, corn, whole ears yet in the trough, and fodder nearby, plainly showed the generosity of the noble little family that took us in and gave us the best they had. After breakfast we bade *adieu* to the good mother and her children, and went on our way, if not rejoicing, at least feeling better for having seen and been with such good people. There was a strong tie between us all. The husband and father was off in the army, like our loved ones.

The generous feeding given to our steed had so braced him up that he began to walk faster, and was keenly appreciative of every kind word; and I and he formed a friendship for each other that continued to his dying day. The road was very rough and hilly, and more than once he showed signs of fatigue; but a word of encouragement seemed to renew his strength, and he walked bravely on. Maggie would perhaps have lightened his load by walking now and then, but the jolting of the wagon kept the trunks in perpetual motion, and the lives of the children would thereby have been jeopardized.

Nothing of special interest transpired this second day of our journey. The same fiend of destruction had laid his ruthless hand upon everything within his reach. The woods had been robbed of their beauty and the fields of their products; not even a bird was left to sing a requiem over the scene of desolation, or an animal to suggest where once had been a habitation. Once, crouching near a standing chimney, there was a solitary dog who kept at bay every attempt to approach— no kind word would conciliate or put him off his guard. Poor, lonely sentinel! Did he remember that around the once cheerful hearthstone he had been admitted to a place with the family group? Was he awaiting his master's return? Ah, who can know the emotions, or the dim reasonings of that faithful brute?

Night again came on and I discovered that we were approaching the hospitable mansion of Mr. Montgomery, an excellent, courtly country gentleman, who was at home under circumstances not now remembered. He and his interesting family gladly welcomed me and my little charge, and entertained us most hospitably. The raiders had been here and helped themselves bountifully, but they had spared the house for another time, and that other time came soon, and nothing was left on the site of this beautiful home but ubiquitous chimneys.

An early start the next day enabled Yankee to carry Maggie and her children and the trunks to Social Circle in time to take the noon train for Madison. So far as Maggie and her children were concerned, I now felt that I had done all that I could, and that I must hasten back to my lonely mother at Decatur; but Maggie's tearful entreaties not to be left among strangers prevailed with me, and I got aboard the train with her, and never left her until I had placed her and her children in the care of good Mr. Thrasher at Madison, to be conveyed by him to the home of Mrs. Reeves, her husband's sister.

In Madison, I too had dear friends and relatives, with whom I spent the night, and the morning's train bore me back to Social Circle, then the terminus of the Georgia Railroad—the war fiend having destroyed every rail between there and Atlanta. Arriving there, imagine my surprise and indignation when I learned that Mr. R——, whom I had paid in advance to care for Yankee while I was gone to Madison, had sent him out to his sorghum mill and put him to grinding cane; and it was with much difficulty and delay that I got him in time to start on my homeward journey that afternoon.

Instead of his being rested, he was literally broken down, and my pity for him constrained me to walk every step of the way back to Decatur. While waiting for the horse, I purchased such articles of food as I could find. For instance, a sack of flour, for which I paid a hundred dollars, a bushel of potatoes, several gallons of sorghum, a few pounds of butter, and a few pounds of meat. Even this was a heavy load for the poor jaded horse. Starting so late I could only get to the hospitable home of Mr. Crew, distant only about three miles from "The Circle."

Before leaving Mr. Crew's the next morning, I learned that an immense Yankee raid had come out from Atlanta, and had burned the bridge which I had crossed only two days ago. This information caused me to take another route to Decatur, and my heart lost much of its hope, and my step its alacrity. Yet the Lord sustained me in the discharge of duty. I never wavered when there was a principle to be guarded or a duty to be performed. Those were praying days with me, and now I fervently invoked God's aid and protection in my perilous undertaking, and I believed that He would grant aid and protection.

That I might give much needed encouragement to Yankee, I walked by his side with my hand upon his shoulder much of the time, an act of endearment which he greatly appreciated, and proved that he did so by the expression of his large brown eyes. One of my idiosyncrasies through life has been that of counting everything, and as I journeyed homeward, I found myself counting my steps from one to a thousand and one. As there is luck in odd numbers, says Rory O'Moore, I always ended with the traditional odd number, and by telling Yankee how much nearer home we were. And I told him many things, among them, *sotto voce*, that I did not believe he was a Yankee, but a captured rebel. If a tuft of grass appeared on the road side, he was permitted to crop it; or if a muscadine vine with its tempting grapes was discovered, he cropped the leaves off the low shrubbery, while I gathered the grapes for my mother at home with nothing to eat save the one article of diet, of which I have told before.

A minute description of this portion of the war-stricken country would fill a volume; but only the leading incidents and events of the journey are admissible in a reminiscence of war times. In the early part of the day, during this solitary drive, I came to a cottage by the wayside that was a perfect gem—an oasis, an everything that could thrill the heart by its loveliness. Flowers of every hue beautified the grounds and sweetened the air, and peace and plenty seemed to hold undisputed sway. The Fiend of Destruction had not yet reached this little Eden.

Two gentlemen were in the yard conversing. I perceived at a glance that they were of the clerical order, and would fain have spoken to them; but not wishing to disturb them, or attract attention to myself, I was passing by as unobtrusively as possible, when I was espied and recognized by one of them, who proved to be that saintly man, Rev. Walter Branham. He introduced me to his friend, Professor Shaw of Oxford. Their sympathy for me was plainly expressed, and they gave me much needed instruction regarding the route, and suggested that I would about get to Rev. Henry Clark's to put up for the night. With a hearty shake of the hand, and "God bless you, noble woman," I pursued my lonely way and they went theirs. No other adventure enlivened the day, and poor patient Yankee did the best he could, and so did I. It was obvious that he had done about all he could. Grinding sorghum under a hard taskmaster, with an empty stomach, had told on him, and he could no longer quicken his pace at the sound of a friendly voice.

At length we came in sight of "Uncle Henry Clark's" place. I stood amazed, bewildered. I felt as if I would sink to the ground, yea, through it. I was riveted to the spot on which I stood. I could not move. At length I cried—cried like a woman in despair. Poor Yankee must have cried too (for water ran out of his eyes), and in some measure I was quieted, for misery loves company, and I began to take in the situation more calmly. Elegant rosewood and mahogany furniture, broken into a thousand fragments, covered the face of the ground as far as I could see; and china and glass looked as if it had been sown. And the house, what of that? Alas! it too had been scattered to the four winds of heaven in the form of smoke and ashes. Not even a chimney stood to mark its site.

Nearby stood a row of negro cabins, intact, showing that while the conflagration was going on they had been sedulously guarded. And these cabins were occupied by the slaves of the plantation. Men, women and children stalked about in restless uncertainty, and in surly indifference. They had been led to believe that the country would be apportioned to them, but they had sense enough to know that such a mighty revolution involved trouble and delay, and they were supinely waiting developments. Neither man, woman nor child approached me. There was mutual distrust and mutual avoidance.

It took less time to take in the situation than it has to describe it. The sun was almost down, and as he turned his large red face upon me, I fancied he fain would have stopped in his course to see me out of this dilemma. What was I to do? The next nearest place that I could remember that would perhaps give protection for the night was Mr. Fowler's, and this was my only hope. With one hand upon Yankee's shoulder, and the ropes in the other, I moved on, and not until my expiring breath will I forget the pleading look which that poor dumb animal turned upon me when I started. Utterly hopeless, and in my hands, he wondered how I could thus exact more of him.

I wondered myself. But what was I to do but to move on? And with continuous supplication for the Lord to have mercy upon me, I moved on. More than once the poor horse turned that look, beseeching and pathetic, upon me. It frightened me, I did not understand it, and still moved on. At last the hope of making himself understood forsook him, and he deliberately laid himself down in the road. I knelt by his side and told him the true state of affairs, and implored him not to desert me in this terrible crisis. I told him how cruel it would be to do so, and used many arguments of like character; but they availed nothing. He did not move, and his large, lustrous brown eyes seemed to say for him: "I have done all I can, and can do no more." And the sun could bear it no longer, and hid his crimson face behind a great black cloud.

What could I do but rise from my imploring attitude and face my perilous situation? "Lord have mercy upon me," was my oft-repeated invocation. The first thing which greeted my vision when I rose to my feet was a very distant but evidently an advancing object. I watched it with bated breath, and soon had the satisfaction of seeing a man on muleback. I ran to meet him, saying: "O, sir, I know the good Lord has sent you here." And then I recounted my trouble, and received most cordial sympathy from one who had been a Confederate soldier, but who was now at home in consequence of wounds that incapacitated him for further service. When he heard all, he said:

"I would take you home with me, but I have to cross a swimming creek before getting there, and I am afraid to undertake to carry you. Wait here until I see these negroes. They are a good set, and whatever they promise, they will, I think, carry out faithfully."

The time seemed interminable before he came back, and night, black night, had set in; and yet a quiet resignation sustained me.

When my benefactor returned, two negro men came with him, one of whom brought a lantern, bright and cheery. "I have arranged for you to be cared for here," said he. "Several of the old house servants of Mrs. Clark know you, and they will prove themselves worthy of the trust we repose in them." I accepted the arrangement made by this good man, and entrusted myself to the care of the negroes for the night. This I did with great trepidation, but as soon as I entered the cabin an assurance of safety filled my mind with peace, and reconciled me to my surrounding's. The "mammy" that presided over it met me with a cordial welcome, and assured me that no trouble would befall me under her roof.

An easy chair was placed for me in one corner in comfortable proximity to a large plantation fire. In a few minutes the men came in bringing my flour, potatoes, syrup, bacon, etc. This sight gave me real satisfaction, as I thought of my poor patient mother at home, and hoped that in some way I should yet be able to convey to her this much needed freight. I soon espied a table on which was piled many books and magazines; "Uncle Henry Clark's" theological books were well represented. I proposed reading to the women, if they would like to hear me, and soon had their undivided attention, as well as that of several of the men, who sat on the doorsteps. In this way several hours passed, and then "mammy" said, "You must be getting sleepy."

"Oh, no," I replied, "I frequently sit up all night reading."

But this did not satisfy her; she had devised in her own mind something more hospitable for her guest, and she wanted to see it carried out. Calling into requisition the assistance of the men, she had two large cedar chests placed side by side, and out of these chests were taken nice clean quilts, and snow-white counterpanes, and sheets, and pillows—Mrs. Clark's beautiful bed-clothing—and upon those chests was made a pallet upon a which a queen might have reposed with comfort. It was so tempting in its cleanliness that I consented to lie down. The sole occupants of that room that night were myself and my hostess—the aforesaid black "mammy." Rest, not sleep, came to my relief. The tramping of feet, and now and then the muffled sound of human voices, kept me in a listening attitude, and it must be confessed in a state of painful apprehension. Thus the night passed.

With the dawn of day I was up and ready to meet the day's requirements.

"Mammy's" first greeting was, "What's your hurry?"

"I am accustomed to early rising. May I open the door?"

The first thing I saw was Yankee, and he was standing eating; but he was evidently too weak to attempt the task of getting that cumbersome vehicle and its freight to Decatur. So I arranged with one of the men to put a steer to the wagon and carry them home. This he was to do for the sum of one hundred dollars. After an appetizing breakfast, I started homeward, leading Yankee in the rear of this turnout. Be it remembered, I did not leave without making ample compensation for my night's entertainment.

No event of particular interest occurred on the way to Decatur. Yankee walked surprisingly well, and the little steer acquitted himself nobly. In due time Decatur appeared in sight, and then there ensued a scene which for pathos defies description. Matron and maiden, mother and child, each with a tin can, picked up off the enemy's camping-ground, ran after me and begged for just a little something to eat—just enough to keep them from starving. Not an applicant was refused, and by the time the poor, rickety, cumbersome wagon reached its destination, its contents had been greatly diminished. But there was yet enough left to last for some time the patient, loving mother, the faithful Telitha, and myself.

A summary of the trip developed these facts: To the faithfulness of Uncle Mack was due the holding together of the most grotesque vehicle ever dignified by the name of wagon; over all that road it remained intact, and returned as good as when it started. And but for the sorghum grinding, poor Yankee would have acted his part unfalteringly. As for myself, I laboured under the hallucination that I was a Confederate soldier, and deemed no task too great for me to essay, if it but served either directly or indirectly those who were fighting my battles.

Chapter 21

A Second Trip For Supplies

At an early hour in the morning of a bright autumnal day, that memorable year 1864—the saddest of them all—Yankee was roped (not bridled, mark you), and crocus sacks, four for him, one for Telitha, and one for myself, thrown over his back, and we three, boon companions in diversified industries, scampered off to a neighbouring cane-brake—a favourite resort in those days, but now, alas for human gratitude! never visited for the sake of "Auld Lang Syne."

Perfect health—thanks to the parents who transmitted no constitutional taint to my veins—unusual strength, and elasticity of motion, soon carried me there, and having secured Yankee to a clump of canes luxuriant with tender twig's and leaves, sweetened by the cool dew of the season, Telitha and I entered upon the work of cutting twigs and pulling fodder.

There being no drainage in those times, I often stepped upon little hillocks, covered with grass or aquatic vegetation, that yielded to my weight, and I sunk into the mud and water ankle deep, at least, and Telitha was going through with similar experiences. I often laughed at her grimaces and other expressions of disgust in the slough of despond, and rejoiced with her when she displayed the trophies of success, consisting of nice brittle twig's, generously clad in tender leaves and full growth; Yankee, too, was unmindful of small difficulties, and did his "level" best in providing for a rainy day by filling his capacious paunch brimful of the good things so bountifully supplied by Providence in the marshes of old DeKalb.

By the time the aforesaid half dozen sacks were filled, the enlargement of that organ of his anatomy suggested that he proposed carrying home about as much inside of him as might be imposed upon his back—of this sagacity he seemed conscious and very proud, and when the sacks of cane were put over his back, pannier fashion, he pursued the path homeward with prouder air and nobler mien than that which marked his course to the cane-brake.

When we three were fully equipped for starting back to the deserted village, Yankee, as already described, and I with a sack of cane thrown over my right shoulder, and reaching nearly to my heels, and Telitha, in apparel and equipment an exact duplicate of myself, I was so overcome by the ludicrous features of the scene that for the time I lost sight of the pathetic and yielded to inordinate laughter. As memory, electrical and veracious, recapitulated the facts and circumstances leading to this state of affairs, I realized that there was but one alternative—to laugh or to cry—but the revolutionary blood coursing through my veins decided in favour of the former, and I laughed until I could no longer stand erect, even though braced by an inflexible bag of cane, and I ignominiously toppled over.

As I lay upon the ground I laughed, not merrily, but grimly, as I fancy a hyena would laugh. The more I sought the sympathy of Telitha in this hilarious ebullition, the more uncontrollable it became. Her utter want of appreciation of the fun, and a vague idea that she was in some way implicated, embarrassed her, and, judging from her facial expression, ever varying and often pathetic, wounded her also. In vain did I point to our docile equine, whose tethering line she held. His enlarged proportions and grotesque accoutrements failed to touch a single risible chord, or convey to her utilitarian mind aught that was amusing, and she doubtless wondered what could have so affected me.

In due time we reached Decatur. After passing the Hoyle place, the residence being then deserted, Telitha indicated by signs too intelligible to be misunderstood that she would go home with her sack of stock provender, leading the horse, and then come back for mine, and I could go by a different route and not be known as a participant in the raid upon the cane-brake; but I was too proud of my fidelity to the Southern Confederacy to conceal any evidences of it that the necessities of the times called into action, and I walked through the stricken village with my sack of cane in my arms instead of upon my back; and would have walked as proudly to the sacrificial altar, myself the offering, if by so doing I could have retrieved the fortunes of my people and established for them a government among the nations of earth.

The lowing of our cow reached me as I entered the court-house square, and I hastened my gait and soon displayed before her, in her stall in the cellar, a tempting repast. And my mother, who possessed the faculty of making something good out of that which was ordinary, displayed one equally tempting to me and Telitha—milk and mush, supplemented by coffee made of parched okra seed.

"*Tired nature's sweet restorer*" faithfully performed its recuperative service that night. When I opened my eyes upon the glorious light of another day, I was so free from the usual attendants upon fatigue that I involuntarily felt for my body—it seemed to have passed away during the night, and left no trace of former existence. I found it, though, perfectly intact, and ready to obey the behests of my will and serve me through the requirements of another day. And my mother seemed to be in her usual health and willing for me to do anything I thought I ought to do. She could not close her eyes to the fact that our store of supplies was nearly exhausted, and that there was only one way to replenish it; and she had the wisdom and the Christian grace to acquiesce to the inevitable without a discouraging word. Telitha, upon whose benighted mind the ridiculous phases of the previous day's adventures had dawned sometime in the interim, laughed as soon as she saw me, and in well-acted pantomime made me fully aware that she enjoyed at this late hour the ludicrous scene that had so amused me. And Yankee evidently smiled when he saw me, and greeted me with a joyous little whicker that spoke volumes.

A good breakfast for women and beast having been disposed of, I wended my way in quest of Uncle Mack. He alone understood the complicated process of harnessing Yankee in ropes to the primitive vehicle manufactured by his own ingenious hands, and to him I always went when this important task had to be performed. On this occasion, as upon others, it was soon executed. When all was ready and the unbidden tears dashed away, as if out of place, I seized the ropes and started? Where? Ah, that was the question. There was only one place that offered hope of remuneration for the perilous undertaking, and forty miles had to be traversed before reaching it. Forty miles through a devastated country. Forty miles amid untold dangers.

But in all the walks of life it has been demonstrated that pluck and energy, and a firm reliance upon Providence, are necessary to surmount difficulties, and of all these essentials I had a goodly share, and never doubted but that I would be taken care of, and my wants and those of others supplied. "*God helps those who help themselves*," is an adage which deserves to be emblazoned upon every tree, and imprinted upon every heart. That vain presumption that folds the hands, and prays for benefits and objects desired, without putting forth any effort to obtain them, ought to be rebuked by all good men and women as a machination of Satan.

These and similar reflections nerved me for the task before me, and I started in earnest. When I got to the "blacksmith shop," I looked back and saw my mother standing just where I left her, following me with her eyes. I looked back no more, lest I dissolve in tears. As I passed the few abodes that were tenanted, my mission "out" was apprehended, and I was besought in tearful tones to bring back with me all I could, by those who told me that they and their children were upon the verge of starvation. I took all the sacks which were handed to me and rolled them together, and by the aid of a string secured them to the cart, and amidst blessings and good wishes pursued my devious way; for, be it remembered, many obstructions, such as breastworks and thorny hedge-wood, presented formidable barriers to rapid travel for a considerable distance from Decatur.

While leisurely walking beside Yankee, I was struck with the agility of his motion and his improved figure since we travelled over these grounds a few weeks before. He had taken on a degree of symmetry that I never supposed attainable by the poor, emaciated animal which I captured in the cane-brake. His hair had become soft and silky, and in the sunlight displayed artistic shades of colouring from light to deepest brown; and his long, black tail, which hung limp and perpendicular, now affected a curve which even Hogarth might have admired, and his luxuriant and glossy mane waved prettily as a maiden's tresses. And his face, perfect in every lineament, and devoid of any indication of acerbity, lighted by large, liquid, brown eyes, would have been a fit model—a thing of beauty—for the pencil of Rosa Bonheur. Rubbing my hand over his silky coat and enlarged muscles, I decided to enjoy the benefit of his increased strength and gently ordered a halt. Stepping from the ground to the hub of the wheel, another step landed me into the cart, vehicle, wagon or landau, which ever you see proper to denominate it; I do not propose to confine myself to any one of these terms.

Yankee understood the movement, and doubtless felt complimented. As soon as I took my seat in the chair—a concomitant part of the equipage—he started off at a brisk gait, which, without a word of command, he kept up until we came to the base of a long hill, and then he slackened his speed and leisurely walked to the summit. I enjoyed going over ground without muscular effort of my own, and determined to remain in the cart until he showed some sign of fatigue. I had only to hold the ropes and speak an encouraging word, and we travelled on right merrily. Ah, no! That was a misnomer. Callous indeed would have been the heart who could have gone merrily over that devastated and impoverished land. Sherman, with his destructive host, had been there, and nothing remained within the conquered boundary upon which "Sheridan's Crow" could have subsisted.

Nothing was left but standing chimneys, and an occasional house, to which one would have supposed a battering ram had been applied. I looked up and down, and in every direction, and saw nothing but destruction, and the gaunt and malignant figure of General Starvation striding over our beautiful country, as if he possessed it. I shook my head defiantly at him and went on, musing upon these things. I never questioned the wisdom or goodness of God in permitting them, but I pondered upon them, and have never yet reached their unfathomable depths.

At the end of the first day's journey, I found myself twenty miles, or more, from the starting point, and tenderly cared for by a good family, consisting, in these war times, only of a mother and several precious little children, who were too glad to have company to consider my appeal for a night's entertainment intrusive. This desolate mother and children thought they had seen all the horror of warfare illustrated by the premeditated cruelty of the Yankee raiders, and could not conceive how it could have been worse. But when I got through with my recital of injuries, they were willing that theirs should remain untold. A delicious supper, like manna from Heaven, was enjoyed with a zest unknown to those who have never been hungry.

The light of another day found us all up in that hospitable household, and an appetizing breakfast fortified me for another day's labour in any field in which I might be called to perform it. The little boys, who had taken Yankee out of the rope harness the evening before, remembered its intricacies and had no difficulty in getting him back into that complicated gear. When all was ready, and grateful goodbyes had been uttered, I again mounted "the hub," and got into the vehicle. After I had taken my seat, the good lady handed me a package, which proved to be a nice lunch for my dinner. She also had a sack of potatoes and pumpkins stored away in the landau; and being a merciful woman, she thought of the horse, and gave some home-cured hay for his noonday meal.

All day I followed in the track of Sherman's minions, and found the destruction greater than when I had passed in this direction before. Coming to a hill, the long ascent of which would be fatiguing to Yankee, I ordered a halt and got out of the wagon. Taking position by his side, we climbed the hill together, and then we went down it together, and continued to journey side by side, I oblivious to everything but the destruction, either complete or partial, on every side. At length we came to a lovely wee bit stream of water, exulting in its consciousness that no enemy could arrest it in its course to the sea, or mar its beauty as it rippled onward.

We halted, and I loosened the ropes so that Yankee might partake of the flowing water before eating his noonday meal. And I am sure epicure never enjoyed luncheon at Delmonico's with more zest than I did the frugal meal prepared for me by the friendly hands of that dear Confederate woman. Much as I enjoyed it, I finished my dinner sometime before Yankee did his, and employed the interim in laving my hands and face in the pure water, and contemplating myself in the perfect mirror formed by its surface. Not as Narcissus did I enjoy this pastime, but as one startled by the revelation. Traces of care; sorrow, apprehension for the future, were indelibly imprinted upon forehead and cheek, and most of all upon that most tell-tale of all features, the mouth. I wept at the change, and by way of diversion turned from the unsatisfactory contemplation of myself to that of Yankee.

This horse, instinct with intelligence, appreciated every act of kindness, and often expressed his gratitude in ways so human-like as to startle and almost affright me. I am sure I have seen his face lighted by a smile, and radiant with gratitude. And no human being ever expressed more forcibly by word or act his sorrow at being unable to do all that was desired of him in emergency, than did this dumb brute when he gave me that long, earnest, pathetic look (mentioned in a former sketch) when, from sheer exhaustion, he lay down near the heap of ashes where once stood the beautiful residence of my friend of honoured memory, Rev. Henry Clark.

The more I contrasted the treatment which I, in common with my country women and my country, had received at the hands of the Yankees (the then exponents of the sentiment of the United States towards the Southern people), and the gentle, friendly demeanour of the animal upon whom I had unthoughtedly bestowed a name constantly suggestive of an enemy, the more dissatisfied I became with it, and I determined then and there to change it. Suiting the action to the decision, I gathered the ropes and led the noble steed to the brink of that beautiful little brooklet, and paused for a name. What should it be? "Democrat?" I believed him to be a democrat, true and tried, and yet I did not much like the name. Had not the Northern democrats allowed themselves to be allured into abolition ranks, and made to do the fighting, while the abolitionists, under another name, devastated the country and enriched themselves by the booty. "Copperhead?" I did not like that much. It had a metallic ring that grated harshly upon my nerves, and I was not then aware of their great service to the South in restraining and keeping subordinate to humanity, as far as in them lay, the hatred and evil passions of the abolitionists. "Johnny Reb?"

Ah, I had touched the keynote at last, and it awakened a responsive chord that vibrated throughout my very being. I had a secret belief, more than once expressed in words, that my noble equine was a captured rebel "held in durance vile" until bereft of health and strength, then abandoned to die upon the commons. "Johnny Reb!" I no longer hesitated. The name was electrical, and the chord with which it came in contact was charged to its utmost capacity. With the placid waters of that ever-flowing stream, in the name of the Southern Confederacy, I christened one of the best friends I ever had "Johnny Reb," a name ever dear to me.

This ceremony having been performed to my satisfaction and to his, too—judging by the complacent glances, and, as I fancied, by the suggestion of an approving smile which he bestowed upon me—I mounted the hub, stepped into the cart, seated myself, and with ropes in hand continued my way to "The Circle," and arrived there before night, Not being tired, I immediately struck out among the vendors of home-made products—edibles, wearing apparel, etc.—for the purpose of purchasing a wagon load to carry to Decatur, not for the ignoble purpose of speculation, but to bestow, without money and without price, upon those who, like my mother and myself, preferred hunger and privation rather than give up our last earthly home to the destroying fiend that stalked over our land and protected Federal bayonets.

Before the shades of night came on I had accomplished my object. As a matter of history I will enumerate some of the articles purchased, and annex the prices paid for them in Confederate money:

One bushel of meal	$10.00
Four bushels of corn	40.00
Fifteen pounds of flour	7.50

Four pounds dried apples	5.00
One and half pounds of butter	6.00
A bushel of sweet potatoes	6.00
Three gallons of syrup	15.00
Shoeing the horse	25.00
For spending the night at Mrs. Born's, self and horse	10.00

Not knowing the capabilities of "Johnny Reb," I feared to add one hundred and thirty-six pounds avoirdupois weight to a cart already loaded to repletion, and the next morning on starting took my old familiar place by his side. To my slightest touch or word of encouragement, he gave me an appreciative look and obeyed to the letter my wishes with regard to his gaits—slow or fast in adaptation to mine. In due time we again rested on the banks of the beautiful little stream hallowed by the memory of repudiating a name, rendered by the vandalism of its legitimate owners too obnoxious to be borne by a noble horse, and by the bestowing upon him of another more in keeping with his respect for ladies and other fine traits of character which he possessed. Neither he nor I had lunch with which to regale ourselves; and whilst he moved about at will cropping little tufts of wild growth and tender leaves, which instinct taught him were good for his species, I abandoned myself to my favourite pursuit—the contemplation of nature.

Like Aurora Leigh, I "found books among the hills and vales, and running brooks," and held communion with their varied forms and invisible influences. To me they ever spoke of the incomprehensible wisdom and goodness of God. My heart, from my earliest recollection, always went out in adoration to Him who could make alike the grand old Titans of the forest and the humblest blade of grass; and now I beheld them under circumstances peculiarly calculated to evoke admiration. Change had come to everything else. The lofty trees stood in silent grandeur, undisturbed by the enemy's step or the harsh clarion of war—as if defiant of danger—and gave shelter and repose to the humblest of God's creatures who sought their protecting arms. Beguiled by the loveliness of the woodland scenery, I often found myself stopping to daguerreotype it upon the tablets of my memory, and to feast my senses upon the aromatic perfume of wildwood autumn flowers. "Strong words of counselling" I found in them and in "the vocal pines and waters," and out of these books I learned the "ignorance of men."

And how God laughs in Heaven when any man
Says, 'Here I'm learned; this I understand;
In that I am never caught at fault, or in doubt.'

A word of friendly greeting and renewed thanks to mine hostess of two nights before, and her dear little children, detained me only a very short and unbegrudged space of time; and during that time I did not forget to refer to the potatoes and the pumpkin so kindly given to me by them on my down trip, and which I could have left in their care until my return, had I thought of it.

Night again came on, and this time found me picking my way as best I could over the rocks shadowed by Stone Mountain. On I plodded through the darkness, guided rather by the unerring step of Johnny Reb than any knowledge I had of the way. At length the poor faithful animal and myself were rewarded for perseverance by seeing glimmering lights of the mountain village. We struck a bee line for the nearest one, and were soon directed to "a boarding house." I was too glad to get into it then, to descant upon its demerits now. I assured the landlady that I needed no supper myself, and would pay her what she would charge for both if she would see that the horse was well fed. I think she did so.

My valuable freight could not remain in the cart all night, and there was no one to bring it in. In vain did she assure me that I would find it all right if I left it there. I got into the cart and lifted the sacks and other things out of it myself, and, by the help of the aforesaid person, got everything into the house. I fain would have lain down by these treasures, for they had increased in value beyond computation since leaving Social Circle, and would have done so but for repeated assurance of their safety.

An early start next morning gave me the privilege of going over the ground familiar to my youth in the loveliest part of the day, and when the sun looked at me over the mountain's crest, I felt as if I was in the presence of a veritable king, and wanted to take my bonnet off and make obeisance to him. His beneficent rays fell alike upon the just and the unjust, and lighted the pathway of the destroyer as brightly as that of the benefactor. Amid destruction, wanton and complete, and over which angels might weep, I stepped the distance off between Stone Mountain and Judge Bryce's; not a living thing upon the face of the earth, or a sound of any kind greeting me—the desolation of war reigned supreme.

I again stopped at Judge Bryce's, and implored his protection to Decatur, but, as on the former occasion, he was afraid to leave his wife to the tender mercy (?) of the enemy. He told me he feared I would not reach home with my cart of edibles, as "Yankee raiders had been coming out from Atlanta every day lately," and that the set that was now coming was more vindictive than any that had preceded it. Good, dear Mrs. Bryce, trusting in the Lord for future supplies, took a little from her scanty store of provisions and added it to mine for her friend, my mother.

With many forebodings of evil, I took up the line of march to Decatur. I looked almost with regret upon my pretty horse. Had he remained the poor ugly animal that was lassoed in the cane-brake, I would have had but little fear of losing him, but under my fostering care, having become pretty, plump and sprightly, I had but little hope of keeping him. Being absorbed by these mournful reflections and not having the ever-watchful Telitha with me to announce danger from afar, I was brought to a full realization of its proximity by what appeared to be almost an army of *blue-coats*, dashing up on spirited horses, and for the purpose of humiliating me, hurrahing "for Jefferson Davis and the Southern Confederacy." As a flag of truce, I frantically waved my bonnet, which act was misapprehended and taken as a signal of approval of their "hurrah for Jefferson Davis and the Southern Confederacy," which was resounding without intermission.

Seeing several very quiet, dignified looking gentlemen, who, although apart from the others, seemed to be exercising a restraining influence, I approached them and told them how I had gone out from Decatur unprotected and all alone to get provisions to keep starvation from among our defenceless women and children, and that I had to go all the way to Social Circle before I could get anything, and that I had walked back in order to save the horse as much as possible. These men, however, although seemingly interested, questioned and cross-questioned me until I had but little hope of their protection. One of them said, "I see you have one of our horses. How did you come by him?"

And then the story of how I came by him was recapitulated without exaggeration or diminution. This narrative elicited renewed hurrahs for Jefferson Davis and the Southern Confederacy. A few minutes private conversation between these gentlemen ensued, and all of them approached me, and the spokesman said, "Two of us will escort you to Decatur, and see that no harm befalls you." It seemed, then, that no greater boon could have been offered under the canopy of Heaven, and I am sure no woman could have experienced more gratitude or been more profuse in its expression.

The sight of my nervous, gray-haired mother, and her pretty mother ways, touched another tender chord in the hearts of these gentlemen, and if constraint existed it was dispelled, and they became genial and very like friends before they left. They even promised to send us some oats for noble Johnny Reb, who displayed the greatest equanimity all through these trying scenes.

CHAPTER 22

News From the Absent Brother

After the majority of these sketches were written, I was permitted by my sister to take a few extracts from the cherished letters of our brother, which she numbered and carefully laid away as her most precious treasure. To these we are indebted for all that we know of his history during those trying days and weeks of which I have just been writing. Where was he, and how did he fare? Few and far between were the letters now, in these dark days of the war. The soldiers themselves had but little opportunity to write, and the mail facilities were poor. But I feel sure that to the survivors of the "Lost Cause," these meagre scraps concerning that brave but disastrous march into Tennessee will be read with melancholy interest:

On the Line of Alabama and Georgia,
Near Alpine, Ga., 8 o'clock at night, Oct. 17, 1874.
My Dear Sister—As there is a probability of the mail courier leaving here early in the morning, I hastily scratch you a few lines that you may know that under the blessings of a kind Providence I am yet alive, and, though somewhat wearied, enjoying good health. Yours of 28th of September has been received, but under circumstances of hard marches, etc., there has been but one opportunity of writing to you since leaving Palmetto, and then had just finished one to Texas, and was fixing to write to you, when the order came to 'fall in.'
Well, leaving camps near Palmetto on the 29th of September, we crossed the Chattahoochee below, marched up to Powder Springs, threatened Marietta, and at the same time threw Stewart's corps around above Big Shanty to cut the railroad, which was torn up for about thirteen miles, French's Division attack-

ing Allatoona, where he sustained some loss, having works to charge. Ector's Texas Brigade, and some Missourians, carried their part of the works, but A———'s Brigade failed to do their part, hence the advantage gained was lost. By this time the enemy were concentrating at Marietta, and General Hood's object being accomplished, he then marched rapidly towards Rome, flanking the place, and making a heavy demonstration as if he intended crossing the river and attacking the place.

The enemy then commenced a concentration at Kingston and Rome. We then moved around Rome and marched rapidly up the Oostanaula, and, on the evening of the 11th inst., sent a division of infantry with some cavalry across the river, and captured Calhoun with some stores. Moved on the next morning by a forced march, flanking Resaca, and striking the railroad immediately above, tearing it up to Tilton where there were about three hundred Yankees in a block-house. A surrender was demanded. A reply was returned: 'If you want us come and take us.' Our artillery was soon in position and a few shots soon made them show the 'white rag.'

We tore up the road that night, and the next morning by nine o'clock, to Tunnel Hill, burning every cross-tie and twisting the bars. Dalton surrendered without a fight, with a full garrison of negroes and some white Yankees. The block-house above, at a bridge, refused to surrender, and we had to bring the artillery into requisition again, which made them succumb. They all seemed to be taken by surprise and were hard to convince that it was a cavalry raid. They evacuated Tunnel Hill. Thus after five months of fighting and running, the Army of Tennessee re-occupied Dalton. Sherman has been taken by surprise. He never dreamed of such a move.

General Hood's plans all being carried out, so far as the State road was concerned, we marched across the mountains to La-Fayette, in the vicinity of which we camped last night, and have marched twenty-three miles today. Tomorrow we cross the Lookout Mountain, and will, I suppose, make directly for the Tennessee River, though of this I'm not certain. Hood has shown himself a general in strategy, and has secured the confidence of the troops. Wherever we go, may God's blessing attend us. Pray for me. In haste.

  Your affectionate brother,   Tom Stokes.

P. S.—Cherokee Co., Ala., Oct. 18, 1864.

The courier not leaving this morning, I have a little more time left. We did not travel so far today as I heard we would, having come only ten miles, and have stopped to rest the balance of the evening. I find you dislike to have your communications cut off, so I see you are below Madison. Would to Heaven that, in one sense of the word my communication was cut off forever; yea, that every channel leading me in contact with *the world*, in any other character than as a minister of 'the meek and lowly Saviour,' was to me forever blocked up. I am tired of confusion and disorder—tired of living a life of continual excitement . . . You spoke of passing through a dark cloud. '*There is nothing true but Heaven*,' and it is to that rest for the weary, alone, to which we are to look for perfect enjoyment. We are to walk by faith, and though the clouds of trouble thicken, yet we should know that if we do our duty we shall see and feel the genial sunshine of a happier time. Yes, my sister, though we knew our lives should be lengthened one hundred years, and every day should be full of trouble; yet if we have a hope of Heaven, that hope should buoy up the soul to be cheerful, even under earth's saddest calamities.

I think we will cross the Tennessee river and make for Tennessee, where it seems to be understood that we will have large accessions to our army, both there and from Kentucky . . . .

The next letter is enclosed in an envelope which came through no post-office, as it was furnished by my sister, and upon it she wrote:

This letter was sent to me on the 27th of November, by someone who picked it up upon the street in Madison. The post-office had been rifled by the Federals who (under command of Slocum) passed through Madison, November 18th and 19th. Though found without an envelope, and much stained, it has reached me, because signed with his full name.

This letter is dated "Near Decatur, Ala., October 28th, 1864." We give a few items:

We invested this place yesterday, and there has been some skirmishing and artillery firing until an hour ago, when it seems to have measurably ceased. We are in line of battle southwest of Decatur, about one and a quarter miles. I went out reconnoitring this morning and saw the enemy's position. They have a large fort immediately in the town, with the 'stars and stripes' waving above. I hear occasional distant artillery firing which I suppose is Forrest, near Huntsville. . . . . . We were several days crossing Sand Mountain. Have had delightful weather until a day or two ago it rained, making the roads very muddy, in consequence of which we have been on small rations, the supply trains failing to get up. We had only half rations yesterday, and have had none today (now nearly three o'clock), but will get some tonight. We try to be cheerful. . . . . No letter from Texas yet. No one of our company has had any intelligence from Johnson county since last May. I can't see what's the matter. I have been absent nearly one year and have received but one letter. (Of course the dear loved ones in Texas wrote to their soldier braves on this side the Mississippi River; but such are the misfortunes of war that these missives were long delayed in their passage).

Saturday, October 29th.—The condition of affairs this morning at sunrise remains, so far as I know, unchanged. . . . . Yesterday evening we drew two ears of corn for a day's ration; so parched corn was all we had yesterday; but we will get plenty today.

And now we come to the last of the letters ever received. It is probable it was among the last he ever wrote. It is dated "Tuscumbia, Ala., Nov. 10, 1864.—

We arrived at this place the 31st of October, and have been here since, though what we are waiting for I can't tell. The pontoons are across the river, and one corps on the other side at Florence. We have had orders to be ready to move several times, but were countermanded. We were to have moved today, and even our wagons started off, but for some cause or other we have not gone. The river is rising very rapidly, which may endanger the pontoons.

November 12th.—I thought to send this off yesterday morning, but, on account of the rain a few days ago, the mail carrier was delayed until last night, which brought your dear letter of date October 31st. It was handed me on my return from the graveyard, where I had been to perform the funeral ceremony of a member of the 6th Texas, who was killed yesterday morning by the fall of a tree. He had been in every battle in which this brigade was ever engaged; an interesting young man, only nineteen years of age.

The scene at the graveyard was a solemn one, being sometime in the night before we arrived. The cold, pale moon shone down upon us, and the deep stillness which pervaded the whole scene, with the rough, uncouth, though tender-hearted soldiers with uncovered heads, forming a large circle around the grave, made it, indeed, a scene solemnly impressive. The print of my Bible being small, I could not read, but recited from memory a few passages of Scripture suitable to the occasion, the one upon which I dwelt chiefly being a declaration of Paul to the Corinthians, *'For we must all appear before the judgment seat of Christ.'*

I then spoke of the certainty of that change from life to death; that with the soldier, even, death is not confined to the battlefield; spoke of our comrade, who but in the morning bade as fair for long life as any of us, but within the space of a few short hours was lying in the cold embrace of death; of another of our brigade who was instantly killed a short time since by a stroke of lightning; closed with an exhortation to all to live nearer to God, and be prepared at all times to meet their God in peace. Oh, how sad! Far away from his home to be buried in a land of strangers. How the hearts of his father, mother and sisters must bleed when they receive the sad tidings.

I expect we will leave here for Middle Tennessee next Monday, as the river will be falling by that time. There is much talk of this brigade being sent home after this campaign. Major Rankin has been exchanged, and is with us. I gave Lieutenant Collins' overcoat to his company to take care of for him.

Am so glad to hear from ma and sister. We get no letters from Texas; but are continually sending some over, as all the disabled of the last campaign are being retired and sent across. Poor Uncle James! His Joseph is gone... Write to me often.

   Affectionately,
    Your Brother.

Ah, could the history of these brave men be written, what a record it would be of endurance, of daring, of heroism, of sacrifice! And the heart-breaking pathos of the last chapters of their experience, ere the furling of the flag they followed! Pat Cleburne and his fallen braves—

On fame's eternal camping ground,
Their silent tents are spread,
And glory marks with solemn round
The bivouac of the dead.

Chapter 23

An Incident of the War
Related to the writer by Hon. Roger Q. Mills, of Texas.

The night was black as Erebus. Not a scintillant of light from moon or star penetrated the dense forest, and no eye save that of God discerned the danger of the situation. Hill and dale, mountain and precipice, creek and surging stream, presented barriers that none but men inured to hardship, and unknown to fear, would have attempted to surmount.

Obedient to the command of the superior officer, the remnant of that magnificent and intrepid army, once guided by the unerring wisdom of Joseph E. Johnston, plodded their way uncomplainingly over these trying difficulties. The Lord must have been amazed at their temerity, and shook the very earth in rebuke, and ever and anon by the lightning's flash revealed glimpses of the peril to which they were exposed; and yet in unbroken lines they groped their way, not knowing whither. At length bewildered, and made aware of impending danger, the general in command ordered a halt. The martial tread ceased, and all was still as death. In the midst of this stillness a voice, sweet as that of a woman, was heard repeating that grand old hymn, which has given comfort to many weary ones treading the wine press:

How firm a foundation, ye saints of the Lord,
Is laid for your faith in His excellent Word!
What more can He say than to you He hath said,
You who unto Jesus for refuge have fled.

In every condition, in sickness, in health,
In poverty's vale, or abounding in wealth,
At home and abroad, on the land, on the sea,
As thy days may demand shall thy strength ever be.

Fear not, I am with thee, O! be not dismayed,
I, I am thy God, and will still give thee aid;
I'll strengthen thee, help thee and cause thee to stand,
Upheld by My righteous, omnipotent hand.

When through the deep waters I call thee to go,
The rivers of woe shall not thee overflow;
For I will be with thee, thy troubles to bless,
And sanctify to thee thy deepest distress.

When through fiery trials thy pathway shall lie,
My grace all sufficient shall be thy supply;
The flame shall not hurt thee; I only design
Thy dross to consume, and thy gold to refine.

E'en down to old age, all My people shall prove
My sovereign, eternal, unchangeable love;
And when hoary hairs shall their temples adorn,
Like lambs they shall still in My bosom be borne.

The soul that on Jesus hath leaned for repose,
I will not, I will not desert to his foes;
That soul, though all hell should endeavour to shake,
I'll never, no never, no never, forsake."

General Mills said that during the rendition of this beautiful hymn, not even the breaking of a twig, or the changing of a footstep broke the silence of the midnight tranquillity. The rain drops ceased to fall; the electricity darted harmlessly through the tree tops; and the muttering of the thunder lulled.

After a most impressive silence of several minutes, the same voice, which had rendered the hymn so effectually, repeated from memory an appropriate passage of Scripture and proceeded to expatiate upon it. He had not uttered a dozen words before another flash of lightning revealed the upturned heads and listening attitudes of the men composing that weird congregation, and each one of them knew as if by instinct that he was going to hear something that would help him on his journey to the Land of Beulah. Strong in the faith, he carried many of the truths and promises of the Holy Word within his mind, and now, as many times before, he opened them by the magic key of memory and unfolded to view their unsearchable riches.

He begged his fellow-men and comrades in arms to accept them without money and without price—to accept them that they might wear kingly robes and royal diadems, and be with Jesus in His Father's regal mansions throughout the grand eternities. And as he told the old, old story of divine love, it assumed a contemporaneous interest and seemed a living present reality. Every man who heard it felt the living force and energizing influence of the theme. And thus by earnest, aggressive appeals, he exerted a wonderful power for good over the minds of his hearers; and those men, even now with phantom hands pointing gaunt fingers at them, by their deep interest testified to the warm suffusing purpose which made itself felt in every word that he uttered, as he told of the Fatherhood of God and the ever-present sympathy of a benignant and infinite parent, who delighted not in the death of sinners, but rather that all should come to Him and have eternal life.

General Mills added that, as the fine resonant voice of the speaker penetrated the dense forest and found its way to his hearers in distinct enunciation of well-chosen words, the deep-toned thunder emphasized the impressive points, and made it a scene which for grandeur and sublimity has never been surpassed, while the vivid flashes of lightning revealed again and again the earnest face and solemn mien of my brother, Lieutenant Thomas J. Stokes, of the Tenth Texas Infantry of Cleburne's Division.

CHAPTER 24

Picking Up Minie Balls Around Atlanta

After mingling renewed vows of allegiance to our cause, and expressions of a willing submission to the consequences of defeat—privations and evil dire, if need be—with my morning orison; yet I could not be oblivious to the fact that I was hungry, very hungry. And there was another, whose footsteps were becoming more and more feeble day by day, and whose voice, when heard at all, was full of the pathos of despair, who needed nourishment that could not be obtained, and consolation, which it seemed a mockery to offer.

In vain did I look round for relief. There was nothing left in the country to eat. Yea, a crow flying over it would have failed to discover a morsel with which to appease its hunger; for a Sheridan by another name had been there with his minions of destruction, and had ruthlessly destroyed every vestige of food and every means of support. Every larder was empty, and those with thousands and tens of thousands of dollars, were as poor as the poorest, and as hungry too. Packing trunks, in every house to which refugees had returned, contained large amounts of Confederate money. We had invested all we possessed except our home, and land and negroes, in Confederate bonds, and these were now inefficient for purchasing purposes. Gold and silver had we none. A more favoured few had a little of those desirable mediums of purchase, and sent a great distance for supplies; but they offered no relief to those who had stayed at home and borne the brunt of battle, and saved their property from the destroyers' torch.

What was I to do? Sit down and wait for the inevitable starvation? No; I was not made of such stuff. I had heard that there had been a provision store opened in Atlanta for the purpose of bartering provisions for munitions of war—anything that could be utilized in warfare. Minie balls were particularly desirable. I therefore took Telitha by the apron, and had a little talk with her, and when I was through she understood that something was up that would bring relief to certain organs that had become quite troublesome in their demands, and she was anxious to take part in the performance, whatever that might be. I went also to my mother, and imparted to her my plans of operation, and she took that pathetic little backward step peculiar to herself on occasions which tried her soul, and with quivering lip she assented in approving, though almost inaudible words.

With a basket in either hand, and accompanied by Telitha, who carried one that would hold about a peck, and two old dull case-knives, I started to the battlefields around Atlanta to pick up the former missiles of death to exchange for food to keep us from starving.

It was a cold day. The wind was very sharp, and over the ground, denuded of forest trees and undergrowth, the wind was blowing a miniature gale. Our wraps were inadequate, and how chilled we became in that rude November blast! Mark you, it was the 30th of November, 1864. But the colder we were, the faster we walked, and in an incredibly short time we were upon the battlefield searching for lead.

I made it a point to keep very near the road in the direction of Atlanta, and soon found myself on the very spot where the Confederate magazine stood, the blowing up of which, by Confederate orders, shook the very earth, and was distinctly heard thirty-five or forty miles distant. An exclamation of glad surprise from Telitha carried me to her. She had found a bonanza, and was rapidly filling her basket with that which was more valuable to us than gold. In a marshy place, encrusted with ice, innumerable bullets, minie balls, and pieces of lead seemed to have been left by the irony of fate to supply sustenance to hungry ones, and employment to the poor, as all the winter those without money to send to more favoured and distant points found sure returns from this lead mine. It was so cold! our feet were almost frozen, and our hands had commenced to bleed, and handling cold, rough lead cramped them so badly that I feared we would have to desist from our work before filling the baskets.

Lead! Blood! Tears! O how suggestive! Lead, blood and tears, mingled and commingled. In vain did I try to dash the tears away. They would assert themselves and fall upon lead stained with blood. "God of mercy, if this be Thy holy will, give me fortitude to bear it uncomplainingly," was the heart-felt invocation that went up to the throne of grace from over lead, blood and tears, that fearful day. For relief, tears did not suffice. I wanted to cry aloud; nature would not be satisfied with less, and I cried like a baby, long and loud. Telitha caught the spirit of grief, and cried too. This ebullition of feelings on her part brought me to a realization of my duty to her, as well as to my poor patient mother to whom the day must seem very long, and I tried to stifle my sobs and lamentations. I wondered if she had the forebodings of coming bereavement that were lacerating my own heart. I did not doubt but that she had, and I cried in sympathy for her.

At length our baskets were filled, and we took up our line of march to the desolated city. There were no labyrinths to tread, no streets to follow, and an occasional question secured information that enabled us to find the "commissary" without delay. Telitha was very ambitious that I should appear a lady, and wanted me to deposit my load of lead behind some place of concealment, while we went on to deliver hers, and then let her go back for mine. But I was too much a Confederate soldier for that, and walked bravely in with my heavy, precious load.

A courteous gentleman in a faded grey uniform, evidently discharged because of wounds received in battle, approached and asked what he could do for me. "I have heard that you give provisions for lead," I replied, "and I have brought some to exchange." What seemed an interminable silence ensued, and I felt without seeing that I was undergoing a sympathetic scrutiny, and that I was recognized as a lady "to the manor born."

"What would you like in exchange," he asked. "If you have sugar, and coffee, and meal, a little of each if you please," I timidly said. "I left nothing to eat at home." The baskets of lead were removed to the rear and weighed, and in due time returned to me filled to the brim with sugar, coffee, flour, meal, lard, and the nicest meat I had seen in a long time.

"O, sir," I said, "I did not expect so much."

"You have not yet received what is due you," this good man replied, and handed me a certificate which he assured me would secure as much more on presentation.

Joy had gone out of my life, and I felt no thrill of that kind; but I can never describe the satisfaction I experienced as I lifted two of those baskets, and saw Telitha grasp the other one, and turned my face homeward.

CHAPTER 25

The Decatur Women's Struggle For Bread

The tug of war was upon us from the mountains to the sea-board, and ingenious was the woman who devised means to keep the wolf, hungry and ravenous, from the door. The depreciation of our currency, and its constant diminution in value, had rendered it an unreliable purchasing commodity, and we had nothing to give in exchange for food. I, therefore, felt that I had literally rubbed against Aladdin's lamp when I saw much needed food, good and palatable, given in exchange for minie balls, and for any kind of metal convertible into destructive missiles, and I was anxious that others should share the benefit accruing from the lead mines mentioned in a former sketch. In pursuance of this humane desire, I proclaimed its discovery and results from house to house; for, mark you, we had no *Daily Courier*, nor messenger boy to convey the glad tidings to the half-famished women and children in and around Decatur. And if my words could have been changed into diamonds by the magic wand of a fairy, not one of those starving people would have accepted the change of diamonds for bread.

It required only a short time to raise a large company of women, girls and little boys, who were ready to do service for themselves and their country by digging lead with case-knives from mines providentially furnished them. And was it not serving the cause of the Confederacy? I thought so; and never walked with more independent step than when acting as generalissimo of that band of devoted, patriotic women, *en route* to the "lead mines" around Atlanta. Telitha, too, evidently felt that she was an important adjunct in the mining enterprise, and a conspicuous personage in the scenes being enacted, and emphasized her opinion by strong and suggestive gesticulation. On this occasion she playfully wrenched from my hand the small vessel with which I had supplied myself and which I carried on the former trip, and substituted a larger one, while for herself she got at least a half-bushel measure.

All who remember the month of December, 1864, know that it abounded in clouds and rain and sleet, and was intensely cold in the Confederate States of America; and in the latitude embracing Atlanta, such severity of weather had never been known to the oldest inhabitant. But what mattered it? Each one in that little band of women was connected by a bright link to the illustrious armies that were enduring greater privation and hardship than those to which she was exposed, and counted it a willing oblation upon his country's altar, and why should she not prove faithful to the end, and suffer the pangs of hunger and privation too?

The work of picking up minie balls began as soon as we reached the battlefield, and, consequently, we carried several pounds some distance unnecessarily. The "mine" proper, I doubt not, could have filled several wagons. As "a little fun now and then is relished by the wisest men," I found a grim smile asserting itself at the quaint and ready wit of those estimable girls, the Misses Morton, whose Christian names I have forgotten and who, alas! have long since joined the silent majority. One of them assumed the character of a Confederate soldier and the other that of a Federal, and the conversation carried on between them, as they "exchanged coffee and tobacco," was rich, rare and racy. The exchange having been effected, the signal of combat was given. "Look out, Billy Yank!" "Look out, Johnnie Reb!" were simultaneous warnings from opposing forces, and minie balls whizzed through the air, much to the merriment of the little boys who wished themselves men, that they might be with their fathers, whizzing minie balls from musket mouths.

The sham battle over, the work of digging lead was resumed, and in an amazingly short time our vessels were filled to overflowing. I watched Telitha with interest. She was eager to fill her basket, and more than once she said, "Me full!" and added a little gutteral laugh that always indicated pleasure. Her attempt to raise the basket from the ground, and her utter failure to do so surprised her amazingly, and her disappointment was pathetic. With great reluctance she saw her treasure reduced to her capacity of handling. Each member of the party experienced similar disappointment on attempting to raise her burden, and we left more exhumed lead and other valuables than we carried away.

We took up our line of march, and as there were no obstructions in the way (for, be it remembered, Sherman had been there, and with torch and explosive removed all obstructions save the standing chimneys and carcasses of horses and cattle shot by his order to prevent the possibility of use to the rebels), we struck a bee-line to the commissary. As the first to take advantage of this industry, I took the lead, and the vigour of young womanhood, and "a heart for every fate," gave elasticity to my steps, and I soon outdistanced even the girls. In due time we reached the commissary, and in a short while a most satisfactory exchange was made, thanks to one whose great heart beat in unison with ours, and in lieu of the heavy burden which we laid down, we picked up food for the nourishment of our tired bodies and those of our loved ones at home. Oh, how light, comparatively, it seemed! I verily believe if it had weighed the same number of pounds, it would have seemed lighter, and the change would have seemed restful. "Goodbye, noble ladies and sisters in a righteous cause," was the parting salutation of our no less noble benefactor.

With our respective packages of food we again turned our faces homeward, solemn as a funeral march, for, strive against them as we would, we all had forebodings of ill, and the swaying of our bodies and our footsteps kept time with the pulsations of our sad hearts. I fancied as I approached standing chimneys and other evidences of destroyed homes, that the spirit of Sherman, in the guise of an evil spirit, was laughing over the destruction his diabolism had wrought. In the midst of these reflections a song, which for sweetness and tranquilizing melody I have seldom heard equalled and never surpassed, broke the stillness of the scene and added to the melancholy interest of the occasion. It was the well known ballad, then familiar to every child in the Confederacy, "When this Cruel War is Over," and sung by those gifted sisters mentioned as a part of the lead digging company.

The pure, sweet *soprano* voice of one of the girls put to flight the spirit of Sherman, and when it was joined by the flute-like alto of the others, every evil spirit within and without was exorcised, and the spirit of submission took its place. And yet as the words rang out and found an echo in my own heart, I had to walk very straight, and turn my head neither to the right nor to the left, lest I betray the copious tears trickling down my cheeks. At length pent-up feelings burst the fetters, and an audible sob removed restraint, and we cried as women burdened with great sorrow. Precious tears! Nature's kind alleviator in time of trouble.

The day was cold and dark and dreary,
And it rained and the winds were never weary,

.... and yet I was nerved for its duties and toil by the consciousness of having met, uncomplainingly, the work which the preservation of my own principles made me willing to endure. Several days subsequent to this trip to Atlanta, the Morton girls came running in and told me that we had some delightful friends at the "Swanton place," who requested to see us. My mother was too much exhausted by anxiety and waiting for that which never came, to go, but approved my doing so. I, therefore, donned my sun-bonnet and went; and whom should I meet but Mrs. Trenholm and her sweet young daughters, Essie and Lila? I was delighted to see them, and invited them to go home with me. Ma received them in a spirit of cordial hospitality, and they were invited to remain at her house. Without hesitation, Mrs. Trenholm accepted the proffered kindness, and returned to her wayside rendezvous only to send her trunks, bedding and other household goods.

And truly the coming of that saintly woman and those lovely girls was a rare benediction, especially at that time. Day by day ma looked in vain for tidings from "the front"—wherever that might be—and day by day her health and strength was perceptibly weakened by disappointment. Mrs. Trenholm's sympathy with her in her suspense regarding the operations of Hood's army, and the fate of her beloved son, was both touching and consoling. Seeing that my mother and myself were hoping almost against hope, she endeavoured to bring us to a realization of that fact, and a complete submission to the will of God, even though that will deprived us of our loved one. All of her Christian arguments and consolations had been pondered over and over by mother and daughter, but they never seemed so sweet and potent as when coming in the chaste and simple language of a precious saintly woman.

With the tact peculiar to the refined of every clime and locality, Mrs. Trenholm assumed management of the culinary department, and her dinner-pot hung upon our crane several weeks, and daily sent forth appetizing odours of bacon and peas. How we enjoyed those peas and that bacon, and the soup seasoned with the only condiments at our command—salt and red pepper—and the good hoe cakes! Mrs. Trenholm had a large sack of cow peas, and a sack of dried fruit, and other articles of food which she had provided for herself and her family before she left Southwest Georgia *en route* to her home in Marietta, which she left in obedience to the order of William Tecumseh Sherman, and which she learned, before reaching Decatur, had shared the fate of nearly all other homes which had to be thus abandoned.

Although magnanimously proffered, we were averse to sharing Mrs. Trenholm's well-prepared and ofttimes tempting *cuisine*, unless our proportion of food equalled hers; and fearing even the appearance of scanty supplies, I set about to gather up "the miners," so that we might appoint a day to again go lead digging, if that which we left in as many little heaps as there were members of the company had been, in the interim, gathered up by others.

On former occasions I had led my company to victory over that malignant general left by Sherman to complete his work, and styled by him "General Starvation," and they were willing to go wherever I led. Now, I had two recruits of whom I was very proud. Telitha, too, had gathered from observation that the sweet young Trenholm girls were going with us, and she set about to provide very small baskets for their use, which, with gestures amusing and appropriate, she made us understand were large enough to contain all the lead that girls so pretty and so ladylike ought to carry. To their credit, however, they repudiated that idea, and carried larger vessels. By appointment the "lead diggers" were to meet at the tan-yard, those arriving first to wait until the entire number came. "*Man proposes and God disposes.*" Just as my last glove was drawn on, Telitha, ever on the alert, said "Morton, Morton," and I looked and saw the girls coming. "We needn't go—the commissary has folded its tents, and silently stolen away," was the voluntary announcement.

Imagine my consternation and disappointment—the last hope of supply cut off! Ma saw the effect upon me, and said in a more hopeful voice than was her wont, "*The Lord is my shepherd, I shall not want.*" And good Mrs. Trenholm said her sack of peas was like the cruse of oil that never seemed to diminish in quantity, however much was taken out of it. An examination, too, of our own resources was quite gratifying; but I knew I ought to be "providing for a rainy day."

I pass now over an interval which brings me to the latter part of January, 1865. My sister returned home from Madison and spent several weeks with us, but had accepted an offer to teach at Grantville, on the LaGrange and West Point Railroad. I had a precious aunt, my mother's sister, Mrs. Annie Watson, whom I loved dearly, and of whom I had not heard a word since the interruption of the mail communication by the siege of Atlanta, and my mother's frequent mention of her determined me to go and see if this beloved aunt was living, and, if so, in what condition. I knew she was one of the favoured ones of earth, viewed from a worldly standpoint, but I knew not what changes had come over her or her worldly possessions. Rumour conveyed startling accounts of the atrocious deeds of Wilson's raiders, and I knew that they were operating in that rich cotton belt of Alabama which embraced my aunt's plantation and beautiful home. I could scarcely hope that that home and its valuable appointments had escaped the cupidity of an organized band of robbers protected by the United States Government.

When I think of my mother's fond affection for her children, and her tender solicitude for their welfare, I am constrained to think that she thought I was endowed with a sort of charmed existence not subject to the perils which beset the pathway of ordinary mortals, and hence her ready acquiescence to my proposition to undertake a journey of many miles, under circumstances of imminent danger, inspired with confidence amounting to certainty that I would be preserved by an All-wise Providence for future usefulness. I had very little preparation to make for the contemplated trip. A pretty, small-checked dress, which had done service through many a changing scene, and was good for as many more, and a hat—well, I beg to be excused from describing it—and gloves upon which I had expended skill in darning until it was difficult to perceive where the darning ceased and the glove began, completed my toilet, and I bade to all appearance a cheerful goodbye to my mother and kind friends, and went by private conveyance to Fairburn. There I took the train for Cowles' Station, Alabama.

Nothing of particular interest transpired on the way. My country was prostrate and bleeding from many lacerations, and my tears flowed so freely that by the time I reached my railroad destination I had a very sick headache. That "there is a providence that shapes our ends" was again illustrated. Some of my aunt's neighbours, who knew me at least by name, were at the station, and kindly offered to carry me to her residence, a distance of ten miles. I found my aunt in feeble health, and all alone save her usual dusky attendant. Her only child, Mrs. Mary E. Seaman, had gone to Tuskeegee to see her little daughter, who was there going to school in care of a friend and relative, Col. Smith Graham. My closest scrutiny failed to detect any change in my aunt's mode of living. The same retinue of servants came into the house to see and shake hands with mistress' niece, and after many questions about "our white folks in Georgia," retired from my presence with the same courtesy that had marked their demeanor towards me in ante-bellum days.

My aunt manifested her joy at seeing me in many ways, and wept and smiled alternately, as I related my adventures with the Yankees. "And my sister, what was their treatment of her?" My evasive answer, "It could have been worse," heightened her desire to learn particulars, and I told them to her. She was grateful for all leniency shown by them, and affected to tears by unkindness. As the day waned, and the middle of the afternoon came on, my aunt proposed walking "to meet Mary." I supported her fragile form, and guided her footsteps in the best part of the road. How like her beloved sister in Georgia she seemed! Accustomed to this little diversion, for she always went to meet Mary, she had reckoned accurately regarding the time of her daughter's coming, and we had not gone far when we saw the carriage descending a declivity in the distance.

Nelson, the coachman, had also recognized "Mistress and Miss Mary," and announced his discovery to my cousin. Increased speed in the gait of the horses soon brought us together, and she opened the door and stepped to the ground. After kissing her dear mother, she encircled me in her arms, and kissed me time and again, and then assisted me into the carriage, and she and her mother followed. I greeted the coachman in a cordial manner, because of past service and present fidelity to "mistress and my white folks" generally.

With my rapidity in conversation, I could scarcely keep up with my cousin's questions. Happy woman! She had never seen any "Bluecoats," or, in the parlance of the times, "Yankees," and she enjoyed my description of them, especially when in answer to the question, "Do they look like our men?" I attempted to define the difference. It was amusing to me to hear her describe the preparations she made for the coming of Wilson and his raiders.

After reaching home, she left her mother and myself only a few minutes. I scarcely perceived her absence, and yet when she returned the disparity in our dress was not so apparent. The elegant travelling suit had been exchanged for her plainest home attire, and every article of jewellery had disappeared. The brief period spent with these dear relatives was spent in mutual efforts to entertain and amuse each other. My aunt's conversation was like sweet music in which minor chords abounded. Her love for her sister, and apprehension of evil, gave a pathetic turn to every conversation she attempted, and it was evident to me that she had given up all hope of my brother's safety, and her resignation under similar circumstances was a great support to me.

Much as I enjoyed this luxurious home, and its refined appointments, there was a controlling motive—a nearer tie—that made me willing to again take up the hardships and perils of warfare, and battle for life with that relentless enemy left by Sherman to complete his cruel work, the aforesaid General Starvation.

After many farewell words were spoken, I left my aunt, accompanied by her daughter, who went with me to the station for the purpose of seeing me on the train bound for Fairburn, then the terminus of the railroad. It was past noon when the train left the station, and in those days of slow railroad locomotion, it was all the afternoon reaching West Point. I learned before reaching there that I would have to remain over until the next morning, and, therefore, as soon as I stepped from the cars, started to hunt a place at which to spend the night. Wending my way, solitary and alone, through the twilight, I saw Mr. John Pate, the depot agent at Decatur, coming towards me.

"Oh, Mr. Pate, have you heard anything from ma in the last week?"

"Yes; it went very hard with her, but she was some better this morning."

I did not have to ask another question. I knew it all, and was dumb with grief. The thought that I would never see my darling brother again paralyzed me. I saw him in the mirror of my soul, in all the periods of his existence. The beautiful little baby boy, looking at me the first time out of his heavenly blue eyes, and his second look, as if not satisfied with the first, followed by the suggestion of a smile. Ah, that smile! It had never failed me through successive years and varying scenes. The boyhood and youth—honest, truthful and generous to a fault—and the noble, genial boyhood, had all developed within my recollection, and I loved him with an intensity bordering on idolatry. These scenes and many others rushed through my mind with kaleidoscopic rapidity and made me so dizzy that I had no knowledge of how I reached the "hotel."

My heart cried and refused to be comforted. From the consolation of religion and patriotism it recoiled and cried all the more. A great tie of nature had been sundered, and the heart, bruised and crushed and bleeding, pulsated still with vitality that would have flickered out but for the hope of giving comfort to the poor bereaved mother and sister in our great sorrow. Good ladies bathed my throbbing temples and kissed my cheeks and spoke comforting words, for they were all drinking the bitter waters of Marah, and knew how to reach the heart and speak of the balm of Gilead.

"Killed on the battlefield, thirty steps from the breastworks at Franklin, Tennessee, November 30th, 1864," was the definite information regarding my brother's death, left for me by Mr. Pate.

Interminable as the darkness of night appeared, it at length gave way to the light of day, and I was ready with its dawn to take the train. But, oh, the weight of this grief that was crushing me! Had the serpents which attacked Laocoon, and crushed him to death by their dreadful strength, reached out and embraced me in their complicated folds, I could not have writhed in greater agony. I did not believe it was God's will that my brother should die, and I could not say to that Holy Being, "Thy will be done." In some way I felt a complicity in his death—a sort of personal responsibility. When my brother wrote to me from his adopted home in Texas that, having voted for secession, he believed it to be his duty to face the danger involved by that step, and fight for the principles of self-government vouchsafed by the Constitution of the United States, I said nothing in reply to discourage him, but rather I indicated that if I were eligible I should enter the contest. These, and such as these were the harrowing reflections which accused me of personal responsibility for the demon of war entering our household and carrying off the hope and prop of a widowed mother.

I found my poor stricken mother almost prostrate. The tidings of her son's tragic death did the work apprehended by all who knew her nervous temperament. Outwardly calm and resigned, yet almost paralyzed by the blow, she was being tenderly cared for by our saintly neighbour, Mrs. Ammi Williams and her family, who will always be held in grateful remembrance by her daughters.

Chapter 26

My Mother's Death

In sympathy with a disappointed people who had staked all and lost all in the vain effort to defend the inherited rights of freemen, and had not yet rallied from the depression occasioned by defeat, the spring of 1866 had withheld her charms, and, instead of donning a mantle of green, decorated with pansies, violets and primroses, hyacinths, bluebells and daffodils, verbenas, phlox and geraniums, and bloom of vine and briar in endless variety, the first day of April found her wounded, bleeding bosom wrapped in the habiliments of sorrow and despondency. A few brave old apple trees, as if to encourage the more timid, had budded and blossomed and sent forth sweet fragrance as of yore, and a few daring sprigs of grass suggested spring-time and sunny skies. Loneliness, oppressive and melancholy, and a spirit of unrest, prompted me to go to the depot in quest of something that never came, and my sister had stepped over to our neighbour, Mrs. Williams'.

Our mother loved the spring-time. It had always been her favourite season of the year. Fifty-nine vernal suns had brought inspiration and hope to her sensitive, tender heart, and given impulse to a checkered life; but now no day-star of hope shed its effulgence for her. As I mentioned in a former sketch, her only son had fallen mortally wounded upon the sanguinary battlefield of Franklin, and she had never recovered from the shock.

After a few months of patient endurance, an attack of paralysis had occurred, and during many days life and death contended for the victory. But the skill of good physicians, among them Dr. Joseph P. Logan, and faithful, efficient nursing, aided in giving her a comfortable state of health lasting through several months. But the fiat had gone forth, and now after a pathetic survey of earth, mingled with thankfulness even then to the God of the spring-time, she succumbed to the inevitable.

Returning from the depot, I espied in the distance the approaching figure of Telitha. As she came up to me she was the very picture of despair. With one hand clasped to her head, she fell on the ground and lay as if dead for a moment. My worst apprehensions were more than realized. I found my mother speechless, and never more heard her voice—never more heard any sound emanating from her lips except laboured, heavy breathing. It was all so sudden and strange and sad, I cannot describe it. Neighbours and friends came in by the score, and did all they could to mitigate our great sorrow. "Johnnie" Hardeman stayed until all was over, and mother never received from loving son kinder care or more unremitting attention.

Paul Winn also remained and manifested deep sympathy, and so did other neighbours. Oh, the sorrow, the poignant sorrow, to see a mother in the embrace of death, and to have no power over the monster! About thirty hours of unconsciousness, and without a struggle, "life's fitful dream was over," about 9 o'clock p. m., April 1st, 1866. The silent hush that ensued was sacred, and scarcely broken by the sobs of those most deeply afflicted.

Loving hands fashioned a shroud, and a beautiful casket was obtained from Atlanta. When all was done, and our mother arrayed for the tomb, she looked like the bride of Heaven. I gazed long and earnestly upon her face and figure, and went away and came back, and gazed again admiringly. For every lineament was formed into a mould that compelled admiration.

During the two days that she lay there, I often lingered by her side; and I recalled the many scenes, ofttimes perilous and sad, and ofttimes joyous and gay, through which we had gone together. Although a wee bit girl, scarcely turned in my fifth year at the time of my mother's second marriage, I remembered her as a bride. I remembered our journey by gig and wagon to Cassville, then, paradoxical as it may sound now, situated in the heart of a wilderness of beauty and savagery. The war-whoop of an uncivilized race of Indians, justly angry and resentful, reverberated though the impenetrable forest that belted the little settlement of white people that had the hardihood and bravery to make their homes among them.

I remembered how she soon became a favourite, and was beloved by everyone in that sparsely-settled locality, and won even the hearts of the Indians, by kindness towards them. She taught them how to make frocks and shirts, and clothes for their children, for the Cherokees were an ambitious people, and aspired to assimilation with the white race; and, to please them, she learned to bead moccasins, and other articles, ornamental and useful, just as they did. She also learned their alphabet, and became able to instruct them in their own language.

I remembered how she had always worked for the poor; not so much in societies (where the good that is accomplished in one way is often more than counterbalanced by the harm that is done in others), as in the quiet of her home, and in the humble habitations of God's poor. I remembered, with a melancholy thrill, how she had worked for our soldiers, and had not withheld good deeds from an invading alien army. Reverently I took in mine her little, symmetrical hand as it lay peacefully over the heart that had ever beat in unison with all that was good. It was weather-beaten, and I could feel the rough places on the palm through the pretty white silk glove in which it was encased. Cold and stark in death, it gave no responsive pressure to my own. I thought of its past service to me in which it never tired. It had trained my own from the rudimentary "straight lines" and "pot hooks," through all the intricacies of skilled penmanship, and from the picturesque letters on a sampler to the complete stitches of advanced embroidery.

The little motionless hand that I now held in my own had picked corn from cracks and crevices in bureau drawers, which served as troughs for Garrard's cavalry horses, to make bread with which to appease her hunger and mine. I gazed upon the pallid face and finely-chiseled features. The nose never seemed so perfect, or the brow so fair, or the snow-white hair so beautiful. The daintiest of mull caps heightened the effect of the perfect combination of feature, placidity and intellectual expression. I fancied I had never seen her look so beautiful, and felt that it was meet that we should lay her away in a tomb where she could rest undisturbed until the resurrection morn, not doubting that the verdict of a great and good God would assign her a place among His chosen ones.

Soothing to our bruised hearts was the sweet singing of those who watched at night beside her lifeless form. With gratitude we remember them still: Laura and Mary Williams, Emma and John Kirkpatrick, Josiah Willard and John McKoy. One of the hymns they sang was "Jerusalem, My Happy Home."

The hour for the funeral service came. Friends and neighbours and fellow-citizens had been assembling for several hours, and now the house was full, and the yard was thronged. Where did this concourse of people come from—old men, war-stricken veterans, and a few young men who had survived the bloody conflict that had decimated the youth of the South, and boys and women and girls! All alike came to pay respect to the deceased friend, and to show sympathy for the bereaved and lonely sisters. That sainted man and friend of ours, Rev. John S. Wilson, took his stand near the casket, and we sat near him, and those who loved us best got very near to us. Ah, well do I remember them! I could call each by name now, and the order in which they came.

An impressive silence ensued, broken by the man of God uttering in hopeful intonation and animated manner, "She is not dead, but sleepeth," and a sermon followed upon the resurrection of God's people, never surpassed in interest and pathos. All felt the power of his theme, and the eloquence of his words. He also spoke of the humble modesty of his friend, who had counted herself least in the congregation of the righteous, and dispensed favours to others in an unobtrusive manner, and who practically illustrated the divine command:"*Do unto others as ye would that others should do unto you.*" This beautiful funeral tribute was succeeded by the hymn—

"*Rock of ages, cleft for me,*"

..... which was sung with an unction which none but Christians can feel.

The last earthly look, solemn and earnest, was taken of our long-suffering, patient, loving mother, and everybody in the house followed our example and gazed reverently upon the pretty face, cold in death. And then the pall-bearers, "Johnnie" Kirkpatrick, "Johnnie" Hardeman, Virgil Wilson and Mr. G. W. Houston, bore her to the grave.

With uncovered head and grey locks fluttering in the vernal breeze, Dr. Wilson repeated the beautiful burial service of the Presbyterian Church. I can never describe the utter desolation of feeling I experienced as I stood clasped in the arms of my sister, and heard the first spadeful of earth fall over the remains of our loved one.

But we had heard above all the glorious words, "*This mortal shall put on immortality,*" and "*O, death, where is thy sting? O, grave, where is thy victory?*"

Chapter 27

A Reminiscence

"Sister, you are not paying any attention whatever to my reading, and you are losing the most beautiful thoughts in this delightful book."

"Yes, and I am sorry to do so; but I think I see one of Rachel's children—Madaline or Frances."

My sister closed her book, and, looking in the direction indicated, agreed with me that the negro woman, clothed in the habiliments of widowhood, who was coming up the avenue with a little boy by her side and one in her arms, was one of Rachel's children; and, although she was scarcely in her teens when she went away, she was a mother now, and traces of care were visible in every lineament of her face. I recognized her, however, as Rachel's youngest daughter, Frances, and went to meet her.

"Is that you, Frances?" I asked.

"Yes, Miss Mary, this is me; your same nigger Frances, and these are my children."

"I am glad to see you and your children;" and I extended my hand in genuine cordiality to her who had once been a slave in my mother's family, and I bade her welcome to her old home. Frances was too demonstrative to be satisfied with simply hand-clasping, and putting her boy on the ground, she threw her arms around me and literally overwhelmed me with kisses. My hands, neck and face were covered with them, and she picked me up and carried me in her arms to the house, her children following in amazed astonishment. She now turned her attention to them, and, after deliberately shaking the wrinkles out of their clothes, she as deliberately introduced them to me. The older of the two she introduced as "King by name," and the younger as "Lewis by name."

"You see, Miss Mary, I named my children King and Lewis 'cause my white folks named my brothers King and Lewis."

The ceremony of introducing her sons to *her* old *white folks* being performed to her satisfaction, she again turned her attention to me, and again literally overwhelmed me with caresses.

Entering the house, I asked Frances and her children to come in too.

"Miss Mary, whar's Miss Polly?"

"Have you not heard, Frances, that ma is dead?"

"Seem to me I has heard somethin' about it, but somehow I didn't believe it. And my poor Miss Polly is dead! Well, she ain't dead, but she's gone to heaven."

And Frances became quite hysterical in demonstrations of grief.

"And Marse Thomie, what about him, Miss Mary?"

"He was killed by the enemy at Franklin, Tenn., the 30th of November, 1864."

"Miss Mary, did them old Yankees kill him?"

"Yes, he was killed in battle."

And again, whether sincere or affected, Frances became hysterical in demonstrations of grief.

"Miss Mary, whar's Miss Missouri? Is she dead too?"

"No; that was she who was sitting in the portico with me as you were coming up the avenue. She always has to go off and compose herself before meeting any of you—ma was that way, too—I suppose you remind her of happier days, and the contrast is so sad that she is overcome by grief and has to get relief in tears."

"Yes'm, I have to cry, too, and it does me a monstous heap of good. I know it's mighty childish, but I jest can't help it. Jest to think all my white folks is done dead but Miss Mary and Miss Missouri!"

"Our brother left a dear little boy in Texas, and I am going after him next winter. He and his mother are going to live with us, and then we will not be so lonely."

"That's so, Miss Mary."

Frances and her children having partaken of a bountiful supper, she resumed, with renewed vigour, her erratic conversation, which consisted, chiefly, of innumerable questions, interspersed with much miraculous information regarding herself since she left her white folks and became a wife, a mother, and a widow.

"Miss Mary, whar's my children going to sleep tonight?"

"With your help I will provide a comfortable place for them, and, also, for you."

And taking a lantern and leading the way to the kitchen, I entered and pointed to a light bedstead, and told her to carry a portion of it at a time to my room, and we would put it up in there.

"Same old room, jest like it was when me and my mammy used to sleep in it.

"Well, things do look mighty nateral if it has been a long time since I seed it.

"And Miss Mary is agoing to let me and my children sleep in her room. Well!"

The bedstead having been placed in position, a mattress and bed clothing were furnished. And soon the little negro children were soundly sleeping under the protecting roof of their mother's former young mistresses.

"Whar's your teakettle, Miss Mary?" Having been told where to find it, Frances took it to the well and filled it with water, and, by adding a little more fuel to the fire, soon had it boiling.

"Whar's your bath-tub, Miss Mary?"

That, too, was soon produced and supplied with hot water, reduced to proper temperature. Memories of the past left no doubt in my mind as to the use to which the water was to be applied, and I determined to gratify every fancy that would give pleasure to our former handmaid, and, therefore, I made no resistance when garters were unbuckled, shoes and stockings removed, and feet tenderly lifted into the tub. She knew just how long to keep them there, and how to manipulate them so as to give the most satisfaction and enjoyment; and how to dry them—a very important process. And then the shoes and stockings were again put on, and giving me an affectionate pat on the head she told me to sit still until she told me to move.

"Now, whar's your comb and brush?"

The force of habit must have impelled her to ask this question, as, without awaiting an answer, she went to the bureau and got the articles about which she had asked, and in a few moments she had my long, luxuriant black hair uncoiled and flowing over my shoulders. She was delighted; she combed and braided it, and unbraided and combed it again and again, and finally, as if reluctant to do so, arranged it for the night.

"Now, whar's your gown?"

"You will find it hanging in the wardrobe."

Having undressed me, Frances insisted upon putting the gown on me, and then wanted to carry and put me in bed; this service, however, I declined with thanks. All these gentle manipulations had a soporific effect upon me, and I fain would have slept, but no such pleasure was in store for me. Frances had an axe to grind, and I had to turn the grindstone, or incur her displeasure. Mark her proposition:

"Miss Mary, I come to give you my children."

"Your what?"

"My children, these smart little boys. I'll go with you to the courthouse in the mornin' and you can have the papers drawn up and I'll sign 'em, and these little niggers will belong to you 'til they's of age to do for theyselves; and all I'll ever ask you to do for me for 'em is to raise them like my Miss Polly raised me."

"That you should be willing to give your children away, Frances, surprises me exceedingly. If you are without a home, and would like to come here and live, I will do all I can for you and your children. The kitchen is not occupied, only as a lumber or baggage room, and you can have that without paying rent; and you can take care of the cow and have all you can make off of her milk and butter, except just enough for the table use of two; and you can have a garden without paying rent, and many other favours—indeed, I will favour you in every possible way."

"Well, I tell you how it is, Miss Mary. You see, mammy wants to open up a laundry, and she wants me to help her. She's done 'gaged several womens to help her, and she wants me to go in with her sorter as a partner, you see. And I wants to get my children a good home, for you knows if I had to take care of 'em I couldn't do much in a laundry."

"And you want me to take care of them?"

"Yes'm; just like you used to take care of your own little niggers before freedom, and after I sign the papers they'll belong to you, *don't you know*."

"I am sorry to disappoint you, Frances, but I cannot accept your offer. If slavery were restored and every negro on the American continent were offered to me, I should spurn the offer, and prefer poverty rather than assume the cares and perplexities of the ownership of a people who have shown very little gratitude for what has been done for them." Without seeming to notice the last sentence, Frances exclaimed:

"Well, it's mighty strange. White folks used to love little niggers, and now they won't have them as a gracious gift."

Under the cover of night she had made her proposition and received her disappointment, after which she lay down by her children and was soon sleeping at the rate of 2:40 per hour, if computed by the snoring she kept up. In due time morning, cheerful, sun-lighted morning, came, and with it many benign influences and good resolutions for the day.

Frances asked where everything was, and having ascertained, went to work and soon had a nice, appetizing breakfast for us, as well as for herself and children. After that important meal had been enjoyed, she inquired about the trains on the Georgia Railroad, and asked what time she could go into Atlanta. I told her she could go at nine o'clock, but I preferred that she should stay until twelve o'clock, m.

"Miss Mary, what was in that trunk I saw in the kitchen last night?"

"I scarcely know; odds and ends put there for safekeeping, I suppose."

"May I have the trunk and the odds and ends in it? They can't be much, or they wouldn't be put off there."

"We will go and see." Again I took the kitchen key, and the trunk key as well, and having unlocked both receptacles, I told Frances to turn the contents of the trunks out upon the floor. When she saw them I noticed her disappointment, and I told her to remain there until I called her. I went in the house and got a pair of sheets, a pair of blankets, a quilt, several dresses and underclothing, and many things that she could make useful for her children, and put them together, and then called her and told her to take them and put them in the trunk.

"Look here, Miss Mary, you ain't going to give me all them things, is you?"

"Yes, put them in the trunk and lock it."

A large sack of apples, a gift also, was soon gathered and a boy engaged to carry it and the trunk over to the depot in a wheelbarrow. Promptly at half-past eleven o'clock the trunk and apples, and Frances and her little boys, were on the way to the depot, *en route* to Atlanta, their future home, and even a synopsis of the subsequent achievements of that woman and her unlettered mother would be suggestive of Munchausen.

CHAPTER 28

How The Decatur Women Kept Up the Sabbath School

Before the war there were in Decatur but two churches, the Methodist and the Presbyterian; although Baptist and Episcopal services were occasionally held. The churches first mentioned had been organized about 1825. The Presbyterians first worshipped in a log church, and afterwards in a frame building, but in 1846 had erected a substantial brick church. In this building was also taught the Decatur Union Sabbath School, organized in 1831, and for twenty-five years preceding the summer of 1864 it had been superintended by that godly man, Mr. Levi Willard.

The Federals had now come in. The church had been rifled of all its contents, including the pews. The faithful Sunday School superintendent with his lovely family soon after went away. Being nearer to our house, I remember more about the dismantling and refurnishing of the Presbyterian church than of the Methodist. So far as can be ascertained, the last sermon at the Presbyterian church had been preached by Rev. James C. Patterson, who was then living at Griffin, but was the stated supply of the pulpit here at that time. He will be remembered as a most godly man, and as a sweet singer of sacred songs.

The Sabbath before the entrance of the Federals, no service was held in the dear old church. The last prayer service had been held on Wednesday afternoon, led by Mr. Levi Willard, who was an efficient elder.

In July, 1864, but few families remained in Decatur; but there was still a goodly number of children and young people whose training must not be neglected. On the southwest corner of the Courthouse stood, and still stands, a long, narrow, two-story house. The lower story was occupied as a residence—the upper storey, for many years preceding and succeeding these times, was the quarters of the Masonic Lodge. In the ante-room of this lodge, Miss Lizzie Mortin taught a day school. The first story of the building was now occupied by the family of Mr. John M. Hawkins. Mr. Hawkins had enlisted in the army early in the war, but for some reason had returned home and been elected clerk of the court, which position he held until forced to leave before the advancing foe.

Mrs. Hawkins, whose maiden name was Valeria A. Perkins, the eldest daughter of Reuben Perkins of Franklin county, gladly opened her house on Sunday mornings that the children might be taught in the Sacred Scriptures. And thus a Sunday School was begun, and Mrs. Hawkins was made the superintendent.

Among the organisers and teachers may be mentioned Miss Cynthia Brown, Mrs. H. H. Chivers, Mrs. Eddleman, Miss Lizzie Morton, and Miss Lizzie McCrary. Mr. and Mrs. Buchanan, Mrs. Ammi Williams, and Mr. Fred Williams acted as a sort of advisory board. Rev. Dr. Holmes and Rev. P. F. Hughes, two elderly Baptist ministers, sometimes came; and Mr. R. J. Cooper, a godly layman, came a few times.

The names of some of these Sabbath school pupils can yet be recalled:—Charley, Guss and Lizzie Hawkins; their Cousins John, Sam, Ellen and Lizzie Hawkins, the children of Mr. Sam Hawkins, who is still living in Summerville, Georgia; the children of Mr. R. J. Cooper, and of Mrs. Eddleman, Mrs. Chivers, and of Mr. Ed Morton. There were others whose names I cannot recall.

The number of pupils increased to forty, and the school, having out-grown its quarters, was moved to the Court House; but when the Federals chose to occupy the Court House, the Sunday school was moved back to Mrs. Hawkins's home. The Bible was the text book; for there were no Sunday-school papers or song books.

Imagine the scene, if you can. Says one of the participants, who was then a young girl:

> We were a peculiarly dressed lot. I had a stand-by suit, the skirt made of a blanket shawl; with this I wore one of my brother's white shirts and a red flannel jacket. I had grown so fast that I was taller than my mother, and there was literally nothing large enough in our house or circle of friends to make me a whole suit. One of the ladies wore a gray plaid silk, a pair of brown

jeans shoes, and a woven straw bonnet. She had nothing else to wear. Many of the children were rigged out in clothes made from thrown-away uniforms, picked up, washed, and cut down by the mothers.

Mrs. Hawkins is still living near Decatur. She remembers that on several occasions the soldiers came in while the school was in session, much to the demoralizing of good order and comfort of mind. On one occasion the raiders piled barrels one on top of another, near the house, and set them afire, frightening the children very much.

When the war was over, the refugees began to return. Among the first were the families of Mr. J. W. Kirkpatrick, Mr. Ezekiel Mason, Captain Milton A. Candler, Dr. W. W. Durham, Dr. P. F. Hoyle, Mrs. Jane Morgan, Mrs. Cynthia Stone, Mr. James Winn, Mr. Benjamin Swanton, Mr. Jonathan Wilson, and Mr. J. N. Pate. But, alas! our faithful old Sunday-school superintendent and his family returned not, but remained in Springfield, Ohio, with the exception of Mr. Josiah J. Willard, who afterwards married Miss Jessie Candler, a sister of Captain Candler.

These returning refugees were devoted to the Sunday-school. Mr. John C. Kirkpatrick, just from the war, and scarce twenty-one, undertook the task of re-seating the Presbyterian church. He went out to a saw-mill and had puncheons sawed and carried to Mr. Kirkpatrick's cabinet shop, where they were fashioned into temporary seats. These were placed in the church, and it was once more opened for the exercises of the union Sunday-school, and also for divine worship. Who conducted those exercises, I can find no one who now remembers. My mother had been stricken in July, 1865, with paralysis, which confined her to her bed for many weeks. It was not to be supposed that her daughters could leave her; so that neither one of them can recollect these sessions of the resumed Sabbath-school.

There lies before me "the Sunday-school register and minute-book of 1866," kindly furnished for inspection by Mr. Hiram J. Williams, who had from early youth been constantly identified with the Sunday-school and church. The Superintendent was Mr. Ben T. Hunter; the librarian, Mr. John C. Kirkpatrick; the treasurer, Mr. John J. McKoy. Mr. Kirkpatrick removed to Atlanta in the August of that year, and Mr. Josiah Willard was elected to fill his place, but resigned in December to go on to Ohio, from whence he soon returned, and died a few years ago in Atlanta.

But I must not forget that I am not writing a history of the Sabbath-school, yet I cannot leave the theme without mentioning the fact that all the faithful ones who had taught in the stormy days of war still came in time of peace, and many others whose hearts had not grown cold by their enforced absence. Let me mention the teachers: Mr. J. W. Kirkpatrick, Dr. P. F. Hoyle, Rev. A. T. Holmes, Mr. W. W. Brimm, Captain Milton A. Candler, Mr. G. A. Ramspeck[1], Dr. John L. Hardman, Mr. H. H. Puckett, Mr. W. A. Moore (afterwards a Superintendent), Miss Cynthia Brown, Mrs. H. H. Chivers, Mrs. Eddleman, Mrs. Catharine Winn, Mrs. Jane Morgan, Miss Lizzie Swanton, Mrs. E. A. Mason, Mrs. Valeria A. Hawkins, Mrs. J. J. McKoy and Miss Lee Moore. Miss M. H. Stokes had been appointed one of the teachers, but her mother's feeble health, and the great shock consequent upon her death, prevented this teacher from attending that year with any regularity.

Among the names of "visitors" we notice those of Mr. Bryce, Rev. P. F. Hughes, Mr. Cooper, and Mr. L. J. Winn.

The re-opening of the Sabbath school at the old church was doubtless a great blessing to many. To one young man the joining of that school, and the acceptance of a teacher's place, meant the first public step to a profession of faith in Christ. Captain Milton A. Candler was the child of pious parents, but so far as he knew, was at this time an unconverted man. He reluctantly and with great diffidence accepted a teacher's place. Said he quite recently: "I attribute my subsequent union with the church to the study of the Bible which I made while teaching a class of little boys, Sabbath after Sabbath, in the old church with its puncheon seats. I taught my pupils, a class of little boys, to read from 'the blue-back speller,' and, when that lesson was over, read to them from the Bible, explaining it to them as best I could in all humility." In a few years he made a public profession of his faith in Christ, and was elected to the Superintendency of the Sabbath-school, (which office he still holds), and has laboured for its interests with a love and an unflagging zeal rarely ever equalled.

How sweet were the voices of many of the teachers and pupils! John C. Kirkpatrick sang a fine tenor; and clear and soft and true were the tones of Josiah Willard, sweet as the lovely character of this sainted one. All who knew Rev. J. D. Burkhead remember his singing, and he often led the music. A little later came Mrs. Mary Jane Wood

---

1. This gentleman, who married sweet Maggie Morgan, (the sister of Dewitt and Billy), has now, (1897), been Sunday school treasurer for twenty-seven years.

with her magnificent voice, and the grand bass of Joseph Morgan, the son of one of the pioneer teachers, Mrs. Martha Morgan. From this Sunday-school, and from its ex-Confederate soldiers, there went into the ministry W. W. Brimm, Paul P. Winn and Sam K. Winn. Promoted to the Glory Land long ago was Mrs. Jane Morgan; and, more recently, Mrs. Catherine Winn.

In the summer of 1866, a Sabbath-school was organized at the Methodist church, which, while a step in the right direction, was the sundering, in one sense, of ties that were very dear.

I cannot ascertain when the first sermon was preached in the church after the war, but think it must have been in August, as there is this entry in the journal of my sister, Miss Stokes, already quoted from in a former part of this volume: "Sunday, August 27th, 1865.—Dr. Holmes preached in the Presbyterian church, which has been re-opened for divine service, being furnished with puncheon seats without backs. There are a few benches with backs. Next Sabbath, Dr. Wilson will administer the communion of the Lord's supper." This was done at the time appointed—the first communion held in the church after the war. (The Dr. Wilson referred to was the venerable Rev. John S. Wilson, D. D., who had organized the church forty years before.)

So far as is known, the only part of the former church furnishings that ever re-appeared was the melodeon (or "seraphine"), which Rosella Stone, a negro woman, had preserved. She must have done this for the sake of Miss Marian Stone, who had formerly played it in church, and who, if I remember aright, played it again after the resumption of church services.

In the winter of 1865 and 1866, there was preaching for a short while by the Rev. Theodore Smith. Then followed Rev. J. D. Burkhead, and under his preaching, in the early spring, there occurred a protracted meeting, at which many persons were added to the church.

Gladly would I recall, if I could, the preachers who supplied the Methodist church at that time, but my memory fails me as to the exact details. I believe, however, that the Rev. William Henry Clarke, referred to in a preceding sketch, was the first Methodist minister who preached there after the war; and that Rev. Mr. Morgan and Rev. William A. Dodge were the first ministers in charge appointed by Conference.

In *ante-bellum* times, on many of the large plantations, special services were held for the negroes—some planters paying a regular salary for this purpose. In pious families, members of the household often taught the slaves, especially the house servants, the Bible and Catechism. So far as I can recollect, certain seats were assigned to them in all churches at all services, besides the special services usually held for them on Sabbath afternoons.

After the war, the negroes of Decatur and surrounding country were organized into a Sabbath-school at the Presbyterian Church, They came in large numbers, and were faithfully taught by the people of Decatur. To the kind courtesy of Mr. George A. Ramspeck I am indebted for the loan of the Minute-book of this school, which seems to have been organized in 1867. The pastor was the superintendent. The vice-superintendent was Mr. Samuel K. Winn, the Treasurer, Mr. George A. Ramspeck, and the Librarian, Mr. Moses S. Brown. But after several months the negroes went off to themselves, and eventually founded the African Methodist Episcopal Church. They have also a Baptist Church. In these undertakings they were assisted by the people of the village.

Chapter 29

Postal Affairs

The north side of the court-house square at Decatur is intersected by a public road leading to North Decatur, Silver Lake, the Chattahoochee River, and points beyond. On the eastern corner of this intersection stands the well-known Bradbury House. The house itself is an unsightly object, being almost untenable through age and neglect, but occupying a most desirable location. From its site lovely views of the surrounding country may be obtained, as the eye sweeps the circle of the horizon which is bounded on the north by distant hills, and on the northwest by the blue peaks of the Kennesaw. In the west is a near-by plateau, crowned with oaks and pines, beautiful in the morning when covered with a filmy mantle of faint purple mist—gorgeous at evening, when overhung by sunset clouds.

In 1860 the lower part of the Bradbury House was occupied as a store and post-office, the proprietor and postmaster being Mr. William Bradbury. His assistant was Hiram J. Williams, then a lad of fourteen years. When Mr. Bradbury enlisted in the DeKalb Light Infantry in 1861, Hiram became in reality the postmaster. At that early age he manifested the same traits which have characterized him to this day—unwearied attention to the business before him, unvarying courtesy, beautiful modesty, calm unbroken serenity of manner, and an unswerving honesty.

During the four years of the war, the mail received and sent out from Decatur was enormous in its quantity, and all the while it was handled by this youth; for when, in 1862, Mr. Bradbury resigned and Mr. John N. Pate was appointed postmaster in his place, Hiram Williams was retained in the office, Mr. Pate simply bringing over the mail from the depot. So great was the quantity of mail matter that sometimes Hiram had to call to his assistance his young friend, John Bowie.

During those war years, there were but few post-offices in DeKalb County, and the people for miles around had their mail sent to Decatur. The soldiers, unless writing to young ladies, rarely ever paid postage on their letters, but left it to be done by their home folks. This unpaid postage had to be collected and kept account of. Often a poor wife or mother, after trudging weary miles to the post-office, would receive a letter from husband or son and, unwilling to return without answering it, would request Hiram to answer it for her, which he always did. With every package of letters sent out, a way-bill had to go, showing the number of letters, how many were prepaid, how many unpaid, etc, etc. Imagine the work this entailed! Imagine the great responsibility! Imagine the youth who bore this labor and responsibility for four years! Small of stature, quiet in manner, but with an undaunted spirit looking out from his steady but softly bright brown eyes. How brave he must have been, and how his good widowed mother and only sister must have doted on him.

In July, 1864, when the booming of the Federal guns is heard from the banks of the Chattahoochee, the post-office is closed and for several months thereafter letters, if sent for at all, are sent by hand.

Our brave little postmaster now hies him away to Augusta, and there acts as mailing clerk for *The Constitutionalist*, and, after the surrender, for *The Evening Transcript*. In 1866 he returns to Decatur and engages in mercantile business with Willard and McKoy, but soon after opens a store of his own.

Early in 1867, Mr. Williams, now arrived at the age of twenty-one, is appointed postmaster at Decatur by Samuel W. Randall, postmaster general of the United States Government. In 1869 Mr. Williams was elected clerk of the Superior Court of DeKalb County, still retaining the office of postmaster, but having an assistant in each position.

In 1871, he was re-elected clerk of the court, and again in 1873. All this time he continued to be postmaster, and was re-commissioned by Postmaster General Jewell in 1875, holding the office up to 1880.

Mr. Williams continued to be Clerk of the Superior Court until 1884, when Mr. Robert Russell, a Confederate veteran, was elected. Mr. Williams then returned for a while to mercantile pursuits. But while pursuing the even tenor of his way, was called to a responsible position in Atlanta (which he still holds) with the G. W. Scott Manufacturing Company, now known as the Southern Fertilizer Company.

From 1870 to 1886, Mr. Williams was a special correspondent of *The Atlanta Constitution*, thus preserving the history of Decatur and of

DeKalb county during that period.

So much for a business career of remarkable success. But is this all? What of the higher and nobler life? This has not been neglected. In 1866 Mr. Williams united with the Decatur Presbyterian church. In 1868 he was appointed Librarian of the Sabbath school, an office he still holds. In 1894 he was elected to the office of Deacon, and also appointed church Treasurer. When the Agnes Scott Institute, for girls, was founded in 1891, he was made Secretary and Treasurer.

Mr. Williams has been twice married—in his early manhood to Miss Jennie Hughes, who lived but a short while. His present wife was Miss Belle Steward, who has been a true help-meet. They have a lovely and hospitable home on Sycamore street, where her sweet face, ever beaming with cheerfulness and loving kindness and sympathy for all, must be to him as a guiding star to lead and bless him with its light, as he returns at evening from the city and its business cares and toils, to the rest and peace of home.

If anyone should say that this is not strictly a war sketch, I would reply, "no, but who could resist following up at least the salient points of such a life—a life that exemplifies the main elements of success." Dear young readers, have you not seen what they are:—perseverance, fidelity to trusts reposed, punctuality, courtesy, honesty and conscientiousness—in other words, adherence to right principles and to Christian duty.

CHAPTER 30

The Tragic Death of Sallie Durham

On the 9th of April, 1865, at Appomattox Court House, Lee had surrendered his army of twenty-five thousand men to Grant with his four-fold forces. One after another of the Confederate generals had been forced to yield to superior numbers, and by the last of May the war was over.

The North had at the beginning of the strife a population of twenty-two millions; the South had ten millions, four millions of whom were slaves. The North had enlisted during the war two million six hundred thousand troops—the South a little more than six hundred thousand. Now the North had a million men to send home—the South but one hundred and fifty thousand.

Jefferson Davis had been captured, and imprisoned in Fortress Monroe. Our worn and ragged soldiers had returned to a devastated country. Our entire people were to begin life over again in the midst of poverty, uncertainty, and under the watchful eye of the conqueror. The war was over, but military rule was not.

It was in these transition days, between the fall of "the Lost Cause" and the more stirring events of "Reconstruction," that there occurred in our little village a most appalling tragedy. To understand it fully, my readers should know something of the young lady's family. Let us pause here and take a backward glance.

About a hundred years ago Lindsey Durham, a Georgia boy of English descent, graduated from a Philadelphia Medical College and located in Clarke county, in his native State. Drugs were expensive, as they could not be obtained nearer than Savannah, Charleston or New York. Being surrounded by frontiersmen and Indians, he could but notice the efficacy of the native barks and roots used by them as medicines. He was thus led to adopt to a large extent the theories of the Botanic School. He began to cultivate his own medicinal plants, and to prosecute with much zeal his botanical studies and researches. He even went to Europe and procured seeds and plants of medicinal value, until finally his garden of medicinal herbs and plants contained thirteen acres. So great was his fame that patients began to come to him from adjoining States, and he had to build cottages on his plantation in order to entertain them. His marvellous success brought to him ample compensation. He became a millionaire, and lived in all the old-time splendour. Once, by a loan of money, he rescued the Athens bank from utter failure.

Dr. Lindsey Durham left several sons, all of whom were physicians. The eldest of these, and the most eminent, was Dr. William W. Durham, who was born on his father's plantation in Clarke county, in 1823. After a collegiate course at Mercer University, he graduated from the Jefferson Medical College of Philadelphia, taking high honours, spending five years in the hospital there, and perfecting himself in surgery. This talented gentleman married Miss Sarah Lowe, of Clarke County, and, four years after her death, he married Mrs. Georgia A. Allen, whose maiden name was Wood, and who was a native of Franklin, Georgia.

With the children of his first marriage and their fair young stepmother, Dr. Durham came to Decatur in 1859. Well do I remember the children; two handsome sons, John and William—two pretty brown-eyed girls, Sarah and Catherine. It is needless to say that a large practice awaited the skilful physician, whose eclectic methods were then comparatively new.

William, the eldest son, went into the Confederate service at the age of sixteen, remaining the entire four years, suffering severely at the siege of Vicksburg, fighting valiantly at the Battle of Atlanta, and coming out of the war the shadow of his former self, with nothing but an old army mule and one silver dollar.

Sarah Durham, called Sallie by her family and friends, was a lovely girl of seventeen. She was tall and graceful; bright, and full of enthusiasm; kind, loving and generous. She had just returned from her grandmother's plantation, for her father had not sooner dared to have his daughters return, such was the insolence of the straggling Federals.

On the morning of September 1st, 1865, this dear girl arose early and noiselessly with a scheme in her kind heart. The former servants were all gone; her mother was not well, and she would surprise the household by preparing for them a nice breakfast. In fancy we see her, as she treads lightly, and chats softly with her tiny half-sister Jennie, and with a little negro girl who in some way had remained with the family.

The Durham residence, which was on Sycamore street, then stood just eastward of where Col. G. W. Scott now lives. The rear of the house faced the site where the depot had been before it was burned by the Federals, the distance being about 350 yards. Hearing an incoming train, Sallie went to the dining room window to look at the cars, as she had learned in some way that they contained Federal troops. While standing at the window resting against the sash, she was struck by a bullet fired from the train. (It was afterwards learned that the cars were filled with negro troops on their way to Savannah, who were firing off their guns in a random, reckless manner.) The ball entered the left breast of this dear young girl, ranging obliquely downward, coming out just below the waist, and lodging in the door of a safe, or cupboard, which stood on the opposite side of the room. (This old safe, with the mark of the ball, is still in the village - as at time of first publication.)

The wounded girl fell, striking her head against the dining table, but arose, and walking up a long hall she threw open the door of her father's room, calling to him in a voice of distress. Springing from bed, he said:

"What is it, my child?"

"Oh, father," she exclaimed, "the Yankees have killed me!"

Laying her upon a small bed in the room, her father cut away from her chest her homespun dress and made a hasty examination of the wound. Her horror-stricken mother remembers to this day that awful scene in all its details. But we will draw a veil over the grief of the smitten family, as they stood half paralyzed at this sudden calamity, and looked upon the loved one whom they were helpless to save. Mrs. Durham recalls the fact that the first person who came in was Rev. Dr. Holmes, and that throughout this great trial he and his family were very sympathetic and helpful.

Every physician in the village and city, and her father's three brothers were summoned, but nothing could be done except to alleviate her sufferings. She could lie only on her right side, with her left arm in a sling suspended from the ceiling. Every attention was given by relatives and friends. Her grandmother Durham came and brought with her the old family trained nurse. Sallie's schoolmates and friends were untiring in their attentions. Some names that have appeared in previous sketches, will now appear again, for they watched with anxious, loving hearts by the couch where the young sufferer lay. Tenderly let us mention their names, as we tread softly in memory's sacred halls. Among the constant attendants at her bedside were Mrs. Martha Morgan, Mrs. Hughes, Mrs. Morton, Miss Laura Williams (Mrs. J. J. McKoy), Lizzie and Anna Morton, Mrs. H. H. Chivers, Dr. Jim Brown and John Hardeman. During the week that her life slowly ebbed away, there was another who ever lingered near her, a sleepless and tireless watcher, a young man of a well-known family, to whom this sweet young girl was engaged to be married.

Writes Mrs. P. W. Corr, of Hampton, Florida, (formerly Miss Lizzie Morton):

"Never can I forget the dreary night when Willie Durham, Kitty Durham and Warren Morton left Decatur with Sallie's body, which was to be buried in the old family cemetery in Clarke county. Mrs. Durham, who was in delicate health, was utterly prostrated and the doctor could not leave her."

So Dr. Charles Durham managed the funeral arrangements, chartering the car, and Sallie was buried from the old church her grandfather Lowe had built on his own plantation in Clarke County, and laid to rest in the Durham cemetery nearby.

Sallie was shot on Friday at 7:30 a. m., and died the following Friday at 3:30 a. m. While she had suffered untold agony, she was conscious to the last. Throughout her illness she manifested a thoughtful consideration for the comfort of others. Especially did she show tender solicitude for her step-mother, insisting that she should not fatigue herself. While anxious to live, she said she was not afraid to die. In her closing hours she told her friends that she saw her own mother, her grandfather Durham, and her uncle Henry Durham (who had died in the Confederate service), all of whom she expected to meet in the bright beyond.

General Stephenson was in command of the Federal Post at Atlanta. He was notified of this tragedy, and sent an officer to investigate. This officer refused to take anybody's word that Sallie had been shot by a United States soldier from the train; but, dressed in full uniform, with spur and sabre rattling upon the bare floor, he advanced to the bed where the dying girl lay, and threw back the covering "to see if she had really been shot." This intrusion almost threw her into a spasm. This officer and the others at Atlanta promised to do all in their power to bring the guilty party to justice, but nothing ever came of the promise, so far as we know.

As a singular coincidence, as well as an illustration of the lovely character of Sallie, I will relate a brief incident given by the gifted pen already quoted from: "One of the most vivid pictures of the past in my memory is that of Sallie Durham emptying her pail of blackberries into the hands of Federal prisoners on a train that had just stopped for a moment at Decatur, in 1863. We had all been gathering berries at Moss's Hill, and stopped on our way home for the train to pass."

Dr. W. W. Durham lived for nearly twenty years after Sallie's death. During the war he had enlisted as a soldier, but was commissioned by Dr. George S. Blackie, a Medical Director in the Western Division of the Confederate Army, to the position of Inspector of Medicines for the Fifth Depot. This position was given him because of his remarkable botanical knowledge and power of identifying medicines. After the war he was prominent in the reorganization of the Georgia Medical Eclectic College, but refused to take a professorship on account of an almost overwhelming practice. He was a quiet, earnest, thoughtful man; and highly sympathetic and benevolent in his disposition. His widow, Mrs. Georgia A. Durham, and their daughter, Mrs. Jennie Findley, still reside in Decatur.

Dr. W. M. Durham is a successful physician in Atlanta. He holds a professorship in the Georgia Eclectic Medical College, and edits the Georgia Eclectic Medical Journal. Kitty is Mrs. W. P. Smith, of Maxey's; and John L. Durham is a physician with a large practice, and a large family, living at Woodville, Georgia.

The Durham residence still stands in Decatur, though not upon the same spot. For years a great stain of blood remained upon the floor, as a grim and silent reminder of this most awful tragedy which so closely followed the horrible and cruel war.

CHAPTER 31

The Death of Melville Clark

The lamented death of Miss Durham was not the only one in our community to be traced to the results of the war.

The period of reconstruction, forcing upon the Southern states the obnoxious Fourteenth Amendment, so humiliating and so unjust, especially at that time, had intensified the prejudices of the negroes against the white people—prejudices already sufficiently aroused by previous abolition teachings and the results of the war.

Several times in this little volume mention has been made of Rev. William Henry Clarke, the staunch patriot and well known Methodist preacher. At this period he had become a resident of Decatur. His son, Melville Clarke, a noble, promising boy, while attempting to rescue a small white child from the abuse of an overgrown negro youth, received wounds from which he died. Memory recalls many other instances of like character, perpetrated at this period, the most disgraceful in the annals of American history.

The subjoined resolutions, passed by the Methodist Sabbath school of which Melville was a beloved scholar, attest the many good traits of his character, and the affection accorded him in the community:

> The committee appointed to draft resolutions on the death of Melville Clarke, one of our scholars, beg leave to submit the following:
> In the wise dispensation of Him that doeth all things well, we are called to pay the last tribute to departed worth. Melville Clark is no more. The vacant seat says he is no more. The hushed voice says he is no more. Yes, the impressive, solemn silence of this moment whispers that another light which shone brightly the brief space allotted it here has flickered out. The

body which encased the spirit of the noble Christian boy has been laid away in the silence of the grave, and his spirit, as we trust, escorted by a convoy of angels, has gone to that bright and better world above.

Therefore, Resolved, That as we gather around the new-made grave and drop a sympathetic tear (which speaks more eloquently than any words mortal lips can utter), we deeply feel the loss of one so full of promise and usefulness—that noble spirit just bursting into manhood, with a mind that would grasp in a moment things that men have passed through life and never comprehended—and a heart lit up with the love of God, and drawn out by the tenderest cords of affection to do little acts of kindness. Language fails us to give utterance to the anguish we feel at sustaining so great a loss.

But he has gone. No more shall we hang upon the eloquence of his gentle, kind words, or see that face which was so often lit up with an expressive sweetness that we could but recognize as the reflex of the lamb-like Christian spirit that reigned within. He has gone, and as we turn from the sad, solemn scene in that faith which 'hopeth all things, believeth all things, endureth all things,' we can but exclaim: '*The Lord gave—the Lord hath taken away—blessed be the name of the Lord!*'

Resolved, That in the death of one of our members, so young, we recognize an admonition that the young, as well as the old, are swiftly passing away, and that we should pause and reflect seriously upon this important subject.

Resolved, That as a school, our warmest sympathy and condolence be tendered to the family of our dear deceased friend in this, their great bereavement, and that a copy of these resolutions be furnished them."

Committee:—
    Dr. Avery,
    John N. Pate ,
    Captain Randall
    J. R. Hampton
August 30th, 1868.

CHAPTER 32

The Morton Family

In several previous sketches references have been made to the Misses Morton. Not only they, but the whole family, bore an interesting and heroic part in the scenes of the war. Mr. Edward L. Morton hoisted the first Confederate flag that ever floated on the breeze in DeKalb county. This he did as soon as he heard that Georgia had passed the ordinance of secession. A few miles from Decatur there was a large mill known as Williams's Mill, situated on Peachtree Creek. At the terminus of the bridge that spanned the creek, near the little hamlet, there grew a tall, graceful Lombardy poplar tree. The flag had been made by Mrs. Morton, Mrs. James Hunter, and other ladies who lived in the neighbourhood, and was hoisted by Mr. Morton from the top of the lofty poplar. When the Federals came in they cut down the tree, but another has grown from its roots.

Mr. Morton enlisted with the first company that went from DeKalb, but returned and organized one of his own—Company F, 36th Georgia. From this command he was sent home on account of lung trouble, and placed on special duty. When Hood fell back to Atlanta, Captain Morton joined White's Scouts, a picked band of men. He was also at one time Morgan's guide.

After Mr. J. W. Kirkpatrick refugeed, his home on Atlanta street was occupied by Captain Morton's family. Here some stirring incidents occurred. Says one of his daughters: "Pa tried to avoid coming within the Yankee lines, but did several times get caught at home, owing to his extreme weakness. Finally, after the 23rd Army Corps was sent back to Tennessee, a raiding party of Federals went out toward Stone Mountain, were fired on a few miles from Decatur, and several killed. They were furious when they got to our house (on their return). Here they found one of 'White's Men' (Pa) ill in bed. They held a court-martial and sentenced him to be hanged as soon as they finished eating dinner. Meanwhile they left a guard in his bed-room. Ma asked the guard to sit in the parlour and leave them alone the short time he had to live. The guard was a kind-hearted man, the house surrounded, the whole detachment eating and feeding their horses on all sides, and Pa was very feeble; so the guard sat in the parlour."

Captain Morton then disguised himself, armed himself, and, passing out a side door, went unchallenged through the crowd of soldiers, by Woodall's tan-yard and out into the woods. Continues his daughter: "But when the guard thought he had better see the prisoner, it was discovered that he was gone. They talked of burning the house and made many other threats. For a long time we did not know whether he had escaped or died in the woods. . . . . No man that served in the Confederate Army more truly laid down his life for the cause than did my father. He never recovered from the lung trouble brought on and aggravated by the exposure and hardships he endured between '61 and '65."

Warren Morton went into the army at the tender age of fifteen, as a private in his father's company. He was in the siege of Vicksburg—was paroled, and re-entered the army in Cumming's Brigade—and was shot at Kennesaw, near Marietta, while acting as Sergeant-Major on Hood's retreat. The ball struck the bone of the outer angle of the left eye, cutting away the temple plate, and came out just over the ear, cutting off the upper half of the ear. The torn nerves and arteries have always caused him pain. The bullet, while it did not touch his eye-ball, paralyzed the optic nerve on that side. The hardships endured when a growing boy, the long marches in Kentucky, the starvation rations in Vicksburg, and the horrible wound, ruined his constitution. Yet he has been an energetic man, and is living now, (as at time of first publication), on a farm near Newnan.

The young ladies—girls they all were at the time of which I write—were Lizzie, Anna, Kelly, Fannie and Eddie.

On the day that Wheeler's Cavalry routed the Federal wagon train at Decatur, Lieutenant Farrar of the 63rd Ohio Regiment was killed on a meadow near Mrs. Swanton's residence, just opposite Mrs. Morton's. There was also another Federal, a mere lad, who was mortally wounded. In some way I discovered the dying boy, and, after carrying him some water, I left him to the care of the nearer neighbours. Mrs. James Hunter, Mrs. Morton and her daughters cared for him as best they could, and sat by him until he died. Miss Lizzie Morton cut from his head a lock of hair and wrote some verses, which Mrs. Swanton kindly sent to his people in Dayton, Ohio. In some way this became known to the Federal officers, and future developments showed that this tender act was much appreciated by them.

On the morning of the 22nd of July, 1864, Mrs. Morton sat on the front steps watching for an officer to whom she might appeal for protection. "Very early General McPherson and his staff rode by. Mrs. Morton ran out and called. General McPherson alighted from his horse, heard her story, bare-headed, with his hat in hand, wrote an order and dispatched it, and then mounting, rode away to his death." That order was to station a guard at the house, and it was never disregarded as long as the Federal line was near. This the family have always attributed to their caring for the dead, and to the kind order of General McPherson.

On the night of the 21st, Mrs. Morton had been badly frightened by some Federal soldiers coming to her house with the accusation that her young daughter "had given information that had led to the capture of their wagon train." Threats of burning the residence were made by the Federals on several occasions. The family feel persuaded that Bill Pittman, a faithful negro, a sawyer who had lived many years at Williams's Mill, prevented these threats from being put into execution.

Soon after the close of the war Captain Morton and his family went to Mississippi. Here he died, and one after another four of the girls, Anna, Kelly, Fanny, and Eddie. Most touchingly Lizzie (Mrs. P. W. Corr) writes: "When my sister and I were little girls in Decatur, we were very fond of private literary entertainments. Anna's favourite declamation (which always brought down the house) was:

They grew in beauty side by side
Around one parent knee;
Their graves are scattered far and wide
O'er mountain, plain, and sea.

"Anna sleeps alone near an old church in Scott county, Mississippi; Kelly, alone at Pickens; Pa, Fanny and Eddie side by side at Shiloh, in Holmes county." Anna married Mr. Kearney; Kelly, Mr. W. S. Cole. Mrs. Morton is still living in the home of her daughter Lizzie, who married Rev. P. W. Corr, of Hampton, Florida. Mrs. Corr is very happily married, being fond and proud of her husband, and her children filling her heart with comfort and pleasure. To crown her earthly blessings, her mother has been spared to her in all life's changing scenes.

Here in her happy Florida home we leave our erstwhile lassie of the war times—now an earnest wife and mother, busy ever with home duties, and also a true helpmeet to her husband in his ministerial and editorial labours.

This sketch, with its incidents, both heroic and pathetic, cannot be more appropriately concluded than by the touching words of Mrs. Corr in a recent letter: "What you say of the 'empty places' is full of suggestiveness. I think I never could have borne my losses and still have moved about among the 'empty places.' But going always among strangers after every loss, being removed at once from the scene of death and not passing that way again, my sisters live in memory as part of the past, always merry, happy girls, never to grow heart-weary, never to fade. We, wandering among strangers in strange and unfamiliar scenes, have kept the memory of our old Decatur home and friends intact. There are no empty places there for us.

"It seems sweet to me to think that in that home to which we are all travelling, we shall find that those dear ones who have preceded us have carried with them that same bright and precious picture, which, however, is not there a picture of memory, but a reality of which the earthly circle was only a shadow or prophecy; and the only empty places there are those which shall be filled when we get home. Something there is in the friendships, even, of other days, that has never died—something that will live again—a root planted here that there blossoms and fruits eternally. How much more true is this—it must be so—of those who were heart of our hearts, our own loved ones. I doubt not that for one sad longing thought of 'brother, mother, nephew,' all that you have loved and lost, they have had many sweet and loving thoughts of you, and joyful anticipations of your coming home 'Some Sweet Day.'"

CHAPTER 33

Hon. Joseph E. Brown's Pikes and Guns

(This chapter, and the succeeding one, were not placed in the chronological order of events, because they would have broken the continuity of personal experiences).

After an appeal to physical force, as the only means of redressing our wrongs, was fully determined upon, we made many important discoveries, chief of which was that we were not prepared for war. This fact had often been impressively and earnestly set forth by our greatest statesmen, Alexander Hamilton Stephens and Benjamin Harvey Hill, who, though reared in different schools of politics, were fully agreed upon this point, and who urged, with all the eloquence of patriotism and profound understanding of existing facts, the importance of delaying the act of seceding from the United States until we were better prepared for the mighty consequences—either beneficial or disastrous. In no way was the wisdom of this advice made more apparent than by our utter want of the appliances of warfare on land and on sea.

The ordinance of secession having been enacted, Georgia found itself confronted by the scarcity of guns and other munitions of warfare. Hon. Joseph E. Brown, our war governor, finding it impossible to secure even shot-guns to equip the many regiments eager for the fray, conceived the idea of arming them with pikes; and, undaunted by the Herculean undertaking, put a large force of the best blacksmiths at the W. & A. R. R. shops to making these primitive weapons. To whose fertile brain belongs the honor of evolving the plan or diagram by which they were to be made, has never been revealed to the writer. The blade of the pike was to be about 16 inches long and 2 inches wide, with a spur of about 3 inches on either side, all of which was to be ground to a sharp edge. The shank was to be about 12 inches long, and arranged to rivet in a staff 6 feet long.

In the memorable year, 1861, J. C. Peck owned a planing mill and general wood-working shop on Decatur street, Atlanta, Ga., on the grounds now occupied by the Southern (old Richmond and Danville) R. R. freight depot. There being no machinery at the railroad shops suitable for turning the handles nor grinding the pikes, Mr. Peck contracted to grind and supply with handles the entire number—he thinks ten thousand. Before he finished this work, Governor Brown called a meeting of the mechanics of Atlanta for the purpose of ascertaining if some arrangement could be made for the manufacture of guns for the army. This meeting was adjourned two or three times, and no one seemed willing to undertake the job.

At the last meeting a letter was received from the Ordnance Department of the Confederate States, containing a "drawing" of a short heavy rifle to be supplied with a Tripod rest, and an urgent request that the governor would encourage the making of twenty-five guns after this pattern, as soon as possible. A liberal premium for the sample was offered by the Confederate Ordnance Department. The barrels were to be thirty inches long with one inch bore, and rifled with three grooves, so as to make one complete revolution in the thirty inches. As no one else would undertake this complicated job, Mr. Peck asked for the "drawing," and announced his willingness to do so. He discovered that it would require iron ¾ by 4½ or 5 inches to make the barrels, and for this purpose he procured enough Swede iron at a hardware store on Whitehall street to make thirty barrels.

He also discovered that the common Smith bellows would not yield a blast sufficient to secure welding heat on so large a piece, and it was suggested that it could be done at W. & A. R. R. shops; he therefore secured an order from Governor Brown authorizing this important work to be done there under his instruction. An old German smith, whom Mr. Peck found at the shops, rendered him valuable aid in the accomplishment of this portion of the work. As rapidly as the welding was done he had them carried to his shop, and a wood-turner, Mr. W. L. Smith, bored them on a wood turning lath. This was a difficult job, as the boring bits caught in the irregular hole and broke; finally he devised a sort of rose bit which steadied itself, and he had no further trouble.

After successfully accomplishing this portion of the work, Mr. Peck found himself confronted by another difficulty. He had no way of turning iron, but his indomitable will shrank not from the task, and he threw out a search-light which enabled him to discern a Savage, who had been superintendent of Pitts & Cook's gin factory, and he engaged him to turn it. Mr. Peck then employed an ingenious blacksmith, who did to his satisfaction all the smith work he wanted. He made his own taps and dies for fitting the breech pieces, putting in the nipples, etc., and forged the hammers, triggers, ramrods, etc. The brass mountings were cast by Gullatte Brothers, who at that time were running a brass foundry. The locks were purchased by Mr. Peck in Macon, but, as already intimated, had to be supplied with new hammers and triggers.

As the plan called for the barrels to be rifled with three grooves, and to make one complete revolution in the length of the barrel, there was none in the employ of Mr. Peck who had any idea how it was to be done. Much perplexed he went to Mr. Charles Heinz, the gunsmith on Whitehall street, who explained the process of rifling done by hand. On this idea Mr. Peck constructed a machine which he attached to a Daniels planer. This was a wood machine, with a bed which travelled backward and forward, similar to the bed of an iron planer—in such a manner that the backward and forward motion of the bed gave, also, a rotary motion to the cutters. By this process each barrel was rifled precisely alike. Mr. Peck had thirty barrels forged, but some of them were defective and would not bore through without breaking, and some were burnt in testing. Only twenty-five of them were finished. He had an abundance of walnut lumber and did not have to contend with any obstacle in making the stocks, but some in clamping them to the barrels.

The plan also showed the usual screw in the extension of the breech pin, and two bands similar to those on the old style musket. Mr. Peck forged iron bands, but with his best effort at finishing them they appeared clumsy. Opportunely he chanced to see a wagon on Pryor street containing a lot of hardware and other things, among which was a large brass kettle. Thinking he could make bands out of this vessel, he purchased it and cut it up into those indispensable parts of his famous job, but another obstacle to success presented itself to his patient vision. He could find no one to braze the joints. By reference to his *Mechanic's Companion* he learned the art, and brazed the bands in a skilful style. This being, done, he gave his finishing touches to the rifles.

The balls were like minie balls, one inch in diameter, and two and one-fourth inches long, and weighed four ounces. Mr. Peck made only one set of bullet moulds, which run two bullets at the same time, and he thinks he made only six of the tripod rests. They were—every lock, stock and barrel—tested by several persons expert in the handling of muskets, rifles, shot-guns, etc., among whom was Mr. Charles Heinz, still living in Atlanta, (as at time of first publication), and who will vouch for the accuracy of this important item of Confederate history, and the utility of the shot emanating from these wonderful guns. To put it mildly, the effect was almost equal to that of a six-pounder. And the recoil! Well! Wonderful to relate! They must have had infused into their mechanism supernatural or national prescience, and peering through the dim vista of the future saw the beacon light of a re-united country, and disdained partiality in the Fratricidal Contest, for every time one of them was shot at a "Yankee," it kicked a "Rebel" down.

P. S.—Mr. Peck has the original "drawing" sent on from the Ordnance Department at Richmond, and also the receipt for the payment for the barrels. He also has a letter from the Chief of Ordnance at Washington, D. C., informing him that the identical guns described in the above sketch had been found in his department, and that two of them would be exhibited in the Government Building of the Piedmont Exposition, Atlanta, Georgia, in 1895.

CHAPTER 34

The Pursuit and Capture of the Andrews Raiders

In the early part of 1862 the army of the Cumberland and also that of the Tennessee had grown to gigantic proportions. The history of that memorable era establishes the fact that in the month of February of that year the army of the Cumberland, commanded by General Buell, had captured Fort Donaldson and several other strong strategic points on the Tennessee and Mississippi Rivers. Numerically the Federal Army was so much stronger than the Confederate that large detachments could easily be made for incursions into the interior and unprotected sections of middle and West Tennessee, while the main army steadily advanced down the Mississippi Valley. By the first of April, General Mitchell had occupied Shelbyville and other cities, including Nashville; and the larger towns and railroad stations in the neighbourhood South and East of Nashville had been occupied by the Federals.

Recognizing the importance of saving to the Confederate cause everything necessary to sustain life both of man and beast, all that could be brought out of Kentucky and Tennessee had been sent South—to Atlanta and other important points—so that those States were literally stripped of all surplus food.

The army of the Tennessee, under the command of General Albert Sidney Johnston, sought to meet General Buell and dispute his further advance. Corinth, Mississippi, was selected by General Johnston as a point beyond which the army of the Cumberland should not go. This position commanded the Memphis and Charleston Railroad, as well as others running south of that point. By the fifth of April General Buell's army had massed at Pittsburg Landing, and along a line reaching south and parallel to that of General Johnston. Relatively the armies stood about five to eight, the Confederate of course being the smaller. They met in battle on the 6th day of April at Shiloh, so-called by the Federals, but Southern historians call it the Battle of Corinth.

The fight was a long and disastrous one—disastrous to both armies—but the Federals, having an unbounded supply of everything needed in war, and being immediately strengthened by large reinforcements which literally poured in, were enabled to rapidly recuperate. The Confederates lost heavily in killed and wounded, and suffered irreparably by the death of General Albert Sidney Johnston. The loss of this noble man was deeply felt and regretted by the entire South. The week following this horrible carnage was mainly taken up by both armies in burying the dead, caring for the wounded, fortifying, receiving reinforcements and manoeuvring for advantageous positions.

General Mitchell, as already stated, had occupied Shelbyville, and had a considerable force. Some cavalry had penetrated as far southeast as Chattanooga, and had several times dropped a few shell into that town.

After the death of General Johnston the Confederate Army at Corinth was put under the command of General Beauregard. There were small detachments of Confederate troops distributed along the Memphis and Charleston Railroad to Stephenson, and from there to Chattanooga; also from Chattanooga to Bristol, on the East Tennessee and Georgia Railroad, and on the Virginia and Tennessee. These were to guard the railroad bridges, depots, and government stores, etc. General Ledbetter was stationed at Chattanooga with about three thousand men. There was a tolerably strong guard at London bridge, where the East Tennessee railroad crosses the Tennessee River; and General E. Kirby Smith occupied Knoxville, with a sufficient force to protect that important point as against General Morgan in his immediate front with a strong force.

East Tennessee was very nearly evenly divided between Federals and Confederate sympathizers. Neither side was safe from betrayal. Those who were true to the Southern cause distinguished themselves as officials and soldiers, and those who were recreant to it were a source of great annoyance and disaster; and this applies to Kentucky and West Virginia as well. During the month of April, 1862, Brownlow, and those of his opinion, were arrested, and imprisoned in Knoxville.

The strict rules of the passport system had not yet been adopted by southern army commanders, and it was no difficult matter for friend or foe to pass the lines.

Thus matters stood at that time. The reader, therefore, may be prepared to appreciate one of the most exciting, thrilling and interesting stories of the Civil Contest.

The Western and Atlantic Railroad (often called the State Road) at the time discussed in the preceding pages, was the only line of communication between the southern centre of the Confederate States and the Army of Tennessee. It was worthy of notice that this road was not paralleled by any of the roads now in existence. The Memphis and Charleston Railroad came into the Nashville and Chattanooga at Stevenson as now, and the latter road reached from Nashville to Chattanooga. The East Tennessee and Georgia Road also came into Chattanooga then as now, and also into Dalton. These three railroad lines were "the feeders" for the Western and Atlantic Railroad at Chattanooga and Dalton. At the south or Atlanta end of that line we had the old Macon & Western (now the Georgia Central), the Atlanta and West Point, and the Georgia Railroad, as feeders for the Western and Atlantic, which reached from Atlanta via Dalton to Chattanooga.

As has been stated, the Army of Tennessee, under General Beauregard at Corinth, the army under General E. Kirby Smith at Knoxville, the army under General Ledbetter at Chattanooga, and all detailed men on duty along the whole front of the Confederates from Corinth to Bristol, depended upon this single line (the old reliable Western and Atlantic Railroad) for army supplies. There was no other road in the whole distance of eight hundred miles, reaching from Mobile, Alabama, to Richmond, Virginia, that ran north and south. These facts were well known to northern commanders, and it has always seemed strange that the road should have been so unprotected. The many bridges on the Western and Atlantic were guarded at the time under consideration, April 1862, by a single watchman at each bridge, and he was employed by the railroad authorities. The bridges were of the Howe Tress pattern, weatherboarded with common wooden boards, and covered with shingles. They were exceedingly inflammable and could easily have been set on fire.

One of the rules for the running of the trains was that "if any two trains failed to make the meeting point they would be considered irregular trains, and the conductor of each train should be required to send a flagman ahead, and thus proceed until the two flagmen met." This cumbersome rule frequently occasioned great disorder, and sometimes many trains of all grades were massed together at one station. Railroad men will understand this condition of affairs. These things were known and understood not only by the Confederates, but by the Federals through their spies. J. J. Andrews especially understood them, as the sequel will prove.

It is beyond the scope of this article to discuss the plans adopted by Captain J. J. Andrews and his twenty-two auxiliaries, to descend into the heart of the South; suffice it to say, their plans were successful, and they passed the Confederate lines and entered the pretty town of Marietta, twenty miles north of Atlanta, unmolested and unsuspected. The solving of the mystery will appear at the proper time. For present purposes it is enough to state that they not only entered the town mentioned, but boarded the north-bound train on the morning of April 12th, 1862. The well-known and intrepid Captain William A. Fuller was the conductor in charge of that train—the now celebrated "General" was his engine—and Jeff Cain his engineer. There was nothing suspicious in the environments of the occasion. In those days it was not unusual, even in a country town, for a large number of men to board a train, and they were coming in from all over the country to join the Confederate army.

There was a Camp of Instruction at Big Shanty, seven miles north of Marietta, and this fact, as well as many others more important, was known to Andrews, who from the beginning of the war had been "a commercial traveller," "in full sympathy with the South," and had ridden over this line many times. The conductor, therefore, took up the tickets as usual, some to one point and some to another, but the most of them to Big Shanty. The raiders were dressed in various styles and appeared like a good class of countrymen. They claimed to be "refugees from beyond the Lincoln lines."

Big Shanty was a mere station, having only one or two business houses, and noted by the travelling public as having a most excellent "eating-house" for the accommodation of the passenger trains. When Captain Fuller's train arrived at Big Shanty, the passengers and train hands went into the hotel for breakfast. The absence from the table of the large crowd that got on the train at Marietta was noticed by the conductor, and just as he took his seat, which commanded a view of his train, the gong on the old "General" rang. It should be stated here that the train was as follows: "The General," three freight cars, one second and two first-class coaches, a baggage car and express car. Andrews had detached the entire passenger train, put his surplus men into the three freight cars, and on "The General" he had with himself his own engineer and fireman.

The very moment the gong rang Captain Fuller sprang from the table, and with a swift run reached the main track and pursued the flying train, which was now fast disappearing around a curve in the road. As he ran out of the hotel Captain Fuller called to his engineer, Jeff Cain: "Someone who has no right to do so has taken our train!" Cain and Mr. Anthony Murphy joined in the race, but were soon distanced by the fleet-footed Fuller. The limestone soil between the tracks was wet and clung to his feet so that fast running was very fatiguing to Captain Fuller, but he ran with a determination that overcame all obstacles. Moon's Station, a little more than two miles from Big Shanty, was reached by him in an incredibly short time. Here he found that the Andrews raiders had stopped and had taken all of the tools from the railroad section hands. They had climbed the telegraph poles, cut the wire, and carried a hundred feet of it along with them to prevent the repair of the line in time to thwart their plans. The track hands were amazed at their conduct, and hurriedly told Captain Fuller what had been done.

Up to this time he had been in doubt as to the true character of the raiders. He had thought that possibly some of the Confederates at Camp McDonald, (the Camp of Instruction at Big Shanty), tired of strict discipline and confinement, might have taken the train in order to enable them to pass the environment of their camp. But from this moment there was no room for doubt. As quickly as possible Captain Fuller and two track hands placed upon the rails an old timber car used for hauling crossties, iron, and other heavy material. This was an unwieldy and cumbersome medium of locomotion, but it rendered good service, nevertheless. Captain Fuller knew that every moment of time was most valuable, as the raiders were speeding along up the road and his chances for overtaking and capturing them were very doubtful. While putting on the hand-car he debated with himself these questions: "Should he proceed immediately in the pursuit, or would it be best to push back and get his engineer?"

He decided to push back for Cain, and when he had gone nearly a mile he met Cain and Mr. Anthony Murphy. They were taken on the hand-car and the pursuit of the raiders, now far ahead, was begun again. Captain Fuller says that if he had not gone back, as above stated, he would have captured the raiders at Kingston, as more than twenty minutes were lost, and he was quite that close to them at Kingston. He says, however, he is now glad he did not do so, as the run from that point furnished the most thrilling event of his life.

Murphy, Cain, the two track hands, and Fuller, pushed and ran, and ran and pushed, alternately, and each and every man on the old hand-car did his full duty. Soon after passing Moon's Station, where Captain Fuller got the hand-car, the pursuers came upon a pile of cross-ties, but they were soon removed from the track and the race resumed.

The intelligent reader will not for a moment suppose that Captain Fuller and his comrades entertained any hope of overtaking the raiders on foot, or even by the hand-car. Captain Fuller's thoughts ran ahead of his surroundings, and he disclosed his plans to his comrades in these words:"If we can get to Etowah by 9:40, we will catch the old Yonah. This we can do by very hard work, unless hindered by obstructions." This suggestion doubled the energy of every man, and they abandoned themselves to the task before them. It is difficult to write, with deliberation, a story so full of push and haste. This run of twenty miles with an old clumsy hand-car, under so many difficulties, is replete with interest.

At length, after Captain Fuller and his comrades were thoroughly exhausted, standing on the turn-table at Etowah more than a mile away, "the old Yonah" was espied. A yell and cry of great joy went up from these gallant men; but, alas, their vision had extended beyond their immediate danger! The raiders had removed an outside rail in a short curve, and unexpectedly the whole party was thrown into a ditch full of water. This, however, was a small matter to men of resolute will and iron nerve. The car was soon carried across the break in the track and put upon the run again.

One of the track hands was left to watch this break, to prevent danger to following trains—the other was left with the hand-car at Etowah. Although the old Yonah was standing on the turn-table at Etowah, her tender was on another track. Willing and eager hands soon had the engine and tender coupled together, and the Yonah was "pressed into service." An empty coal car was taken on, and a few Confederate soldiers, who were at the station waiting for a south-bound train, volunteered to join in the chase. The engineer of the Yonah, Mr. Marion Hilly, and his own hands, ran the Yonah from Etowah to Kingston, and Captain Fuller gives them great credit for their loyalty and faithful service.

A more dangerous run was never made. The track was in a bad condition, and the line quite crooked; and the pursuers could not tell at what moment they might be thrown into a ditch by a removal of rails, or obstructions placed upon the track; but they were absolutely blind to all personal danger or considerations. The Yonah had only two drivers and they were six feet, and she had a very short strike. She was built for fast running with a small passenger train on an easy grade. Under all the difficulties by which he was surrounded, Hilly ran the Yonah from Etowah to Kingston, thirteen miles in fourteen minutes, and came to a full stop at Cartersvile, and also at Kingston. Several crossties had been put upon the track, but the pursuers said "they were literally blown away as the Yonah split the wind."

At Kingston, Captain Fuller learned that he was only twenty minutes behind the raiders. At this point, Andrews had represented himself as a Confederate officer. He told the railroad agent that he "passed Fuller's train at Atlanta, and that the cars which he had contained fixed ammunition for General Beauregard at Corinth." He carried a red flag on "The General," and said that "Fuller's train was behind with the regular passenger train."

This plausible story induced the agent to give him his keys to unlock the switch at the north end of the Kingston railroad yard. Several heavy freight trains were at Kingston, bound southward. Those furthest behind reached a mile or so north of the switch on the main line. Owing to Andrews's "fixed ammunition" story, the agent, being a patriotic man, ordered all trains to pull by, so as to let Andrews out at the north end of the yard. This was done as quickly as possible, though it was difficult to make the railroad men understand why the great haste, and why Andrews should be let pass at so much trouble when Fuller's train would soon be along, and both could be passed at the same time. But Andrews's business was so urgent, and so vitally important, as a renewal of the fight between Beauregard and Buell was expected at any hour, the freightmen were induced to pull by and let him out. This delay gave Captain Fuller an inestimable advantage, and but for the delay at Moon's Station, Andrews and his raiders would have been captured at Kingston.

When Fuller arrived at Kingston on the Yonah, he was stopped by a flagman more than a mile south of the depot, on account of the trains that had pulled by to let Andrews out. He saw at once that he would have to abandon the Yonah, as he could not get her by without much delay. So taking to his feet again, he ran around those freight trains to the depot and held a short conversation with the agent from whom he learned the particulars of Andrews's movements and representations, etc. He then ran to the north prong of the Rome railroad "Y," where that road intersected with the Western and Atlantic mainline.

There he found "The Alfred Shorter," the Rome railroad engine, fired up and ready to move. He hurriedly told Wyley Harbin the engineer of "The Alfred Shorter," about the raiders, and he and his fireman, noble fellows, at once put themselves and their engine at his service. The pursuers were gone in thirty seconds. Captain Fuller says that Jeff Cain got into the train, but that Mr. Murphy who was in another part of the car yard, considering some other plan, came near being left; but Fuller saw him and held Harbin up until he ran up and got on.

Captain Fuller rode on the cowcatcher of the "Shorter," that he might remove crossties and other obstructions that would probably be put on the track. Further down the road, when Andrews was running more at leisure, he loaded the three box cars with ties and other timber, and when he feared pursuit he punched out the rear end of his hindermost car and dropped obstructions in the way of his pursuers. The Alfred Shorter had drivers only four feet—6—, and could make only ordinary time; but Captain Fuller did not consider that of any great disadvantage, as she ran as fast as it was safe to do on account of the many obstruction dropped by raiders upon that part of the road.

Six miles north of Kingston, Captain Fuller found it necessary to abandon the "Shorter," because at that point several rails of the track had been taken up and carried away by the raiders. Knowing the schedule as he did, and seeing he could not get by in less time than thirty minutes, Captain Fuller decided that the best thing to be done was to go to Adairsville, four miles north, where he hoped to find a south-bound train, "tied up" because of the delay of his train. Possibly he might meet this train before reaching Adairsville. Leaving the "Shorter," he called upon all who wished to join in one more effort to follow him, and started in a run on foot for another four miles. There were none to follow—all preferred to remain in the Rome passenger coach. (It is not amiss here to state that, at Kingston, Fuller took on one coach belonging to the Rome Railroad, and that some thirty or forty persons had volunteered and boarded the Rome car; but, when invited to join in a four-mile foot race, they preferred to remain in the coach.)

When Fuller had run about two miles he looked back and saw Murphy just rounding a curve about three hundred yards behind. When he had run about a mile further, to his great delight he met the expected south-bound freight train. Fuller gave the signal, and, having a gun in his hand, was recognized by the conductor, who stopped as quickly as possible. Fortunately Peter I. Brachen was the engineer of the freight, and had "The Texas," a Danforth & Cook, 5 feet 10 driver, as his engine. Captain Fuller knew that Brachen was a cool, level-headed man, and one of the best runners that ever pulled a throttle. As soon as the train stopped, Fuller mounted and was about to back it, when, seeing Murphy coming, he held Brachen a few seconds until his comrade got on "The Texas." Then the long train was pushed back to Adairsville, where Fuller changed the switch, uncoupled the train from the engine, and pushed in upon the side track. In the further pursuit of the raiders, Captain Fuller never changed his engine or his crew again.

From hence "The Texas" is after "The General"—both are new, both 5 feet 10 driver, with the same stroke—"The General" a Rogers, "The Texas" a Danforth & Cook. But "The General" was forward, while "The Texas" had to back.

Captain Fuller rode on the back end of the tender, which was in front, and swung from corner to corner, so that he could see round the curves and signal to Brachen. His only chance to hold on was by two hooks, one at each corner of the tender, such as were formerly used to secure "spark catchers." Many times he bounced two feet high when the tender ran over obstructions not seen in time to stop the engine. The ten miles from Adairsville to Calhoun was made in twelve minutes, including the time consumed in removing obstructions. (Here it may be in order to state that when Andrews had met Brachen at Adairsville, on his south-bound trip before being met by Fuller, that he told him to hurry to Kingston, as Fuller would wait there for him. This Brachen was doing, when Captain Fuller met him a mile south of Adairsville. But if Fuller had not met and stopped him, he would not have gone on to Kingston, but would have plunged into the break in the railroad where the raiders had taken up the rails at the point where the "Shorter" was abandoned. This was one of Andrews' best moves. He hoped to occasion a disastrous wreck, and block the road.)

As Captain Fuller with "The Texas" and her crew figure exclusively in the remainder of this wonderful chase, he thinks it eminently due them that the names of those actually engaged on the engine should be given. Federal reports of the affair have put under the command of Fuller a regiment or more of armed soldiers. Some illustrations show long trains of cars packed to overflowing with armed men.

From the time he stopped Brachen, a mile south of Adairsville, to the point where Andrews abandoned "The General," three miles north of Ringgold, he had with him only Peter J. Brachen as engineer, Henry Haney, fireman of the engine (who, at the suggestion of Brachen, stood at the brakes of the tender, and had for additional leverage a piece of timber run through the spokes of the brake-wheel), Flem Cox, an engineer on the road, who happened to be along, and fired the "Texas," and Alonzo Martin, train hand of the freight train left at Adairsville, who passed wood to Cox. Thus it is seen that Captain Fuller, Peter J. Brachen, Flem Cox, and Alonzo Martin were the members of the pursuing party *in toto*, during the last fifty-five miles of the chase.

As has been stated, Mr. Anthony Murphy, of Atlanta, rode on "The Texas" with Brachen from Adairsville to the point at which the Andrews raiders were caught, and there is no doubt he would have aided in their capture at the forfeit of his life had he been called upon to do so.

As the pursuers ran past Calhoun, an enthusiastic old gentleman, Mr. Richard Peters, himself a Northern man, and who died an honored citizen of Atlanta, offered a reward of a hundred dollars each for all the raiders captured. Had this promise been fulfilled Captain Fuller would have received $2,300, which no doubt he would have divided with his comrades in the pursuit.

At Calhoun Captain Fuller met the south-bound "day passenger train," delayed by his unexpected movements. He had his engine run slowly by the depot, and exchanged a few words with the excited crowd of people, who were amazed at the sudden appearance and disappearance of the runaway train which had passed there a few moments before. Here he also saw Ed Henderson, the telegraph operator at Dalton. Discovering that the line was down below Dalton, Henderson had gone down on the passenger train to try to repair the break in the wire. Seeing him, Fuller reached out his hand as he was running by and took the operator into the tender, and as they ran at the rate of a mile a minute he wrote the following dispatch:

> To General Ledbetter, Chattanooga:
> My train was captured this morning at Big Shanty, evidently by Federal soldiers in disguise. They are making rapidly for Chattanooga, and will no doubt burn the Chickamauga bridges in their rear, if I should fail to capture them. Please see that they do not pass Chattanooga.
> Signed, W. A. Fuller.

He handed this dispatch to the operator, and instructed him to put it through at all hazards when he should arrive at Dalton.

Just at that moment the pursuers came in sight of the raiders for the first time. They had halted two miles north of Calhoun and were removing a rail from the track. As the pursuers hove in sight, the raiders detached their third car and left it before Captain Fuller could reach them. Coupling this abandoned car to "The Texas," Captain Fuller got on top of it and began the race again. The rails had only been loosened and the intrepid conductor took the chances of running over them. From this point the raiders ran at a fearful rate, and the pursuers followed after them as fast as "The Texas" could go.

One mile and a half further up, the raiders detached another car in the front of the pursuers. This was witnessed by Fuller, who was standing on the rear end of the car he had coupled to when the raiders were first seen. He gave Brachen the signal, and he advanced slowly to the abandoned car and coupled it to the first one obtained in this way. Then getting on top of the newly captured one he was off again in the race with scarcely the loss of a moment's time.

Just in front of the raiders, and not more than a mile away, was an important railroad bridge over the Oostanaula river at Resaca. The pursuers had greatly feared that the raiders would gain time to burn this bridge, after passing over it. But they were pressed so hotly and so closely that they passed over the bridge as rapidly as the "General" could carry them. The pursuers were, therefore, greatly rejoiced on their arrival at Resaca to see that the bridge was standing, and that it had not been set on fire. The two cars picked up as described were switched off at Resaca, and the pursuers again had "The Texas" untrammelled. The race from Resaca to Dalton has seldom been paralleled. It is impossible to describe it.

At Dalton the telegraph operator was dropped, with instructions to put the dispatch to General Ledbetter through to the exclusion of all other matter. All was excitement at this point. The unusual spectacle of a wild engine flying through the town with only one car attached was bewildering indeed; and when Captain Fuller arrived and ran through, slacking his speed just enough to put the operator off the train, the excitement became intense. The operator was besieged on every side for an explanation, but he knew nothing save that contained in the dispatch.

Two miles north of Dalton, Andrews stopped. Some of his men climbed telegraph poles and cut the wire, while others were engaged in an effort to take up the track behind them. The operator at Dalton had sent the dispatch through to Ledbetter at Chattanooga; but just as he had finished and was holding his finger on the key, waiting for the usual "O. K," click went the key, and all was dead. He did not know until the next day that Captain Fuller's dispatch had reached its destination. Had the raiders been thirty seconds earlier in cutting the wire, the dispatch would not have gone through.

As it was Ledbetter received it, and not being able to hear anything further by telegraph or otherwise he had a regiment placed in ambush (some of the soldiers on either side of the track), and had a considerable part of the track taken up. This was about a mile from Chattanooga, so that by the intervention of the telegram Fuller had Andrews both front and rear.

Andrews was run away from the point where the wires were cut before any material damage was done to the track. The rails had been partially removed, but not so much as to prevent the safe passage over them of "The Texas" and her crew.

Now the last long race begins. The pursued and the pursuers are in sight of one another. In every straight line of the road, Andrews was in plain view. This tended to increase the interest and excitement, if, indeed, the thrilling scenes and incidents of the seconds as they flitted by could have been heightened. I say seconds, because minutes in this case would be too large to use for a unit of time. The experience, practice, and knowledge of machinery possessed by the engineers was brought into full play. "The Texas" was kept at a rate of one hundred and sixty-five pounds of steam, with the valve wide open. Brachen would appear a little pale sometimes, but he was encouraged by Fuller standing the full length of the tender before him, and watching around the curves. At every straight line in the road Andrews was sighted, and a yell went up from the throats of the pursuers, but they did not lose their wits.

Their aim was forward, onward, at all hazards. They were now convinced that Andrews had exhausted his supply of obstructive material, and were not so uneasy on that account. But as prudence is the better part of valor, and as they had so few men on board, they dared not approach too close, lest their little band should be fired upon; or what appeared to be a greater danger, Andrews might suddenly stop and give fight. Captain Fuller had only five person on "The Texas" besides himself, and all accounts heard by them at points below had placed Andrews's party as high as twenty or twenty-five. Fuller knew that the fire-arms he had gathered up early in the race, such as "squirrel guns," and most of them unloaded, would have but little showing in a hand-to-hand contest; so these things had to be considered as they sped along so swiftly. Another danger was to be feared—Andrews might stop, abandon "The General," let her drive back, and thus force a collision with the pursuers.

In approaching the tunnel, seven miles north of Dalton, our brave conductor slackened speed until he could see dimly through the smoke of "The General," which had only passed out of the further end by a few seconds, and was in sight beyond. For the next seven miles from Tunnel Hill to Ringgold, nothing occurred except a race between engines such as has never been excelled. When Ringgold was reached, both engines literally flew through the town, the "Texas" only about one-fourth of a mile behind. When the pursuers were passing through the north end of the town, Captain Fuller noticed a company of militia drilling. Their horses were hitched to the small shade trees near the muster grounds, and this fact fastened itself upon his mind.

In a few minutes the pursuers swung around the second short curve north of Ringgold, just in time to see Andrews slack his speed, and himself and his men jump off the "General" to seek concealment in the dense woods. The foliage of the trees and undergrowth was about half grown, and it would have been an easy matter to hide in the forest. When the raiders were first seen north of Ringgold, it was obvious that the heroic old "General" was almost exhausted. Her smoke was nearly white, and ran up at an angle of 45 degrees, while before that it lay flat, and appeared to the eyes of the pursuers as if fresh from the stack. When Andrews abandoned the "General," his engineer threw the lever back and gave the engine all the steam it had, but in his haste the brake was left on, so the engine was unable to drive back and collide with the "Texas," as Andrews had hoped it would.

The pursuers ran up to the "General" to which was attached one box car—the one historians and statesmen have so often said was fired and left to burn in a bridge below Ringgold. This car had been fired, but was easily extinguished. It had never been uncoupled from the "General" since Fuller left Atlanta with it that morning. Brachen hastily coupled the "Texas" to this car and the "General." Captain Fuller reminded Brachen of the militia company they had seen drilling at Ringgold a few minutes before, and encouraged him to go back there as soon as possible and tell of the capture of the "General," and to beseech the soldiers to mount their horses and come to his aid, as he, Flem Cox, and Alonzo Martin were already chasing through the woods after Andrews and his men. Mr. Murphy and Henry Haney went back to Ringgold with Brachen after the militia.

It was probably three minutes after the "General" was overtaken before Captain Fuller and his two comrades were ready to take to the woods, as they assisted in getting the car and two engines started back to Ringgold. The raiders, therefore, had the advantage and were deep in the forest before the woodland chase began. Besides, the reader will see at once that the raiders were fresh—that they had done no really hard work, except the fireman and engineer. They had not already run on foot more than twenty miles, as Fuller had done. After the pursuing party had gone about two miles through the woods, they came to a fifty-acre wheat field just in time to see the raiders cross the fence at the further side. It had been raining nearly all day, and the ground was wet. It was limestone soil, and almost as sticky as tar. The boots of the pursuers would clog up, and the mud on them would sometimes weigh doubtless two or three pounds. Another source of annoyance was the growing wheat, which was half leg high and very difficult to tread. Captain Fuller has said that it appeared to be up-hill every way that he ran.

Finally the woods beyond were reached, and, by accident, Captain Fuller and his two comrades got separated. In the afternoon four of the raiders were captured. About 8 p. m. Captain Fuller became completely exhausted. Some old farmers put him on a mule and carried him back to Ringgold, distant seven miles direct route, but by the one he was carried three times that distance. He lay down on the mule's back, and a man on either side held him on.

Soon after they arrived at Ringgold the down night passenger train came, and Captain Fuller was put on board and carried to Atlanta. At Tunnel Hill, seven miles south, a train of soldiers passed them on the way to the scene of interest. The Andrews Raiders had already been captured, and the "General" was safe on the side track at Ringgold, eight hours before. And this train of soldiers just spoken of is "the second pursuing train" that Pittenger so often speaks of in his "Capturing a Locomotive," and "Daring and Suffering."

We have followed Captain Fuller and his wise and intrepid men, in the pursuit of spies no less wise and intrepid, from the first step in an act which, under the usages of war in all countries, meant death to them if captured; and over that lamentable scene we drop the curtain. We have the testimony of reliable men that they were humanely treated while in prison. After a trial, conducted on the highest principles of military law and honour, eight of these spies were condemned and executed.

The following list gives the names of the Andrews raiders, all of whom were captured in the manner described:

J. J. Andrews,
Wilson Brown,
Marion Ross,
W. H. Campbell,
John Scott,
Perry G. Shadrack,
George D. Wilson,
Samuel Slavens.
These were tried and executed.
S. Robinson,
Ed. Mason,
Wm. Knight,
Robert Bruffum,
William Pittenger,
M. J. Hawkins,
I. Parroth,
W. Bensinger,
A. Wilson,
W. Reddie,
D. A. Dorsey,
I. R. Porter,
M. Wood,
W. Brown.
The last named fourteen were never tried.

Confederate Love Song.
Over the mountains of Winter,
And the cold, cold plains of snow,
Down in the valleys of Summer,
Calling my love I go.

And strong in my woe and passion,
I climb up the hills of Spring,
To listen if I hear his voice
In songs he used to sing.

I wait in the fields of Autumn,

And gather a feast of fruit,
And call my love to the banquet;
His lips are cold and mute.

I say to the wild bird flying:
"My darling sang sweet as you;
Fly o'er the earth in search of him,
And to the skies of blue."

I say to the wild-wood flowers:
"My love was a friend to you;
Send one of your fragrant spirits
To the cool Isles of Dew,"

"Gold-girt by a belt of moonbeams,
And seek on their gleaming shore
A breath of the vanished sweetness
For me his red lips bore."

I stand at the gates of Morning,
When the radiant angel, Light,
Draws back the great bolt of darkness,
And by the gates of Night,

When the hands of bright stars tremble
While clasping their lanterns bright;
And I hope to see him passing,
And touch his garments white.

O, love! if you hear me calling,
Flee not from the wailing cry;
Come from the grottoes of Silence
And hear me, or I die!

Stand out on the hills of Echo;
The sensitive, pulsing air
Will thrill at your softest whisper—
Speak to me, love, from there!

O, love, if I hear you calling,
Though far on the heavenly side,
My voice will float on the billow:
"Come to your spirit bride."

—Mary A. H. Gay.

To the Reader,

Who has kindly perused these sketches, I would say, as they have already attained length and breadth not anticipated from the beginning, I will withhold the sequels to many of them for, perhaps, another volume of reminiscences.

Were I possessed of the Sam Weller genius and versatility, and the happy faculty of making the reader wish I had written more, I would throw open the doors of the store-house of my war memories, a structure as capacious as the "Southern Confederacy" and canopied by the firmament, and invite the public to enter and share with me the treasures hidden there. The coruscations of wit and the profound displays of wisdom by many who donned Confederate grey and went forth in manhood's prime to battle for the principles of their country, would employ the minds and feast the intellect of the most erudite. There are living, glowing pictures hanging upon the walls which delineate the mysteries of humanity in all its varied forms, and, by example, demonstrate that we often spurn with holy horror that which is better far than that which we embrace with all the fervour of affection.

I would resurrect the loftiest patriotism from the most humble graves in the Southern land, and prove by heroic deeds and noble acts that valour on the battlefield was as often illustrated by the humble soldier whose name has not been preserved in "storied urn," as by the gallant son of chivalrous ancestors who commanded the applause of an admiring multitude. I would place by the side of those greatest of chieftains, Robert E. Lee, and our impregnable "Stonewall" Jackson and Albert Sidney Johnston, many of our soldiers "unknown to fame," in faded grey jackets and war-worn pants, and challenge the world for the difference. I would dwell with loving interest upon the innumerable sad, sweet faces of the mighty throng of bereaved mothers, sisters and aunts, out of whose lives all light had gone, and who, though hopeless, uttered no words of complaint against our cause or its leader, but toiled on with unswerving faith and souls that borrowed the lustre of heaven.

All these sad things in my gallery I would clothe in living form and glowing colour. And, saddest of all, I would live over with them that melancholy period when the very few, comparatively, that were left of the noble defenders of our principles, came back, not with buoyant step and victor crown, but with blighted hopes and despondent mien to desolated homes and decimated families. Under the new regime I would tell of despair and suicide, of hope, energy and success; I would tell how I have lived in this gallery—its silent occupants my companions and friends, my inspiration to useful deeds.

There is not a day that I do not arouse by muffled tread the slumbering echoes of this past, and look upon the cherished souvenirs of the patriotic friends now roaming the beautiful gardens of Paradise, or sleeping the mystic waiting of the resurrection. I ponder upon their lives, their ambitions, their disappointments, and it requires no effort of the imagination to animate those dead forms and invest them with living attributes. And daily, in imagination I weave for them a laurel crown that shall grow greener and greener as the cycles of Time speed on to Eternity.

Appendix

The author has selected the article, "Gleanings from General Sherman's Despatches," as an appendix for these sketches, not because of a desire to keep up the issues of the war between the States (for she would gladly bury them so deep they could never be resurrected until the great Judge of all issues calls them up to receive sentence by his unerring judgment), but rather, because of the persistent insistence of Northern Republicans to make it appear to the world that the Southern people are a semi-barbarous people, solely responsible for the war and altogether unworthy fraternal consideration in the compact called the Union.

The article mentioned, "Gleanings from General Sherman's Despatches," is to be found, word for word, in *The Southern Magazine*, May, 1873, Vol. XII. Baltimore: Turnbull Brothers.

GLEANINGS FROM GENERAL SHERMAN'S DESPATCHES.

Those thick, loosely-bound octavos printed on soft and rather dingy paper, which Congress publishes and distributes under the name of Public Documents, are not generally considered very entertaining reading. But there are exceptions; and one of these is the report of the joint committee of Congress on the conduct of the war. Indeed, compared with such mild pastorals as "Some Accounts of the Cheese Manufacture in Central New York," or "Remarks on the Cultivation of Alfalfa in Western Tennessee," it is quite luridly sensational, and in parts reminds us of those striking reports of the Duke of Alva to his royal master, which have been disinterred in the dusty archives of Simancas. As a study of congressional nature, military nature, and human nature generally, in its least attractive aspects, these eight stout volumes are richly worth perusal.

Here the reader is allowed to peep behind the scenes of that portentous drama; here he may see the threads of the intrigues that centred in Washington; may hear a petty newspaper correspondent demonstrating, with an animation that we can scarcely ascribe to fervid patriotism, the incapacity, the ignorance and even the doubtful "loyalty" of the commander-in-chief; may see private malignity and vindictiveness putting on grand Roman airs, and whispering debaters draping themselves in the *toga* of Brutus.

However, it is not with these aspects of the reports that we at present have to do, but with the despatches of General Sherman on his march through Georgia and South Carolina. A great deal of fiction and some verse,[1] we believe, have been written about this famous march or grand foray; but here we have the plain matter-of-fact statement of things as they were, and they form a luminous illustration of the advance of civilization in the nineteenth century as exemplified in the conduct of invasions, showing how modern philanthropy and humanitarianism, while acknowledging that for the present war is a necessary evil, still strive to mitigate its horrors and spare all avoidable suffering to non-combatants. For this purpose we have thought it worthwhile to reproduce a few of the most striking extracts illustrating the man, his spirit, and his work.

A kind of keynote is sounded in the despatches to General Stoneman, of May 14, which, after ordering him to "press down the valley strong," ends with the words, "Pick up whatever provisions and plunder you can."

On June 3, the question of torpedoes is discussed, and General Stedman receives the following instructions: "If torpedoes are found in the possession of an enemy to our rear, you may cause them to be put on the ground and tested by wagon loads of prisoners, or, if need be, by citizens implicated in their use. In like manner, if a torpedo is suspected on any part of the railroad, order the point to be tested by a carload of prisoners or citizens implicated, drawn by a long rope." "Implicated," we suppose here meant "residing or captured in the neighbourhood."

On July 7, we have an interesting dispatch to General Garrard on the subject of the destruction of the factories at Roswell.

> Their utter destruction is right, and meets my entire approval; and to make the matter complete, you will arrest the owners and

---

1. One of these poems, "*Marching Through Georgia*," we learn by the evidence, was a favourite canticle of Murray, the kidnapper and butcher of Captain Polynesius.

employees and send them under guard charged with treason, to Marietta, and I will see as to any man in America hoisting the French flag and then devoting his labour and capital to supplying armies in open hostility to our government, and claiming the benefit of his neutral flag. Should you, under the impulse of anger, natural at contemplating such perfidy, hang the wretch, I approve the act beforehand.... I repeat my orders that you arrest all people, male and female, connected with those factories, no matter what the clamour, and let them foot it, under guard, to Marietta, whence I will send them by cars to the North. Destroy and make the same disposition of all mills, save small flouring mills, manifestly for local use; but all saw mills and factories dispose of effectually; and useful labourers, excused by reason of their skill as manufacturers, from conscription, are as much prisoners as if armed.

On the same day he further enlarges on this subject in a despatch to General Halleck:

General Garrard reports to me that he is in possession of Roswell, where were several very valuable cotton and wool factories in full operation, also paper mills, all of which, by my order, he destroyed by fire. They had been for years engaged exclusively at work for the Confederate government; and the owner of the woollen factory displayed the French flag, but, as he failed to show the United States flag also, General Garrard burned it also. The main cotton factory was valued at a million of United States dollars. The cloth on hand is reserved for the use of the United States hospitals; and I have ordered General Garrard to arrest for treason all owners and employees, foreign and native, and send them to Marietta, whence I will send them North. Being exempt from conscription, they are as much governed by the rules of war as if in the ranks. The women can find employment in Indiana. This whole region was devoted to manufactories, but I will destroy everyone of them.

There are two points specially worth notice in this despatch. The first, that *since* these men and women, by reason of sex, or otherwise, are exempt from conscription, they are, therefore, as much subject to the rules of war as if in the ranks. Why not do less violence to logic and state frankly that factory hands were in demand in Indiana? The next point is that the Roswell factories, whether French property or not, were destroyed because they were making cloth for the Confederate government, followed presently by the declaration that every manufactory in that region shall be destroyed, evidently without reference to its products or their destination. How much franker it would have been to have added to this last sentence, "and thus get rid of so many competitors to the factories of the North." The South must learn that while she may bear the burden of protective tariffs, she must not presume to share their benefits. Another despatch to General Halleck, of July 9, again refers to these factories. After referring to the English and French ownership, comes this remark:

> I take it a neutral is no better than one of our citizens, and we would not respect the property of one of our own citizens engaged in supplying a hostile army.

This is the kind of logic proverbially used by the masters of legions. A despatch to General Halleck, of July 13, gives General Sherman's opinion of two great and philanthropic institutions. Speaking of "fellows hanging about" the army, he says

> The Sanitary and Christian Commission are enough to eradicate all traces of Christianity from our minds.

July 14, to General J. E. Smith, at Allatoona:

> If you entertain a bare suspicion against any family, send it North. Any loafer or suspicious person seen at any time should be imprisoned and sent off. If guerrillas trouble the road or wires they should be shot without mercy.

September 8, to General Webster after the capture of Atlanta:

> Don't let any citizens come to Atlanta; not one. I won't allow trade or manufactures of any kind, but you will remove all the present population, and make Atlanta a pure military town.

To General Halleck he writes:

> I am not willing to have Atlanta encumbered by the families of our enemies.

Of this wholesale depopulation, General Hood complained, by flag of truce, as cruel and contrary to the usages of civilized nations and customs of war, receiving this courteous and gentlemanly reply (September 12):

I think I understand the laws of civilized nations and the 'customs of war;' but, if at a loss at any time, I know where to seek for information to refresh my memory.

General Hood made the correspondence, or part of it, public, on which fact, General Sherman remarks to General Halleck: "Of course, he is welcome, for the more he arouses the indignation of the Southern masses, the bigger will be the pill of bitterness they will have to swallow."

About the middle of September, General Sherman, being still in Atlanta, endeavoured to open private communication with Governor Brown and Vice-President Stephens, whom he knew to be at variance with the administration at Richmond on certain points of public policy. Mr. Stephens refused to reply to a verbal message, but wrote to Mr. King, the intermediary, that if the general would say that there was any prospect of their agreeing upon "terms to be submitted to the action of their respective governments," he would, as requested, visit him at Atlanta. The motives urged by Mr. King were General Sherman's extreme desire for peace, and to hit upon "some plan of terminating this fratricidal war without the further effusion of blood." But in General Sherman's despatch of September 14, to Mr. Lincoln, referring to these attempted negotiations, the humanitarian point of view is scarcely so prominent. He says:

> It would be a magnificent stroke of policy if I could, without surrendering a foot of ground or principle, arouse the latent enmity to Davis.

On October 20, he writes to General Thomas from Summerville, giving an idea of his plan of operations:

> Out of the forces now here and at Atlanta, I propose to organize an efficient army of 60,000 to 65,000 men, with which I propose to destroy Macon, Augusta, and it may be, Savannah and Charleston. By this I propose to demonstrate the vulnerability of the South, and make its inhabitants feel that war and individual ruin are synonymous terms.

Despatch of October 22, to General Grant:

> I am now perfecting arrangements to put into Tennessee a force able to hold the line of the Tennessee, while I break up the railroad in front of Dalton, including the city of Atlanta, and push into Georgia and break up all its railroads and depots, capture

its horses and negroes, make desolation everywhere; destroy the factories at Macon, Milledgeville and Augusta, and bring up with 60,000 men on the seashore about Savannah and Charleston.

To General Thomas, from Kingston, November 2:

Last night we burned Rome, and in two more days will burn Atlanta (which he was then occupying).

December 5:

Blair can burn the bridges and culverts and burn enough barns to mark the progress of his head of columns.

December 18, to General Grant, from near Savannah:

With Savannah in our possession, at some future time, if not now, we can punish South Carolina as she deserves, and as thousands of people in Georgia hope we will do. I do sincerely believe that the whole United States, north and south, would rejoice to have this army turned loose on South Carolina, to devastate that State in the manner we have done in Georgia.

A little before this he announces to Secretary Stanton that he knows what the people of the South are fighting for. What do our readers suppose? To ravage the North with sword and fire, and crush them under their heel? Surely it must be some such delusion that inspires this ferocity of hatred, unmitigated by even a word of compassion. He may speak for himself:

Jefferson Davis has succeeded perfectly in inspiring his people with the truth that liberty and government are worth fighting for.

This was their unpardonable crime.

December 22, to General Grant:

If you can hold Lee, I could go on and smash South Carolina all to pieces.

On the 18th General Halleck writes:

Should you capture Charleston, I hope that by some accident the place may be destroyed; and if a little salt should be sown upon its site, it may prevent the growth of future crops of nullification and secession.

To this General Sherman replies, December 24:

> This war differs from European wars in this particular—we are not only fighting hostile armies, but hostile people; and must make old and young, rich and poor, feel the hard hand of war, as well as their organized armies. I will bear in mind your hint as to Charleston, and don't think *salt* will be necessary. When I move, the Fifteenth corps will be on the right of the right wing, and their position will naturally throw them into Charleston first; and, if you have studied the history of that corps, you will have remarked that they generally do their work up pretty well. The truth is, the whole army is burning with insatiable desire to wreak vengeance upon South Carolina. I almost tremble for her fate, but she deserves all that seems in store for her.
> I look upon Columbia as quite as bad as Charleston, and I doubt if we shall spare the public buildings there as we did at Milledgeville.

And now we look with interest for the despatches that would settle the vexed question as to whether Sherman or his officers, acting under his orders, burned Columbia on the 17th of February. Unfortunately, a paternal government, not thinking it good that the truth should be known, has suppressed all the despatches between the 16th and the 21st, and every other allusion to the transaction.

On the 23rd, he writes to General Kilpatrick: "Let the whole people know the war is now against them, because their armies flee before us and do not defend their country or frontier as they should. It is pretty nonsense for Wheeler and Beauregard and such vain heroes to talk of our warring against women and children and prevent us reaching their homes."

If, therefore, an army defending their country can prevent invaders from reaching their homes and families, the latter have a right to that protection; but if the invaders can break through and reach these homes, these are justified in destroying women and children. Certainly this is a great advance on the doctrine and practice of the dark ages. Another extraordinary moral consequence flows from this insufficiency of defence:

> If the enemy fails to defend his country, we may rightfully appropriate what we want." Here, now, is a nice question of martial law or casuistry, solved with the simplicity of an ancient Roman. In other words, when in the enemy's country, the army

shall be strictly careful not to seize, capture or appropriate to military or private uses, any property—that it cannot get.

They (the Southern people) have lost all title to property, and can lose nothing not already forfeited.

What, nothing? Not merely the houses we had built, the lands we had tilled, the churches we worshipped in—had we forfeited the right to drink of the streams, to behold the sun, to breathe the free air of heaven? What unheard of, what inconceivable crime had we committed that thus closed every gate of mercy and compassion against us, and provoked an utterance which has but one parallel—the death warrant signed by Philip II. against all Netherlanders? General Sherman has himself told us what it was: We had dared to act on the "truth that liberty and government are worth fighting for."

On March 15, he writes to General Gillmore, advising him to draw forces from Charleston and Savannah (both then in Federal hands) to destroy a railroad, etc.:

As to the garrisons of those places I don't feel disposed to be over-generous, and should not hesitate to burn Savannah, Charleston and Wilmington, or either of them, if the garrisons were needed.

Such are some of the results of our gleanings in this field. Is it any wonder that after reading them we fervently echo General Sherman's devout aspiration:

I do wish the fine race of men that people the United States should rule and determine the future destiny of America.

Sherman's March to the Sea

It is a proud thing for Americans to feel that there is little to bring the blush of shame to their cheeks in the contemplation of their country's history. It is a glorious thing for our young manhood to know that the annals of their race tell of the earnest and upward progress of a people, Christian from the first, toward an ever higher civilization. It is well to reflect that when the ruthless hand of war has turned American citizenship from the paths of peace it could do little more than array strong man against sturdy foeman in an honest battle for principle, and that outrage and pillage in our broad domain have been the almost undisputed heritage of the Aborigines.

Enduring with patient fortitude the raids of savage foes upon our early frontiers, meeting the armed invasion of foreign hosts with a resistance vigorous but manly, pressing our own victorious arms to the very citadel of our Mexican neighbours without spoliation or rapine, it is sad to realize that it remained for an internecine conflict, where brother stood against brother, for an invasion by an army void of pretext of reprisal or revenge, to write upon American warfare the stigma of vandalism, rapacity and theft.

The movement from Atlanta to Savannah, which figured in history as "The March to the Sea," was, from the standpoint of the tactician, no great achievement; it involved no more than the passage of an invincible army across some three hundred miles of country, where it could gather supplies upon its way, to effect a junction with its naval allies at a practically defenceless city. It was peculiarly lacking in the daring which is customarily ascribed to it, for it was made, practically, without resistance and along a route where no considerable force of the enemy could have been encountered. It was not a venture in the dark with a conclusion to be determined by circumstances; for the authorities at Washington were fully advised of its author's purpose, and Gen. Sherman was assured that he would meet a formidable fleet at Savannah before he undertook it.

It was no more nor less than the yielding, by this most typical barbarian conqueror of the Nineteenth century, to the spirit of pillage and excess which distinguished his prototypes in the days of the Goths and Vandals, when the homes and firesides of their enemies were at their mercy. It was a campaign remarkable only for the revival of military methods abandoned since Attila the Hun. It was, nevertheless, as carefully planned as it was ruthlessly executed. It was no sudden impulse which laid the torch to every roof-tree upon the invading army's path. It was no spirit of retaliation for vigorous but ineffective resistance which goaded these conquerors to excess, for out of 62,204 men who began the march but 103 lost their lives before they reached Savannah. It was simply the grasping of the amplest opportunity by a man who glories in looting and destruction, and to whom human misery was a subject for jest.

At the outset let us understand that General Sherman, through all that portion of his career which began with the destruction of Atlanta, was acting upon a plan and a theory devised and adopted weeks before; that his own actions and that of his army were in no sense impulsive, but in every way controlled by premeditation, and that our authority for such a conclusion lies in the repeated statements of the general himself.

With the brutal frankness which was one of his characteristics, he wrote on September 4th, 1864, in a letter to General Halleck, which he reproduces in his autobiography:

> If the people raise a howl against my barbarity and cruelty, I will answer that war is war and not popularity-seeking.
>
> I knew, of course that such a measure would be strongly criticized, but made up my mind to do it with the absolute certainty of its justness, and that time would sanction its wisdom. I knew that the people of the South would read in this measure two important conclusions; one that we were in earnest, and the other that if they were sincere in their common and popular clamour *'to die in the last ditch,'* the opportunity would soon come.

The cold-blooded candour of this statement leaves little doubt of the temperature of the well-springs which fed that organ of General Sherman corresponding to the heart of an ordinary man; but if evidence were wanting of his absolute unconcern for the sufferings of others when his own plans might be interfered with to the slightest degree, it might be found in his answer to General Hood's proposition for an exchange of prisoners. "Some of these prisoners," he says, "had already escaped and got in, and had described the pitiable condition of the remainder." He had at that time about two thousand Confederate prisoners available for exchange.:

> These I offered to exchange for Stoneman, Buell, and such of my own army as would make up the equivalent; but I would not exchange for his prisoners generally, because I knew these would have to be sent to their own regiments away from my army, whereas all we could give him could at once be put to duty in his immediate army.

No possible suffering which his unfortunate companions in arms could be forced to bear by reason of the Confederates' lack of supplies with which to feed and clothe them, could induce him to exchange for men who would not strengthen his own immediate army!

Geneseric, the Vandal, is said to have been "cruel to blood thirstiness, cunning, unscrupulous and grasping; but he possessed great military talents and his manner of life was austere." Let the impartial reader of history say how nearly the barbarian who marched to the sea in the nineteenth century, approached to his prototype of the fifth century. One is not surprised, therefore, to find this man writing to General Hood on September 7th, 1864, that he "deemed it to the interest of the United States that the citizens now residing in Atlanta should remove."

In the midst of a region desolated by war, their fathers, husbands, brothers, sons, in the army hundreds of miles away, it was "deemed to be in the interest of the United States" that the helpless women and children of Atlanta should be driven from their homes to find such shelter as God gives the ravens and the beasts of the wood. It was a course that wrung from General Hood these forceful words of reply:

> Permit me to say that the unprecedented measure you propose transcends, in studied and ingenious cruelty, all acts ever before brought to my attention in the dark history of war. In the name of God and humanity I protest, believing that you will find you are expelling from their homes and firesides the wives and children of a brave people.

To this burning arraignment General Sherman could find no better answer than argument concerning the right of States to secede. But it was followed on September 11th by an appeal from the mayor and councilmen of Atlanta which would have touched a heart of stone. It was humble, it was earnest, it was pitiful. It provoked these words in reply:

> I have your letter of the 11th in the nature of a petition to revoke my orders removing all the inhabitants from Atlanta. I have read it carefully, and give full credit to your statements of distress that will be occasioned, and yet shall not revoke my orders, because they were not designed to meet the humanities of the case, but to prepare for the future struggles in which millions of good people outside of Atlanta have an interest.

The same unalterable resolution must have dominated Geneseric, the Vandal, when he prepared for his fourteen days sacking of Rome. The vandal of the fifth century had at least the pretext of reprisal for his actions; the vandal of the nineteenth century could find no better plea for his barbarity than that it might wring the hearts of absent men until they would sacrifice principle and honour for the relief of their loved ones.

President Davis says:

> Since Alva's atrocious cruelties to the non-combatant population of the low countries in the sixteenth century, the history of war records no instance of such barbarous cruelty as this order designed to perpetrate. It involved the immediate expulsion from their homes and only means of subsistence of thousands of unoffending women and children, whose husbands and fathers were either in the army, in Northern prisons, or had died in battle.

At the time appointed the women and children were expelled from their houses, and, before they were passed within our lines, complaint was generally made that the Federal officers and men who were sent to guard them had robbed them of the few articles of value they had been permitted to take from their homes. The cowardly dishonesty of the men appointed to carry out this order, was in perfect harmony with the temper and the spirit of the order.

It was on the 12th day of November, 1864, that "The March to the Sea" began. Hood's army had been followed to Tennessee, and Sherman's forces had destroyed the railroad during their return trip to Atlanta. They were now ready to abandon the ruins of the Gate City for fresher and more lucrative fields of havoc. It is fair to General Sherman to say that his plans and intentions had been fully communicated to the authorities at Washington, and that they met with the thorough approbation of General Halleck, then Chief of Staff.

General Halleck will be remembered as the hero who won immortal fame before Corinth. With an immensely superior force he so thoroughly entrenched himself before that city that he not only held his position during General Beauregard's occupancy of the town, but retained it for several days after the Confederate evacuation. He retired from active service after this, his only piece of campaigning, to act in an advisory capacity at Washington, and it was he who wrote these encouraging words to Sherman at Atlanta:

> The course which you have pursued in removing rebel families from Atlanta, and in the exchange of prisoners, is fully approved by the War Department.... Let the disloyal families thus stripped go to their husbands, fathers, and natural protectors in the rebel ranks.... I would destroy every mill and factory within reach, which I did not want for my own use.... I have endeavoured to impress these views upon our commanders for the last two years. *You are almost the only one who has properly applied them.*

These words of encouragement fell upon willing ears. No one knew better than Sherman how to read the sentiments between those lines; he understood the motives which moved their doughty author as thoroughly as when later the same hand gathered courage to advise him in plain unvarnished words to wipe the city of Charleston off the face of the earth, and sow her site with salt. The valiant chief of staff, who urged on campaigns from a point sufficiently to the rear, had found at last a man who would carry out his instructions, and the war upon women and children was about to begin.

General Halleck was not the sole confidant of General Sherman's plan. Less than a month before the memorable march was undertaken, he telegraphed to General Grant:

> I propose that we break up the railroad from Chattanooga forward, and that we strike out for Milledgeville, Millen and Savannah. Until we can repopulate Georgia, it is useless for us to occupy it, but the utter destruction of its roads, houses and peo-

ple will cripple their military resources. I can make this march, and make Georgia howl!

Sir Walter Raleigh conceived and attempted to execute the plan of exterminating the Irish race, and colonizing their lands from England. The Sultan of Turkey is about to carry out a similar policy with his Armenians.

The difference between these other exterminators and Sherman, is that they expected to be met at the doors of the homes they intended to destroy by men capable of offering resistance, while the American General knew he would have to do with women and children alone.

He evidently met with some expostulation from General Grant, for he afterwards telegraphed him that he would:

> Infinitely prefer to make a wreck of the road and the country from Chattanooga and Atlanta, including the latter city, send back all wounded and unserviceable men, and with the effective army move through Georgia, smashing things to the sea.

Receiving no answer to this latter dispatch, he did not hesitate to execute the campaign as he had planned it, and in his own language proceeded to "make the interior of Georgia feel the weight of war."

Sherman and his staff rode out of the Gate City at 7 o'clock in the morning of the 16th.

> Behind us lay Atlanta, smouldering and in ruins, the black smoke rising high in the air and hanging like a pall over the ruined city. Some band, by accident, struck up the anthem of '*John Brown's soul goes marching on*'. The men caught up the strain, and never before or since have I heard the chorus of '*Glory, glory, hallelujah!*' done with more spirit or in better harmony of time and place.

To the credit of the slandered soul of that other marauder, let us say, that John Brown's lawless warfare was upon men alone, and that booty formed no part of his incentive.

Knowing that no effective resistance was to be expected, Sherman so scattered his columns that the sixty-mile "swath" which it was his purpose to devastate, was covered by them with ease. In order that the work might be thoroughly and effectively done, a sufficient number of men were detailed for that branch of military service peculiar to Sherman's army, and known as "bummers." The general says:

These interesting individuals alway arose before day and preceded the army on its march."

Although this foraging was attended with great danger and hard work, there seemed to be a charm about it that attracted the soldiers, and it was a privilege to be detailed on such a party.

No doubt (with that same blunt frankness), many acts of pillage, robbery and violence were committed by these parties of foragers usually called 'bummers'; for I have since heard of jewellery taken from women, and the plunder of articles that never reached the commissary.

But these playful fellows, in spite of such indiscretions, were never more to the general than an exhibition of that charming humour invariably apparent in him in the presence of human suffering.

We may gather an idea of them from the following description given by a correspondent of the *New York Herald,* who accompanied the army:

Any man who has seen the object that the name applies to will acknowledge that it was admirably selected. Fancy a ragged man, bleached by the smoke of many a pine-knot fire, mounted on a scraggy mule without a saddle, with a gun, a knap-sack, a butcher-knife and a plug hat, stealing his way through the pine forests far out in the flanks of a column, keen on the scent of rebels, or bacon, or silver spoons, or coin, or anything valuable, and you have him in your mind. Think how you would admire him if you were a lone woman, with a family of small children, far from help, when he blandly inquired where you kept your valuables! Think how you would smile when he pried open your chests with his bayonet, or knocked to pieces your tables, pianos and chairs, tore your bed clothing into three-inch strips and scattered them about the yard. The 'bummers' say it takes too much time to use keys. Colour is no protection from the rough raiders. They go through a negro cabin in search of diamonds and gold watches with just as much freedom and vivacity as they 'loot' the dwelling of a wealthy planter. They appear to be possessed of a spirit of 'pure cussedness.'

One incident, illustrative of many, will suffice. A bummer stepped into a house and inquired for sorghum. The lady of the house presented a jug, which he said was too heavy, so he merely filled his canteen. Then taking a huge wad of tobacco from his mouth he thrust it into the jug. The lady inquired, in wonder, why he spoiled that which he did not want. 'Oh, some feller'll come along and taste that sorghum and think you've poisoned him, then he'll burn your d——d old house.' There are hundreds of these mounted men with the column, and they go everywhere. Some of them are loaded down with silverware, gold coin, and other valuables. I hazard nothing in saying three fifths (in value) of the personal property of the country we have passed through was taken by Sherman's army.

In an address delivered before the Association of the Maryland Line, Senator Zeb Vance, of North Carolina, has laid the vigorous touch of his characteristic English upon the void until it stands out in barbarous bold relief, so far beyond the pencil of the present writer that he best serves his readers by quoting:

> With reference to his famous and infamous march, I wish to say that I hope I am too much of a man to complain of the natural and inevitable hardships, or even cruelties of war; but of the manner in which this army treated the peaceful and defenseless inhabitants in the reach of his columns, all civilization should complain.
>
> There are always stragglers and *desperadoes* following in the wake of an army, who do some damage to and inflict some outrages upon helpless citizens, in spite of all efforts of commanding officers to restrain and punish; but when a general organizes a corps of thieves and plunderers as a part of his invading army, and licenses beforehand their outrages, he and all who countenance, aid or abet, invite the execration of mankind. This peculiar arm of military service, it is charged and believed, was instituted by General Sherman in his invasion of the Southern States. Certain it is that the operations of his 'Bummer Corps' were as regular and as unrebuked, if not as much commended for efficiency, as any other division of his army, and their atrocities are often justified or excused, on the ground that '*such is war.*'

In his own official report of his operations in Georgia, he says:

> We consumed the corn and fodder in the region of country thirty miles either side of a line from Atlanta to Savannah, also the sweet potatoes, hogs, sheep and poultry, and carried off more than ten thousand horses

and mules. I estimate the damage done to Georgia at one-hundred million dollars, at least twenty million of which inured to our benefit, and the remainder was simply waste and destruction!

The 'remainder' delicately alluded to, that is say damage done the unresisting inhabitants to over and above the seizing of necessary army supplies, consisted in private houses burned, stock shot down and left to rot, bed clothes, money, watches, spoons, plate and ladies' jewellery stolen, etc., etc. A lane of desolation sixty miles wide through the heart of three great states, marked by more burnings and destructions than ever followed in the wake of the widest cyclone that ever laid forest low!

And all done, not to support an invading army, but for 'pure waste and destruction'; to punish the crime of rebellion, not in the persons of those who had brought these about, but of peaceful non-combatants, the tillers of the soil, the women and the children, the aged and feeble, and the poor slaves! A silver spoon was evidence of disloyalty, a ring on a lady's finger was a sure proof of sympathy with rebellion, whilst a gold watch was *prima facie* evidence of the most damnable guilt on the part of the wearer. These obnoxious earmarks of treason must be seized and confiscated for private use—for *'such is war!'* If these failed, and they sometimes did, torture of the inhabitants was freely employed to force disclosure. Sometimes with noble rage at their disappointment, the victims were left dead, as a warning to all others who should dare hide a jewel or a family trinket from the cupidity of a soldier of the Union.

No doubt the stern necessity for such things caused great pain to those who inflicted, but the Union must be restored, and how could that be done whilst a felonious gold watch or a treasonable spoon was suffered to remain in the land, giving aid and comfort to rebellion? For *'such is war.'* Are such things war indeed? Let us see. Eighty-four years before that time, there was a war, in that same country; it was a rebellion, too, and an English nobleman led the troops of Great Britain through that same region, over much of the same route, in his efforts to subdue that rebellion. The people through whose land he marched were bitterly hostile, they shot his foraging parties, his sentinels and stragglers, they fired upon him from every wood.

He and his troops had every motive to hate and punish those

rebellious and hostile people. It so happens that the original order-book of Lord Cornwallis is in possession of the North Carolina Historical Society. I have seen and read it. Let us make a few extracts and see what he considered war, and what he thought to be the duty of a civilized soldier towards non-combatants and the helpless:

> Camp Near Beatty's Ford,
> January 28, 1781.
>
> Lord Cornwallis has so often expressed the zeal and good will of the army that he has not the slightest doubt that the officers and soldiers will most cheerfully submit to the ill conveniences that must naturally attend war, so remote from water carriage and the magazines of the army. The supply of rum for a time will be absolutely impossible, and that of meal very uncertain. It is needless to point out to the officers the necessity of preserving the strictest discipline, and of preventing the oppressed people from suffering violence by the hands from whom they are taught to look for protection.

Now, General Sherman was fighting, as he said, for the sole purpose of restoring the Union, and for making the people of the rebellious States look to the United States alone for protection; does any act or order of his anywhere indicate a similar desire of protecting the people from suffering at the hands of those whose duty it was to protect them? Again:

> Headquarters, Lansler's Plantation,
> February 2, 1781.
>
> Lord Cornwallis is highly displeased that several houses have been set on fire today during the march—a disgrace to the army—and he will punish with the utmost severity any person or persons who shall be found guilty of committing so disgraceful an outrage. His lordship requests the commanding officers of the corps will endeavor to find the persons who set fire to the houses today.

Now think of the march of Sherman's army which could be discovered a great way off by the smoke of homesteads by day and the lurid glare of flames by night, from Atlanta to Savannah, from Columbia to Fayetteville, and suppose that such an order as this had been issued by its commanding officers and rigidly executed, would not the mortality have been quite equal to that of a great battle?

Arriving in Fayetteville on the 10th of January, 1865, he not only burned the arsenal, one of the finest in the United States, which perhaps he might properly have done, but also burned five private dwelling houses nearby; he burned the principal printing offices, that of the old 'Fayetteville Observer;' he burned the old Bank of North Carolina, eleven large warehouses, five cotton mills and quite a number of private dwellings in other parts of the town, whilst in the suburbs almost a clean sweep was made; in one locality nine houses were burned. Universally houses were gutted before they were burned, and after everything portable was secured the furniture was ruthlessly destroyed, pianos on which perhaps rebel tunes had been played—'Dixie' or 'My Maryland'—disloyal bureaus, traitorous tables and chairs were cut to pieces with axes, and frequently, after all this damage, fire was applied and all consumed.

Carriages and vehicles of all kinds were wantonly destroyed or burned; instances could be given of old men who had the shoes taken from their feet, the hats from their heads and clothes from their persons; and their wives and children subjected to like treatment. In one instance, as the marauders left they shot down a dozen cattle belonging to an old man, and then left their carcasses lying in the yard. Think of that, and then remember the grievance of the Pennsylvania Dutch farmers who came in all seriousness to complain to General Longstreet in the Gettysburg campaign, of the outrage which some of his ferocious rebels had committed upon them *by 'milking their cows.'* On one occasion, at Fayetteville, four gentlemen were hung up by the neck until nearly dead to force them to disclose where their valuables were hidden, and one of them was shot to death. Again:

> Headquarters Dobbins House,
> February 17, 1781.
>
> Lord Cornwallis is very sorry to be obliged to call the attention of the officers of the army to the repeated orders against plundering, and he assures the officers that if their duty to their king and country, and their feelings for humanity are not sufficient to force their obedience to them, he must, however reluctantly, make use of such

powers as the military laws have placed in his hands.... It is expected that captains will exert themselves to keep good order and to prevent plundering. Any officer *who looks on with indifference and does not do his utmost to prevent shameful marauding, will be considered in a more criminal light than the persons who commit these scandalous crimes,* which must bring disgrace and ruin on His Majesty's Service. All foraging parties will give receipts for supplies taken by them.

Now, taking it for granted that Lord Cornwallis, a distinguished soldier and a gentleman, is an authority on the rights of war, could there be found anywhere a more damnatory comment upon the practices of General Sherman and his army? Again:

> Headquarters, Freelands,
> February 28, 1781.
>
> Memorandum:—A watch found by the regiment of Bose. The owner may have it from the adjutant of the regiment upon proving property.'

Another:

> Smith's Plantation, March 1, 1781.
>
> Brigade Orders. A woman having been robbed of a watch, a black silk handkerchief, a gallon of peach brandy and a shirt, and as, by the description, by a soldier of the guards, the camp and every man's kit is to be immediately searched for the same by the officers of the brigade

Are there any poets in the audience, or other persons in whom the imaginative faculty has been largely cultivated? If so, let me beg him to do me the favour of conceiving, if he can, and make manifest to me, the idea of a notice of a lost watch being given, in general orders, by William Tecumseh Sherman, and the offer to return it on proof of property by the rebel owner! Let him imagine, if he can, the searching of every man's kit in the army for a stolen watch, a shirt, a black silk handkerchief and a gallon of peach brandy! Sherman says 'such is war.' I venture to say that up to the period when that 'great march' taught us the contrary, no humane general or civilized people in Christendom believed that *'such was war.'* Has civilization gone backward since Lord Cornwallis' day? Have arson and vulgar theft been ennobled into heroic virtues? If so, when and by whom? Has the art of discovering a poor man's hidden treasure by fraud or torture been elevated into the strategy which wins a campaign? If so, when and by whom?

No, it will not do to slur over these things by a vague reference to the inevitable cruelties of war. The time is fast coming when the conduct of that campaign will be looked upon in the light of real humanity, and investigated in the real historic spirit which evolves truth; and all the partisan songs which have been sung, or orations which subservient orators have spoken about that great march to the sea; and all the caricatures of Southern leaders which the bitterness of a diseased sectional sentiment has inspired; and all the glamour of a great success, shall not avail to restrain the inexorable, the illuminating pen of history. *Truth, like charity, never faileth.* Whether there be prophecies, they shall fail, whether there be tongues they shall cease; whether there be knowledge, it shall vanish away; but when the truth, which is perfect, has come, then that which is in part shall be done away.

Now let us contrast General Sherman with his greatest foe; likewise the greatest, the most humane general of modern times, and see whether he regarded the pitiless destruction of the substance of women and children and inoffensive inhabitants a legitimate war:

> Headquarters Army of Northern Va.,
> June 27, 1863.

General Order No. 73. The commanding general has observed with marked satisfaction the conduct of troops on this march. There have, however, been instances of forgetfulness on the part of some that they have in keeping the yet unsullied reputation of this army, and that the duties exacted of us by civilization and Christianity are not less obligatory in the country of an enemy than in our own. The commanding general considers that no greater disgrace could befall the army and through it our whole people, than the perpetration of barbarous outrages upon the unarmed and defenceless, and the wanton destruction of private property, that have marked the course of the enemy in our country.... It will be remembered that we make war only upon armed men.

> R. E. Lee, General.

The humanity and Christian spirit of this order was such as to challenge the admiration of foreign nations. The *London Times* commented upon it, and its American correspondent said:

> The greatest surprise has been expressed to me by officers from the Austrian, Prussian and English armies, each of which has representatives here, that volunteer troops, provoked by nearly twenty-seven months of unparalleled ruthlessness and wantonness, of which their country has been the scene, should be under such control, and willing to act in harmony with the long-suffering and forbearance of President Davis and General Lee.

To show how this order was executed, the same writer tells a story of how he witnessed with his own eyes General Lee and a surgeon of his command repairing the damage to a farmer's fence. Colonel McClure, of Philadelphia, a Union soldier himself, bears witness to the good conduct of Lee's ragged rebels in that famous campaign. He tells of hundreds of them coming to him and asking for a little bread and coffee, and others who were wet and shivering asking permission to enter a house, in which they saw a bright fire, to warm themselves until their coffee should be ready. Hundreds of similar instances could be given, substantiated by the testimony of men on both sides, to show the splendid humanity of that great invasion. Blessed be the good God, who, if in His wisdom denied us success, yet gave to us and our children the rich inheritance of this great example.

Major General Halleck, the commander-in-chief, under the President, of the armies of the Union, on the 18th of December, 1864, dispatched as follows to Sherman, then in Savannah:

> Should you capture Charleston, I hope that by some accident the place may be destroyed; and if a little salt should be sown upon its site it may prevent the growth of future crops of nullification and secession.

On December 27th, 1864, Sherman made the following answer:

> I will bear in mind your hint as to Charleston, and don't think "salt" will be necessary. When I move, the 15th corps will be on the right of the right wing, and their position will bring them naturally into Charleston first,

and if you have watched the history of the corps you will have remarked that they generally do their work up pretty well. The truth is, the whole army is burning with insatiable desire to wreak vengeance upon South Carolina. I almost tremble at her fate; but feel that she deserves all that seems to be in store for her.... I look upon Columbia as quite as bad as Charleston.'

Therefore Columbia was burned to ashes. And though he knew what was in store for South Carolina, so horrible that he even trembled, he took no steps to avert it, for he felt that she deserved it all. Did she, indeed? What crime had she committed that placed her outside the protection of the law of civilized nations? What unjust, or barbarous, or brutal conduct had she been guilty of to bring her within the exceptions laid down by the writers on the laws of war as authorizing extraordinary severity of punishment? They are not even imputed to her. South Carolina's crime, and the crime of all the seceding States, was that of a construction of the constitution of the United States differing from that of General Sherman and the 15th corps—which 'always did up its work pretty well.' Happily the Divine Goodness has made the powers of recuperation superior to those of destruction; and though their overthrow was so complete that 'salt' was not needed as the type of utter desolation, Marietta and Atlanta are thriving and prosperous cities.

Governor Vance does not wish to confine himself, in quoting, to Southern testimony. There are plenty of honest and truthful soldiers in the Federal army, who served in its ranks, to tell all we want and more. This is what one of them says, writing to the *Detroit Free Press* of that campaign:

One of the most devilish acts of Sherman's campaign was the destruction of Marietta. The Military Institute and such mills and factories as might be a benefit to Hood could expect the torch, but Sherman was not content with that; the torch was applied to everything, even the shanties occupied by the negroes. No advance warning was given. The first alarm was followed by the crackling of flames. Soldiers rode from house to house, entered without ceremony and kindled fires in garrets and closets, and stood by to see that they were not extinguished.

Had one been able to climb to such a height at Atlanta as to enable him to see for forty miles around, the day Sherman marched out, he would have been appalled at the destruction. Hundreds of houses had been burned; every rod of fence destroyed; nearly every fruit tree cut down, and the face of the country so changed that one born in that section could scarcely recognize it. The vindictiveness of war would have trampled the very earth out of sight, had such a thing been possible.

One cold and drizzly night in the midst of this marching General Sherman found shelter and warmth beneath the roof of a comfortable plantation home.

> In looking around the room I saw a small box, like a candle box, marked 'Howell Cobb,' and, on inquiring of a negro, found we were at the plantation of General Howell Cobb, of Georgia, one of the leading rebels of the South, then a general in the Southern Army, and who had been Secretary of the Treasury in Mr. Buchanan's time. Of course we confiscated his property, and found it rich in corn, beans, peanuts, and sorghum molasses. Extensive fields were all around the house. I sent word back to General Davis to explain whose plantation it was, and to instruct him to spare nothing. That night huge bonfires consumed the fence-rails, kept our soldiers warm, and the teamsters and men, as well as slaves, carried off an immense quantity of corn and provisions of all sorts.

Do the records of civilized warfare furnish a parallel to this petty and mercenary wreaking of spite upon the helpless home of a gallant foeman?

The general furnished us with proof of how worthy of their selection his staff-officers proved during that memorable raid. While camped that night on Cobb's plantation, Lieutenant Snelling, who was a Georgian commanding his escort, received permission to visit his uncle, who lived some six miles away. The general says:

> The next morning he described to me his visit. The uncle was not cordial by any means to find his nephew in the ranks of the host that was desolating the land, and Snelling came back, having exchanged his tired horse for a fresher one out of his uncle's stables, explaining that surely some of the 'bummers' would have got the horse had he not.

It was the eternal fitness of things that the staff-officers of this prince of free-booters should be renegades capable of stealing from their nearest kin.

The unfailing jocosity of this merry marauder breaks out in his recital of a negro's account of the destruction of Sandersville: "First, there came along some cavalrymen, and they burned the depot; then came along some infantrymen, and they tore up the track and burned it, and, just before they left, they set fire to the well!" The well, he explains, was a boxed affair into which some of the debris was piled, and the customary torch was applied, making the negro's statement literally true. This was one of the incidents to leaving the pretty town of Sandersville a smoking mass of ruins.

But why enumerate further details of an unresisted movement which cost Sherman one hundred and three lives, and the State of Georgia one hundred million dollars, twenty millions of which he frankly states he carried off, and eighty millions of which he destroyed? It began in shame at Atlanta—it passed with a gathering burden of infamy to Savannah. Starvation, terror, outrage hung upon its flanks and rear. Its days were darkened by the smoking incense from unparalleled sacrifices upon the altar of wantonness; its nights were lurid with flames licking the last poor shelter from above the heads of subjugated wives and children.

Its history is the strongest human argument for an orthodox hell.

A Virginia Girl in the Civil War

Contents

Introduction	275
Home Life in a Southern Harbour	277
How I Met Dan Grey	282
The First Days of the Confederacy	287
The Realities of War	294
I Meet Belle Boyd and See Dick in a New Light	300
A Faithful Slave and a Hospital Ward	304
Travelling Through Dixie in War Times	309
By Flag of Truce	316
I Make Up My Mind to Run the Blockade	320
I Cross the Country in an Ambulance and the Pamunkey on a Lighter	325
The Old Order	330
A Dangerous Masquerade	335
A Last Farewell	342
The Little Jew Boy and the Provost's Deputy	345
I Fall Into the Hands of the Enemy	348
The Flower of Chivalry	358
Prisoners of the United States	365

Within Our Lines	376
My Comrade General Jeb Stuart	385
"Whose Business 'Tis To Die"	392
Rescued by the Foe	400
With Dan at Charlottesville	410
"Into the Jaws of Death"	416
By the Skin of Our Teeth	424
The Beginning of the End	431
How We Lived in the Last Days of the Confederacy	439
Under the Stars and Stripes	446

Introduction

This history was told over the teacups. One winter, in the South, I had for my neighbour a gentle, little brown-haired lady, who spent many evenings at my fireside, as I at hers, where with bits of needle-work in our hands we gossiped away as women will. I discovered in her an unconscious heroine, and her Civil War experiences made ever an interesting topic. Wishing to share with others the reminiscences she gave me, I seek to present them here in her own words. Just as they stand, they are, I believe, unique, possessing at once the charm of romance and the veracity of history. They supply a graphic, if artless, picture of the social life of one of the most interesting and dramatic periods of our national existence.

The stories were not related in strict chronological sequence, but I have endeavoured to arrange them in that way. Otherwise, I have made as few changes as possible. Out of deference to the wishes of living persons, her own and her husband's real names have been suppressed and others substituted; in the case of a few of their close personal friends, and of some whose names would not be of special historical value, the same plan has been followed.

Those who read this book are admitted to the sacred councils of close friends, and I am sure they will turn with reverent fingers these pages of a sweet and pure woman's life—a life on which, since those fireside talks of ours, the Death-Angel has set his seal.

Memoirs and journals written not because of their historical or political significance, but because they are to the writer the natural expression of what life has meant to him in the moment of living, have a value entirely apart from literary quality. They bring us close to the human soul—the human soul in undress. We find ourselves without preface or apology in personal, intimate relation with whatever makes the yesterday, today, tomorrow of the writer. When this current of events and conditions is impelled and directed by a vital and formative period in the history of a nation, we have only to follow its course to see what history can never show us, and what fiction can unfold to us only in part—how the people thought, felt, and lived who were not making history, or did not know that they were.

This is the essential value of *A Virginia Girl in the Civil War*: it shows us simply, sincerely, and unconsciously what life meant to an American woman during the vital and formative period of American history. That this American woman was also a Virginian with all a Virginian's love for Virginia and loyalty to the South, gives to her record of those days that are still "the very fibre of us" a fidelity rarely found in studies of local colour. Meanwhile, her grateful affection for the Union soldiers, officers and men, who served and shielded her, should lift this story to a place beyond the pale of sectional prejudice.

Myrta Lockett Avary.

New York, November 1, 1902.

Chapter 1

Home Life in a Southern Harbour

Many years ago I heard a prominent lawyer of Baltimore, who had just returned from a visit to Charleston, say that the Charlestonians were so in the habit of antedating everything with the Civil War that when he commented to one of them upon the beauty of the moonlight on the battery, his answer was, "You should have seen it before the war." I laughed, as everybody else did; but since then I have more than once caught myself echoing the sentiment of that Charleston citizen to visitors who exclaimed over the social delights of Norfolk. For really they know nothing about it—that is, about the real Norfolk.

Nobody does who can not remember, as I do, when her harbour was covered with shipping which floated flags of all nations, and her society was the society of the world. Milicent and I—there were only the two of us—were as familiar with foreign colours as with our own Red, White, and Blue, and happily grew up unconscious that a title had any right of precedence superior to that of youth, good breeding, good looks, and agreeability. That all of these gave instant way to the claims of age was one of the unalterable tenets handed down from generation to generation, and punctiliously observed in our manner and address to the older servants. The "uncle" and "aunty" and "mammy" that fall so oddly upon the ears of the present generation were with Southern children and young people the "straight and narrow" path that separated gentle birth and breeding from the vulgar and ignorant.

My girlhood was a happy one. My father was an officer of the Bank of Virginia, and, according to the custom that obtained, he lived over the bank. His young assistant, Walter H. Taylor (afterward adjutant to General R. E. Lee), was like a brother to Milicent and me. Father's position and means, and the personal charm that left him and my mother cherished memories in Norfolk till today, drew around us a cultivated and cosmopolitan society. Our lives were made up of dance and song and moonlit sails. There were the Atlantic Ocean, the Roads, the bay, the James and Elizabeth Rivers, meeting at our very door. And there were admirals, commodores, and captains whose good ships rode these waters, and who served two sovereigns—the nation whose flag they floated and a slim Virginia maiden. In all the gatherings, formal and informal, under our roof, naval and military uniforms predominated. Many men who later distinguished themselves in the Federal and Confederate armies, sat around our board and danced in our parlours; others holding high places in Eastern and European courts were numbered among our friends and acquaintances.

Some years after Commodore Perry through a skilful mixture of gunpowder and diplomacy had opened the ports of Japan to the commerce of all nations, Ito and Inouye—not then counts—had brought into existence an organized Japanese navy which sailed out of these same ports to the harbours of the world on tours of inspection. One of my most vivid memories is of the Japanese squadron which lay at anchor in our harbour, of the picturesque dress and manners of these Eastern strangers, and the polished courtesy of the two men whose names are now a part of history.

But the handsomest sailors I ever saw were the Prussians. When the Prussian navy was in its infancy two Prussian vessels, the frigate *Gaefion* and a *corvette*, dropped anchor in Norfolk harbour; they, too, were visiting the ports of different nations on tours of inspection. All the officers on these vessels, including the midshipmen, were noblemen, and all of them were magnificent-looking men. Then, too, their brilliant uniforms and the state and ceremony with which they invested every-day life made them altogether charming to a young, romantic girl. I shall never forget how they used to enter the room. They would appear in full regimentals, march in military form, the frigate's captain in command, and salute Milicent before they permitted themselves to talk, dance, and sing.

Upon leaving, the same order was observed. They went out into the hall, donned their hats, sword-belts, and swords, returned, saluted, and withdrew in military form. At this time I was a little girl who played on the piano for grownup people to dance. On formal occasions we had military bands, but for the every-evening dance my playing did well enough. When the Prussians were our guests, one of them always sat by me while I played. Baron von der Golz, since Admiral of the German Navy, was the gentleman who was oftenest kind enough to turn over my music. I play now, for my children to dance, a Prussian gallop he taught me, with some of the music I played for those officers, and some which they used to play when they took my place at the piano that I might have my share of the dancing. Another Prussian officer of whom I was very fond was Count von Monts, afterward Admiral of the German Navy, Von der Golz succeeding at his death.

I shall never forget the day my Prussian friends sailed away. From the roof of our residence over the bank, there was a good view of the harbour and river: Milicent, Emily Conway, and a number of girls who wanted to see the last of the gallant, handsome Prussians went up on the roof, and I was permitted to go with them. We turned our spy-glasses on their ships as they sailed toward Hampton Roads, and there were our friends on deck, their glasses turned upon the housetop where we stood in the full glare of the midday sun. Even I was visible to them. Milicent placed me in front of our spy-glass, and I looked through and singled out Baron von Golz, to whom I waved my handkerchief vigorously. A little snow-storm fluttered on the deck, and the baron not only waved, but saluted.

According to the fashion of the time, young ladies wore low-necked dresses in the middle of the day—never, however, at any hour, so low as ladies at the opera wear them now. Milicent and her friends who went to the housetop were bare-necked, and the sun blistered their throats and shoulders; and mother had to bathe Milicent with buttermilk all the afternoon to make her presentable for the dance that night, which, by special permission, Count von Monts attended, coming up from Fortress Monroe to escort Milicent. They made a pretty picture when they danced their last dance together. The count would not permit their friendship to cease with that last dance, and a correspondence was long kept up between them. At parting, she gave him her little Catholic prayer-book with her name on the fly-leaf, and years after, when revisiting Norfolk, he had that prayer-book and tried to find her; but times were changed, and Norfolk no more our home. Many a titled sailor sought my sister's favour, but in our day Virginia's daughters, undazzled by coronets, were content to wed Virginia's sons.

The almost limitless hospitality of those days made all the sharper the distinction between "open house" and open hand. In the forties, the reserve of the American girl was more like that of her English sister than it is at the present day: Society did not sanction the freedom which it countenances now. The gentlewoman of the old South was a past mistress in the art of tact, but had little knowledge or practise in it to further her own private ends. Its office, as she understood it, was to relieve painful situations not her own, to contribute to the comfort and pleasure of others. To rid herself of a disagreeable third person to secure a *tête-à-tête* with a lover was not within its province. Lovers had to make their own opportunities—indeed it was not her part even to conceive that they wanted to make opportunities. Taking all this into consideration, the freedom with which Southern children entered into the social life must have often made them thorns in the flesh of their elders. I have often wondered since those happy days if my favourites among my sister's visitors did not find me a great nuisance in spite of the caresses they lavished upon me.

The New Year's reception of that period was not an afternoon and evening affair. It began in the morning and lasted all day; it meant pretty girls fluttering in laces and ribbons and feathers and sparkling with jewels and smiles; stately matrons who, however beautiful and young they were, never indulged even in the innocent coquetry that neither deceives a man nor wounds a woman—the married *belle* was unknown to Virginia; and gallant men, young and old, ready to die for them or live for them; it meant the good things to eat for which Virginia is famous, and, I am sorry to say, often more than enough of good things to drink. I remember one of these New Year's days when the ardour of my affections prevented a young officer who had come to bid us goodbye from exchanging a word with anybody unhampered by my close attendance.

I was brimful of nine-year-old love for him. I proposed to him and was promptly accepted; I made him drink punch with me dipped from the old punch-bowl that had been presented to father by the military companies of Norfolk, and I told him how Admiral Tucker had made the presentation with flags flying and bands playing and wine flowing, and how the admiral tried to ride his horse up the front steps into the house, and how the sober animal wisely and firmly refused to perform the feat. Through a long day he did not once escape me. This young officer was Lieutenant John L. Worden. He was one of the gallant "boys in blue" who made my sister's girlhood happy. A most charming gentleman he was, and everybody in my father's house loved him.

Another young sailor—the handsomest of them all, whom everybody in my father's house loved—was Captain Warren. How well

I remember that evening when the order came bidding him report at once to his ship, which was to set forth on a long cruise in Eastern waters! Shall I ever forget the look in his eyes as he turned them upon Milicent! How beautiful she was that night! How gracious and sweet, how greatly to be desired! And how many desired her!

Milicent had been married several years and I was in the raptures of my first winter in society when my father died, and mother decided that we should leave Norfolk—Norfolk where river and bay and ocean had sung our cradle-songs—and go to Petersburg to live. In this day of independent women it sounds absurd to say that it was scarcely considered wise or delicate for women to live without the protection of a male relative in the house, and to add that as far as possible they were shielded from the burden of business responsibilities. Uncle Henry considered it imperative that we should be under his care; he could not come to Norfolk, so we went to him. We could scarcely have been strangers anywhere in Virginia, and in Petersburg we had many friends. The Lees and the Randolphs, the Pegrams and the Pages, the Stringfellows, the Hamiltons, the Witherspoons, the Bannisters, the Donnans, the Dunlops, and a score of others made it easy to exercise the genius for friendship which in Virginia hands down that relation from generation to generation.

It was in Petersburg that my *trousseau* was made. Much of it was the work and embroidery of loving, light-hearted girls whose feet were set to music and dancing, and most of it was worn by women who trod in stead fields red with the blood of their friends and kinsmen. During the long, dreary years in which the Northern ports were closed, and the South clothed itself as best it could, or went in rags, that *trousseau* constituted my sole outfit, and it reinforced the wardrobes of some comrades in war and want.

CHAPTER 2

How I Met Dan Grey

"Have you met Dan Grey?"
Charlie Murray and I were galloping along a country road.
"I haven't, Charlie. I met his brother Dick in Norfolk, and didn't like him at all."
"Well, Nell, you'd like Dan—everybody does. I wonder you haven't met him. Dan never fails to meet every pretty girl that comes here."
I had heard that before. Indeed, I had heard a great deal about Dan Grey that made me long to get even with him. Everybody had a way of speaking as if Petersburg wasn't Petersburg with Dan Grey left out.
"You ought to meet Dan Grey," Charlie repeated.
"I don't think so," I rapped out. "I think I can get along very nicely without meeting Dan Grey"—Dan Grey seemed to be getting along very nicely without meeting me—"I know as many nice men now as I have time to see."
So I dismissed Dan, whipped up my horse, and raced Charlie along the old Jerusalem Plank Road—that historic thoroughfare by which the Union troops first threatened Petersburg, and near which Fort Hell and Fort Damnation are still visible. We ran our horses past the old brick church, built of bricks brought from England to erect a place of worship for the aristocratic colonists, past the quiet graves in Blandford; and turning our horses into Washington Street, slackened their pace and, chatting merrily the while, rode slowly into the city toward the golden sunset. A few years later I was to run along this street in abject terror from bursting shells.
"You ought to meet Dan Grey."
It came from George Van B—— this time. George was the poet laureate of our set. Afterward he was Colonel Van B——, and as gal-

lant a soldier as ever faced shot and shell. I had been playing an accompaniment for him; he was singing a popular ditty of the day, "Sweet Nellie is by my Side;" I wheeled around on the piano-stool and faced him.

"What is the matter with that man? He must be a curiosity?"

"He is just the nicest fellow in town," George asserted with mingled resentment and amusement.

"He must be something extraordinary. One would think there was just one man in town and that his name was Dan Grey."

Before the week was out I heard it again. This time it was Willie. He spoke oracularly, and as if he were broaching an original idea. Page, the best dancer in our set, repeated the recommendation, looking as if I were quite out of the swim in not knowing Dan Grey. (If Governor —— reads this chapter, will he please overlook the familiar use of his name? Boys and girls who have played mumble-peg together and snowballed each other, do not attach handles to each other's names until they are more thoroughly grown up than we were then.)

"I am sure it must be my duty to meet Dan Grey," I said gravely. "I am continually being told that I 'ought to meet Dan Grey' just as I might be told that I ought to go to church."

"Dan isn't a bit like a church, Nell," laughed Willie. "But he is a splendid fellow, generous to a fault—and then, you know, Dan is the handsomest man in town."

"Oh, no" I retorted, "I left the handsomest man in town in Norfolk."

I can't begin to tell how terribly tired I got of "You ought to meet Dan Grey," "Haven't you met Dan Grey?" Evidently Dan Grey was in no hurry to meet me. I knew that he was the toast of our set and that he ignored me as completely as if I were not in it—and I had never been ignored before. I also knew, without being continually told, that he was a broad-shouldered, magnificent-looking fellow, fair-haired, blue-eyed, and "the handsomest man in town." My girlfriends talked about him almost as much as the men did. And I did not even know the lion! I took great pains not to want to know him. I impressed it upon Willie and Charlie and George and the rest that they were not to bring Dan Grey to see me.

"Why, what will we say if he asks us to bring him? You are unreasonable, Nell. How did you ever pick up such a prejudice against Dan? Nobody can object to Dan Grey. If he asks any of us to bring him, I don't know what we can do."

"Oh, of course you can't be rude. If you are asked to bring him, you will have to do as you are asked, but I don't think you will be asked. I'm sure I hope you won't, for I have heard of Dan Grey until I am sick of the very name."

Meanwhile I resolved privately if I ever did lay my hands on Dan Grey I would wreak a full vengeance. He says that I have done it.

A Catholic fair was to be held in Petersburg, but as dearly as we loved Father Mulvey (all Petersburg loved him), and as much as we longed to do everything possible for our poor little Church of St. Joseph, we could not go to the fair rooms and sell things and make merry. We were in deep mourning; mother said that our going was out of the question. Then her old friend, Mrs. Winton, came out to persuade and convince.

"I really cannot let the girls go," mother protested. "They can make fancy articles and send them to the fair, or do any homework that you can put them to; we are willing to help just as much as we can. I will send pickled oysters and shrimp salad after my Norfolk recipes, and cake and cream and anything you like that I can make."

"We want the oysters and the salad and the cake and everything else you choose to send, but above all things we want the girls. I didn't come here for your pickled oysters and shrimp salad, if they are the best I ever tasted. I want Milicent and Nell—I want Nell for my booth and Milicent for Mrs. Lynn's. Mrs. Lynn has set her heart on Milicent—but, there! Mrs. Lynn may do her own begging. Do let me have Nell."

"My dear, I don't see how I can."

"Oh, you must! We really need them. You know how few girls there are in our little congregation."

Mother was too good a Catholic not to yield—Milicent and I were given over to the cause of St. Joseph's.

"But they are to work, not to amuse themselves," she stipulated. "They are not to promenade—just to stand behind tables and sell things."

"Just send them," pleaded Mrs. Winton. "I'll promise not to let them enjoy themselves. I'll keep Nell busy, and Mrs. Lynn will do her duty by Milicent."

But work is fun when you are young enough, and there was plenty of both in getting the booths ready. The old Library Hall on Bollingbrook Street was a gay and busy scene for several days before it was formally opened to the public who came to spend money and make merry.

On one never-forgotten morning the hall was filled with matrons and maidens weaving festoons of pine-beard, running cedar, and ivy. I had purposely donned my worst dress, and was sitting on the floor Turkish fashion, with evergreens heaped around me, when I saw a party of gentlemen entering the hall.

I tried to sink out of sight, but they saw me, demolished my barricade, and began to tease me. The quartet were Charlie Murray, George Van B——, Willie, and Page.

Behind them came a fifth gentleman, and before this fifth gentleman and I knew what was happening we were being presented to each other. And that is how I met Dan Grey—sitting on the floor in my shabbiest dress and half hidden by evergreens. I soon had the whole party hard at work festooning the hall, and what a good, if late, labourer, Dan Grey made in my vineyard!

"You see how useful I am," he said—he was standing on a box and I was handing up wreaths of cedar which he was arranging on the wall. "Now, why didn't you let me come to see you?"

"Me?" I asked in utter bewilderment.

"Yes, 'me'!"

"Why, I never had a thing to do with your not coming to see me."

He gave George, Charlie, and Willie a withering look.

"I reckon somebody else didn't want me to."

The boys looked dumfounded.

"I heard," said Dan from his box, "that you didn't want me to come to see you, that you had an unaccountable prejudice against me because you didn't like Dick, that you asked all your friends by no means to bring me to see you."

I was as mad as I could be with George, Willie, and Charlie.

"Why," I said, "you are not your brother Dick. And then, I don't dislike Dick at all."

Again the trio looked at me as if they doubted the evidence of their senses.

"Nell, what did you tell such a story for?" George asked me privately later.

"Why, I didn't tell any story at all," I declared. "He isn't his brother Dick, is he? And I don't dislike Dick now."

The night of the fair I wore a black bombazine, cut low in the neck and with long angel sleeves falling away from my arms above the elbow to the hem of my dress, and around my neck a band of black velvet with a black onyx cross. I sat or stood behind Mrs. Winton's booth, and Mr. Grey haunted the booth all the evening, and bought quantities of things he had no use for.

After the fair he saw me or reminded me of his existence in some way every day. Mother took me, about this time, on a visit to some cousins in Birdville, and every day Mr. Grey rode out on Dare Devil, the horse that he was to ride into his first fight. There was another fair. I went in from Birdville to help, and had the same *coterie* of assistants. "Ben Bolt" was a great favourite then. It was a new song and divided honours with "Sweet Nellie is by my Side." My assistants used to sit on a goods box that was later to be converted into an ornamental stand, and sing, "O don't you Remember Sweet Alice, Ben Bolt?"

Well, to make a long story short—as Dan and I did—we were married in exactly four months and a half from the day on which he was introduced to me as I sat cross-legged among the evergreens; and when Willie and George and Charlie came up to congratulate us, every wretch of them said, "Didn't I tell you you ought to meet Dan Grey?"

Chapter 3

The First Days of the Confederacy

Soon after my marriage my brother-in-law moved to Baltimore, and my mother decided to go with Milicent and her little boy. I had never really been separated from them before; I was only seventeen, a spoiled child, but though I loved them dearly, after the first I scarcely missed them. I had my husband, and ah! how happy we were—how glad we both were that I had met Dan Grey!

We did not go to housekeeping at once. In the first place, I did not know anything about housekeeping and I didn't want Dan to find it out; in the second place, we wanted to look around before we settled upon a house; and in the third, and what was to me the smallest place, the country was in a very unsettled condition.

The question of State's rights and secession was being pressed home to Virginia. The correspondence between the commission at Washington and Mr. Seward was despatched to Richmond, and Richmond is but twenty miles from Petersburg. There were mutterings that each day grew louder, signs and portents that we refused to believe. Local militia were organizing and drilling—getting ready to answer the call should it come. Not that the people seriously thought that it would come. They believed, as they hoped, that something would be done to prevent war; that statesmen, North and South, would combine to save the Union; that, at any rate, we should be saved from bloodshed. As for those others who prophesied and prayed for it, who wanted the vials of God's wrath uncorked, they got what they wanted. Their prayers were answered; the land was drenched in blood. But for the most of us—the Virginians whom I knew—we did not, we would not believe that brothers could war with brothers.

Then something happened that drove the truth home to our hearts. The guns of Sumter spoke—war was upon us. But not for long; the differences would be adjusted. Sumter fell, Virginia seceded. Still we befooled ourselves. There would be a brief campaign, victory, and peace. North and South, we looked for anything but what came—those four long years of bloody agony; North and South were each sure of victory. In Virginia, where the courage and endurance of starving men were to stand the test of weary months and years, we scoffed at the idea that there would be any real fighting. If there should be, for Virginia who had never known the shadow of defeat, defeat was impossible.

One day my brother-in-law, Dick, walked in.

"I've come to tell you goodbye, Nell—I'm off tomorrow."

"Where?"

"Norfolk."

"What for?"

"Infantry ordered there. The Rifles go down tonight, the Grays tomorrow."

I looked serious, and Dick laughed.

"Don't bother, Nell, we'll be back in a few days. There won't be any fighting."

Dick was a good-looking fellow, and I liked him much better than I had once said I did. He was the dandy of the family, and on the present occasion was glorious in a new uniform.

"Dick," I said, "please don't get in a fight and get shot."

"Not if I can help it, Nell! There won't be any fighting. We're going to protect Norfolk, you know. Just going there to be on the spot if we're needed, I suppose."

He went away laughing, but I wasn't convinced. When Dan came, I was almost too weak with fear to ask the question that was on my tongue.

"Is Norfolk to be bombarded?"

"No, I think not," he spoke cheerily. "The boys will be back in a few days."

Oh, I hoped they would! Many of my friends were among "the boys."

"Do—do you think your company will have to go?"

I was only seventeen; mother and Milicent were away; my young husband was my life.

"The cavalry have not been ordered out," he said. "I don't think we will be sent for. Cheer up, Nell! The boys will be back in a few days, and won't we have a high old time welcoming them home!"

Dick had broken it to me gently. All the infantry went down together. Soon after my husband came in, looking very pale and quiet.

"Dan," I said, "I know what it is."

"The cavalry are ordered to Norfolk," he said in a low voice. "It's only a few days' parting, little wife. I don't think there will be any fighting. Be brave, my darling."

I had thrown myself into his arms with a great cry.

"I can't, Dan! I can't let you go!"

He did not speak. He only held me close to his breast.

"Mother and Milicent are gone," I cried, "and I can't let you leave me to go and be killed! I couldn't let you go if they were here."

There was silence for a little while, then he said:

"I belong to you, little wife—I leave it to you what I shall do. Shall I stay behind, a traitor and a coward? Or shall I go with my company and do my duty?"

I couldn't speak for tears. I felt how hard his heart beat against mine.

"Poor wife!" he said, "poor little child!"

When I spoke, I felt as if I were tearing my heart out by the roots.

"I—I—must—let—you—go!"

"That is my own brave girl. Never mind, Nell, I will make you proud of your soldier!"

"Oh, Dan! Dan!" I sobbed, "I don't want to be proud of you! I just don't want you to get hurt! I don't want you to go if I could help it—but I can't! I don't want fame or glory! I want you!"

He smoothed my hair with slow touches, and was silent. Then he spoke again, trying to comfort me with those false hopes all fed on.

"I still doubt if there will be any fighting. But if there is, I must be in it. I can't be a coward. There! there! Nellie, don't cry! I hope for peace. The North and the South both want peace. You will laugh at all of this, Nell, when we come back from Norfolk without striking a blow!"

"Dan, let me go with you."

"Dear, I can't. How could you travel around, with only a knapsack, like a soldier?"

"Try me. I am to be a soldier's wife."

I was swallowing my sobs, sniffling, blowing my nose, and trying to look brave all at once. Instead of looking brave, I must have looked very comical, for Dan burst out laughing. The next moment we were silent again. The chimes of St. Paul's rang out upon the air. It was neither Sabbath nor saint's day. We knew what the bells were ringing for. Not only St. Paul's chimes, but the bells of all the churches had become familiar signals calling us to labour as sacred as worship. Sewing machines had been carried into the churches, and the sacred buildings had become depots for bolts of cloth, linen, and flannel. Nothing could be heard in them for days but the click of machines, the tearing of cloth, the ceaseless murmur of voices questioning, and voices directing the work. Old and young were busy. Some were tearing flannel into lengths for shirts and cutting out havelocks and knapsacks. And some were tearing linen into strips and rolling it for bandages ready to the surgeon's hand. Others were picking linen into balls of lint.

"I must go make you some clothes," I said, getting up from Dan's knee.

"But I have plenty," he said.

"It doesn't matter. I must make you some more—like the others."

Before the war was over I had learned to make clothes out of next to nothing, but that morning, except for fancy work, I had never sewed a stitch in my life. I could embroider anything from an altar cloth to an initial in the corner of a handkerchief, but to make a flannel shirt was beyond my comprehension. Make it, however, I could and would. I never hinted to Dan that I didn't know how, for I was determined that nobody but me should make his army shirts—I must sew them with my own fingers. I went down town and bought the finest, softest flannel I could find. Then I was at my wits' ends. I looked at the flannel and I looked at the scissors. Time was flying. I picked up my flannel and ran to consult my neighbour, Mrs. Cuthbert. She showed me how to cut and fashion my shirts, and I made them beautifully, feather-stitching all the seams.

Next day came and Dan made me buckle on his sword.

"If you stay long in Norfolk may I come?" I sobbed.

Poor Dan didn't know what to say.

"I'm a soldier's wife," I said with a mighty effort to look it. "I can travel with a knapsack—and," with a sob, "I can—keep—from crying."

"I'm going to have you with me if possible. There! little wife, don't cry, or you'll make a fool of me. Be brave, Nell. That's it! I'm proud of you."

But there was a tremor in his voice all the same. He put me gently away from him and went out, and I lay down on the sofa and cried as if my heart would break. But not for long. Captain Jeter's wife came for me; her eyes were red with weeping, but she was trying to smile. We were to go to the public leave-taking—there would be time enough for tears afterward. Everybody was on the streets to see the troops go off, and I took my stand with the others and watched as the cavalry rode past us. We kept our handkerchiefs waving all the time our friends were riding by, and when we saw our husbands and brothers we tried to cheer, but our voices were husky. The last thing I saw of my husband he was wringing the hand of an old friend who was not going, tears were streaming down his cheeks and he was saying, "For God's sake, take care of my wife."

They were gone, all gone, infantry and cavalry, the flower of the city. But they would be back in a few days, of that we were sure—and some of them never came back again.

I was in a city of mourning and dread, but my own suspense measured by days was not long, though it seemed an age to me then. A week had not passed when I got a telegram from Dan:

"Come to Norfolk. We are camped near there."

It was near train time when I got it. I snatched up my satchel, put in a comb and brush and toothbrush—not even an extra handkerchief—and almost ran to the depot. I could not have carried all my clothes, I know, for part of them were with the laundress, and packing a trunk would have taken time; but why on earth I did not put a few more articles into my satchel I cannot tell. It is a matter of history, however, that I only took those I have named. The first thing Dan did was to get me some handkerchiefs.

"Why, Nell," he said, "you are taking this thing of being a soldier's wife too seriously."

It was delightful to be in my old home once more. Friends and kindred crowded around me, the river and bay and ocean sang my old cradle-songs to me again, and, above all, Dan was near and came in from camp as often as he could. Then he was ordered away to Suffolk, which is twenty miles from Norfolk, and there, of course, he could not ride in to see me. But that was not so bad as it might have been. I could hear from him regularly, he had not yet been in any actual engagement, my fears were subsiding, or I was getting accustomed to them. I had, of course, telegraphed to Petersburg for my baggage and had made myself as comfortable as possible. An old uncle had taken it into his head to become quite fond of me, and altogether I was very far from unhappy. This uncle was eccentric and had eccentric ways of comforting me when I had the blues.

"Why, Nellie, my dear," he used to say, "you ought to be playing dolls, and here you are a wife, and if Dan gets killed you will be a widow."

On the heels of which cheerful observation this despatch came from Suffolk:

Come by next train. Dan slightly hurt.
Jack.

When I got to Suffolk four of the company met me.

"Don't be alarmed, Miss Nell," said the great fellows, sympathy and desire to cheer me blending in their eyes. "Dan will pull through all right."

Then Jack Carrington took me aside and explained as gently and tenderly as if he had been my brother:

"It happened yesterday, Miss Nell, but we wouldn't let you know because there was no way for you to get here then. We thought it wouldn't be so hard on you if we waited and sent the telegram just before train time. Your uncle got one before you did, but we told him not to tell you till just before train time, and he wired us back to tell you ourselves, that he couldn't tell you. Dan is getting all right now—he'll soon get well, Miss Nell, indeed he will. But the doctor said I must warn you—Miss Nell, you must be brave, you see—or I can't tell you at all. The doctor said I mustn't let you go in there unless you were perfectly calm. The wound is nothing at all, Miss Nell."

Poor Jack was almost as unnerved as I was. He mopped my face with a wet handkerchief, and made somebody bring me some brandy.

But the words ringing in my head, "A soldier's wife," pulled me together more than the brandy, and I made Jack go on.

"It's nothing but his arm. We were out on vidette duty yesterday and we got shot into. You see, Miss Nell, you *must* be brave or I can't tell you!"

I pulled myself together again and insisted that I *was* brave.

"You don't look like it, Miss Nell. I declare you don't."

"But I am. See now."

Jack didn't seem to see, but he went on, looking scared himself all the time.

"The real trouble was Dare Devil. You see, after Dan's arm got hurt—I wish it had been me or George who had caught that shot, but, hang the luck! it was Dan. You know Dare Devil's old trick—catching the bit in his teeth. Well, he did that and ran away. Dan held on with his good arm until that d——d horse (excuse me, Miss Nell!) wheeled suddenly and dashed into the woods. The limbs of the trees dragged Dan out of his saddle, and his foot caught in the stirrup and Dare Devil dragged him (take some brandy, Miss Nell) until the strap broke. We picked Dan up insensible; he was delirious all night, and we thought for a time that he was done for, but, thank God! he's all right now. I hate to tell you, Miss Nell, but—you'll see how his head is—and the doctor said we mustn't let you go in if you couldn't be calm."

"I understand," I said, "I will be very careful—"

And to prove how careful I could be, I broke down crying.

They didn't know what to do with me, poor fellows. They begged me not to cry, and then they said crying would do me good, and I had four pairs of broad shoulders to cry on. They were all as gentle and pitiful with me as a mother is with a baby. One of them got out his nice fresh handkerchief and wiped my eyes with it. I had come off the second time without a change of handkerchiefs, and this time without even a toothbrush. When I had cried my trouble out and was quite calm, I told them I was ready to go to my husband. They took me to the door and I went in quietly, and seeing that he was awake, bent over him.

"I am here, Dan," I said smiling.

He tried to smile back.

"Take my head in your hands, Nell," he whispered, "and turn it so I can kiss you."

I laid my hands softly and firmly on each side of his head and turned it on the pillow. As I did so, a quantity of sand fell away.

I don't know whether his head had been properly dressed or not, but I know that for a number of days the sand fell away from it whenever I took it into my hands to turn it.

"After I fell," he told me, when he was allowed to talk, "my head was in the dirt, of course, and it was beat first against one tree and then against another. When I felt my senses leaving me, I clasped my arms tight around my head. I don't know how I managed it, but I got hold of my crippled arm with my good one, and when I was picked up my arms were locked in some way about my head. That is all that saved me."

I took the law into my own hands. Before Dan got well Dare Devil had been shot.

Chapter 4

The Realities of War

When Dan recovered I returned to Norfolk, and there I stayed for some time, getting letters from him, taking care of uncle and developing a genius for housekeeping. One day I was out shopping when I saw everybody running toward the quay. I turned and went with the crowd. We saw the *Merrimac* swing out of the harbour—or did she crawl? A curious looking craft she was, that first of our ironclads, ugly and ominous.

She had not been gone many hours when the sound of guns came over the water followed by silence, terrible silence, that lasted until after the lamps were lit. Suddenly there was tumultuous cheering from the quay. The *Merrimac* had come home after destroying the *Cumberland* and the *Congress*.

"Well for the *Congress!*" we said. Her commander had eaten and drunk of Norfolk's hospitality, and then had turned his guns upon her—upon a city full of his friends. Bravely done, O *Merrimac!* But that night I cried myself to sleep. Under the sullen waters of Hampton Roads slept brave men and true, to whom Stars and Stripes and Southern Cross alike meant nothing now. The commander of the *Congress* was among the dead, and he had been my friend—I had danced with him in my father's house. Next day, the *Monitor* met the *Merrimac* and turned the tide of victory against us. Her commander was John L. Worden, who had been our guest beloved.

During all this time I had been separated from my husband. He had been detailed to make a survey of Pig Point and the surrounding country, and it was not until he reached Smithfield that he sent for me. We were beginning now to realize that war was upon us in earnest. There was the retreat from Yorktown; Norfolk was evacuated. Troops were moving. Everything was bustle and confusion. My husband went off with his command, the order for departure so sudden that he had not time to plan for me.

As Northern troops began to occupy the country, fearing that I would be left in the enemy's lines and so cut off from getting to him, I took the matter into my own hands and went in a covered wagon to Zuni, twenty miles distant, where I had heard that his command was encamped for a few days. After a rough ride I got there only to find that my husband had started off to Smithfield for me. We had passed each other on the road, each in a covered wagon. There was nothing to do except to wait his return that night.

As my husband's command had been ordered to join the troops at Seven Pines, I took the train for Richmond the next day, stopped a few hours, and then went to Petersburg. When I got there the Battle of Seven Pines was on. For two days it raged—for two days the booming of the cannon sounded in our ears and thundered at our hearts. Friends gathered at each other's houses and looked into each other's faces and held each other's hands, and listened for news from the field. And the sullen boom of the cannon broke in upon us, and we would start and shiver as if it had shot *us*, and sometimes the tears would come. But the bravest of us got so we could not weep. We only sat in silence or spoke in low voices to each other and rolled bandages and picked linen into lint. And in those two days it seemed as if we forgot how to smile.

Telegrams began to come; a woman would drop limp and white into the arms of a friend—her husband was shot. Another would sit with her hand on her heart in pallid silence until her friends, crowding around her, spoke to her, tried to arouse her, and then she would break into a cry:

"O my son! my son!"

There were some who could never be roused any more; grief had stunned and stupefied them forever, and a few there were who died of grief. One young wife, who had just lost her baby and whose husband perished in the fight, never lifted her head from her pillow. When the funeral train brought him home we laid her in old Blandford beside him, the little baby between.

Now and then when mothers and sisters were bewailing their loss and we were pressing comfort upon them, there would be a whisper, and one of us would turn to where some poor girl sat, dumb and stricken, the secret of her love for the slain wrenched from her by the hand of war. Sometimes a bereaved one would laugh!

The third day, the day after the battle, I heard that Dan was safe. Every day I had searched the columns of "Killed and Wounded" in the *Richmond Despatch* for his name, and had thanked God when I didn't find it. But direct news I had none until that third day. The strain had been too great; I fell ill. Owing to the general's illness at this time his staff was ordered to Petersburg, and Dan, who was engineer upon the staff, got leave to come on for a day or two in advance of the other members of it; but while I was still at death's door he was ordered off. When I at last got up, I had to be taught to walk as a child is taught, step by step; and before I was able to join my husband many battles had been fought in which he took part. I was at the breakfast-table, when, after months of weary waiting, he telegraphed me to come to Culpeper Court-house.

This time I packed a small trunk with necessary articles, putting in heavy dresses and winter flannels. The winter does not come early in Petersburg; the weather was warm when I started, and I decided to travel in a rather light dress for the season. I did not trouble myself with hand-baggage—not even a shawl. The afternoon train would put me in Richmond before night; I would stop over until morning, and that day's train would leave me in Culpeper. Just before I started, Mr. Sampson, at whose house I was staying, came in and said that an old friend of his was going to Richmond on my train and would be glad to look after me. I assented with alacrity. Before the war it was not the custom for ladies to travel alone, and, besides this, in the days of which I write travelling was attended with much confusion and many delays.

I reached the depot a few minutes before train time, my escort was presented and immediately took charge of me. He was a nice-looking elderly gentleman, quite agreeable, and with just a slight odour of brandy about him. He saw me comfortably seated, and went to see after our baggage, he said. He did not return at once, but I took it for granted that he was in the smoking-car. Travelling was slower then than now. Half-way to Richmond I began to wonder what had become of my escort. But my head was too full of other things to bother very much about it. The outlook from the car window along that route is always beautiful; and then, the next day I was to see Dan. Darkness, and across the river the lights of Richmond flashed upon the view. Where was my escort? I had noticed on the train that morning a gentleman who wore the uniform of a Confederate captain and whom I knew by sight. He came up to me now.

"Excuse me, madam, but can I be of any assistance to you? I know your husband quite well."

"Do you know where my escort is?" I asked.

He looked embarrassed and tried not to smile.

"We left him at Chester, Mrs. Grey."

"At Chester? He was going to Richmond."

"Well—you see, Mrs. Grey, it was—an accident. The old gentleman got off to get a drink and the train left him."

I could not help laughing.

"If you will allow me, madam," said my new friend, "I will see you to your hotel. How about your baggage?"

"Oh!" I cried in dismay, "Mr. C—— has my trunk-check in his pocket."

My new friend considered. "If he comes on the next train, perhaps that will be in time to get your trunk off with you to Culpeper. If not, your trunk will follow you immediately. I'll see the conductor and do what I can. I'm going out of town tomorrow, but Captain Jeter is here and I'll tell him about your trunk-check. He'll be sure to see Mr. C——."

I was to see Dan the next day, and nothing else mattered. I made my mind easy about that trunk, and my new friend took me to the American, where I spent the evening very pleasantly in receiving old acquaintances and making new ones.

But with bedtime another difficulty arose: I had never slept in a room at a hotel by myself in my life. Fortunately, Mrs. Hopson, of Norfolk, happened to be spending the night there. I sent up a note asking if I might sleep with her, and went up to her room half an hour later prepared for a delightful talk about Norfolk. When we were ready for bed, she took up one of her numerous satchels and put it down on the side where I afterward lay down to sleep.

"I put that close by the bed because it contains valuables," she said with an impressive solemnity I afterward understood.

Of course I asked no questions, though she referred to the valuables several times. We were in bed and the lights had been out some time when I had occasion to ask her where she had come from there.

"Oh, Nell!" she said, "didn't you know? I've been to Charlottesville and I've come from there today. Didn't you know about it? John" (her son) "was wounded. Didn't you know about it? Of course I had to go to him. They had to perform an operation on him. I was right there when they did it." Here followed a graphic account of the operation. "It was dreadful. You see that satchel over there?" pointing to the one just beneath my head on the floor.

"Yes, I see it."

"Well, John's bones are right in there!"

"Good gracious!" I cried, and jumped over her to the other side of the bed.

"Why, what's the matter?" she asked. "You look like you were scared, Nell. Why, Nell, the whole of John wouldn't hurt you, much less those few bones. I'm carrying them home to put them in the family burying-ground. That's the reason I think so much of that satchel and keep it so close to me. I don't want John to be buried all about in different places, you see. But I don't see anything for you to be afraid of in a few bones. John's as well as ever—it isn't like he was dead, now."

I lay down quietly, ashamed of my sudden fright, but there were cold chills running down my spine.

After a little more talk she turned over, and I presently heard a comfortable snore, but I lay awake a long time, my eyes riveted on the satchel containing fragments of John. Then I began to think of seeing Dan in the morning, and fell asleep feeling how good it was that he was safe and sound, all his bones together and not scattered around like poor John's.

I reached Culpeper Court-house the next afternoon about four o'clock. Dan met me looking tired and shabby, and as soon as he had me settled went back to camp.

"I'll come to see you as often as I can get leave," he said when he told me goodbye. "We may be quartered here for some time—long enough for us to get ourselves and our horses rested up, I hope; but I'm afraid I can't see much of you. Hardly worth the trouble of your coming, is it, little woman?"

"Oh, Dan, yes," I said cheerfully; "just so you are not shot up! It would be worth the coming if I only got to see you through a car window as the train went by."

A few days after my arrival a heavy snowstorm set in. As my trunk had not yet come, I was still in the same dress in which I had left Petersburg, and, though we were all willing enough to lend, clothes were so scarce that borrowing from your neighbour was a last resort. I suffered in silence for a week before my trunk arrived, and then it was exchanging one discomfort for another, for my flannels were so tight from shrinkage and so worn that I felt as if something would break every time I moved.

During this snowstorm the roads were lined with Confederate troops marching home footsore and weary from Maryland. Long, hard marches and bloody battles had been their portion. In August they had come, after their work at Seven Pines, Cold Harbor, and Malvern Hill, to drive Pope out. of Culpeper, where he was plundering. They had driven him out and pressed after, fighting incessantly. Near Culpeper there had been the Battle of Cedar Mountain, where Jackson had defeated Pope and chased him to Culpeper Court-house. Somewhat farther from Culpeper had been fought the second battle of Manassas, and, crowding upon these, the battles of Germantown, Centreville, Antietam—more than I can remember to name. Lee's army was back in Culpeper now with Federal troops at their heels, and McClellan, not Pope, in command. Civilians, women, children, and slaves feared Pope; soldiers feared McClellan—that is, as much as Lee's soldiers could fear anybody.

I found our tired army in Culpeper trying to rest and fatten a little before meeting McClellan's legions. Then—I am not historian enough to know just how it happened—McClellan's head fell and Burnside reigned in his stead. Better and worse for our army, and no worse for our women and children, for Burnside was a gentleman even as McClellan was and as Pope was not, and made no war upon women and children until the shelling of Fredericksburg.

CHAPTER 5

I Meet Belle Boyd and See Dick in a New Light

The tallow candles were lighted on each side of my bureau—the time came when I remembered those *two* tallow candles as a piece of reckless and foolish extravagance—when there was a rap at my door and Mrs. Rixey entered to ask if I would share my room with a lady who had come unexpectedly. A heavy snow was falling, and the wind was blowing it into drifts. The idea of sending anybody out in such weather was not to be thought of for a moment, so saying yes I hurried through with my dressing and went down to the parlour. Mrs. Rixey's house was filled with Confederates who were there either because it was near the army or because they were awaiting an opportunity to run the blockade. Our evenings were always gay, and when I entered the parlour this evening there was as usual a merry party, and, also as usual, there were several officers of rank in the room. I was so busy sending messages to mother and Milicent by a little lady who meant to run the blockade to Baltimore as soon as possible, that I did not catch my roommate's name when Mrs. Rixey introduced her.

She seemed to be nineteen, or, perhaps, twenty—rather young, I thought, to be travelling alone. True, I was not older, but then I was married, which made all the difference in the world. What made her an object of special interest to every woman present, was that she was exceedingly well dressed. It had been a long, long time since we had seen a new dress! She was a brilliant talker, and soon everybody in the room was attracted to her, especially the men. She talked chiefly to the men—indeed, I am afraid she did not care particularly for the women—and at first we were a little piqued; but when we found that she was devoted to The Cause we were ready to forgive her anything.

She soon let us know that she had come directly from Washington, where she had been a prisoner of the United States. She showed us her watch and told us how the prisoners in Washington had made the money up among themselves and presented it to her just before she left. I wish I had listened better to her account of her prison life and her adventures; but I was on the outer rim of the charmed circles, my head was full of Milicent and mother, Dan was at camp, and I couldn't see him.

I got sleepy, slipped quietly out of the room, and went upstairs and to bed. My roommate undressed and got to bed so quickly that night that I did not wake. The next morning when the maid came in to make the fire, we woke up face to face in the same bed, and then she told me that her name was Belle Boyd, and I knew for the first time that my bedfellow was the South's famous female spy. When we got up she took a large bottle of cologne and poured it into the basin in which she was going to bathe. It was the first cologne I had seen for more than a year, and it was the last I saw until I ran the blockade.

That day, while we were at dinner, a servant, behind my chair, whispered:

"Somebody out dar wan' ter see you right erway, mistis—er solger."

When I went out into the hallway, there stood the most abject, pitiable-looking creature—a soldier, ragged and footsore! He was at the end of the hall farthest from the dining-room, and looked as if he didn't wish to attract attention.

He wore gray trousers patched with blue—or were they blue patched with gray?—and a jacket which had as much Federal blue as Confederate gray in it. From the colour of his uniform, he belonged equally to both armies. His trousers were much too short for him, and altogether too small. His shoes were heavy brogans twice too large for him, and tied on with strings. He was without socks and his ankles showed naked and sore between trousers and shoes. He had on a bed-ticking shirt, a tobacco-bag of bed-ticking hung by a string from a button of his shirt—a button which, by the way, was doing more than double duty—and an old slouch hat was pulled over his face.

"You wanted to see me, sir?" I asked, stopping at a short distance from him.

He looked up quickly.

"How do you do, Nell?" he said. "I got leave to come from camp to see you today. My company got in from Maryland yesterday."

"Dick!" I cried in amazement; and then I burst into tears. Dick, our dandy, to look like this! Laughter mingled with weeping.

"Good gracious, Nell! what is the matter?" he said.

"Dick, Dick, how you look!"

"Hush, Nell! Good gracious! You'll have everybody in the dining-room out here to look at me."

Then I began to beg incoherently that he would go in and dine with me. I think Dick was hungry, but he was not *that* hungry. In his present garb starvation would not have driven him into a dining-room where ladies were. He looked toward the door with abject terror, and tried to hide himself behind the hat-rack. I was puzzled to know what I should do with him. As a young lady was my roommate it was out of the question to take him to my room, and he positively refused to go into the parlour. While we debated, the dining-room door opened and the ladies filed out into the hall. Unkempt, unshorn, patched, ragged, and dirty, a very travesty of his former foppish self, Dick went through the introductions with what grace he might.

Fortunately my friends who surrounded him were in sympathy with the threadbare Confederate soldier, and ready to help him to the extent of their power. One friend, whose husband had a shirt to spare, gave that to him; another lady found him a pair of socks; some one else contributed a pair of homespun drawers. I was drawn aside and consulted as to the best and most graceful way of conveying these presents to him. They feared that he might be wounded and insulted if the matter were not delicately managed. But Dick was past all that. He accepted the goods the gods provided in the spirit in which they were bestowed, and was radiant with his good luck, and with gratitude to the fair donors. While we held council he had been in Mrs. Rixey's and Miss Boyd's hands, and had had a good dinner.

As he stood in the hall ready to go back to camp, Belle Boyd came down the staircase, carrying a large new blanket shawl.

"You must let me wrap you up, lieutenant," she said, putting the shawl around Dick's shoulders and pinning it together.

Dick blushed and demurred. A shawl like that was too much—it was a princely gift, a fortune.

"I can't let you go back to camp in this thin jacket," she said, "while I have this shawl. It is serving our country, lieutenant, while it protects her soldier from the cold. I may need it? No, no, I can get others where this one came from."

There was nothing for him to do but to accept it. He looked at me with something of his old humour in his eyes as he started off.

"I'll be sure to come to see you again, Nell," he said.

After he left the house we saw him stoop, take off his shoes, and walk off with them in his hands. His feet left marks of blood in the snow. Shoes had been dealt out to the army only that morning, and his feet were so sore that his heavy, ill-fitting brogans were unendurable.

I have heard of many generous deeds like this done by Belle Boyd. Once, when riding out to review some troops near Winchester, she met a soldier, a mere boy, trudging along painfully on his bare feet. She took off her own shoes and made him put them on; they were fine cloth gaiters laced at the side, and trimmed with patent leather. Some one remonstrated; the shoes would not last the boy long enough to pay for her sacrifice.

"Oh," she said, "if it rests his poor young feet only a little while, I am repaid. He is not old enough to be away from his mother."

She did not spend another night with us. She seemed to feel that she had the weight of the Confederacy on her shoulders, and took the afternoon train for Richmond.

Chapter 6
A Faithful Slave and a Hospital Ward

Not long after this I had to give up my room to Governor Bailey of Florida and his family. They had come on in search of their son, whom they had for months believed to be dead, and who, they had only recently learned, was alive and in the mountains near Culpeper Court-house.

It seems that young Bailey had been shot at the battle of Cedar Mountain and left on the field for dead. An old negro, his body-servant, had carried him off by stealth to a hut in the woods, and there, with such simple resources as he had, had dressed and bandaged the wound. The hut was a mere shell of a house, a habitation for bats and owls; it had been unused so long that no paths led to it, and Uncle Reuben's chief object in carrying his master there was to hide him from the Yankees. He had no medicine, no doctor, no help, the master was ill for a long time from his wounds and with a slow fever, and through it all Uncle Reuben never left him except at night to forage for both. Food in the Confederacy was far from plentiful, and under the circumstances almost impossible to get. The hardships they endured seem inconceivable today.

Afraid to show himself lest in doing so he should turn his master over into the hands of the dreaded Yankees, the faithful old servant saw no way of communicating with the family. He was in a strange country; he could not leave his charge, alone and desperately ill, long enough to seek advice and assistance, and, besides, how was he to know the friend who would help him from the man who might betray him? He knew but one token—the Confederate uniform, and that was not always to be trusted, for spies wore it.

Confederate troops must have passed near his hiding-place several times, but in his anxiety to save his master from the Federals, the negro hid him from the Confederates as well.

It happened at last that a party of skirmishers who had frequently deployed along the obscure roads intersecting the country, noticed, rising from the depths of the forest, a thin streak of smoke suggesting deserters or spies, and began to investigate. So, it happened that they came upon the hut, and a poor, old, half-starved negro watching what seemed to be little more than a human skeleton. When convinced that his discoverers were really Confederates, his joy and eagerness knew no bounds.

"Ef any uv you gentlemen will jes send a 'spatch to Ole Marster," he said tremulously, "Ole Marster'll be hyer torecky. He'll be hyer jes ez quick ez de kyars kin git him hyer. We ain't got no money. But Ole Marster'll pay fur de 'spatch jes ez soon ez he comes. Ole Marster's rich. He'll pay fur anything anybody do fur Mars Hugh, an' be thankful ter do it. Ole Marster'll come arter Mars Hugh jes ez quick ez I kin git him word. He'll pay anybody fur evvything."

The soldiers hardly knew what to do; perhaps they never considered that they could do anything but what they did: ride away and leave behind them the pair in the hut. Perhaps, poor fellows, there was nothing else they could do. Comfortable hospitals for Southern soldiers were scarce, and the Confederate soldier had little to give to anyone, even to his sick comrade.

The negro, the guardian in this instance, was not anxious to have his charge moved. His whole concern was "to git word to Ole Marster."

"I kin take kyeer uv him," he insisted, "jes lak I bin doin' 'twell Ole Marster come. Den he'll know what to do. Mars Hugh ain't fitten to move now. Ef twarn't done jes right, he couldn't stan' it, case he's too weakly. 'Twon't do fur no strange folks to tech him nor 'sturb him, lessen dey knows how. Mars Hugh jes same ez er baby."

They gave the negro the rations they had with them, and the whisky in their canteens—it was all they had to give except their scant clothes—and rode on to Culpeper Courthouse, where one of them sent the despatch to "Ole Marster," according to the directions Uncle Reuben had given. And our Florida party was "Ole Marster" and his wife, and poor Hugh Bailey's young wife and her uncle.

It was well into the night after their arrival when four soldiers carried up to my room a stretcher holding a skeleton of a man. A gaunt, ragged old negro followed.

The next day the party started for home, but they never got poor Hugh as far as Florida. They stopped in Richmond at the Exchange, and there Hugh Bailey died the next day.

And now began for me the nursing in hospital wards that made up so large a part of our lives during the war.

"Jeter shot, perhaps fatally. Go to the hospital and see what you can do for him. I have telegraphed to his wife and mother.

"Dan."

The orderly who brought me this message from my husband said that Captain Jeter's command had been in a skirmish that day, and that the captain had fallen, mortally wounded, it was thought.

I went to him at once. He was lying unconscious across the bed as if he had fallen or been dropped there, dressed in full uniform with his coat buttoned up to his throat, breathing stertorously, and moaning. There was a small black hole in his temple. I thought he must be uncomfortable with his clothes on, and proposed to the nurse that we should try to undress him, but she said he was dying and it would only disturb him. All that day and until late that night I stayed with him, changing the towels on his head, wiping the ooze from his lips, listening to that agonizing moaning, and thinking of the wife and mother who could not reach him. About ten o'clock he seemed to be strangling.

"It's phlegm in his throat," the nurse said. She ran her finger down his throat, pulling out a quid of tobacco that had been in his mouth when he was shot and that had lain there ever since.

He died at midnight, and his mother came the next day at noon. I don't know which was the hardest to stand, her first burst of agony or her endless questions when she could talk.

"Did he suffer much, Nell?"

"Not much, I think. He was unconscious from the time he was shot."

"Nell, did he send me any message? Did he call for me?"

"He was unconscious," I repeated gently, "and we must be thankful that he was. If he had been conscious he would have suffered more."

"Yes, yes; I reckon I am thankful. I don't know how I am now. But I'm trying to submit myself to the will of the Lord. Nellie, you don't know what a sweet baby he was! the prettiest little fellow! as soon as he could walk, he was always toddling after me and pulling at my skirts."

I turned my head away.

"Last night I dozed for a minute and I dreamed about him. He was my baby again, and I had him safe in my arms, and there never had been any war. But I didn't sleep much. I couldn't come as soon as I got the telegram. I had to wait for a train. And I was up nearly all night cooking things to bring him."

She opened her basket and satchel and showed me. They were full of little cakes and crackers, wine jellies and blancmange, and other delicacies for the sick.

"Do you think if I had gotten here in time he could have eaten them?" she asked wistfully.

"He could not eat anything," I said, choking back my tears.

"You don't think he was hungry at all, Nell? The soldiers have so little to eat sometimes—and I have heard it said that people are sometimes hungry when they are dying."

"Dear Mrs. Jeter, he looked well and strong except for the wound. You know the troops had just returned from the valley, where they had plenty to eat."

"I am glad of that. I was just getting a box ready to send him full of everything I thought he would like. And I had some clothes for him. I began making the clothes as soon as I heard the troops had come back to Culpeper. You say he was wounded in the head?"

Neither of us closed our eyes that night. She walked the floor asking the same questions over and over again, and I got so I answered yes or no just as I saw she wanted yes or no and without regard to the truth.

Several months after this I saw Captain Jeter's widow. She was surrounded by his little children—none of them old enough to realize their loss.

"Nell," she said, "you remember the day in Petersburg when we stood together and watched the troops start off for Norfolk—and everybody was cheering?"

"Yes."

"Well, war does not look to me now as it did then. God grant it may spare your husband to you, Nell!"

I shivered.

I called on another widowed friend. Her husband—a captain, too—had been sent home, his face mutilated past recognition by the shell that killed him. Her little ones were around her, and the captain's sword was hanging on the wall. When I spoke to her of it as a proud possession, her eyes filled. His little boy said with flashing eyes:

"It's my papa's s'ode. I wants to be a man. An' I'll take it down and kill all the Yankees!"

"H-sh!" his mother put her hand over his mouth."God grant there may be no war when you are a man!" she said fervently.

"Amen!" I responded.

"Oh, Nell," she said, "when it's all over, what good will it do? It will just show that one side could fight better than the other, or had more money and men than the other. It won't show that anybody's right. You can't know how it is until it hits you, Nell. I'm proud of him, and proud of his sword; I wouldn't have had him out of it all. I wouldn't have had him a coward. But oh, Nell, I feel that war is wrong! I'm sorry for every Northern woman who has a circle like this around her, and a sword like that hanging on her wall."

The little boy put his arm around her neck. "Mamma," he said, "are *you* sorry for the *Yankees?*"

"My dear," she said, "I am sorry for all little boys who haven't got a papa, and I'm sorry for their mammas. And I don't want you ever to kill anybody."

CHAPTER 7

Travelling Through Dixie in War Times

Our troops had to get out of winter quarters before they were well settled in them. I am not historian enough to explain how it was, but the old familiar trip "On to Richmond "had been started again, Burnside directing it. Every new Federal commander-in-chief started for Richmond as soon as he was in command. There was a popular song called "Richmond is a Hard Road to Travel." They always found it so, though they got there eventually.

The cavalry, as usual, were on the wing first. General Rooney (W. H. F.) Lee's division was sent to Fredericksburg in November, I think. My husband, of course, went with it. I was to go to Richmond and wait until I heard whether it would be safe for me to join him.

From Richmond I ran over to Petersburg, saw many old friends and ran back to Richmond again, fearful lest a message should come from Dan and I should miss it. I looked for a telegram every day, and kept my trunk packed. It was well that I did.

One morning my door was burst open unceremoniously and Dan rushed in.

"Ready to go, Nell?"

"Yes."

"Come. Now."

I put on my bonnet, caught up my satchel, stuffed brush, toothbrush, and comb into it and was ready. Dan had stepped into the hall to call a porter to take the trunk down. We followed it, jumped into the omnibus, and it rolled off— all this in about five minutes from the time he burst my door open. On the omnibus, among other passengers, was a gentleman who had a brother in Dan's command. This gentleman had so many questions to ask about the army, and so many messages to send his brother that Dan and I hardly exchanged a dozen sentences before we were at the depot. He established me in my seat, got my baggage checked, sat down, and then exclaiming:

"Good gracious! I forgot that bundle for General Lee. It's on top of the omnibus, Nell. I'll be back in a minute," and darted off.

At the next station, when the conductor came for my ticket, I said:

"See my husband, please. He must be in the smoking-car."

A gentleman across the aisle remarked:

"Excuse me, madam, but I think the gentleman who came in with you got left. I saw him get off the omnibus with a bundle in his hand and run after the car, but he missed it."

"Then I don't know what to do," I said in despair to the conductor. "I haven't a ticket, and I haven't any money."

"Where are you going?" he asked kindly.

"I don't know!" I gasped.

The conductor looked blank. I explained the manner of my starting to him.

"Do you know where your husband's command is stationed?"

"No, I don't know that either. You see," I explained, "as he belongs to the cavalry it is much harder to keep up with his whereabouts than if he were in the infantry."

"What division is he in?"

"General Rooney Lee's."

"Do you know what brigade?"

"Chambliss's."

"All right. I know what to do with you, then. You stop at Milford. Your husband will come on the freight this afternoon—at least, that's what I expect him to do. Your best plan is to wait at Milford for him."

When we reached Milford the conductor took me out and introduced me to the landlord of the tavern, and I was shown into what I suppose might be called by grace the reception-room. It was literally on the ground floor, being built on native brown earth. The ceiling was low, the room was full of smoke, and rough-looking men sat about with pipes in their mouths. I asked for a private room, and was shown into one upstairs, but this was so cold that I went out into the porch which overhung the street and walked up and down in the sun to keep myself warm. Very soon the gong sounded for dinner. I went down, sat with a rough crowd around a long table, swallowed what I could, and went back to my promenade on the porch. After a time an ambulance drove up and stopped under the porch, and an orderly sang out:

"Adjutant of the Thirteenth here?"

I leaned over the railing.

"I am his wife," I said.

He saluted. "Can you tell me where the adjutant is, ma'am?"

"He will be here on the next train."

"That might be midnight, ma'am, or it might be tomorrow. My orders were to meet the adjutant here about this time."

"The adjutant got left by the regular passenger. But a freight was to leave Richmond soon after the passenger, and the adjutant will come on that."

"The freight?" the orderly looked doubtful. "Maybe so."

"What do you mean?" I asked.

"Well, ma'am, all trains are uncertain, and freight trains more so. And sometimes freight trains are mighty pertickular about what kind of freight they carry."

I laughed, but the orderly did not see the point. Dan's body-servant was to drive the ambulance back, so the orderly, turning it over to a man whom he picked up in the tavern, went back to camp according to instructions. As soon as he was out of sight I began to repent. If Dan *shouldn't* come on that freight, what would I do with myself and that strange man and the ambulance and the mules? It was getting late when the welcome sound of a whistle broke upon my ear and the freight came creeping in. On the engine beside the engineer stood my husband, with that abominable little bundle of General Lee's in his hand.

"Josh got left somewhere," Dan said of his servant, "the man will have to drive"

At last we were off, Dan and I sitting comfortably back in the ambulance. I was very cold when I first got in, but he wrapped me up well in the blanket and I snuggled up against him, and began to tell him how nice and warm he was, and how thankful I was that there was no possibility of his getting left from me between here and camp.

"I had a time of it to come on that freight," he said.

"The orderly said you would." I repeated the orderly's remark, and Dan laughed.

"He told the truth. I had to do more swearing to the square inch than I have been called upon to do for some time. I knew you didn't even know where you were going, and that I *must* get here tonight. As soon as I heard about the freight, I went to the conductor. He said passengers couldn't be taken on the freight, it was against orders. 'I belong to the army as you see,' I urged, 'I am an officer and it is important for me to rejoin my command.' He insisted still that I couldn't go, that it was against orders. I told him that it was a bundle for General Lee that had got me left, and I pictured your predicament in moving colours. He was obdurate. 'If the freights begin to take passengers,' he said, 'there would soon be no room for any other sort of freight on them.' I felt like kicking him.

"It was then that I told him that orders were not made for fools to carry out, and the swearing began. I threatened to report him. He looked uneasy and was ready to make concessions which politeness had not been able to win, but I walked off. Evidently, like a mule, he respected me more for cursing him. I had my plan laid. Just as the train moved out of the station I swung on to the engine, and politely introduced myself to the engineer. He had overheard my conversation with the conductor—the first part of it, not the part where the swearing came in—and he invited me to get off the engine. While we were debating the engine was travelling. I saw that he was about to stop it.

"Quick as a flash I had my pistol at his head.

"' Now,' I said, 'drive on with this engine, or I'll kill you and run it myself!' I am not telling you *all* the words I used, Nell, you'll forgive me this time, I had to get to you, and honest English is wasted on fools and mules. 'Hold off!' he said, 'and don't put that d—d thing so close to my head, and you can ride up here and be d—d to you.' The invitation was not very polite, but I accepted it. I gave him some good tobacco, and we got to be friends before I got off."

The short day was done. I was tired and warm and sleepy and went to sleep while Dan was talking. I don't know how long I had dozed when the driver doubled up suddenly and turned head over heels backward into my lap. I struggled from under him, and Dan gave him a push that helped to free me and at the same time jumped on to the driver's seat and caught up the lines.

"Lord-a-mussy on me!" I heard the man groaning, "dat ar d—n mu-el! she have kicked me in de pit er my stummick!"

He gathered himself together in a corner of the ambulance, and continued to express forcible opinions of the mule.

"Dan," I said, "please get away from there! That mule might kick you."

"Don't be silly, Nell! Somebody's got to drive."

"But, Dan, if you get kicked, you *can't* drive."

"I won't get kicked. I know how to talk to a mule. Just shut your ears, Nell, if you don't want to hear me. I've got to convince this mule. She's just like that engineer and conductor. As soon as I get through giving her my opinion in language she can understand, she'll travel all right."

Presently Dan called out: "You can unstop your ears now, Nell—I think she understands."

"Dan," I said, "are you cold out there?"

"Not a bit of it! This isn't anything to a soldier. But a soldier's wife, eh, Nell? Getting to be rather hard lines, isn't it?"

"Dan," I said, my teeth chattering, "don't it seem that I have had more adventures in one day than I am entitled to?"

"Rather! By the way, Josh got on that same freight. How he managed it, the Lord only knows! Worked himself in with the brakeman, I suppose. But he got off—to look around, I reckon—just like him!—at some station before Milford and got left. He'll come straggling into camp tomorrow. You see there's another accident you can credit your account with. Josh could have driven these mules instead of that fool white man over there who don't know what to do with a mule. Then I would have been back there entertaining you, and you would have been complimenting me by going to sleep." He drove on singing:

Sweet Nellie is by my side!

We caught up with another ambulance. In it were an army friend of Dan's and his wife, and she proved the straw that broke the back of my endurance. She played the martyr. She had rugs, and shawls, and blankets. I cross-examined her and made her show that she hadn't been left on a car by herself without a ticket or a cent of money, and with no knowledge of where she was going, that the driver of her ambulance hadn't been kicked in the stomach and tumbled himself backward into her lap and nearly broken her bones, and that my case was far worse than hers. But in spite of it, she complained of everything, and had Dan and her husband sympathizing so with her that they had no time to sympathize with me. I sat, almost frozen, huddled up in the one shawl that answered for shawl, blanket, and rug, and tried to keep my teeth from chattering and myself from hating that whining Mrs.

Gummidge of a woman.

At last our ambulance drew up in front of the Rev. Mr. McGuire's, where we were to stop. There was a hot supper ready, in parlour and dining room cheerful flames leaped up from hickory logs on bright brass fire-dogs, and our welcome was as cheery as the glow of the fire. As our ambulance had driven into the gate a few minutes in advance of the other, and as Dan had also engaged board for me several days before, I had a right to the first choice of rooms. One of these was large with a bright fire burning in the fireplace, and a great downy feather-bed on the four-poster; the other was small, and had neither fireplace nor feather-bed. Of course "Mrs. Gummidge" got the best room. Dan had to go back to camp. I slept on my hard bed in my cold room and cried for Milicent and mother; and the next morning I broke the ice in my bowl when I went to take my bath.

I was very, very miserable that morning. I was not out of my twenties, I had been a spoiled child, I had not seen Milicent or mother since my marriage, I had nearly lost my husband, and I had been ill unto death. Following my husband around as I did, I yet saw very little of him, and I endured hardships of every sort. I was in the land of war, and in spite of all his efforts to protect me life was full of fears and horrors. I do not mean that it was all woe. There were smiles, and music, and laughter, too; my hosts were kind, Dan came over from camp whenever he could, and life was too full of excitement ever to be dull. During the day I managed fairly well—it was at night that the horrors overwhelmed me. My room was cheerless, my bed was hard and cold—I wanted Milicent, I wanted mother. I felt that the time had come when I must see them and I couldn't: there was no way!

The longing grew upon me the more I struggled against it, until there was no risk I would not have run to see them. I was sitting in the parlour one night thinking with indescribable longing of the happy, care-free days in Norfolk, and seeing dissolving pictures of home in the hickory fire. Tears were rolling down my cheeks, for while I was living over those dear old days I was living in the present,. too. Suddenly I heard a voice in the hall—Dan's and another's!

I sprang up. And there was Dan, and behind him in the doorway stood a graceful figure in a long wrap. And a face—Milicent's face—pale and weary, but indescribably lovely and loving, was looking toward me with shining eyes.

"Millie!"

"Nell!"

That was one time I forgot Dan, but he didn't mind. He stayed with us as long as he could, and after he left Milicent and I talked and talked. Milicent—she was a widow now—had come all the way from Baltimore to see me—she had left mother and Bobby to come to see me! My little bed wasn't hard any more, my room wasn't cheerless any more; I didn't mind having to break the ice for my bath. Ah, me, what a night that was and how happy we were until Dan's command was moved!

Millie and I—Catholics—wish to pay tribute to the sweet piety of that Protestant home which sheltered us. Every evening the big Bible was brought out and prayers were held, the negro servants coming in to share in the family devotions.

Chapter 8

By Flag of Truce

Milicent tells how she got from Baltimore to Dixie.

The War Department of the United States issued a notice that on such a date a flag-of-truce boat would go from Washington to Richmond, and that all persons wishing to go must obtain passes and come to that city by a certain date.

I had not heard from my sister, Mrs. Grey, for some time. We were very anxious about her, and I determined to seize this opportunity to get to her.

I was fortunate in making one of a party of three ladies, one of whom was Mrs. Montmorency, the widow of an English officer, and the other Mrs. Dangerfield, of Alexandria, Virginia. On our arrival at Washington late at night, we found all the hotels crowded and were told that it would be impossible to get a room anywhere. Fortunately for us, Mrs. Dangerfield was acquainted with the proprietor of one of the hotels where we inquired, and here, after much difficulty, we secured two small rooms. As he left us the old lady said triumphantly:

"Now, see what's in a name! If my name hadn't been Dangerfield none of us could have gotten a place to sleep in tonight."

The next morning we started for the flag-of-truce boat. Immediately upon our arrival our baggage was weighed and all over two hundred pounds refused transportation. The confusion was indescribable. As soon as the steamer cleared the wharf every stateroom was locked, and the five hundred passengers on board, with the exception of the children, were subjected to a rigid examination—their persons, their clothing, their trunks were all thoroughly searched. We were marched down two by two between guards, and passed into the lower cabin, where four women removed and searched our clothing; our shoes, stockings, and even our hair were subjected to rigid inspection.

Mrs. Dangerfield being the oldest lady on board was by courtesy exempted. As for myself, I fell into the hands of a pleasant woman, who looked ashamed of the office she had to perform. She passed her hand lightly over and within my dress, and over my hair; touched my pockets and satchels, which I willingly showed her, and dismissed me with a smile and the kind remark, "Oh, I know you have nothing contraband," while around me stood ladies shivering in one garment.

I had tea and sugar, both contraband articles, in a large satchel upstairs in the care of the provost marshal. I out-Yankeed the Yankees this trip. As soon as I had heard that we were to be searched and have our things taken from us, I had walked up to the provost marshal, told him I had tea and coffee—a small quantity of each—and asked to be allowed to use them. In the gruffest manner he bade me bring them immediately to him. My dejected looks must have inspired him with some pity, for when I went off and brought back my satchel and handed it to him, he turned and said in the kindest manner:

"Now I have saved them for you. After the search is over come to me and I will return them to you."

I thanked him and hurried off to impart the good news to my friend Mrs. Dangerfield. I found her in a most animated discussion with an officer who had just pronounced her camphor-bottle contraband. The old lady was asserting loudly her inability to stand the trip or to live without her camphor-bottle. After much argument and persuasion she was allowed to retain it.

The scenes on deck at this time were too painful to dwell upon. Mothers who had periled everything and spent their last dollar in buying shoes for their children had to see them rudely taken away. Materials for clothing, and pins, needles, buttons, thread, and all the little articles so needful at home and so difficult to obtain in the Confederacy at that time were pronounced contraband. Men went about with their arms filled with plunder taken from defenceless women who stood wringing their hands and pleading, crying, arguing, quarrelling.

By this time we were far down the Potomac. Weak, hungry, and seasick, we were glad when dinner-time drew near. The official notice had stated that food would be provided, which we, of course, had construed into three meals a day of good steamboat fare. The bell rang out loudly at last, and we all rushed to the cabin, where to our utter consternation we saw nothing whatever to eat, no set table, and nothing that looked like eating. Coming up the steps was a dirty boat-hand with a still dirtier bucket and a string of tin cups. He deposited these on a table and then called upon the ladies to help themselves to atrocious coffee, without milk, sugar, or spoons. Down he went again, and came up laden with tin plates piled one on the other, and containing what he called a sandwich. This sandwich was a chunk—not a slice—of bread, spread with dreadful mustard, a piece of coarse ham and another chunk of bread. Each person was generously allowed one of the tin plates and one sandwich. The very thought of swallowing such food was revolting, and more particularly so because we were tantalized with odours of beefsteak and chicken and other appetizing delicacies prepared for the officers' table.

How thankful I was to the provost for confiscating my tea and coffee and sugar and crackers and ginger-cakes! Each of our party had something to add. Down upon the lower deck we had seen an immense pile of loaves of bread, and near them a large stove. We coaxed the sailor in charge to get us a clean loaf from the centre of the pile and to put our tea on his stove to draw. In a few moments we disappeared to enjoy in our stateroom the luxury of a cup of tea! How others fared I do not know. We were the only people, I think, who had saved any tea. Almost every one had brought a few crackers, or cakes of some kind which they had managed to keep, and these they must have lived on with the abominable coffee.

When we reached the boat that morning only one stateroom was vacant, and this we contrived to secure. It was crowded comfort for three persons, but we were thankful. When night came our less fortunate fellow travellers were scattered in every direction on the floor, their only accommodations filthy camp mattresses without sheets, pillows, or covering of any kind except their own cloaks and shawls.

We travelled slowly and cautiously, fearing that in the night our flag might not be distinctly seen and we might be fired upon. The provost and his officers were in most things polite and kind. The men got up a little play between decks for the amusement of the ladies; but our party was too ultra-Southern even to look on.

We remained off Fortress Monroe all night, only starting at daylight for the James River. The trip up the James was accomplished in safety and without incident of special interest, if we except a very sudden and desperate love affair between a Southern girl and a Federal officer and the amusement which it afforded us.

As our boat neared the wharf at City Point, on all sides were heard cries of:

"Here we are in Dixie!"

As soon as we were landed a rush was made for the cars, and after everybody was seated the provost marshal came through bidding us goodbye, shaking hands with many and kissing the pretty young girls. He had been very kind, and, as far as lay in his power, had done so much for the comfort of all and for the pleasure of the young people that most of us felt as if we were parting from a friend. Indeed, some were so enthusiastic that before we reached City Point they went among the passengers begging subscriptions to a fund for purchasing the provost a handsome diamond ring as a testimonial. Many, however, refused indignantly, declaring that they did not feel called upon to reward the provost for confiscating every article possible, and for giving us for seven consecutive meals spoiled bacon, mustard, and undrinkable coffee.

In Petersburg little or no preparation had been made for us, although the hotel proprietors knew the truce boat was expected that afternoon at City Point. We were scarcely able to secure an ordinary supper, and had to sleep, eight or ten in a room, on mattresses laid on the floor, and which, though clean and comfortable enough, were without covering. The next day we parted to go in different directions.

Chapter 9

I Make Up My Mind to Run the Blockade

Late one day we saw an ambulance driving up to the gate through the pouring rain. A few minutes after, Patsy, the housemaid, came in to say that the adjutant had sent for his wife and her sister. We supposed that the two men with the ambulance were rough and common soldiers—one of them, in fact, the one who had given the message to Patsy, was a negro driver—and sent them around to the kitchen to warm and dry themselves. Very soon Aunt Caroline, the cook and a great authority, came in hurriedly and attacked Mrs. McGuire.

"Law, mistess! Y'all sholy orter ax one er dem men in de house. He sholy orten ter bin sont to de kitchen. He ain't got no bizness in de kitchen. He's quality. You orter ax him to come to de parlour. He specks you gwine ter ax him to come to de parlour, he done bresh hissef up, and he's puttin' sweet grease on his har, and he say he kin play on de orgin."

Such accomplishments as these changed the whole situation. Aunt Caroline was sent to fetch him. When she threw open the door and announced him and he entered, bowing low and gracefully, we could hardly restrain a laugh, for we had a good view of the top of his head, and it was fairly ashine! He was Lieutenant Dimitri of New Orleans, my husband's courier, who had been sent as our escort. A most efficient and agreeable one he proved.

If I had only been a young lady following my father or brother around, how interesting these memoirs might be made, for Lieutenant Dimitri was only one of many charming men I met. Available heroes pass through, bow, and make their exits. And I am afraid of boring my friends with the one hero who remains because he is my husband;

consequently I keep him as modestly as possible in the background. He had risen steadily in rank, and I was proud of him, but I must say that my memory is less vivid as to his deeds of gallantry than it is to what might have been reckoned minor matters by an older woman. The greatest crosses of my life were separation from my mother and sister, telling my husband goodbye, and beholding him in a hopelessly shabby uniform. The greatest blessings of my life were found in the little courtesies and kindnesses of life and in getting my husband back to me, safe and sound.

When morning came it was still raining, and the roads in such a condition that Mr. McGuire, fearing our ambulance would break down, opposed our going. But I knew that the men and team must return to camp according to orders, so we started off in spite of the weather and Mr. McGuire's protest.

We had not gone far when our driver was halted by a vidette who barred the way.

"Is Adjutant Grey's wife in the ambulance?"

"Yessuh."

"Turn back. Smallpox ahead."

The driver turned another road. It was only a short distance before we were halted again.

"Adjutant Grey's wife in the ambulance?"

"Yessuh, she sho is."

"Turn around. Smallpox this way."

"Lord! how is I ter go?" groaned the driver.

At the next fork the driver paused with a look of utter distraction.

"I don't kyeer whicherway we go, dar'll be smallpox in de road sayin' we can't go datter way." And he drove recklessly on the way the mules seemed to prefer. The mules struck it.

A vidette halted us again, but it was to say that we were travelling in the right direction and to give minute directions for the rest of our journey. There was a village and its neighbourhood to be avoided, and we had to make a wide detour before the driver put us down, according to orders, at Mr. Wright's.

Dan came in quite soon, looking as shabby as one of his own orderlies, but glad enough to see me. For some time here I was in a fool's paradise in spite of the war and the fact that mother was far away in Baltimore, ignorant of what might be happening to us, for camp was very near, there were no active hostilities, and Dan came to see me every day.

Then the cavalry received marching orders. The night after I heard it I determined to tell Dan of a decision I had come to. Milicent had not spoken, but I knew the drift of her thoughts and purposes. We had not heard once from mother and Bobby since she left them in Baltimore. Milicent was going to them, and I had made up my mind to go with her. There was no return to Baltimore by flag of truce; the only way to get there was to run the blockade, a most dangerous and doubtful undertaking at this period of the war. But Milicent's boy was in Baltimore, and mother was there. She had come to me; she would go to them, and I intended to go with her.

My heart was set on seeing mother. To be left alone now by both Milicent and Dan would drive me crazy; for Milicent to run the blockade alone would serve me as ill. Besides, I wanted some things for myself, some pins and needles, and nice shoes and pocket handkerchiefs and a new hat and a new cloak, and I wanted a new uniform for Dan. Dan had had no new uniform since his first promotion, a long time ago. He was an officer of high rank, and he was still wearing his old private's uniform. He had travelled through rain and snow and mud, and had slept on the ground and fought battles in it. Though I had many times cleaned that uniform, darned it, patched it, turned it, scoured it, done everything that was possible to rejuvenate it, my shabby-looking soldier was a continual reproach to me. When Dan would come to see me I used to make him wrap up in a sheet or blanket while I worked away on his clothes with needle and thread, soap and water and smoothing irons. I was ready to run the blockade for a new uniform for Dan if for nothing else, but to tell him that I was going to run the blockade—there was the rub! Evening came and Dan with it, and the telling had to be done somehow.

"Dan," I began, patting the various patches on his shabby knee, "I want you to have a new uniform."

"Wish me a harp and a crown, Nell! One's about as easy as the other. You'll have to take it out in wanting, my girl."

"I expect I could buy Confederate cloth in Baltimore."

"Maybe—if you were there."

"Dan, I think I'll slip across the border and buy you a Confederate uniform, gold lace and all, from a Yankee tradesman, and then slip back here with it, and behold you in all the glory of it. Wouldn't that be nice, Dan?"

"Rather!"

Dan took in his patches at a glance, perhaps by way of mental comparison between himself in this and himself in the imaginary new uniform. But I saw he did not understand me at all—I had to make things plain.

"Dan," I said, "I am going to Baltimore."

"What?" he thundered.

"I am going to run the blockade with Millie."

"Have you lost your senses?"

"No, Dan. But I'm going to run the blockade with Millie— to get you a new uniform."

"Nell, don't be a goose!"

"And some shirts and some socks and some pins and needles—and I want to see mother—and Bobby—and—I'm going."

"I'm not going to allow you to attempt such a thing!" he said gravely.

"I want to see mother—and to get a new uniform—and other things."

Dan looked at me as if he thought I was crazy.

"Milicent is going—and I think I ought to go with her."

"I don't want Millie to go—I don't think she ought to try it; and I won't permit you to go off on such a wild-goose chase."

I was silent a minute, trying to think how to tell him as respectfully as I could that I differed with him on this point. It all ended by my repeating in a stupid, poll-parrot fashion:

"I'm going with Millie to Baltimore."

Dan looked at me as if he would like to spank me! Here was his obedient, docile girl-bride blossomed into a contumacious, rebellious wife!

I was ready to cry—nay, I was crying—but I still affirmed that I must go to Baltimore. Dan reasoned and argued, but that didn't do any good. Then he swore, but swearing didn't alter the case. The case was, indeed, beyond Dan, but he made a long and hard fight, and didn't surrender for a long while. I cried all night, and he reasoned all night. When he saw that the case was hopeless, he started us to Petersburg under suitable escort. We had to go first to Petersburg in order to get the money which we wished to take North to exchange for all the goods and chattels we might be able to smuggle South.

Dan detailed a driver and an ambulance for our service and Lieutenant Johnston to act as escort. The morning we started it looked cloudy. Dan tried to dissuade us. I said I had always been a good weather prophet and I didn't think it would rain. Millie reinforced me.

But when it actually came to telling Dan goodbye, I broke down. His threadbare clothes plead with me both ways. I hung around his neck and did so much crying that he got sorry for me and helped me off.

"When I get you a new uniform, Dan——" I sobbed, as he tucked the old blanket shawl about me where I sat in the ambulance.

"Uniform be——!" growled Dan. Then, seeing my crestfallen look, "I reckon I'll like it well enough, Nell—when it comes. Goodbye, girls. You're mighty big geese. God bless you! If you change your minds in Petersburg—but, Lord! an earthquake wouldn't change you! Goodbye, my darling—God bless you! I reckon you'll get along all right."

The rusty coat-sleeve was out of sight, and I was on my way.

Chapter 10

I Cross the Country in an Ambulance and the Pamunkey on a Lighter

As we travelled along farther and farther from Dan, I kept on crying softly to myself now and then, turning my face from Milicent. Presently her arm stole around me.

"Do you feel so badly, darling?"

"I hate to leave Dan—I can't bear it!"

"Then we'll turn back, Nell."

And our astonished driver and escort received orders to turn back toward camp.

"But in a few days," I sobbed, "Dan—will—be—gone. And you—will be—gone. And I can't stand that!"

And to the further confusion of escort, driver, and mules, we were turned again.

"Better not to do dat too often, lessen we won't git nowhar!" our driver muttered to himself. "Dese mules is clean upsot in dar min's."

I was upset in my mind, too. I continued to cry in a helpless, hopeless fashion, and was feeling that nothing on earth could make me more wretched than I already was when it began raining. Lieutenant Johnston, who had the soul of Mark Tapley, prophesied a shower and refused to leave his seat with the driver, but in a little while he was driven inside with us. It rained harder and harder—it poured. The ambulance began to leak and the straw on the floor got wet. Milicent and I huddled together under the old blanket shawl and drew over that a ragged piece of oilcloth; but the rain soaked through. Where Lieutenant Johnston sat there was a steady dripping, bursting now and then into a stream. But he was not to be daunted by discomforts or difficulties. He invented a trough for carrying off the water by making a dent in his broad-brimmed hat, pulling the brim into a point, and sticking it through a rent in the ambulance cover; and he was so merry over it all, and so convinced that things might be far worse and would soon be much better, that we were beginning to laugh at our own expense, when a sullen rushing and roaring reminded us that the worst of our troubles were still before us. We looked out of our ambulance upon the swollen waters of the Pamunkey River.

The thing on which we were to cross it was moored to the bank by a great chain. It was a lighter crowded with men and horses. There were soldiers at the ends and sides holding long sticks which they used as poles to direct and govern the craft. Our ambulance and mules were driven on along with other teams, and we walked into the midst of rearing and plunging horses, that threatened every minute to back off the lighter into the river and drag us with them, while our craft was making its slow way to the opposite bank.

I stood between two horses that reared and plunged the whole time. The men who held them had hard work to control them, and, I must add, that they swore roundly, and confess that this was the one occasion of my life when I did not undervalue that accomplishment or wish to put any restraint upon its free exercise. The truth is I was so scared that I was ready to help along with either the work or the swearing, if I had only known how.

As one of the men was trying his best to keep the horse he was holding from plunging and kicking itself into the river, or plunging and kicking itself on me, he caught my eye in the middle of an oath, and interrupted himself to begin an apology. The horse took advantage of this to make more vigorous demonstrations.

"Oh! oh!" I cried in terror, "finish—finish what you were saying to the horse! He's going to jump on me, and I'll have to say it myself if you don't!"

I didn't realize what I was saying until I heard a chuckle from the men within hearing distance. They knew that I was beside myself with terror, and did their best to smother their laughter. But I was past caring for public opinion. I was in an agony of terror. There was no other place for me to stand—horses, kicking, plunging, rearing horses were crowded everywhere. A lighter is the rudest excuse for a boat. Ours was made of planks crossed and nailed together, and between their wide spaces, just under my feet, I saw the swollen waters, upon which we seemed to be tossed, and careened, and whipped about without the control or guidance of those on board. Never before or since, never during any period of the war, was I in such a state of helpless fright as on that day when I crossed the mad Pamunkey on a lighter with swearing men and kicking horses around me and the water bubbling up against my feet.

Appearances to the contrary, our soldiers with the poles were directing our craft and turning the will of the tide to our profit, and at last we were on the shore. Safe in our wet ambulance, we started on our way again. I was never so cold, so wet, so everything wretched in my life, and what should Lieutenant Johnston do but propose to go out of our way to see St. Peter's Church.

"An old colonial relic," he said. "You ladies ought not to miss it now that you are so near."

"I don't want to see any relics," I answered promptly. "The only thing I want to see is a fire and something to eat."

But he would drive out of our way to show us that old church. I was too wretched and miserable to look at it with proper interest. I don't remember how it looked—I only know that I had to go there and see it whether I would or no. George Washington had done something or other there—got married, I believe. I think the church had some very fine ivy on it, but I am not sure. I thought it was old and small, and that it might do very well in summer, but that under present circumstances Washington himself would forgive me for being wholly in the thought of getting to a fire. Hunger and cold, cramped positions and rain dripping in on me had blunted everything in me except longings for creature comforts. The lieutenant drove all around the church religiously before starting on our way again.

"I don't believe you saw it at all," he said to me with real concern.

"Oh, yes, I did!" I answered promptly, terrified lest we should be turned back to look at it again, "I saw it thoroughly."

Of course, Milicent had looked the old church over and talked intelligently about it, but for the life of me, I couldn't remember whether it was made of brick or wood. And I didn't care, either.

The rain had dwindled into a drizzle, night was coming on, and I began to grow more and more anxious to find a stopping-place.

"I do hope we shall get into a place where they keep good fires," I said. "If we should get into a place where they burn green pine, I should lie down and die. Wet, green pine," I continued dolorously, "that smokes and never burns, and raw, clammy biscuit is about what we'll get tonight."

The lieutenant looked as if he was very sorry for me.

"I wish," he said unhappily, "I wish I knew how to tell a place where they burn green pine." Suddenly he brightened.

"I have it!" he exclaimed. "We won't stop at any house where there isn't a big wood-pile. We don't stop anywhere until we find a big white house, a big wood-pile and a nigger chopping wood."

We passed several dwellings, but the lieutenant wouldn't stop. "I don't see any wood-pile," or "The wood-pile ain't big enough," he would say.

At last we came upon what we wanted—a large white house, a wood-pile nearly as high as the house and a negro man chopping wood for dear life.

Through a big front yard full of shrubbery, a wide gravelled walk and circular drive-way led up to the house, and in a few minutes our ambulance was in front of the veranda. The lieutenant sprang out and went up the steps.

A gray-headed negro butler answered his knock.

"Wanter see master, sah? Yes, sah. Won't you step right in, sah?"

"I haven't time to stop a minute unless I can get lodgings for the night. I have ladies in the ambulance. Ask your master if he will be good enough to see me at the door for a minute."

Sambo bowed, made haste backward, and almost immediately an old gentleman appeared.

"Certainly, sir, certainly," he said, interrupting the lieutenant in the middle of his application. "Bring the ladies right in, sir."

And he helped to bring us in himself. Servants of all kinds appeared as if by magic from all quarters, and took charge of our trunks, satchels, ambulance, and driver.

The Virginia gentleman of those days was hospitable, as men are truthful, for his own sake first. His hospitality was spontaneous, unconscious, and free as heaven itself with its favours. All it asked in return was that you should come when you pleased, go when you pleased, stay as long as you pleased, and enjoy yourself to the top of your bent.

The house was a house of spindle-legged chairs, spindle-legged piano, brass fire-dogs, fine dark woodwork, candelabra of brass and crystal, and tall wax candles. Through the gloom the eyes of old portraits looked down upon us. In the wide fireplace of our bedroom crackled a mighty fire of oak and hickory; over the fire hung a bright brass kettle singing merrily; there were the ever-present fire-dogs and fender of burnished brass, and on the mantle two wax lights burning in silver candlesticks. Two smiling negro maids stood ready to minister to us.

In opposite corners of the room stood two large, canopied, mahogany bedsteads, with great, downy feather-beds and counterpanes, sheets and pillows as white as snow and smelling of lavender. The undiminished length of the table at which we sat down that night bore testimony not only to the good cheer it had given, but to that which it was ready to give. It was of dark rich mahogany, polished to the fineness of a mirror, that reflected the tall silver candlesticks holding wax candles. The silver service and beautiful old china rested on white mats that were not visible except where encircling fringes of gleaming damask suggested nests of snow. On a quaint buffet stood cut-glass decanters holding topaz and ruby wines and brandy and whisky.

The great mahogany sideboard—a small house in itself—nearly reached the ceiling. The upper half was a cabinet with glass doors shaped like the doors of a Gothic cathedral. The lower half had drawers with white knobs, and bellied doors of the most beautiful dark wood, reflecting, like the table, the glow of the wax lights. The glass cabinet glittered with silver and crystal, and here and there was clouded with the rich maroon and saffron of rare old china. Our hostess was a stately and beautiful old lady in black silk (much worn), with fichu and cuffs of real old lace. Our host wore fine black broadcloth, threadbare and of ancient cut.

Such a soft, shining picture as that supper-room was! I wish I could paint it as I saw it that night! And what a delicious supper! There was tea, sure enough; tea of delicious aroma; and sure enough sugar, too, in fine white lumps which had to be picked up with silver tongs. There were little teacakes and fairy-like puffs and wafers, and delicious hot rolls! creamy and velvety, and light as a breath.

In crystal dishes gleamed the rich, clear red and amber of preserved fruits, and crystal-clear sweetmeats were set before us in crystal dishes. These were cut in designs of leaf and flower, fish and bird, squirrels, rabbits, and acorns—really too elaborately cut and too beautifully transparent to be eaten. And in then there was Virginia fried chicken—of such a delicate rich brown! and such juicy sweetness! At last we each lay covered up in a great downy bed, and went to sleep, and slept as if we never expected to wake up.

Chapter 11

The Old Order

We found fresh straw and hot bricks in the bottom of our ambulance when we were ready to leave the next morning, an excellent luncheon and two bottles of wine. Soon after we started the wind changed, the clouds disappeared, and the sun came out. By the time we reached the Chickahominy there was sunshine in plenty—and wind, too.

Not a boat was in sight, and no figure on either bank of man or beast. I thought the lieutenant and the driver would split their lungs hallooing, but there was no response. Nobody answered and nobody came. We waited on the bank an hour without seeing anybody. Then an Indian came by in a skiff and we hailed him. He paddled to the shore, and we asked him if he knew where we could get a boat and some one to put us across. He knew of nothing and nobody of the kind within reach.

"I must hire your skiff then," said the lieutenant.

The Indian grinned.

"You no get cross in it. You spill out."

"Never mind that, so you get paid for your skiff. I am an old sailor."

Powhatan didn't think the lieutenant could manage that skiff; however, he got his price and gave in.

When he saw the three of us squeezing ourselves into the skiff he remonstrated again.

"Squaws spill out. Squaws git sick," he insisted. He told the lieutenant that we would be frightened out of our lives before we got across the river. He didn't know that Millie and I had been brought up on the coast and were as used to water as ducks.

Whoever has rowed an Indian skiff may have some idea of what a cockle-shell it was that took us across the Chickahominy. I sat in one end, Milicent in the other, and Lieutenant Johnston in the middle, paddle in hand, while our little craft switched and wriggled and rocked itself about in a manner that was as extraordinary as it was dangerous, and that was nearer perpetual motion than anything I ever saw.

At last the lieutenant stood up and straddled the boat to balance her. How he ever balanced himself I can't say, but he stood with one foot on each of her sides and managed her somehow. No one but an old sailor could have done it. I expected every minute to see him fall over into the water.

The sun was shining down, silvering the waters of the Chickahominy. The strong winds churned the waves and blew our hats and veils almost off our heads, and almost blew our breath away—when the rocking skiff left us any. And out on the wide, turbulent, bright river we tossed and tumbled, and laughed and got wet and came near drowning. I never had more fun in any sail. But at last we were safely across, and waiting by the York River Railroad for our train. The half-breed gave us our trunks, and took back his skiff and our money. In a few hours we were in Richmond, where the lieutenant saw us to our hotel, and left. I sent a letter by him to Dan, begging Dan's pardon for having my own way.

The next day found us in Petersburg. Our business here was to provide ourselves with money with which to buy Yankee goods—particularly a Confederate uniform—in Yankeeland. I wanted as much gold as our broker could let me have, but he advised me against taking more than enough to make the trip with, and a small margin for contingencies.

"It will be in your way and increase your danger," he said. "Confederate notes will get you to the Potomac. From there you need a little gold to take you to Baltimore. After you are there I will contrive any sum you want to your trustees in Norfolk. They, being inside the Yankee lines, can send it to Baltimore."

Our next objective point was Mrs. Rixey's in Culpeper. Blockade-runners were continually setting out from there, and we thought we would have no difficulty in attaching ourselves to a party. After a rest in Petersburg of a day and a half, we started for Culpeper, reaching Mrs. Rixey's at nightfall. We told her husband that we wanted to join a party of blockade-runners.

"Mrs. Otis and her two daughters start north tomorrow; perhaps you can go with them," he said, and went out to see about it.

Unfortunately—or fortunately—the Otis party was complete—there was no vacant seat in their wagon.

"I will be on the lookout for you," Mr. Rixey said. "Somebody else will be along soon."

Before breakfast he knocked at our door.

"There are two gentlemen downstairs who are going north," he said, when Millie stuck her head out. "They give their names as Captain Locke and Mr. Holliway, and they seem to be gentlemen. That is all I know about them. You might see them and talk the matter over."

We finished dressing hurriedly and went down to the parlour, where we met Captain Locke and Mr. Holliway, and after a brief talk decided to go with them.

The best vehicle we could get was a wagon without springs, and instead of a body four planks laid across the axles, one plank set up on each side, and no ends at all.

Over the rude floor we had a quantity of straw piled, and two chairs were set up for Milicent and me. The gentlemen seated themselves on our baggage, which consisted of two small trunks into which we had crowded a few articles for each of them. The wagoner, a rough mountaineer, sat on a plank which had been laid across the two uprights at the sides.

It was a bitterly cold day. Milicent and I wore thick cloaks, and the wagoner supplied a blanket which we wrapped about our feet. In addition, the gentlemen contributed a large blanket shawl which they insisted upon folding about our shoulders, declaring that their overcoats protected them sufficiently. Now and then they got out of the wagon and walked and stamped to keep their legs from getting stiff with cold, and at last Milicent and I were reduced to the same device for keeping up our circulation. We got so stiff we couldn't move, and the gentlemen had to lift us out of the wagon, pull us about, and drag us into a walk and a run.

It was dark when we reached the house at which it had been suggested we should stop. Lights were in every window and we could see much moving about. Mr. Holliway went in to ask for lodgings.

He returned quickly and jumped into the wagon, saying to the wagoner:

"Drive on."

Milicent and I were almost freezing.

"What's the matter?" we asked in keen disappointment.

Just then the wagon made a turn, and we saw distinctly into the house through an uncurtained window. There was a long white object in the middle of the floor and over it stood a weeping woman.

"Why," I exclaimed, "somebody's dead there."

"Yes, I didn't want to tell you," he said. "It's a dead soldier. I was afraid it might make you feel badly. Ladies are sometimes superstitious, and I feared you might take it as a bad omen for our journey."

But we found out afterward that it was he who had taken it for a bad omen. He was going north to see his family, and he was so anxious about them that he talked of little else. Captain Locke's mission was not so clear. He called it business—we little knew what dangerous business it was!—and we troubled our heads no further about it.

It was very late when we at last came upon a tumble-down farmhouse, where we were taken in for the night. The family who lived there did their best for us, but they were far from being comfortable themselves. By this time, however, any quarters and any fare were acceptable. We slept in the room with a goodly company, all fortunately of our own sex, and the gentlemen, as we heard afterward, in even more crowded quarters.

Our poverty-stricken hosts did not wish to charge us, but before we left the next morning we insisted upon paying them.

That morning a little Jew boy was added to our party. Just how, or when, or where we picked him up, I can not recall, and I should probably never have thought of him again if he had not impressed himself upon me most unpleasantly afterward at Berlin.

Our second night we spent according to our program, in Fauquier County, with Mr. Robert Bolling, a friend of my husband's.

"I am astonished at your trying to run the blockade, Mrs. Grey," he said.

"Why?" I asked. "And why are you more astonished at me than at Milicent?"

I had been hearing similar remarks, and was becoming curious.

"Because you look like a little girl. I am surprised at such nerve in so youthful a lady."

"I want a new uniform for Dan," I said. "He's promoted."

Mr. Bolling laughed heartily.

"And I am quite as brave as Milicent," I insisted.

"Well, I am surprised at you both. It is a dangerous undertaking."

Our wagoner was invited to take supper with us. He was rough and ill-clad, and he felt out of place, but Mr. Bolling charmed him into ease and talked over our prospective journey with him.

"It is well for you to be on good terms with your wagoner," he said to us privately, when he sent out the invitation.

Mr. Bolling was old and gray-haired, or he would have been in the field. His home was one of the most celebrated country-seats in Fauquier, and he himself full of honours and one of the best-known men in the State.

The night we spent at this old Virginia homestead was repetition of a night previously described, with variations. Here were the same old-fashioned mahogany furniture with claw feet and spindle legs, and wax lights in brass and silver candelabra, and rare old china, and some heirlooms whose history we were interested in. Several of these had come with the first Bollings from England. There was a sword which had come down from the War of the Roses, and on the wall, in a place of special honour, hung the sword of a Bolling who had distinguished himself in the Revolution. Mr. Bolling took it down and laid it in Milicent's outstretched hands with a smile.

"I am a believer in State's rights, and I am a Secessionist, I suppose," said the old man with a sigh, as he hung the sword back in its place. "But—I hate to fight the old flag. I hate that."

Above the sword was the portrait of the Bolling who had worn the sword, a soldierly looking fellow in the uniform of a Revolutionary colonel.

"He saved the old flag once at the cost of his life," the aged man said, sighing again. "He is buried out yonder in the graveyard, wrapped in the folds of the very flag he snatched from the hands of the British. If we were to open his grave tonight, we would find his bones and ashes wrapped in that flag he died to save. Yes, I am sorry to fight the old flag."

"Then," I said innocently and without thinking, "it is well that you are exempted from service in the field."

His eyes flashed.

"Ah, no, my dear! Since fighting there is, I wish I could be in it. If I were young enough and strong enough I'd take that sword down and follow Robert Lee. Virginia is invaded."

Chapter 12

A Dangerous Masquerade

The night of our third day found us at the wagoner's cottage on the top of the Blue Ridge Mountains. As we climbed our slow and painful way up to the ruddy little light that beckoned us from its wild and eerie perch, moonlight and starlight fell upon snow-capped cliffs and into deep valleys, touching them into solemn, mystical beauty. It was as if we had lost ourselves in the clear, white stillness of the enchanted Snow Kingdom that had enthralled and terrified us in the happy days of fairy tales. But there was nothing magical about the cottage when we finally got there, or the welcome, or the supper. Instead of fairies and cowslip dew and, bread of lily pollen, we had a delightfully wholesome, plump Virginia housewife, a Virginia welcome, and, above all, a Virginia supper.

The cottage was plainly furnished, but it was neat as a pin. The mountaineer's wife and mother served us, the one waiting on us, the other cooking. We sat at table in the kitchen, and such a feast as we had! There was nice apple-butter on the table, and delicious milk and cream, fresh eggs and hot buckwheat cakes, and genuine maple syrup, of course. I have never tasted such buck-wheats anywhere. And how fast the old lady fried them, and the wife handed them to us, piping hot! and how fast we ate! and how many!

The furniture in our bedroom, as everywhere else, was exceedingly plain, but so deliciously clean. And such a bed! such a downy, fragrant bed! The sheets were snowy, the coverlet was spotless. As I went to sleep I had an idea that the feathers in that bed must have come from the breasts of mountain birds that had never touched the earth. In the morning the mountaineer took us to a point near his house, where we could stand and look into—I have forgotten how many States, and out upon snowy peaks, and mountain streams, and lovely shadowed vales.

We lost our Confederate captain when we started down the mountain that day; Mr. Holliway had all along been in civilian's dress, and now Captain Locke changed his uniform for citizen's clothes, leaving the uniform at the cottage, to be called for on his return.

The fourth night we reached Berryville.

Here it was necessary to hold a council with closed doors, for the presence of the little Jew boy had for several days prevented us from talking freely.

He seemed to have eyes and ears all over him, and we felt vaguely that he would use both to our disadvantage. So we shut him out of the little room at the inn in Berryville where we held our secret council. The morrow would find us inside the Federal lines—it was necessary to prepare our story. We agreed that Captain Locke was to be our brother, because he had fair hair and blue eyes like ourselves. Mr. Holliway was of too entirely different a type to be claimed for a nearer relationship than that of cousin. We were young ladies of Baltimore who had been visiting at Mr. Robert Bolling's in Fauquier, and our brother and cousin had come south to take us home, not being willing that we should undertake such a journey alone. Captain Locke gave Milicent some papers to be concealed in the lining of her muff. I, too, had some papers to hide for him. Fortunately we did not know until afterward that Captain Locke was a Confederate spy, and that the papers we carried were official documents of importance to the Confederacy, and that if discovered the captain would be strung up in short order and every one of us sent to prison.

If we had known what he was and the nature of the papers, I think our patriotism would have risen to the occasion, but we should have been more nervous and more likely to betray ourselves. So I think he was wise to take the liberty of counting on our patriotism, and also to keep us in the dark as a safeguard for both ourselves and the papers.

The next forenoon we reached the Potomac River, and found ourselves in Federal lines. Our wagoner bade us goodbye and left us there on the bank. In the river below lay the lighter on which we were to cross the Potomac. It was crowded with Federal soldiers. There was no way to reach it except to slide down the bank, and the bank was steep. To slide down, it was neither a graceful nor a dignified thing to do. I drew back. The captain took me by the hand to pull me over. I still drew back. I did not want to slide down that bank.

"Come on, sister!" he exclaimed with brotherly crossness.

I grinned broadly, but the captain, his back to the lighter, gave me such a serious look that I sobered in an instant.

"Sister, come along! Don't be a goose!" he said, and giving me a jerk pulled me over.

The Federal soldiers on the lighter could see and hear. One blunder now and we were lost. I yielded to the inevitable and slid down the bank with the captain; Mr. Holliway followed with Milicent. Another minute, and we stood on the lighter in the midst of Yankee soldiers and Yankee horses. A horse's nose was over my shoulder the whole way. Soldiers were crowded up against me, there was ample occasion for swears, but I don't think I heard an oath the entire distance, and they were courtesy itself to Milicent and me.

Landing at Berlin, we walked into the office of the provost marshal. The provost was out, and the deputy who was at his desk looked at us with cool, inquisitive eyes. He put the usual questions and received readymade answers.

"Who are you?" he asked Captain Locke in a very suspicious tone.

"Charles D. Moore, of Baltimore."

"Occupation?"

"I am studying law."

"Humph!" with a glance that made me keenly alive to the lameness of that story told by the martial-looking captain.

"What are you doing down here?"

"Taking my sisters back home."

"Humph! Who are you?" turning to Mr. Holliway.

"William H. May, of Baltimore."

"Studying law too?"

"No. I expect to study medicine."

"Are you taking these ladies back home too?"

"I am accompanying them, certainly," said Mr. Holliway with asperity.

"Who *are* these ladies?"

"My sisters," said Captain Locke firmly, "and I am here to protect them on their way back home."

"Where have they been?"

"They are from Mr. Robert Bolling's in Fauquier County, Virginia. They have been visiting at his house. We wished them to return to Baltimore, and I came south for them. My cousin, Mr. May, joined us."

"And you—what are you doing down here?" with a touch of irony to Holliway.

"Got caught this side by the war, and am trying to get back home."

"Ah, yes, of course. I can't pass you. Take seats, please. The marshal will be in directly."

Our evidence was too smooth.

It was plain the deputy didn't believe in us, and we felt uneasy and miserable to the soles of our boots—except Captain Locke, who looked thoroughly at his ease.

It was an hour or longer before the marshal came in. It seemed a great deal more, yet I can't say that I longed to see him.

"What's all this?" he asked his deputy as he took in our party, braced up against the wall.

"A party who crossed from Virginia this morning. They have been visiting in Fauquier—*they say*—and want to get back to Baltimore. A lame tale, I call it. I would send them straight back if I had my way with them."

The provost's eyes had rested first on me, as I happened to be more conspicuously placed than the others. I have been accredited with a most ingenuous countenance. I returned his gaze with a regard utterly "childlike and bland," looking up into his face with eyes as frank and trusting as a baby's. Past me his gaze went to Milicent—I have said before that Milicent had the face of a Madonna; then the manly and straightforward eyes of Locke held him; and last Mr. Holliway's reserved and gentlemanly countenance met his scrutiny with a quiet dignity that disarmed suspicion. He began by interviewing Milicent and me. When he questioned me I said plaintively:

"I have been here an hour, sir, and I am very tired. I would be so much obliged if you would send us on home. I am almost sick with the journey I have taken, and I should so like to get home tonight."

"That is impossible," he said; "but," he continued kindly, "I do not think you will be detained later than tomorrow morning."

He conversed in a low tone with his deputy, and then I heard him say: "Let them spend the night at the old German's on the hill, and tomorrow we will see about it."

Then turning to us, he said that an orderly would conduct us to a place where we would be lodged for the night. When an officer asked about our baggage, I extended my keys quickly, saying:

"We have two small trunks."

He took the keys with an apology. As I was passing out of the door

I turned back and held out my satchel.

"I forgot that you have to examine this."

"It is not necessary, miss," he said, smiling.

The old Dutchman was out, but his wife received us and made us comfortable. While we were at supper he came in. "I speeks *mit* you after supper," he said solemnly, and sat in silence until we had finished.

Then he took us into a room, closed and locked the door, came close to us, and whispered:

"I knows dat you haf run te plockate. You bees in ver' mooch tancher. Town te stdreet I hears you vas at mine house, unt I hears ver' mooch talk, unt I lis'en. I vill help you if you vill let me."

He now addressed himself particularly to Captain Locke and Mr. Holliway:

"You, shentlemen, mus' leave mine house, shoost as soon as you can, or you vill be daken brisoners. I vill help you to get avay."

"We can't do it," said Locke promptly. "I cannot leave my sisters alone and unprotected."

Milicent and I were trembling with fear.

"Brother," said Milicent, "you and Cousin William must leave us and save yourselves."

"Please go," I begged. I could not keep my eyes off the door. I feared every moment to hear the rap of the sergeant come to arrest our friends. But the captain and Mr. Holliway reiterated their determination not to leave us in our present situation. If I had not been scared almost to death I could have laughed at the perfect brotherliness of Locke's protestations.

"Tere is tancher, shentlemen. I hears te talk town te street," urged the Dutchman with every appearance of earnestness and good-will.

"What did you hear?" asked Locke nonchalantly.

"Oh, tey tinks you haf not tolt vat you vas. Tey tinks you be Secesh—unt I ton't know vat tey tinks."

"I can't help what they think," said Locke. "I am going to protect my sisters."

"How you brotect tem ven you be brisoners, *hein?*"

"I don't know," answered Locke, smiling, "but I certainly shall not leave them."

"Vat goot you do? I vill take care of te ladies. Nopody vill hu't tern, unt I vill see dat tey gets off all right. Tere is no tancher for tem."

"Thank you, my friend," said the captain simply and heartily. "But we can not accept your kind offer. We must take my sisters home ourselves."

"I ver' sorry," said the Dutchman sadly.

As soon as the door closed behind him, we began to plead.

"Captain," said Milicent, "you and Mr. Holliway must go. We will not consent to anything else."

"We should be regular deserters to do that," said Locke contemptuously. "I think the old fellow is exaggerating. Or maybe he is pumping us. Holliway and I will walk down the street and see."

We thought this was madness, and we were miserable from the moment they left until they were safely back. Captain Locke was, as always, at his ease, but Mr. Holliway was very pale. He knew, as Milicent and I did not, the risk we were all running, and he was more concerned perhaps for Locke's safety than for his own. For him arrest meant prison at the worst—for Locke, a halter.

"The Dutchman is right," he said in answer to our questions. "We stopped outside several places and heard them talking about us and our arrest. We are practically prisoners."

He tried to speak cheerfully and as if it would be a sure and easy matter to find some way out of our predicament; but the truth was that he had been struggling all along against great depression of spirits; his health was bad, the incident of the first night of our journey had impressed him, and he had evidently felt himself under a cloud ever since our experience at the provost's.

"That talk doesn't amount to much," said Captain Locke carelessly.

The room in which we were sitting was that which had been taken for Milicent's and my bedroom. Captain Locke got up, walked to the door and locked it.

"You have needles and thread, I think, ladies?"

Milicent and I immediately produced them and slipped on our thimbles. He handed Milicent his open knife.

"Rip the papers out of your muff, Mrs. Norman, and you, little madam, let me have those I gave you."

The two I had were hidden in my sleeve. While Milicent and I were getting the papers out, I heard Mr. Holliway say:

"Burn those papers, Locke. You can never get them to Baltimore, and you know in what fearful peril they keep us."

"I might as well turn back if I burn them," said the captain. "I take those papers to Baltimore, or I die trying—and I won't die."

"Excuse the trouble I give you, ladies," he said, leaning back in his chair and putting his feet on another. "Will you open the hems of my trousers and sew those papers inside? It is a great favour."

We ripped each hem, folded the papers inside as flat as possible, and sewed the hems up again. I had not made over Dan's old uniform for nothing, and Milicent was always a skilful needlewoman—our hems looked quite natural and not at all "stuffed." But we were so nervous that we worked very slowly, for we felt that a wrong stitch might cost Captain Locke his life.

He had worn his trousers turned up around the bottom to keep them out of the mud. When we had finished he carefully turned them back again, Mr. Holliway looking on gloomily.

"Now, ladies," said the captain cheerfully, "we will all retire and get a good night's rest. You have had a hard day and I am sure you must be tired."

"Aren't you going away?" we asked anxiously. "What did you take the papers for?"

He smiled.

"Little madam," he said, "you had best go to bed and get a good night's rest. That is what I am going to do. Mrs. Norman, make this poor child go to bed. And you will promise me to try to rest too, won't you?"

There was a rap on the door.

Chapter 13

A Last Farewell

Mr. Holliway opened it to admit the Dutchman.

"Shentlemen," he began earnestly, "tey haf got te leetle Chew poy trunk mit giffin' him visky, unt he haf tolt everyding. I pe your vrent. You mus' get avay pefore mitnight."

"The little Jew knows nothing to tell," said the captain. "His drunken babble is not worth attention. We cannot leave my sisters."

"How you help tem by stayin'? I gif you my vort dat tey vill get to Paltimore all right. I hates to see tern Yankees takes you up in mine house."

Milicent and I believed in the German.

So I think did both gentlemen by this time, but we had come this far under their care, and they were loath to leave us unless entirely convinced that it was for our safety as well as their own. Mr. Holliway was no less concerned about us than Captain Locke was, but he took a darker view of the situation. He drew Locke aside and they talked together in low tones. I caught the word "reckless "and "those papers," and "a disadvantage to them," "safer without us." When they turned back to us Captain Locke said:

"We leave the question in your hands, ladies. Perhaps we—and more particularly I—endanger you by remaining. But I hate to leave you alone this way, and I am not afraid of anything that can happen to me. If the worst came to the worst, and we were arrested, I have some influence in the North which might still be of benefit to us all."

"Use it for yourself and Mr. Holliway," we said, "and go."

"Think well, ladies. You want us to go now, but when we are gone and you are here alone, won't you feel desolate and deserted?"

"We will only be glad you're gone," I said.

"I don't think I ever heard such a polite speech in my life," said

Captain Locke, laughing. "Holliway, I think we had better leave immediately."

He stood cool and smiling, but Mr. Holliway, whose health was not robust, and upon whom the hardships of the journey and the excitement had told, was ghastly. Not that he lacked courage. He would have stayed and died for us, as far as that was concerned; but his physical endurance was not great, and from the first he had been oppressed with a presentiment of evil.

Milicent had drawn Captain Locke aside, and was urging him to go, as I knew, and, as I think, to destroy the papers which Holliway felt imperilled him. He gave her a smiling negative.

"You must go yourself, and please help us make the captain go," I was saying to Mr. Holliway.

"You will have to do that," he replied. "I have said what I could. It is madness for us to stay, as I am thoroughly convinced now. You would be safer without us. Locke doesn't think so, but I know it. His character and the papers he carries increase the danger for us all."

Captain Locke and Milicent had finished their conference.

"We will go," he said quietly. "A pen and ink, my friend," to the Dutchman.

"Make haste and go," we pleaded.

But he waited for the pen and ink.

"We have time enough," he said, consulting his watch very coolly. "It is not yet half-past eleven."

He wrote a note and gave it to the Dutchman to be mailed that night.

"If you get into any trouble," he said to Milicent, "telegraph to this address."

And he gave her a slip of paper on which was written: "Gov. ———, Baltimore, Md."

"The letter is to my uncle, and if you are in any trouble he will help you out. The governor will be advised of your situation, and a telegram to him will be understood."

"Goodnight, ladies, and *au revoir*" he said gaily, bowing over our hands. "We will meet in Baltimore."

"I echo that," said Mr. Holliway with assumed cheerfulness. "It has been a great pleasure and privilege to know you, ladies. With all its shadows, this journey will always be one of my sweetest memories."

We might never see them again. We knew it as we looked into Locke's bonnie blue eyes and Holliway's dark sad ones. They had been our brave and gentle knights, shielding us and enduring all the hardships cheerfully. One of them was weaker, we knew, because he had given his blanket to keep us warm. We looked bravely back into the two brave faces that looked into ours—one sign of faltering and they would not leave us.

"I will say a 'Hail Mary' for each of you every night," I said.

"I, too," said Milicent softly.

"Thank you," there was a quiver in each voice now. "We will try to deserve your prayers, dear ladies."

Then they bowed themselves out with smiling faces. One of them we never saw again.

CHAPTER 14

The Little Jew Boy and the Provost's Deputy

The Dutchman went with them to show them the way he said they must take. His wife came in and gossiped with us.

According to her account, it was a miracle that we had passed through the provost's hands as well as we had.

"If de vimmins had peen dere, dey vould haf pult your close off, unt dey vould haf search you all ofer. I ton't know as you haf anyding you not vant dem to see, but if you haf anyding, tey pe zhure to fint it. Te vimmins tat haf to pe dere totay vas gone avay somevare. If she had peen dere, you vas haf harter times tan you vas haf."

I thought with a shudder of our muffs and satchels, our pictures in Confederate uniform, and those papers.

"Mine man say some volks vas arrested town te river totay. Dere vas dree laties unt von shentleman. Tey dry to cross at de Boint of Vrocks [Point of Rocks] unt tey vas took up unt sent pack."

"What were their names?" we asked eagerly.

We remembered that the Otis party consisted of three ladies and one gentleman. We had kept in sight of their ambulance for some time. But at the parting of our ways, when they had taken one road and we another, our driver had said: "They are going to try to get across at the Point of Rocks, and they'll sure be turned back or took up, one."

"I ton't know vat dere names," said the Dutchwoman. "Mine man vill know. He forgets notding."

When he came in he thought a little, and then he said he thought the name was "Odis." So we had been luckier than we thought in the chance that prevented us from joining their party.

The old German had directed our friends as best he could, and started them on their way. They were to keep to the woods and walk to Frederick, from where, he thought, they might reach Baltimore. He told us that they had not gone away immediately after leaving us, although he had urged them to do so. They had said they wouldn't go away until they saw how we took being left alone. They had gone around to the window of the room in which we were sitting, and had spied upon us. When they saw us gossiping with the old woman, they had gone off satisfied that we would not break down after their departure.

"Tey vas not so vraid vor her," he said, indicating Milicent. "It vas you, te leetle matam, as he call you, dat he vas vraid vor. He vraid you vould cry pecause you vas so leetle, unt pecause you vas so ver' younk. I ask him vat he do if you cry, unt I dry to make him come avay, unt he say: ' If she cry I von't go. I vill go in tat room unt I vill dake her up in mine arms unt I vill not stop until I put her safe in Captain Grey's arms! Dot is vot I vill do.' He titn't leaf you off," to Milicent, "put he dort you pe mo' prave."

If he had been at the window then he would have seen tears in our eyes. But I bore a grudge.

"Milicent," I said, as soon as we were alone, "I don't see why people should make of me just the exception that they always do. I may be a little younger, but I am married, and I have got just as much sense about some things and I'm just as brave as you are. I'm a soldier's wife, the wife of a Confederate officer. I wonder how I have behaved that everybody expects me to be a coward."

And Milicent comforted me.

The next morning an orderly rapped at the door of the German's house and asked for us.

The German answered.

"Tell the *ladies*," with an emphasis on the word, "the provost says they can go on. The train leaves in fifteen minutes. They will find their bagagge at the station. Here are their keys."

"You see it is veil tat te shentlemen tit not vait vor bermission," said the German as we hurried into our wraps.

We heard afterward that following our departure a sergeant-at-arms called for the "shentlemen." Our train was late coming in. As we stood on the platform waiting we saw that wretched little Jew boy fooling around and watching us. We pretended not to see him. Suddenly I felt a tremor in Milicent's arm which was linked in mine.

"Do you see who is on the platform talking with the little Jew boy? No, don't turn your head—don't look suddenly—don't look at all. It is the provost's deputy who didn't believe in us yesterday."

Oh, if the train would only come, and we were on it and gone! As it rolled up beside the platform we had to restrain ourselves from getting on it too eagerly. But we were at last in our seats; the whistle blew, and the train moved out of the station.

The station was behind us, out of sight, and we were leaning back enjoying ourselves, when Milicent glanced behind her. I was looking out of the window when I felt her hand on my arm.

"Don't look suddenly. But when you can, glance behind us."

Three seats behind us sat the provost's deputy. He was reading a paper, or, rather, watching us over a paper which he held up before him. He kept us under close observation the whole way. We had no opportunity to consult about the difficulties of the situation, but we felt that we were to elude our shadow in Baltimore or not at all. Carriages stood thick around the depot. Drivers were cracking their whips and importuning the public for patronage. We stepped off the platform into the midst of them, got to haggling about prices, and found ourselves mixed up in a lot of carriages, the yelling and screaming drivers having closed up behind us around the platform to which they had turned their attention. There we saw the deputy's hat revolving rapidly, as if he were turning himself about to catch sight of us. Chance stood our friend. We happened to stand between two carriages, the doors of which hung open. A party of two ladies stepped into one. Instantly we took the other.

"Drive fast to No.— Charles Street," Milicent said to the driver. Several carriages rolled out of the depot with our own, and before we reached Mrs. Harris's we felt that we had escaped the deputy. Once with mother and Bobby we forgot him.

Chapter 15

I Fall Into the Hands of the Enemy

Mrs. Harris kept a select and fashionable boarding-house. There were many regular boarders and a stream of people coming and going all the time. She was a Southern sympathizer, and her house was a hotbed of sedition and intrigue for both sides. Among her guests were three Yankee officers, whom I made up my mind—or, rather, my mind needed no making up—to dislike. Uniform and all, I objected to them. The day after we came Mrs. Harris was chatting with us in mother's room.

"I must introduce you to those Federal officers who are in the house," she remarked.

"I beg you will not!" I replied indignantly. "I will have nothing to do with them."

"Then you will make a grave mistake, my child. That course would betray you at once. You've put your head into the lion's mouth, and prudence is the better policy until you get it out again. If you meet these officers and are civil to them they may be of assistance to you when you want to go back."

Accordingly, when our household met as usual in the parlours that evening, Captain Hosmer, Assistant Adjutant-General William D. Whipple, of Schenck's command, and Major Brooks—also, I think, of Schenck's command—were presented to me.

Major Brooks had such a keen, satirical way of looking at me that I immediately took a violent prejudice against him, though I tried hard to conceal it. Schenck's adjutant I did not like much better. Captain Hosmer was objectionable on general principles as a Yankee, but he was really a handsome fellow and a most charming gentleman, and though I had hard work overcoming my prejudices sufficiently to be quite civil at first, I ended by becoming warmly attached to him. My impulse was to avoid these gentlemen and to show my colours in a passive way. I say in a passive way, because anything approaching discourtesy Dan would have condemned. On duty, he would have shot a Yankee down quickly enough; off duty, he would never have failed in politeness to a gentleman in any uniform. As I could not well appear here as a Confederate officer's wife, I was introduced to these gentlemen as Miss Duncan. The day after our arrival we mailed Captain Locke's picture, which he had given us for the purpose, to his sister in Harrisburg, and called to see Mr. Holliway's mother and sisters. They were charming women, and entertained us in true Baltimore fashion.

Indeed, I soon found myself in a whirl of gaiety. Mrs. Harris's house was a merry one. Of course, being in Baltimore, its politics were mixed, as we have said, but as far as social position and culture were concerned, the guests were above reproach. The parlours in the evening reminded one of those of a fashionable pleasure resort.

Next door was another boarding-house. Mother's windows overlooked the entrance, and we amused ourselves—according to boarding-house custom and privilege—by watching our own and our neighbours' callers and guests, and by nicknaming them. There was one of the next-door boarders who entertained us greatly. We dubbed him "the Professor." He had a funny way of wearing his green goggles as if they were about to fall off his nose. He had long, snaky curls which looked very greasy and glossy, and he walked with a slight stoop, using a gold-headed cane; and he always carried a book under his arm.

In our own house were two ladies who afforded us much amusement. They were sisters, as Captain Hosmer took occasion to inform me early in our acquaintance, but they were politically so opposed to each other that they did not speak.

Mrs. Bonds was a black Republican, Mrs. Lineman a red-hot rebel. This latter fact we discovered by degrees. Women did not gossip in those days—not to talk was a necessary evil—very evil and very necessary in a boarding-house of mixed politics in Baltimore during war times.

Mrs. Harris kept a private parlour for herself and daughters, and here we poor rebels met every now and then with a little less restraint, though even here we had to be very careful. One day a note was brought me.

Happy greetings, dear friends! Can you arrange without inconvenience to yourselves for me to call, and will you allow me that pleasure? Do not hesitate to decline if you feel so disposed. I will understand.

L.

There was no other signature, but we knew the hand. Thank God! He was alive and well! We took the note to Mrs. Harris. Of course we would see him if we could make a way. After a little consultation it was arranged that we receive him in the little parlour upstairs. We addressed an envelope to ourselves, put a blank sheet of paper in it, sealed it, and enclosed it in a note to the captain. The latter we did not know how to address; we were merely to give it to his messenger, who was waiting. We wrote:

Delighted. Come to side entrance at half-past eight; present enclosed and you will be shown up.

N. & M.

At half-past eight we were waiting in Mrs. Harris's private parlour—there were several ladies there beside ourselves. Of all nights, why couldn't they keep away this night?—when Mrs. Harris's maid brought up the envelope we had addressed to ourselves.

"Show him up," we said.

Why in the world wouldn't those other women go? And would there be any callers in the private parlour tonight?

"Dr. Moreau!" announced Mrs. Harris's maid.

Into the room walked the "Professor," green goggles and all. Who in the world was *he* coming to see? What was he doing here any way? And on this night of all nights when we were looking for Captain Locke and wishing for as few witnesses as possible! Through the open door behind the "Professor," we caught a glimpse of Mrs. Bonds out in the hall, following him with curious eyes. If we could only slip downstairs and keep the captain from coming up tonight! And why didn't the girl bring the captain in? Milicent was rising to go out into the hall, when the "Professor," having glanced around the room, approached us.

"I was invited to call on some ladies here this evening? Am I in the wrong room?" said a perfectly strange voice, the voice you would expect to hear from a fossil.

We looked up in confusion. If we could only get him out of the way before the captain entered! He waited while we pondered how to answer.

"What ladies do you wish to see?" I asked.

"Well, this *is* good! Little madam, may I take this seat beside you?"

He dropped into the chair between us and we caught for an instant his old merry laugh, "nipped in the bud," it is true, for we gave him a warning glance. Mrs. Harris was considerate and tactful, and we not only had our corner to ourselves, but attention and observation diverted from us as much as possible. We were much amused at Captain Locke's "make-up," and he was evidently very proud of it.

"It must be very clever for *your* eyes not to have seen through it," he said. "I have been looking up at your window and watching you every day. I saw, too, that you made merry at my expense. It was a great temptation to speak to you many times, but I didn't want to make advances nor to ask permission to call until I knew something about how the land lay over here."

"You don't know how anxious we have been about you, or how glad and thankful we are to see you," we assured him. "We have been very uneasy at not hearing from you. Where is Mr. Holliway?"

"God knows!" he answered gravely. "He was afraid to follow my fortunes, I think. He left me at Frederick. He ought to be here by now, but if he is he is keeping very close."

"He is not here," we answered. "We have been to see his mother and sister, and they know nothing of him."

"Then something is wrong. He had an idea that we might be tracked to Frederick very easily from Berlin, and from Frederick to this place if we came by the direct route; so he branched off into West Virginia, intending to reach Baltimore by a more roundabout route than mine. Poor Holliway! he was not well, and he was nervous and unstrung over this trip from the first. He felt that I was reckless and that I was throwing away my own chance and his."

Someone in the room came near us and we returned to generalities. Very soon after Captain Locke made his *adieux*, promising to call again when we could arrange it.

Captain Hosmer had sought opportunities for showing special courtesies to me, but I had rather repelled him. He was good enough, however, to ignore my bad manners and to persist in turning my music for me. We had dances very often in the evenings, I playing the same tunes for folks to dance by that I played for the Prussians and that I play for my children. One night, I had the audacity to rattle off the Virginia reel, and they danced it with spirit, every Yankee of them.

My fingers were just itching to play *Dixie*, and I don't know what foolhardiness I might have been guilty of if Captain Hosmer, who was turning my music, had not bent over me and said:

"I would like to have a little private talk with you, Miss Duncan. I know who you are. You are from the South and you have run the blockade. Your position is not free from danger. You are suspected. Pray be careful. When you have finished this, go upstairs and I will follow you."

His manner was so serious that it took all the saucy daring out of me. Perhaps it saved me from playing *Dixie*. As soon as I could do so without attracting observation, I got Milicent to take my place, and went upstairs to the private parlour.

I had hardly taken my seat when he came in.

"I was sorry to attack you so suddenly," he said, "but you were so shy of me that it was my only chance."

I had learned to like and to trust him; he was honest and kind, and I told him my situation frankly. Of course I didn't explain Captain Locke.

"It is not so bad as it might be," he said, "But you must have a care about your associates. People in this house are always more or less under observation, and arrest on charge of treason is not an unknown thing in it."

"I am married—" When I came to that part of my confession the captain looked surprised indeed.

"Didn't you guess from the dignity I have displayed that I was a matron?"

"I never dreamed it! I don't mean that you were not dignified," he added quickly, and in some confusion.

"My husband is a staff-officer in the rebel army," I added proudly.

"Lucky fellow!"

"I think he is a lucky fellow to be a staff-officer in the rebel army."

"To be your husband, I meant."

"I wonder if he would agree with you there!" We were on a subject very interesting to me now.

"I will show you his picture in the morning," I volunteered.

"Better not," Captain Hosmer said promptly.

I suppose I must have shown how hurt I was, for he added quickly: "Of course I'll be glad to see his picture. Don't forget to bring it down at breakfast."

But he had frozen me for the time being. I could not talk about Dan to him when I saw it bored him to listen, so we went back to the original subject of our conversation. Among other persons he spoke of Mrs. Lineman.

"I see that you are inclined to form an intimacy there. Mrs. Lineman is in perfect sympathy with the South, but, as you know, her sister is not. They do not speak now, but family differences are frequently made up. Then confidences ensue. And Mrs. Bonds is really a political spy for the North. She thinks the mystery about you is deeper than it is, and you will do well to be on your guard before her and my brothers in arms whom you meet in this house. Major Brooks already has suspicions about you."

"I don't like him," I said viciously.

"Disguise that fact a little better if you can. I don't think any of the gentlemen whom you meet here are malicious, or that they will go out of their way to harm you, but it is good policy to temper your cold civility toward them with a little more warmth."

"You are very good," I said humbly, "and I really mean to act according to your advice."

He smiled. "You are not good at playing the hypocrite, are you?"

"I must improve. But I really must tell you—I don't need to be a hypocrite with you, you know—I believe Major Brooks is malicious."

He laughed outright. "Be careful not to offend him, then. Ah, I am afraid my first lesson in diplomacy will only have skin-deep results."

The next morning I did not forget Dan's picture. I brought it down with me, and slipped it into Captain Hosmer's hand as I passed behind him to my seat at the breakfast table. I was very much pleased later when he told me what a fine fellow he thought Dan must be, and that he thought the picture very handsome. Then I talked about Dan again until he was bored—when I shut up. After this I saw a great deal of Captain Hosmer. He was always so thoroughly well-bred that his attentions were very agreeable to me in spite of his uniform, and I formed a warm personal friendship and attachment for him. We were also seeing a good deal of Captain Locke.

I thought him very reckless in visiting us as he did, and I told him so frankly. He had doffed his disguise, wig and all, and appeared now every day, and sometimes oftener, at Mrs. Harris's in his own proper person, dressed in citizen's clothes. He came openly to the parlour in the daytime immediately after breakfast or lunch; and he was always there after dinner when the parlours were thronged. Several times he had joined the dance, selecting, by the way, Mrs. Bonds for a partner more than once. In fact, he singled this lady out for a number of pleasant courtesies. I could not keep him out of the way of the Yankee officers, and Major Brooks was always starting up at us somewhere like a Banquo's ghost. His eyes got sharper and sharper until I thought they would cut me in two. In halls and by-ways I was always coming upon him and always getting out of his way, and I was always surprising a cynical little grin on his face. One day I encountered him on the first landing of the stairway, squarely face to face. He addressed me, wishing me good morning gruffly, and standing in such a position that I could not pass him without rudeness unless he moved to one side. He did not move, and I was at bay.

"I know who you are, Miss Duncan," he said mischievously. "You are a good rebel now, aren't you?"

"Yes, I am a good rebel, as you call it. I'm a Virginian—and a rebel like Washington was, and like Lee is."

"I thought so. And you ran the blockade to get here."

"That's so, too. I got across at Berlin."

"I wish you'd tell me how."

I told him how. I sat down on the stairs to talk, and my enemy sat down beside me. Captain Hosmer came in, looked up, and saw the confidential and apparently friendly situation, laughed, and went on to breakfast.

"I don't call that running the blockade," he said. "I call that storming it. I didn't think it possible to cross at Berlin or, indeed, at any other point. Our line at the Potomac has been greatly strengthened and the rules are very rigid and inspection most thorough."

"I managed to cross at Berlin because you had such a nice provost marshal there. He knew two little women couldn't do any harm."

"Humph! He doesn't know women as I do, then!"

"Perhaps he had always known only very lovely ladies," I said with the softness of a purring cat.

He grinned. "You'll be wanting to run back soon, I dare say."

"I reckon I will. I wish you'd help me. Can't you tell me how?"

He laughed outright. "You are cool!" he said.

"You know what my duty is?" he added after a pause.

"Yes," I answered. "To fight on the right side, but I'm afraid you'll never do that. Now, I have been wanting to play *Dixie* ever since I've been here, and I'm afraid of nobody but you. Tonight I mean to play it." But I did not. That afternoon a card was brought up to Milicent and me. Major Littlebob, U. S. A., was sorry to disturb us, but would we please step down a minute. "Major Brooks came in with him," said the servant who brought the message.

"Major Brooks is going to have us arrested," I thought in terror. Milicent also was frightened by the message and by a call from an unknown officer of the United States Army who came accompanied by Major Brooks. Mother followed us in fear and trembling to the parlour door as we went in to behold—Milicent's own curly-headed Bobby, all rigged out in Major Brooks's regimentals! There he was, all swallowed up in sash, sword, and hat of a United States major of infantry; beside him was the major, laughing merrily. Milicent, in her relief, bent over and kissed again and again the fairest, softest, cutest, sweetest Major Littlebob that ever wore the regimentals of the U.S.A.; and it is needless to say that after this we were never again afraid of Major Brooks.

"So, the whole purpose of your running the blockade was a visit to your mother?" Major Brooks had asked.

"And to accompany my sister. And—to buy a few things—needles, pins, and so forth," I added in confusion.

Again the major laughed at my expense. Should I confide the Confederate uniform to him and Captain Hosmer? I decided to draw the line at this, as I had drawn it at Captain Locke. Of course, Captain Locke's story was his, not mine, and the uniform—well, the uniform was Dan's, or, rather, I hoped it would be. It was never out of my mind. I would have failed in half my mission if I did not buy it and get it across the Potomac to Dan. To buy shoes, gloves, ribbons, etc., was an easy matter, but to buy a Confederate uniform in Yankeeland, that was a more delicate affair.

It was Captain Locke who helped me out. He told me, where I could buy it, and offered to get it for me himself, but he was taking so many risks on his own account that I was determined he should take none on mine. He directed me to a tailoring establishment on the corner of Charles and St. Paul's Streets. The head of this establishment sympathized with the South and had supplied many Southern uniforms, and his store had a convenient double entrance, one on St. Paul's and one on Charles Street. One morning I went in at the Charles Street entrance. I had chosen an early hour, and I found no one in but the tailor.

"I want to buy a Confederate uniform," I said. "Captain Locke referred me—"

"Walk straight on out at the other door," he whispered. "I see two soldiers coming in from the Charles Street side."

Without looking behind me I walked straight on as if I had merely passed through the store to get to the other sidewalk. I heard some one coming rapidly behind me, and then I was joined by Captain Hosmer.

"What are you in such a hurry for?" he asked. "Wait a minute and I can walk home with you. I have a commission to execute back here."

Accordingly I returned to the store with him, was introduced to the friend accompanying him, and after a few moments walked home between the two. But the tailor had given me a hint—I was to come still earlier next day.

The next morning, however, he signalled me to pass on as I was about to enter. At last one morning I caught him alone long enough to get my uniform.

"I have to be very careful lately," he apologized for waving me off the previous day. "These Yankees suspect me and are always on the lookout. Now we will get the uniform in a hurry. I have several pieces of fine Confederate cloth just in that I will show you. Is your husband a private?"

"Oh, no-o!" I exclaimed indignantly.

"I thought not," he said suavely. "What is his rank?"

"He is a captain of cavalry now. That is—he was when I left home. But I haven't heard from him since. He may be major or colonel by now. Can't you fix up a uniform that would do for him if he is a captain or a colonel or a major when I get back, or—that would do for a general?"

"Certainly, certainly, madam. Very wise of you to think of that."

He showed me several pieces of very fine and beautiful cloth of Confederate gray, and I made my selection.

"The question is, how are you to get it across the line. In what way will you carry it?"

"Ah, that I don't know. Captain Locke advised me to consult you."

The tailor, who seemed to have had a liberal experience in such matters, considered for a moment.

"Are other ladies going with you?"

"My mother."

"It is easy then. I will cut this cloth into lengths that will be all right for the tailor who makes the uniform. You and your mother can make it into two Balmoral skirts. That's the way you get your cloth home. Now for the buttons and gold lace. Will you travel in the wrap you have on?"

"In one like it; I shall pack this in my trunk. The inspectors will not be so likely to condemn this if they find it in a trunk as they would be to condemn a new one. So I will get a new cloak South; mother will wear another."

"I see." He was impressed with the scheme and made a mental note of it. "Send me your cloaks and I'll fix the buttons all right."

Cloaks of the period were long, *sacque*-like affairs, double-breasted and with two rows of buttons. The tailor changed the buttons on our cloaks for Confederate brass buttons covered with wadding, and then with cloth like the wrap. The gold lace was to be folded flat and smooth. Mother was to rip the lining from the bottom of her satchel, lay the lace on the bottom, and carefully paste the lining back. We wanted to take Dan some flannel shirts, and again fashion favoured us. Ladies wore wide plaid scarfs passed around their necks and falling in long ends in front. We got seven yards of fine soft flannel in a stylish plaid and cut it in two lengths. Mother, being quite tall, could wear a longer scarf than myself, so, between us, we managed to carry around our necks two good shirts for Dan.

CHAPTER 16

The Flower of Chivalry

In the meantime we were growing more and more uneasy about Captain Locke. We felt that he was suspected and covertly watched, but he laughed at our fears.

He and I had begun to discuss ways and means of getting back to Virginia. One day, as usual, he was sitting beside me in the parlour after dinner, and, as usual, we were talking together in low tones, and again, as usual, the parlours were full. At one end of the room sat Major Brooks and Colonel Whipple, honouring us now and then with the covert and curious observation to which I could never become hardened. Captain Hosmer was walking restlessly up and down the floor, and casting uneasy glances toward us. He was too much of a gentleman to catechize me about my friend, but I knew he was not only curious but concerned in regard to my intimacy with Captain Locke.

Captain Locke was saying to me that he was in favour of our taking some schooner going down the bay and landing somewhere in Gloucester County, when I became so painfully conscious that the eyes of the enemy were upon us that I could not attend to what he was saying.

"What is the matter with you?" he asked. "You are not thinking at all of what I am saying. I reckon your mind is on Dan Grey."

"I am thinking about you," I said, on the verge of tears. "If you are not more careful, you won't get back home at all, I'm afraid."

"Why?" he asked innocently, and as if he were the most prudent person in the world.

"Only what Milicent and I have been telling you all along. You come here openly and boldly in the presence of all these Yankees. You visit us, and we feel responsible for any misfortune that might come to you through it. It is well known now, I think, by everybody in the house that we are Southerners and blockade-runners. No one in the house except ourselves and Mrs. Harris knows who you really are. Don't you suppose people wonder?"

He had been introduced several times to ladies as Mr. Moore, but we had not introduced him generally. We did not know what to do with him. For ourselves, we felt safe by this time, but I never sat on that sofa by Captain Locke's side without the fear in my heart that a sergeant-at-arms might walk in and lay hands on his shoulder.

"Don't you see," I went on, "how Captain Hosmer is watching you?"

For Hosmer was watching him with a scrutiny which could be felt in spite of all his courteous efforts at concealment. "And can't you see with what suspicious looks those officers across the room regard you?"

"That's so. You must introduce me to some of these people."

I was dumfounded. So this was the result of my caution!

"By which of your names shall I call you?" I asked satirically, but the satire was lost on him.

"The last one. That is a good name. It is nearly as common as Smith. Besides, I really have a right to it. I came by it honestly. I have a friend in New York by that name and he has kindly lent it to me for emergencies. So if anybody wants to write or telegraph to New York about it, they will find me all right. My cousin in New York—who really is my cousin many degrees removed—will acknowledge me. He is well known in business circles there."

"Whom shall I introduce you to?"

"I would rather meet those officers."

"Good gracious!"

He smiled. "They can give me more, and more accurate, information than anybody else, and of just the kind I want."

"You are going to get yourself shot before you start home. I won't be responsible for you."

"They don't shoot spies—they hang 'em," he said cheerfully.

I believe his cheerful ease carried us safely through this conversation under the eyes of the enemy, as it had done before.

"Those gentlemen would hardly think me entitled to the courtesy of a bullet," he went on with the utmost *sang-froid*. "A rope is more in accordance with my expectations if I am caught. But I do not expect to be caught. Really, little madam, the frank and open plan is the best. If I were to visit you clandestinely it would create more suspicion. Don't you see the fact that you haven't presented me to those gentlemen is in itself suspicious? Call those officers up and do the honours."

"I will call Captain Hosmer," I said faintly. "I really haven't the nerve to summon the other two.—Captain Hosmer!" I called.

He came instantly, and I saw that he was glad to be called.

"Captain Hosmer, let me introduce you to my friend, Mr. Moore."

"Mr. Moore "rose, and the two gentlemen bowed and shook hands with each other. Then they sat down, the Federal captain on one side of me, the rebel captain on the other, and we had a pleasant chat. Captain Hosmer asked "Mr. Moore "if he was related to Henry P. Moore, of New York, and "Mr. Moore" replied in the affirmative. Captain Hosmer knew this gentleman very well. Captain Locke was introduced to Major Brooks and Colonel Whipple, and it ended by Captain Locke and Schenck's adjutant walking down the street together. Captain Hosmer and I watched them from the window as they strolled past, smoking their cigars.

"Your friend is a very handsome man," he said.

"You think so? Dan is ever so much handsomer."

"No doubt of it," he laughed.

The next day I said to Captain Locke: "You—you wouldn't have to use information received from these gentlemen in any way that might ever hurt them, would you? We wouldn't have to do that, would we?"

"Dear little madam, it is not probable that they will honour me with too much confidence. No hurt could ever come to one who is kind to you through me. My first duty is to the South; so is yours. But honour between man and man is honour, and friendship is friendship, even in war times. In my life it has sometimes been very hard to know the line."

And there rested on his face at this moment the nearest thing to a shadow that I had ever seen there.

"I don't want you to think I have been reckless of your safety in coming here to see you. I am quite sure of my ground. You are not involved in any of my operations. And if anything *were* to happen, I have friends here who could extricate you even if they could not save me. The principal thing I wish to find out, now, from your Federal friends here is how you may get back to Virginia safely—since you will go.

If I find out that my attendance on you will be to your disadvantage, little madam, we must give that up."

It was I who had shown most anxiety that we should go together. While we were talking Captain Hosmer came in, and I made room for him on the other side of me. The two men greeted each other cordially. They had taken a liking to each other, and the rebel captain said to the other:

"My friend here has just been consulting me as to the route she had best take in getting home. I suggested that you might advise her to better purpose."

"I deplore Miss Duncan's determination to go," said Captain Hosmer. "Almost any route is unsafe just now—if possible. However, I will be glad to do anything I can. Have you any plan under consideration?"

"Wait a minute, captain," I said, rising. "I will go and get a little map I have, and show you the route which Mr. Moore advised me to take."

I went out, leaving the two officers together. When I returned I resumed my seat between them, spread the map open upon my lap, and they bent over it, Federal and Confederate heads touching, while I traced the route with my finger.

"You see, Mr. Moore thinks I might go down the bay in a schooner and land somewhere here in Gloucester County."

"No! no! you mustn't go that way!" exclaimed Captain Hosmer quickly. "You are sure to be taken up if you try that. With all due deference to you, Mr. Moore, my knowledge of the position of our forces convinces me that that is impossible."

"Of course, as an officer in the army, you must be better informed than I am," Captain Locke said simply. "That is why I advised Miss Duncan to consult you."

"Your best plan is to go by Harper's Ferry. It is a difficult matter to get through anywhere now, but if you get to Virginia at all I think it must be by way of Harper's Ferry."

Major Brooks and Colonel Whipple joined us, and the matter ended as on the previous day, by Captain Locke and Colonel Whipple walking off down the street together.

"Moore is a splendid fellow," Captain Hosmer said to me, when we had the sofa to ourselves. "I am glad you introduced us. Your not doing so looked suspicious, and I was troubled for fear he would get you into some scrape or other."

Dear, generous fellow, how I hated to deceive him, and how it was on the tip of my tongue to tell him who Captain Locke was, until I remembered what his duty would be if I told him! And Captain Locke's secret was mine to keep. He had been ready to risk his life rather than leave me alone at Berlin! Then, too, poor fellow, he had such a slender chance, I thought, of getting" home alive that not even an enemy would care to make it worse. I used to look at his bonnie white throat and shudder.

"God bless you," he said to me once, "for all your goodness to a poor, lonely, stray fellow! You shouldn't be afraid for me. You say your 'Hail Marys' for me, you know."

I had been telling him I was afraid for him, and he had, as usual, tried to reassure me and to laugh me out of it. He was never afraid for himself—I believe he would have stood up to be shot with a laugh on his lips. I wonder if he *was* laughing when they shot him—my dear, brave friend!

In the meantime we had heard that Mr. Holliway had been arrested in West Virginia, was lying in prison somewhere, and that his friends were trying to get him out, and before I left Baltimore we heard that he had died in prison just as an exchange had been arranged.

My return to Virginia was the subject of daily discussions between me and my two captains, and in this way Captain Locke continued to find out ways that he must not go, and eventually that we must not go together. It was he who first said it.

"I should be no earthly good, but a disadvantage to you, little madam. Hosmer is going to see you through this thing all right."

Then, seeing my downcast look, he went on cheerily: "I'll get through somehow all right, sooner or later, and we'll meet in Old Virginia. Don't bother your dear little head about me."

Captain Hosmer tried in vain to dissuade me from going. He felt that the journey under present conditions would be uncomfortable and unsafe, and that it was in every way advisable for me to stay where I was. But I was beginning to be very uneasy about Dan. I had heard from him only once since reaching Baltimore. Then his letters came in a batch, and I received them through the kindly agency of Mr. Cridland, British consul at Richmond, who had been my father's personal friend and frequent guest, and who had dandled a small person named "Nell "on his knee many times. Captain Hosmer still insisted that I must go by Harper's Ferry if I went at all, and he said that a pass was necessary.

"How on earth am I to get it?" I asked.

"I must arrange that for you," he said.

I think one reason that Captain Hosmer was so good to me was because his wife was a Southern woman. Her parents were Southern, her brothers were in the Southern army, and her husband was a Federal officer. They loved each other, but somehow they were separated, she living South with her parents. Under the pressure of the times there was a sectional conscience, and people did things which they did not wish to do, because they thought it was right. I don't know what I should have done then if I had been situated as Mrs. Hosmer was, but I know that at the present time I should stick to Dan, no matter what flag he fought under. Perhaps we are not as great or good in peace as in war times.

The captain had a beautiful country-seat several miles out of town. We had heard much of this place and its old-time hospitalities; and we also heard that it had been virtually closed since Captain Hosmer's separation from his wife. The captain went there frequently alone, and occasionally with a few friends, but the place had known no festivity since its mistress had gone away on that visit from which, by the way, she returned before we left Baltimore.

But before she came back there was a stag party at the captain's country place, given in honour of General Fish, the provost marshal at Baltimore, and other prominent officers.

The next time I saw Captain Hosmer he had a smile for me.

"You will get your passes," he said. "I have spoken to General Fish for them."

Milicent had decided that she could not risk little Bobby on such a journey and at this season, but mother was to go with me. The day before we were to start she and I went down to General Fish's office. He was out, but an orderly told us rather rudely to sit down and wait, which invitation or command we humbly acted upon. Presently General Fish entered. We stated our case.

"We are Southerners, general, and we wish to go south by way of Harper's Ferry."

"Mrs. and Miss Duncan, I think you said?"

"Yes, general."

"You are the ladies I heard of from Captain Hosmer, then?"

We gave him a note from Captain Hosmer.

"Excuse me, ladies, while I read this, and I will see what I can do for you."

He finished the note and then said:

"That's all right. I will make out your passes, ladies," and in a few minutes the important papers were in our hands.

"These will take you to General Kelly at Harper's Ferry. There my power ends. You will find General Kelly courteous and considerate, though I make no promises for him, understand. I will furnish you an escort to Harper's Ferry, and an officer will be sent to your boarding-house this afternoon to examine your baggage. Your address, please." He wrote a few words rapidly, and called the orderly:

"Take that order," he said.

The orderly saluted and got as far as the door, then he turned.

"Do these women go?" he asked of the general.

"These *ladies* go. Obey my order, sir!"

Upon which the orderly went quickly about his business.

When the officer came to examine our baggage I was on thorns. I had come north intending to make certain purchases, and I had made them, and the fruit of my money and labours was in those two trunks of mother's and mine. Mother's trunk was quite a large one, and both of those honest-looking trunks to which I yielded the keys so freely were crammed with dishonest goods—that is, dishonest according to blockade law. I had paid good gold for them, and anxiety enough, Heaven knows, for them to be properly mine.

I had shoes in the bottom of those trunks, and on top of the shoes cloth made into the semblance of female wear and underwear; and, lastly, I had put in genuine every-day garments. There were hand-kerchiefs, pins, needles, gloves, thread, and all sorts of odds and ends between the folds of garments, here, there, and everywhere in those trunks. They were as contraband trunks as ever crossed into Dixie. But, again, my Yankee was a *gentleman*.

"This is an unpleasant duty, miss," he said when I handed him my keys, "but I will disarrange your property as little as possible. It is only a form."

The orderly lifted the trays and set them back again, scarcely glancing underneath. What a dear, nice Yankee, I thought! He locked the trunks and sealed them.

"Will those seals be broken anywhere, and my trunks examined again?" I asked in some trepidation—this examination was so satisfactory to me that I wanted it to do for one and all.

"I cannot tell, miss. They may be at Harper's Ferry. But I hardly think so. I think this seal will carry you through."

CHAPTER 17

Prisoners of the United States

The officer who had examined our trunks the previous day took the trunks to the depot in a wagon, mother and I going in a hack. After we got on the train, our officer, Lieutenant Martin, joined us, and made himself very agreeable. The beginning of that journey was most pleasant. The scenery along the road to Harper's Ferry is at all times beautiful, and as we drew nearer to the ferry our car ran by the side of the Potomac, so that from one window we looked across the river to the Virginia Heights, and from the other to the Heights of Maryland. It was afternoon and growing dark when we reached Harper's Ferry.

There we found something like a riot going on, shouting and noises of all sorts, and the town full of drunken soldiers. We were told that there had been fighting in the valley, that the Federals had won, and that the men had just been paid off, and were celebrating victory and enjoying pay and booty in regular soldier fashion. Through this shouting, rowdy mob mother and I passed under our Federal escort to the tavern.

When we reached the tavern, a miserable little place full of drunken soldiers, our kind escort told us that his duty was at an end, and that he must take the return train to Baltimore. I think he hated to leave us under such unsafe circumstances, but he scarcely had time to settle us in the reception-room, shake hands, and catch his train. Here mother and I sat, debating what we should do. Of course, we were extremely anxious to get out of the place. We called a waiter and asked him if he could tell us where we could hire a vehicle to take us a part of our journey, or the whole of it. He knew of nothing that we could get. Then we went out on the porch, disagreeable as this was, and made inquiries of everybody who seemed sober enough to answer, but to no purpose. We could find no way of getting out of Harper's Ferry that night.

Thoroughly frightened, we asked to be shown to the commanding officer of the place, and were ushered into General Kelly's office, which, fortunately, was attached to the tavern—really a part of it.

General Kelly rose when we entered, saw us seated, and was as courteous as possible, while we stated the case and asked his advice. He heard us patiently, and was very sympathetic.

"I don't know what to say, ladies. I have no authority to send you on."

"Then what will we do, general?"

"I cannot say. I can, of course, give you passes, but you will find it impossible to hire anything here to travel in just now. The best you could get would be an ox-cart or a broken-down wagon, and the roads are almost impassable for good strong vehicles. And, besides, it is not safe for you to travel except under military escort, which, as I have said, I have no authority to furnish. There has been a great deal of fighting in the valley, and the roads are lined with stragglers. If you were prisoners now I could put you under escort and send you through our lines easy enough, but as it is I don't see what I can do."

We felt inclined to cry.

"And this is not a fit place for you to spend the night in, as you can see for yourselves," he pursued, very much in the manner of a Job's comforter. "The tavern is thronged with drunken men, and the whole town is overrun with them."

"Would it not be best for us to return to Baltimore?" we asked humbly. We had almost made up our minds to going back.

"That would be best, certainly—if you can.'"

"Why, can't we go back? We had no idea that we wouldn't be allowed to go back if we wanted to."

"Well, you see, ladies, you are in the position of Southerners sent south. The policy of the government encourages the sending of all Southerners in Maryland south to stay. I am only explaining, that you may understand that it may be difficult for me to assist you, in spite of my willingness to do so. I can not send you back without authority from General Fish. I will telegraph to him at once, and do my best for you. My orderly will see you back to the tavern. And I will notify you when I hear from General Fish."

So we returned to the reception-room of the tavern. Among the groups thronging the tavern were a few graycoats who had been captured the day before. One of these prisoners, a tall, handsome man, walked restlessly up and down the room where we sat, his guard keeping watch on him. As he passed back and forth I looked at him sorrowfully, putting into my eyes all the sympathy and encouragement I dared.

There was something in his look when he returned mine that made me think he wanted to speak to me. Every time he passed I thought I saw his eyes growing more and more wistful under their drooping lids.

Without seeming to notice him I moved about the room until I got to a window which was in the line of his restless beat. I stood there, my back turned to him, apparently looking out of the window, until I disarmed the suspicion of the guard. Then I settled down into a seat, my side to the window, my back to the guard, my face to the prisoner when the turn in his beat brought him toward me. A swift glance showed him that I was on the alert. Not a muscle of his face changed—he was facing the guard—but when he turned and came back, as he passed me he dropped these words.

"Going south?"

He walked to the end of the room and turned. Coming back, he faced me and the guard. As he passed I said:

"Yes."

When he came back, he said—always with his head drooped and speaking below his breath and so that his lips could hardly be seen to move:

"Take a message?"

When he passed back I said:

"Yes."

Returning: "Get word to Governor Vance of North Carolina "

To the end of his beat, turning and passing again in silence, then as he walked with his back to the guard:

"You saw Charlie Vance here—"

To the end of beat one way, to the end another, and back again:

"Prisoner—captured in fight yesterday—"

Several beats back and forth in silence, then:

"Carried north—"

Again:

"Don't know where."

This was the last he had opportunity to say. I saw the orderly coming in. Before Lieutenant Vance was near enough to catch another word from me, the orderly stood before me, a telegram in his hand. It was from General Fish to General Kelly:

"The ladies were sent south at their own request. I decline further connection with the matter."

"Why—why," I cried in desperation, "we can't go south, we can't go north, and we can't stay here!"

There was a pert little Yankee in the room who had been watching us for some time. He, like everybody else around us, understood by this time our dilemma.

"I'll tell you how to get sent on, if you will listen," he said.

"I will," I said clearly and firmly, and looking straight into the eyes of Lieutenant Vance, who was then passing close by me.

The little Yankee was staggered by the unnecessary amount of resolution expressed in my reply. I kept my eyes focused on the spot where Mr. Vance had been for some seconds after he had passed. Then I turned to my little Yankee. I had snubbed him severely heretofore, but I was humbled by extremity, and willing enough now to listen if he could tell us how to get away from this place.

"Tell us how we can get sent on," I asked.

"Just step out there in the street and holler for Jeff Davis, and you'll get sent on quick enough!"

We withered him with a stare, and then turned our backs on him, and at the same moment two ladies entered the room whom we recognized. They were Mrs. Drummond and Miss Oglesby, whose acquaintance we had made in Baltimore, and they, too, were going south. They explained that they had been in this wretched place since yesterday, and that they were not allowed to return to Baltimore and were unable to go home. They had been out trying to find a conveyance of some sort, but had been able to secure only the promise of an oxcart, and hearing that we were here had come in to consult with us. During all this time the orderly, whom I had detained, was waiting impatiently. We decided to go with him and make another appeal to General Kelly. Accordingly the whole party filed into General Kelly's office again.

"What *are* we to do, general?" I cried out in desperation. "We can't go back, we can't go on, and we can't stay here!"

The kindly general did honour to the stars he wore—he was a gentleman, every inch of him. It happened later that he was captured and held in Libby Prison in Richmond, and I was in Richmond and didn't know it. I have held a grudge against fate ever since. If I had only known, he would have been reminded by every courtesy that a Southern woman could render of how gratefully his kindness was remembered.

"I hardly hoped for a different answer from General Fish, ladies. The regulations on this point are very stringent. And I cannot return you to Baltimore unless you take the oath of allegiance."

"What?" we asked eagerly.

"If you take the oath of allegiance, I can send you back."

We decided to do this.

We didn't know exactly what the oath was, but we thought we could take anything to get us out of our scrape. We told General Kelly we would take it, and we were conducted into another room, which I can only remember as being full of Federal soldiers. We were marched up to a desk where a man began reading the oath to us. It was the famous "ironclad." We did not wait for him to get through. Without a word each of us turned and marched back into General Kelly's office, as indignant a set of women as could be found.

He was looking for us—doubtless he knew by previous experience the effect the reading of that oath produced upon Southern women—and he burst out laughing as our procession filed back into his room.

"Why, general," we began, "we couldn't take that horrid thing! We are Southerners, and our kinsmen and friends are Southern soldiers."

"I almost knew you wouldn't take that oath, ladies, when I sent you there."

"General," I said, "this is the most remarkable position I ever knew people to be in—where you can't go back, and can't go forward, and can't stay where you are. I don't know what you are to do with us, general, unless you hang us to get us out of the way."

He laughed heartily.

"I must do something a little better than that for you. My orderly will take you back to the tavern, and you will hear from me in an hour."

We went with Mrs. Drummond and Miss Oglesby to their room. Before the hour was up we were escorted to another interview with General Kelly. The general beamed on us.

"Here is a telegram I received in your absence," he said, handing it to us:

> Mrs. and Miss Duncan are dear friends of mine. Can you see them through? If not, tell them I will be in Harper's Ferry tonight. Answer.   Hosmer.

"Here is my answer," said the general:

Stay where you are. Will see them through all right.

Kelly.

"How could he have found out the trouble we were in?" we asked in wonder.

"I don't know. News of the fighting in the valley and the condition of things here reached Baltimore soon after you left there. Hosmer perhaps got an idea of your situation through General Fish. He may have gone to Fish's office to inquire. Hosmer is a capital fellow and an old friend of mine. I had about determined on what to do for you before I heard from him, but I thought it would please you to know of his message. I will ask you to return to the tavern, ladies, and exercise a little further patience. You will hear from me soon."

This time we waited only a little while before an orderly rapped at the door to say that an ambulance was in waiting for us below. We hurried down with him, and in ten minutes were inside the ambulance, and prisoners of the United States.

Behind us into the ambulance stepped a dashing young officer, all brass buttons and gold lace.

"I am Captain Goldsborough," he said, saluting, "commissioned by General Kelly to attend you."

Our escort consisted of five soldiers who followed us, sitting in a wagon on our baggage. That afternoon we passed through Charlestown, and there Captain Goldsborough pointed out to us the house in which John Brown had lived—an ordinary two-story frame house.

As well as I can remember we reached Berryville about nine o'clock. Our ambulance drew up in front of the tavern, and Captain Goldsborough went in to see about getting accommodations for us. He came out quickly and said, "This is no fit place tonight for you, ladies. I am informed that there is an old couple on the hill who may take us in. I hear, too, that they are good Confederates," he added mischievously. Of course lights were out and everybody asleep when we drove up, but our driver went in and beat on the door until he waked the old people up. They received us kindly, and the old lady got a supper for us of cold meats and slices of loaf bread, butter, milk, preserves, and hot coffee which she must have made herself as no servants were in the house at that hour; and we had a comfortable room with two beds in it.

The old lady came in and chatted with us awhile, telling us all she knew about our army's movements, and listening eagerly to what people in Maryland had to say about the war. We were very tired, but I am sure it must have been one o'clock when we went to sleep. At daybreak there came a great banging at the front door. Mother put her head out of the front window and inquired who was trying to break the door down.

It was our driver, and there at the gate stood our ambulance. The driver hurried us desperately, saying we had not a moment to lose. The noise had aroused our hosts, and when we got down the old lady had spread us a cold lunch and made us a cup of coffee.

"I was hoping to have you a nice hot breakfast," she said, "but since you must go in such a hurry this is the best I can do. If I had known you were going to make such an early start I would have got you a hot breakfast somehow."

We swallowed our food hurriedly, but this did not satisfy our driver. Every few minutes he came down on the door with the butt end of his whip. Finally we left off eating, ran upstairs, and gathered up our bags. As we hurried down, almost falling over each other in our haste, we saw a magnificent-looking soldier standing in the hall. He was in the full uniform of a colonel of cavalry, glittering with gold lace, with gauntlets reaching his elbows, and high military boots.

"Mrs. Duncan and Miss Duncan, I suppose," he said with a sweeping bow, "and—"

"Mrs. Drummond and Miss Oglesby," we said of the ladies who came behind us.

"I am Colonel McReynolds, commandant at this place, and at your service, ladies," he continued. "I have to apologize for not paying my respects to you last night upon receipt of General Kelly's letter asking me to take charge of you. The lateness of the hour must be my excuse. At the time Captain Goldsborough presented it I had a number of important despatches to attend to, and I supposed you were tired out and in need of rest."

We expressed our appreciation of his courtesy and General Kelly's thoughtfulness.

"What is all this?" he asked, pointing to our ambulance, baggage wagon, and impatient driver.

We explained that they were the conveniences furnished us by General Kelly.

"But you surely do not propose starting off in such weather as this, ladies?"

I have neglected to say that it had been storming since daybreak.

"The driver has been beating on the doors since before day," somebody said.

"He has, has he? Then he has exceeded his instructions. He had no right whatever to disturb you, ladies. I will see that he is reported."

He called the driver and reprimanded him sharply.

"Pray don't feel that you must leave us in such weather as this, ladies," he continued with the utmost kindness. "Stay here a week if you like. That ambulance and wagon and those men and horses are at your service as long as you choose to keep them here, and we will be glad to do whatever we may for your comfort or pleasure until it suits your own convenience to leave us."

We hardly knew how to thank this princely young enemy, but we insisted that the driver should not be punished, and that we should be allowed to proceed on our journey, as we were anxious to reach our friends and kindred.

He rode in our ambulance with us to his headquarters, where we were joined by our other charming enemy, and, making our *adieux* to the gallant and handsome colonel, continued our journey.

During the day something happened to Captain Goldsborough's watch, and it stopped running, much to his annoyance.

"I should like to know what time it is," he said.

I pulled my watch out and held it open for him to see the time. I could have told him what hour it was. I don't know what made me such a reckless little creature in those days. The watch I held to him had a tiny Confederate flag pasted inside. My companions had either secreted their watches or were not travelling with them. I had been urged to do the same, but had openly worn my watch ever since leaving Baltimore. Captain Goldsborough saw the hour, and he saw the flag also. He stared at me in utter amazement.

"You are brave—or reckless," he said.

"I know this is contraband goods, and, according to your ideas, treasonable. Will you confiscate it?" quietly holding it out again.

His face flushed.

"Not I! but someone else might. You are not prudent to wear that openly."

And I was so ashamed of myself for hurting his feelings that I made amends in rather too warm terms, I am afraid, considering that he didn't know I was married and a privileged character.

"You are travelling in the wrong direction, *I* think, Miss Duncan," he ventured to say after awhile. "You shouldn't leave the North and go south now."

"Why?"

"I—I shouldn't think you would receive the attention there just now that is your due. You are young and fond of society, I imagine. And—there are so few *beaux* in the South now—I shouldn't think you would like that."

"Really?"

"I mean that I wish you would stay up North where it is pleasanter. It's so—uncomfortable down South. You are so young, you see, you ought to have a chance to enjoy life a little. I—I wish you were up here—and I could add a little to your happiness. I—I mean," catching a glance which warned him, "it is must be dull for you in the South—no *beaux*—no nothing."

"All the *beaux* are in the field," I retorted, "where they ought to be. I wouldn't have a *beau* who wasn't, and if I were a Northern girl I wouldn't have a man who didn't wear a uniform—though, I think, it ought to be gray."

"I expect you have a sweetheart down South whom you expect to see when you get home. That is why your heart has been so set on getting back."

"If I had a sweetheart down South I couldn't see him when I got back home, for he would be in the field."

"So, your sweetheart is a Southern soldier?" wistfully.

"I wouldn't have a sweetheart who wasn't a soldier—a Southern soldier."

In the other side of my watch I had pasted a small picture of Dan in uniform. I opened this side and held it out to my companion.

"That's my sweetheart's picture."

He looked at it long and hard. "A good-looking fellow," he said, "and I have no doubt a gallant soldier. If I ever meet him in battle—he will be safe from *my* bullet."

Behind our wagon all the way from Harper's Ferry had come a party equipped like Ourselves. They were Jews, and, as we were informed, were prisoners of the United States. They had an ambulance like ours, a baggage wagon like ours, and a similar escort of five infantry perched on trunks. Their escort who rode inside, however, was not so attractive as ours. We felt and expressed much commiseration for them because they were prisoners—"those poor Jews," we called them.

We were all suffering the consequences of late and early hours, and of the worry and excitement at Harper's Ferry. I felt almost ill, and when Miss Oglesby, whose home was in Winchester, invited us to spend a week with her, we concluded that we would accept her hospitality until better able to continue our journey.

Winchester was the most difficult of all places for Southerners to pass through at this time, and we could not possibly have gotten through if we had been left to our own resources. Milroy was commandant, and his name was a terror. He belonged to the Ben Butler of New Orleans type. Some time near the middle of the day we drew up in front of Milroy's headquarters.

Immediately behind us came the Jews and their belongings. They did not go in with us, and I supposed they were awaiting their turn. General Milroy was absent, off on a fight, and we fell into the hands of his adjutant, a dapper little fellow. We heard him talking to Goldsborough of the recent fight and victory, and heard him making arrangements for our transportation.

Here we thought it proper to inform him that we were going to remain a week in Winchester.

"You can not remain here," he said. "You go on immediately."

"Oh, no!" we said, "we're not going on now. We are going to stop here for a visit and until we are rested."

"You are prisoners and under orders. You go at once—" he began brusquely.

"Oh, no!" we interrupted, eager to enlighten him, for we saw he had made a very natural mistake. "We are not prisoners. Those poor Jews out there, they are prisoners. We are going to stop here on a little visit."

"You don't stop here an hour. This is Miss Oglesby's destination, and she stops, but the rest of you go on—now."

He looked as if he thought us demented. Goldsborough kept making faces at us, but we were so anxious to correct the adjutant's mistake that we had no attention to bestow elsewhere. We thought we had never seen so stupid a man as that adjutant.

"*We* are not the prisoners," we insisted. "Those Jews out there—"

Here he told Captain Goldsborough to conduct "these prisoner" downstairs and into the ambulance provided for them. "You will not go far before you meet a detachment of cavalry on their way to this place," he informed Captain Goldsborough, and then instructed him to turn back of these a sufficient escort for our party.

We were in a perfect rage as Captain Goldsborough led us downstairs. We thought Milroy's adjutant the very rudest and stupidest person we had ever seen.

Chapter 18

Within Our Lines

After leaving the saucy and peremptory adjutant we were shown into the handsomest ambulance I have ever seen. I suppose the one we had been using was returned to Harper's Ferry or left at Winchester for the horses to rest until Captain Goldsborough's return. At any rate, we were in new quarters, and very elegant ones they were. The sides and seats were cushioned and padded, and it was really a luxurious coach. It was drawn by four large black horses with coats like silk. There was a postilion on the seat, and beside him sat a small boy who kept peeping behind us and into the woods on all sides, and as far ahead as possible. I didn't know what he was trying to see or rind out, but I came to the conclusion that he was there to "peep" on general principles.

As soon as we were seated we asked Captain Goldsborough what upon earth that impertinent adjutant meant by referring to us as "prisoners," and ordering us about so.

Whereupon he explained with much embarrassment and many apologies that we were really prisoners—that General Kelly could not have sent us through without the formality of putting us under arrest.

"I wish," he said in an aside to me, "that I didn't have to release you."

Of course we were perfectly satisfied to be General Kelly's prisoners under such circumstances. In fact, we charged Captain Goldsborough to tell him how nice we thought it was to be put under arrest by him.

We withdrew our charges against the adjutant, and even acknowledged that there was kindness in the pert little Yankee's telling us to "holler for Jeff Davis and we'd get sent on quick enough."

Six miles from Winchester we met the detachment of cavalry to which Milroy's adjutant had referred. It was a magnificent-looking body of men, handsomely uniformed and mounted. As they were about to dash past us Captain Goldsborough halted them, gave an order, and instantly thirty riders wheeled out of line and surrounded the ambulance, the others riding on without a break in their movements. Captain Goldsborough had gotten out of the ambulance some minutes before we met the detachment of cavalry, and was sitting with the driver, having sent the little boy inside. It sounds rather a formidable position for a Southern woman, a blockade-runner, in a Yankee ambulance, and surrounded by thirty Yankees armed to the teeth; but I was never safer in my life. The little boy was in a state of terror that would have been amusing if it had not been pitiful.

"What are all these men around the ambulance for?" I asked. He didn't look as if he could get his wits together at once.

"Are they afraid we will get away?" I continued.

"Oh, no'm! no'm!" he answered, his eyes as big as saucers. "There's been lots of fightin'—an' there's rebels all along here in the woods—and they'd come out and take this here ambulance an' these here horses—an' we all, an' you all, an' all of us!"

A novel position, truly, Yankees protecting us against our own soldiers! We met another company of soldiers, and alas! we could turn back none of them. They were not mounted, they were not handsomely uniformed. From the windows of our ambulance we looked out on them with tearful eyes, and waved our handkerchiefs to them; but their heads were bowed, and they did not see us. They would hardly have believed we were prisoners if they had seen us, for our escort of Union cavalry the whole time they guarded us treated us as if we were queens. Not one profane word did we hear—not a syllable that breathed anything but respect and kindly feeling.

At Newtown we were released and were Union prisoners no longer, but Southern travellers close to the Southern lines and on our own responsibility. Captain Goldsborough bade us *adieu*, saying that he was sorry he could not take us farther, but that his orders compelled him to turn back here, and we poured out our gratitude to him and to Colonel McReynolds and General Kelly by him. He put a little sentiment into a farewell pressure of my hand, and I am afraid I put a great deal too much gratitude and penitence into my eyes. My genius for friendship had asserted itself, and I was fast learning to give him a companion niche in my heart with Captains Hosmer and Locke.

Another day with him, and I would have told him I was married, showed him Dan's picture, bored him with Dan, and found in him all the better friend and good comrade.

Our hearts sank as our gallant bluecoat, our cosy ambulance, and our cavalry guard left us, three lonely women in the tavern at Newtown. We spent the night there, and the next morning secured, with much difficulty, a small, uncovered, one-horse wagon to take us on our journey. We were very much crowded. Our trunks were piled up in it—mother's, Mrs. Drummond's, and my own. I made mother as comfortable as possible, and Mrs. Drummond carefully made herself so, while I sat on the seat with the driver, a trunk sticking in my back all the way. I had to sit almost double because of the trunk, the wagon being so small that no other arrangement was possible.

Rain had fallen plentifully here. The day was one of fogs and mists with occasional light showers, the roads were muddy and seamed with ruts, over which the wagon jogged up and down, and I jogged with it, feeling as if my back would break in two and almost wishing it would and end my misery. About nine of that miserable wet night we hailed with eager, glad, tired hearts and eyes the lights of Woodstock. Here we knew we should find Southern forces encamped, here we knew we should be at home among our own people. Just outside the town a voice rang through the darkness:

"Halt!"

A sentry stood in our path.

"We are *Southerners*," we said. "Let us pass."

"Where are your papers?"

"Papers? We haven't any papers. We are Southerners, we tell you—Southern ladies, and we are in a hurry, and you must let us pass right now."

"I can't do it. Show your papers or turn back."

We set up a wail.

"Here, we've come all the way from Baltimore, and the Yankees have sent us and have brought Us all the way in a fine ambulance and cavalry escorts and big horses and gold lace and everything, and now we've got home, and our own people won't let us in! tell us to turn back!"

The sentry seemed impressed. Rags and musket, he was a pathetic if stern figure as he stood in that lonely, muddy road in the glare of our driver's lantern.

But he was firm. He told us that he was obeying orders and could not let us by since we had no passes.

"I'm so tired, and my back is almost broken with this trunk sticking into it," I moaned.

"That *ain't* comfortable," he admitted, but his resolute position in the middle of the road showed that we couldn't pass, all the same.

"Look here," I said, plucking up some of my accustomed spirit, "do you know that my husband is an officer in the Confederate army? My husband is Captain Grey."

"Can't help it. Got to obey orders."

"And *my* brother," said Mrs. Drummond, "is a colonel in the Confederate Army. To think that *I*—I, the sister of Colonel ——, am told that I can't pass here!"

"Law, ma'am! that's my colonel!" said the man. "I tell you what I'll do, ladies. I'll send a note in to the colonel and see what he says about it."

So we waited till he found a passer-by who would be a messenger; and then we waited until the messenger replied to the note, and we were permitted to pass.

Soon after we reached the tavern the news of our arrival and exploits got abroad and soon the little tavern parlour was filled with people listening to the tales of the blockade-runners who were just from Yankeeland, bringing a trunk or two full of clothes. The news of our doughty deeds spread from house to house, and soldiers gathered in front of the tavern and gave us ringing cheers, and welcomed us home with all their lung power. Poor, ragged fellows! how I did wish that mother and I had worn home a hundred or two more Balmorals!

The next morning we left Woodstock.

We were travelling now in a comfortable spring wagon, and made good time, reaching Harrisonburg in time to take the train for Staunton.

As we sat in the parlour of the hotel in Staunton who should walk in but an old friend and cousin of Dan's, Lieutenant Nelson! But he could tell me nothing about Dan—he did not even know where he could be found. This was just before the second battle of the Wilderness, and the cavalry was being shifted constantly from place to place. But if Lieutenant Nelson could tell us nothing, he was greatly interested in our exploits. We told him of the Balmorals with pride.

"And here are two shirts for Dan," I said, pulling at our long scarfs. "Just think of our getting through with a full uniform—cloth, brass buttons, gold lace, and all!"

As at Woodstock, the story of our prowess spread. It went from one person to another until the soldiers got hold of it, and gathered around the hotel and more ringing cheers were given us.

The next morning we took the train for Richmond—but we did not get there.

At Lindseys Station, just before we reached Gordonsville, a man in the uniform of the Thirteenth got on.

I called him to me.

"Can you tell me where the Thirteenth is?"

"Yes'm. We lef' 'em 'bout the aige of Culpeper, yistiddy. Lor'm! we've had times!"

"What was the matter?"

"We been havin' a heap o' fightin'. The kurnel, he warn't thar at Beverly Ford, an' we didn't have but one squadron, an' the adjutant, he led the charge an' he sholy come mighty nigh gittin' killed. Lor'm! what's the matter with ye?"

"Nothing! Go on! Make haste, tell me—make haste. The adjutant—"

"His horse got shot under him, an' his courier ridin' right 'longside o' him got killed, an' the adjutant warn't hurt, not a mite. But, Lor'm! that was sholy a narrer wcape! An' they say that the adjutant'll git promoted."

Didn't I say so? Didn't I think of that when I got the uniform?

"Thank you," I said to the man. "You bring me the first news I have had of my husband for a long time."

"Good gracious! you ain't our adjutant's wife?"

"Yes, I am. And I am glad to meet one of his soldiers. And you are the first to tell me good news."

"Lor'm, now, ain't I proud o' that! An' you our adjutant's wife. You don't say! An' I jes been a-tellin' you how it was a'mos' a miracle that you warn't a widder 'oman! An' you never let on! But I see you changed your face, marm, when I tole 'bout his pretty nigh gitting shot. Yes, marm; the adjutant charged beautiful! he jes rid right squar into 'em, an' he made the Yankees git!"

"How long do you think the Thirteenth will remain in Culpeper?"

"That I couldn't say for certain, marm. They mought be thar for a day or two, an' they mought be thar longer. You can't always tell much 'bout what the cavalry gwine to do. But we's sho proud o' the adjutant, marm. Ginral Lee an' Ginral Stuart an' Kunnel Chambliss all give him the praise."

It was after this battle that Dan was promoted to the rank of major, "for gallant conduct."

I bade the soldier a hurried goodbye and went to the conductor.

"My husband's regiment is in Culpeper," I said; "I have just heard it from one of his men, and I want you to put me off at Gordonsville. I have decided not to go on to Richmond, but to take the next train to Culpeper."

"The next train to Culpeper, ma'am—I think the next train for Culpeper passes Gordonsville at four in the afternoon. There's no train before that, I know, and I am not sure that there's one at four. There's no tavern nor anything to put you down at—I'll just have to set you out on the roadside."

And it was on a red roadside that we and our baggage were set down, on a bank of red mud, and there sat we on top of them as the train rolled away. The conductor left us regretfully.

"Maybe you might get accommodations at that house up there, ma'am," he had said, pointing to the only house in sight, a two-storey white dwelling about a quarter of a mile distant. "I don't know what else you'll do if that train don't come along at four."

This was ten o'clock in the morning. Four o'clock came, but no train. We waited faithfully for it, but it did not come at all. At last we gave up hope and paid a boy to carry our trunks to the house on the hill. I shall never forget our reception at that house. At first they refused to take us at all. After arguing the point with them and placing our necessities before them, and promising to pay them anything they might wish, we were thankful to get a gruff:

"Come in."

We were shown to a room and shut in like horses. There was not even a fire made for us. We had been warmer sitting on the roadside in the sunshine. I will pass over the supper in silence. We had had no dinner and were hungry, and we ate for our part of that supper the upper crust of a biscuit each. A hard bed, the upper crusts of two biscuits, no fire—this was what we got at that house. The next morning we left before breakfast and went back to our mud-bank in the sun, first asking for our bill and paying it. It was two dollars apiece in gold!

The train came along early, however, and we were on it, and off to Culpeper, all our troubles forgotten, for every mile was bringing us nearer to Dan. As soon as we got off I saw quite a number of soldiers belonging to Dan's command. Many of them were known to me personally. They came up and welcomed me back to Dixie, and congratulated me on my husband's gallantry and probable promotion, and I sent word to Dan by them that I was there.

He came—the raggedest, most widowed-looking officer! But weren't we happy!

"Oh, Dan!" I cried, after the first rapture of greeting, "I got it so it would do for a captain or a major or a colonel or a general. Didn't I do right?"

"What are you talking about, Nell? Got what?"

He looked as if he feared recent adventures had unsettled my intellect.

"Your uniform, Dan," I answered, but my countenance fell.

"My—uniform."

Just like a man! He had forgotten the principal thing—next to seeing mother, of course—that I had gone to Baltimore for.

"Your uniform, Dan. I've got it on. Here it is," and I lifted my skirt and showed him my Balmoral. "Isn't it a beautiful cloth? And I have kept it just as nice—not a fleck of mud on it. And here are the buttons on my cloak, and I have the gold lace in mother's satchel, and—"

"Nell, dear, I haven't time to talk about uniforms now. You will sleep here tonight. Tomorrow I will try to get a room for you at Mr. Bradford's. I will come in the morning or send you word what to do. I am so sorry to go, but I can't stay a minute longer. Goodbye, my darling."

I was waked the next morning by a voice under my window calling:

"Miss Nell! O Miss Nell!" and looking out I saw Dan's body-servant, Sam, successor to poor Josh, who had died of smallpox.

"Mars Dan say, I fotch his love to you, an' tell you you git right on dem nex' kyars an' go straight on ter Orange Court-house, case dar's too much fightin' 'roun' here. An' he gwine notify you dar when you kin come back. But he say dat if you hear dar's fightin' 'roun' Orange Court-house, den you go straight on ter Richmond, an' don't you stop untwell you git dar."

"But I don't want to go, Sam."

"But Mars Dan he say tell you p'intedly you mus'."

"Ain't he coming to tell me goodbye, Sam?"

"Law, Miss Nell! how he gwine do dat when de Yankees is er—overrunnin' de whole yuth? What's guine ter become uv de country ef de major leave off fitten de Yankees to humorfy you?"

I could not for the life of me, sad as my heart was, keep from laughing at being taken to task by Sam.

"Is it so bad as that, Sam?"

"Yes'm, dat 'tis! Mars Dan say he 'fraid de Yankees git in de town hyer fo' night. De Yankees is er pressin' we all close."

"I can't see your master at all before I go, Sam?"

"Law, Miss Nell; ain't I done tole you dat? De country will go to de dawgs ef de major stop fitten de Yankees to humorfy you."

"If your master gets hurt, Sam, will you get me word?"

"Law, yes, Miss Nell! I sholy will."

"And you'll take care of him, Sam?"

"Dat's jes what I gwine to do, Miss Nell. *Me* lef' de major ef he git hu't! shuh!"

"Goodbye, Sam. Tell your master I'm gone."

"Yes'm. He'll sho be p'intedly glad ter heah dat!"

Just fifteen minutes in which to catch the train. We threw things pell-mell into our trunks—there was no vehicle to be had—paid a man to drag them to the depot, and were on our way to Orange in less than half an hour. And I had seen Dan, all told, perhaps fifteen minutes!

At Orange we found everything in confusion, and everybody who could get out leaving the town. The story went that the Yankee cavalry under Stoneman would soon be in possession of it. We were glad enough to keep our seats and go straight through to Richmond, and it was well that we did, for behind us came Stoneman's cavalry close on our heels and tearing up bridges as they came. The railroad track at Trevillian's was torn up just after we passed over it. Richmond was in a state of great excitement. Couriers were passing to and fro between the army and the executive offices, stirring news kept pouring in, and the newspapers were in a fever. Tidings from the first battle of the Wilderness began coming in.

Lee's army and "Fighting Joe" Hooker's were grappling with each other there like tigers in a jungle. Stuart, our great cavalry leader, had caught up Jackson's mantle as it fell, and was riding around in that valley of death, charging his men to "Remember Jackson!" and singing in that cheery voice of his which only death could drown: "Old Joe Hooker, won't you Come Out of the Wilderness?" Then came news of victory and Richmond was wild with joy and wild with woe as well. In many homes were vacant chairs because of that battle in the

Wilderness, and from Petersburg, twenty miles away, came the sound of mourning, Rachel weeping for her children and refusing to be comforted because they were not.

It was from Petersburg that I was summoned to Culpeper by Dan, who felt that the army might have a long enough breathing spell there for me to pay him at least a visit. When I got to Mr. Bradford's, where he had engaged board for me, I found General Stuart's headquarters in the yard. He and his staff were boarders at Mr. Bradford's, and I ate at the same table with the flower of the Southern cavalry. Unfortunately for me, Dan's command was stationed at a distance of several miles, and I could not see as much of him as I had hoped. He met me the day of my arrival, rode by once or twice, took one or two meals with me, and then it seemed that for all I saw of him I might as well have remained in Petersburg.

My seat at table was next to that of General Stuart, and for *vis-à-vis* I had Colonel John Esten Cooke. Colonel Cooke was a glum old thing, but General Stuart was so delightful that he compensated for everything. In a short time I was completely at my ease with him, and long before he left I had grown to love and trust him.

CHAPTER 19

My Comrade General Jeb Stuart

One day General Stuart asked me in a teasing way:
"You wouldn't really like to see Dan Grey, would you?"
"Oh, but I would, general," I said, in too dead earnest to give raillery for raillery.
"I don't believe you really want to see Dan Grey."
"Well, I don't, then," a bit sullenly.
"What a pity! You might see him now, if you really wanted to."
I wouldn't notice such a frivolous remark.
Dinner over, we went out on the veranda, as usual, and General Stuart dropped into a chair beside me.
"I really thought you rather liked Dan Grey, but it seems I was mistaken. And you really don't want to see him? Sad—I must tell him and condole with him."
I tried to bury myself in a book I was reading, and to pay no attention to him. A miserable old book it was—Children of the Abbey, or something like it—that I had picked up somewhere at Mr. Bradford's. Hereafter, if I write "Aunt Sally's" instead of Mr. Bradford's, please understand that one and the same place is meant. Aunt Sally was Mr. Bradford's wife, and I reckon the first term best describes the place.
"You wouldn't really rather have Dan Grey sitting here in this chair beside you than me?" continued my tease.
I lifted to him eyes wet with vexation and longing.
"I'll make you smile now!" he said. "*Do* you want to see Dan?"
"Yes, I do. I want to see him dreadfully, but I am not going to tell you so again."
"You will if I command you to, won't you? If you are in the cavalry I am your superior officer, you know. I can even make Dan mind what I say, can't I? If you are refractory, I can command Dan to bring

you to terms."

"I'd like to see Dan do it! You may be commander-in-chief of the cavalry, but you aren't commander-in-chief of me—you or Dan either."

"It seems not," he commented meekly. "You are the most insubordinate little rebel I ever saw. I have a great mind to court-martial you—no, I believe I'll send for Dan and let him do it."

He called a courier, and wrote a despatch in regular form, ordering Major Dan Grey to report at once to General Stuart. Then he added a little private note to Dan which had for a postscript:

Sweet Nellie is by my side.

"That will bring him in a hurry!" laughed Stuart.

The courier, not knowing but that the fate of the Confederacy depended upon that despatch, put spurs to his horse, galloped down the road and out of sight. I suppose he ran his horse all the way, and that Dan ran his all the way back, for before General Stuart left the veranda Dan galloped into the yard.

"I'll get the first kiss!" said General Stuart, still teasingly.

He leaped from the porch and ran across the yard, I tearing after him. I caught up and passed him, and looking back at him from Dan's arms, into which I had stumbled, breathless and panting, I laughed out: "I can beat the Yankees getting out of your way!"

Perhaps this race and General Stuart's love of teasing may seem undignified conduct for the chief of the Southern cavalry, but it is history and it is fun, and those who knew him did not fail in respect to Stuart. Many of us loved the ground he walked on. His boyish spirits and his genial, sunny temperament helped to make him the idol of the cavalry and the inspiration of his soldiers, and kept heart in them no matter what happened.

That was a lovely evening. General Stuart had Sweeny, his banjo-player, in. Sweeny was a dignified, solemn-looking man, but couldn't he play merry tunes on that banjo, and sad ones too! making you laugh and cry with his playing and his singing.

When the sad, chilly winds of December
Stole my flowers, my companions, from me.

That was one of his mournful favourites. And you heard the jingle of spurs in his rollicking:

If you want a good time,

Jine the cavalry,
Bully boys, hey!

We called for "Old Joe Hooker, won't you Come Out of the Wilderness?" and "O Johnny Booker, help this Nigger!" and "O Lord, Ladies, don't you mind Stephen!" and "Sweet Evelina," and—oh! I can't remember them all, but if you choose to read Esten Cooke, he will tell you all about Sweeny's songs and banjo. Stuart sang "The Dew is on the Blossom "and "The Bugles sang Truce." He made Sweeny give, twice over, "Sweet Nellie is by my Side," and sat himself down beside me, and tried to tease Dan because he sat at table with me every day and Dan couldn't. Inspite of everything I was very happy in those old days at the Bradfords'! I was not yet out of my teens, you know; so I hope I was not very much to blame because I was always ready for a romp across that lawn at Mr. Bradford's with the commander-in-chief the Southern cavalry. His was the gentlest, merriest, sweetest-tempered soul I ever knew. He was always ready to sympathize with me, to tease me, and to help me. Whenever he teased me out of conceit with myself or him, he always would put me in a good humour by saying nice things about Dan, or sending a courier after him.

He had an idea that I was very plucky, and in after days when I was ready to show the white feather, Dan would shame me by asking, "What would General Stuart say?"

Mr. Bradford and his wife, "Aunt Sally," were characters. Mr. Bradford was a very quiet, peaceable man; Aunt Sally was strong-minded, and had a tongue and mind of her own. Mr. Bradford had a good deal of property and stayed out of the army to take care of it. I think Aunt Sally made him stay out of the war for this reason, but she made home about as hot for him as the field would have been. I can't think he stayed at home to keep out of war, for he was in war all the time. Aunt Sally continually twitted him with staying at home, although she made him do it. She was always sure to do this when the table was filled with Confederate officers.

"The place for a *man*," she would say, "is on the field. Just give me the chance to fight! Just give me the chance to fight, and see where I'll be!"

And General Stuart would convulse me by whispering: "I don't think she needs a chance to fight, do you?"

Sometimes when Aunt Sally's harangue would begin the general would whisper, "Aunt Sally's getting herself in battle array," or "The batteries have limbered up," or "Aunt Sally's scaled the breastworks," and Mr. Bradford's meek and inoffensive face would make the situation funnier. He would mildly help the boarders to the dish in front of him and endeavour feebly to turn the conversation into a peaceful and safe direction, though this never had the slightest effect upon his belligerent wife.

One day—it was about the time of Stuart's historical grand review—Mr. Bradford invited all the cavalry generals whose forces were stationed around us to dine with the commander in chief of the cavalry. He would never have dared to do this if Aunt Sally had been at home, but Aunt Sally at this auspicious moment was in Washington, where we all hoped the fortunes of war and shopping would keep her indefinitely. Her niece, Miss Morse, and I sat down, the only ladies present, at a table with eighteen Confederate generals. Miss Molly and I were at first a trifle embarrassed at being the only ladies, but they were all refined and well-bred, and soon put us at our ease. General Wade Hampton led me in to dinner, and I sat between him and General Ramseur. General Ramseur was young and exceedingly handsome, and a paralysed arm which was folded across his breast made him all the more attractive.

"If you sit next me, Mrs. Grey," he said with a little embarrassment, "you will have to cut up my dinner for me. I am afraid that will be putting you to a great deal of trouble. Perhaps I had better change my seat."

"Oh, no!" I said, "I will be very glad— if I can be satisfactory."

He smiled. "Thank you. I am always both glad and sorry to impose upon a lady this service. I am sorry, you know, to tax a lady with it, but then, she always does it better than a man."

I had been studying his face, and now, for want of something more sensible I said:

"If I am to feed you, General Ramseur, I must measure your mouth."

It happened that there was dead silence at the table when this silly speech of mine was made. Everybody was listening.

"Madam," said the handsome general, blushing and smiling, "I am entirely willing that you should."

I caught a mischievous light in General Stuart's merry eyes, and blushed furiously. Then I followed his laugh, and the whole table roared.

"I will tell Dan Grey!" cried Stuart.

"I will tell Dan Grey!" ran around the table like a chorus.

But I fed my handsome general all the same.

It was while I was at Mr. Bradford's that one of the most stirring events in Confederate history occurred. This was the trampling down of John Minor Botts's corn. good corn it was, dropped and hilled by Southern negroes and growing on a large, fine plantation next to Mr. Bradford's; and a very nice gentleman Mr. Botts was, too; but a field of corn, however good, and a private citizen, however estimable, are scarcely matters of national or international importance. The trouble was that John Minor Botts was on the Northern side and the corn was on the Southern side, and that Stuart held a grand review on the Southern side and the corn got trampled down.

The fame of that corn went abroad into all the land. Northern and Southern papers vied with each other in editorials and special articles, families who had been friends for generations stopped speaking and do not speak to this day because of it, more than one hard blow was exchanged for and against it, and it brought down vituperation upon Stuart's head. And yet I was present at that naughty grand review—which left sorrowful memory on many hearts because of the battle following fast upon it—and I can testify that General Stuart went there to review the troops, *not* to trample down the corn.

Afterward John Minor Botts came over to see General Stuart and to quarrel about that corn. All that I can remember of how the general took Mr. Botts's visit and effort to quarrel was that Stuart wouldn't quarrel—whatever it was he said to Mr. Botts he got to laughing when he said it. Our coloured Abigail told us with bated breath that "Mr. Botts ripped and rarred and snorted, but Genrul Stuart warn't put out none at all."

There had been many reviews that week, all of them merely by way of preparation and practise for that famous grand review before the Battle of Brandy or Fleetwood, but it is only of this particular grand review I have many lively memories. Aunt Sally was away, and we attended it in state. Mr. Bradford had out the ancient and honourable family carriage and two shadowy horses, relics of days when corn was in plenty and wheat not merely a dream of the past, and we went in it to the review along with many other carriages and horses, whose title to respect lay, alas! solely in the past.

That was a day to remember! Lee's whole army was in Culpeper. Pennsylvania and Gettysburg were before it, and the army was making ready for invasion. On a knoll where a Confederate flag was planted and surrounded by his staff sat General Lee on horseback; before him, with a rebel yell, dashed Stuart and his eight thousand cavalry. There was a sham battle. Charging and counter-charging went on, rebels yelled and artillery thundered. Every time the cannons were fired we would pile out of our carriage, and as soon as the cannonading ceased we would pile back again. General Stuart happened to ride up once just as we were getting out.

"Why don't you ladies sit still and enjoy the fun?" he asked in amazement.

"We are afraid the horses might take fright and run away," we answered.

I shall never forget his ringing laugh. Our lean and spiritless steeds had too little life in them to run for anything—they hardly pricked up their ears when the guns went off.

How well I remember Stuart as he looked that day! He wore a fine new uniform, brilliant with gold lace, buff gauntlets reaching to his elbows, and a canary-coloured silk sash with tasselled ends. His hat, a soft, broad-brimmed felt, was caught up at the side with a gold star and carried a sweeping plume; his high, patent-leather cavalry boots were trimmed with gold. He wore spurs of solid gold, the gift of some Maryland ladies—he was very proud of those spurs—and his horse was coal black and glossy as silk. And how happy he was—how full of faith in the Confederacy and himself!

My own cavalry officer was there, resplendent in his new uniform—I had had it made up for him in Richmond. Dan was very proud of the way I got that uniform. He was almost ready to credit himself with having put me up to running the blockade! He told General Stuart its history, and that is how a greatness not always easy to sustain had been thrust upon me. General Stuart thought me very brave—or said he thought so. The manoeuvres of Dan's command were on such a distant part of the field that I could not see him well with the naked eye, and General Stuart lent me his field-glasses. The next morning, just as gray dawn was breaking, someone called under my window, and gravel rattled against the pane. I got up and looked out sleepily. My first thought was that it might be Dan. There was not enough light for me to see very well what was happening on the lawn, but I could make out that the cavalry were mounted and moving, and under my window I saw a figure on horseback.

"Is that Mrs. Grey?"

"Yes. What is the matter?"

"General Stuart sent me for his field-glasses. I am sorry to disturb you, but it couldn't be helped."

I tied a string around the glasses and lowered them.

"What's the matter? Where is the cavalry going?"

"To Brandy Station. Reckon we'll have some hot fighting soon," and the orderly wheeled and rode away.

I stayed up and dressed, and thought of Dan, and wished I could know if he was to be in the coming engagement, and that I could see him first. But I didn't see him all day.

CHAPTER 20

"Whose Business 'Tis To Die"

In forty-eight hours we knew that the surmise of the orderly was correct—there was enough righting. The first cannon-ball which tore through the air at Brandy was only too grave assurance of the fact. All day men were hurrying past the house, deserters from both armies getting away from the scene of bloodshed and thunder as quickly as possible. Then came the procession of the dead and wounded, some in ambulances, some in carts, some on the shoulders of friends.

In the afternoon we began to hear rumours giving names of the killed and wounded. I listened with my heart in my throat for Dan's name, but I did not hear it. I heard no news whatever of him all day—all day I could only hope that no news was good news, and all day that ghastly procession dragged heavily by. Among names of the killed I heard that of Colonel Sol Williams.

A day or two before the Battle of Brandy he had returned from a furlough to Petersburg, where he had gone to marry a lovely woman, a friend of mine. The day before he was killed he had sat at table with me, chatting pleasantly of mutual friends at home from whom he had brought messages, brimful of happiness, and of the charming wife he had won! As the day waned I sat in my room, wretched and miserable, thinking of my friend who was at once a bride and a widow, and fearing for myself, whose husband even at that moment might be falling under his death wound. I was aroused by hearing the voices of men, subdued but excited, on the stairway leading to my room. I ran out and saw several men of rank and Mr. Bradford on the stairway talking excitedly, and I heard my name spoken.

"What's the matter, gentlemen?" I asked with forced calmness.

They looked up at me in a stupid, masculine sort of way, as if they had something disagreeable to say and didn't want to say it. I could shake those men now, when I think of how stupid they were! They were listening to Mr. Bradford, and I don't think they really caught my question, nor did my manner betray to them how fast my heart was beating, but they were stupid, nevertheless. I could hardly get the next words out:

"Is Dan hurt?"

This time my voice was so low that they did not hear it at all.

"For God's sake, gentlemen," I cried out, "tell me if my husband is wounded or dead."

"Neither, madam!" several voices answered instantly, and the officer nearest me, thinking I was going to fall, sprang quickly to my side. I gathered myself together, and they told me their business, and I saw why my presence had embarrassed them—they wanted my room for the wounded. A funny thing had happened, incongruous as it was, in their telling me that my fears for Dan were groundless. When I asked, "Is Dan hurt?" one of them had answered, "No, ma'am; it's General Rooney Lee;" and I had said, "Thank God!" I can't describe the look of horror with which they heard me.

"These gentlemen," began Mr. Bradford, who was always afraid to speak his mind, "wanted to bring General Lee here, and I didn't have a place to put him, and I was telling 'em that I thought that— maybe—you would give him your room. I could fix up a lounge for you somewhere."

"Of course I will! I shall be delighted to give up my room, or do anything else I can for General Lee."

I busied myself getting my room ready for General "Rooney," but he was not brought to Mr. Bradford's, after all; his men were afraid that he might be captured too easily at Mr. Bradford's. As night came on the yard filled up with soldiers. In the lawn, the road, the backyard, the porches, the outhouses, everywhere, there were soldiers. You could not set your foot down without putting it on a soldier; if you thrust your hand out of a window you touched a soldier's back or shoulder, his carbine or his musket. The place was crowded not only with cavalry, but with infantry and artillery, and still they kept on coming. I had not heard from Dan. It was late supper-time. I had no heart for supper, and I felt almost too shaken to present myself at the table, but as I passed the dining-room in my restless rovings I saw General Stuart's back, and went in and sat by him.

"General," I said, "can you tell me anything of Dan?"

"He is neither killed nor wounded. I know that much. Is not that enough?"

"Yes, thank God!

"Oh, general! I wish this war was over!" I said again.

"I, too, my child!" He spoke with more than Stuart's sadness and gravity, then, remembering himself, he added quickly in his own cheery fashion, "But we've got to whip these Yankees first!"

He finished his cup of coffee (the kind in common use, made of corn which had been roasted, parched, and ground), and then went on telling me about Dan.

"He has borne himself gallantly, as he always does, and as you know without my telling you. I don't know where he is, but he will be along presently."

And at that moment Dan walked in, without a coat, and with the rest of that new uniform a perfect fright. He was covered with dust and ashes and gunpowder, and he looked haggard and jaded. He sat down between General Stuart and me, too tired to talk; but after eating some supper, he felt better, and began discussing the battle and relating some incidents. He took a card out of his pocket and handed it to General Stuart.

"A Federal officer who is about done for, poor fellow, handed me that just now. I don't know the name. He couldn't talk."

"I do!" General Stuart exclaimed, with quick, strong interest. "Where did you see him? This is the name of one of my classmates at West Point."

"I saw him on the roadside as I came on to supper. While riding along I heard a strange sound, something like a groan, yet different from any groan I ever heard—the strangest, most uncanny sound imaginable. I dismounted and began to look around for it, and I found a Yankee soldier lying in a ditch by the roadside. I couldn't see that any legs or arms were broken, nor that he was wounded at all. I felt him all over, and asked what was the matter. He didn't speak, and I saw that he had been trying to direct my attention to his face. He tried very hard to speak, but only succeeded in emitting the strange sound I had heard before; and on examining his face closely, and moving the whiskers aside, I found that he was shot through both jaws. He made the same noise again, put his hand in his pocket, and gave me this card, with another pitiful effort to speak. I put my coat under his head, laid some brush across the ditch to hide him, and promised to go back for him in an ambulance."

"Thank you, in my own behalf!" General Stuart said warmly.

"Perhaps, poor fellow," said Dan, "he took chances on that card's reaching you. Seeing my uniform of major of cavalry, he may not have considered it impossible that you should hear of his condition through me.

"When you have finished your supper, major, we will go after him."

Tired as they both were, they went out and attended personally to the relief of the poor fellow by the roadside. General Stuart had everything done for him that was possible, smoothed his last moments, and grieved over him as deeply as if his classmate had not been his enemy.

Another sad thing among the sorrows of that supper was when Colonel Sol Williams's brother-in-law, John Pegram, came in, and sat down in our midst. General Stuart went up to him, and wrung his hand in a silence that even the dauntless Stuart's lips were too tremulous at once to break. When he could speak he said:

"I grieve for myself as for you, lieutenant, but it was a death that any one of us might be proud to die."

Even then the shadow and glory of his own death was not far from him.

Colonel Williams had been Lieutenant Pegram's superior officer as well as brother-in-law. It had been his sorrowful lot to take the body of his colonel on his horse in front of him, and carry it to a house where it could be reverently cared for until he could send it home to bride and kindred. He had cut a lock of hair from the dead, and when the troops went off to Pennsylvania, he gave it to me for his sister. I shall never forget that supper hour, or how the unhappy young fellow looked when he came in among us after his ride with the dead, and I shall never forget how I felt about that poor young Federal soldier who was wounded in the jaws and couldn't speak, and how I felt about the women who loved him far away; I began to feel that war was an utterly unjustifiable thing, and that the virtues of valour, loyalty, devotion which it brings out had better be brought out some other way.

If General Rooney Lee didn't take my room, I gave it up all the same. Two wounded men were put into it. There were a number of wounded men in the house, and, of course, everybody gave way to their comfort. All but my two were removed in a day or two, but here these two were, and here they were when Aunt Sally came home. Her homecoming was after a fashion that turned our mourning into righteous and wholesome wrath. We were sitting on the porch one afternoon, free and easy in our minds and believing Aunt Sally away in distant Washington, when we noted a small object far off down the road. As it crawled nearer and nearer we perceived that it was an ox-cart; we saw the driver, and behind him somebody else sitting on a trunk.

"Good gracious! that's Aunt Sally!" cried Mr. Bradford in consternation.

We were all dreadfully sorry, but it couldn't be helped.

She climbed off the cart at the gate, and called for some negro to come get her trunk. Mr. Bradford had already found one, and was running to the rescue. In fact he had been running in a half dozen different directions ever since he had spied Aunt Sally. He looked as if his wits had left him and as if he were racing around in a circle.

"You orter been on hand to he'p me off o' that kyart," she told him. "It do look like when a man's wife's been away this long time he might be on hand to he'p her off the kyart."

As she came up the walk she said the yard looked awful torn and "trompled down;" that she was afraid she would find it so soon as she heard that the place had been camping ground for the whole army and her away and nobody there to manage the army as she could have done. She greeted me and her niece, and in the same breath told her niece that there was some mud on the steps which ought to be washed off. Then she went into the house, taking off her things and remarking on "things that ought to be done." Presently there was a great stir in the house; she had found out the wounded men. She commented on their presence in such a loud voice that we heard it on the porch, and the men themselves must have heard it.

"Just like Mr. Bradford! If I had been here it wouldn't have happened. The idea! Turning the house into a hospital! I won't have it! Nobody knows who they are. I can't have 'em on my best beds, and between my best sheets and blankets. Dirty, common soldiers! I never heard of such a thing!"

And she got them out before supper.

There was an office in the yard and she had them taken to this. They had to be carried past us, and I can see them now, poor, mortified, shame-faced fellows! I was as afraid of Aunt Sally as of a rattlesnake, but I think I could have shaken her then!

Little it was that I saw of Dan or any of my army friends after the Battle of Brandy. The cavalry was too busy watching Hooker's, while our infantry was pushing on toward Pennsylvania, to spare any time to lighter matters. Every day the boys in gray marched by on their way North.

I watched from the porch and windows if by any means I might catch sight of Dan. But his way did not lie by Bradford's. One morning, however, I saw General Stuart riding by at the head of a large command. I thought they were going to stop and camp at Mr. Bradford's, perhaps, but I was mistaken. As soon as I saw that they were going by without stopping, I ran to the fence and beckoned to General Stuart. He had seen me on the porch, and rode up to the fence at once.

"Aren't you going to stop at all?" I asked.

"Not today. In fact we're off for some time now."

"Is Dan going?"

"Yes. He's ahead now with General Chambliss."

"Am I not to see him at all, General Stuart?" I said, trying hard to keep my lip from quivering—I had a reputation to keep up with him.

But he saw the quiver.

"You can go on with the army if you want to," he said in quick sympathy. "I will give you an ambulance. You can carry your own maid along, have your own tent, and have your husband with you. I will do anything I can for your comfort. You would nurse our poor fellows when they get hurt, and be no end of good to us. But it would be awfully hard on you."

"I wouldn't mind the hardships," I answered, "but you know Dan won't let me go. I have begged him several times to let me live in camp with him. I could nurse the sick and wounded, and take care of him if he was shot, and I wouldn't be a bit of trouble; and I could patch for the soldiers. Oh, I'd love to do it! If you come up with him, General Stuart, ask him to let me go, and if he says yes, send the ambulance."

"I'll promise him what I promised you," he said, smiling kindly. "Goodbye now. I'll ride on and send him back to say goodbye to you, if I can manage it. Then you can talk him into letting you come with us."

I climbed up on the fence to shake hands with him and to say goodbye, and I had another word for him. Beneath my dress and next my skin was a little Catholic medal which had been blessed by my confessor. It hung around my neck by a slender chain. I unclasped the chain, drew forth the medal and gave it to him, my eyes brimming with tears.

"It has been blessed by Father Mulvey," I said. "Wear it about your neck. Maybe it will bring you back safe."

I was leaning upon the horse's neck, crying as if my heart would break. General Stuart's own eyes were dim.

"Goodbye," I said, "and if you can send Dan back I thank you for us both—I thank you anyway for thinking of it; but—the South and his duty first. Goodbye, and God bless you, General Stuart!"

That was the last time I ever saw him, the last time that knightly hand clasped mine. Before he rode away he said some cheerful, hopeful words, and looked back at me with the glint of merry mischief in his eyes, threatening to tell Dan Grey that I was losing my good repute for bravery. Dan did not come back to say goodbye. I had a little note which he contrived to send me in some way. It was only a hasty scrawl, full of goodbyes and God bless yous.

After saying goodbye to General Stuart I returned to the house. Esten Cooke sat at a table writing. He was preparing some official papers for General Stuart, I think, and had been left behind for that purpose. I understood him to answer one of my questions to the effect that he was going to follow the cavalry presently.

"Colonel Cooke," I asked humbly enough, for I was ready then to take information and advice from anybody, "how long do you think it will be before the army comes back?"

"Can't say, madam."

"Would you advise me to wait here until its return?"

"Can't say, madam."

"Would you advise me to go to Richmond?"

"Madam, I would advise you to go to Richmond."

"You think then it will be some time before the army returns?"

"I can't say, madam?"

I felt like shaking him and asking: "What can you say?" He may have been a brave soldier and written nice books and all that, but I think John Esten Cooke was a very dull, disagreeable man.

I waited several days, but as I got nothing further from Dan than the little note—which was bare of advice because, perhaps, he didn't have time to write more, and because he may not have known how to advise me—I took John Esten Cooke's advice and went to Richmond. I stopped there only a very short time, and then went on to Petersburg, where mother was. Reunion with her was compensation for many troubles, and then, too, she needed me. She had not heard from Milicent since my departure for Culpeper. Then a letter had reached us through the agency of Mr. Cridland, in which Milicent had stated her purpose of coming to us as soon as she could get a pass—a thing it was every day becoming more difficult to secure—for she was determined upon reaching us before the cold weather came again. Since that letter there had been absolute silence.

Then came upon us that awful July of 1863, and the Battle of Gettysburg, the beginning of the end. Virginians fell by hundreds in that fight, and Pickett's charge goes down to history along with Balaklava and Thermopylae. There were more vacant chairs in Virginia, already desolate—there were more broken hearts for which Heaven alone held balm. "When Italy's made, for what good is it done if we have not a son?" Again the angel of death had passed me by. But my heart bled for my friends who were dead on that red field far away—for my friends who mourned and could not be comforted.

One of our wounded, whose father brought him home to be nursed, bore to me a letter from my husband and a package from General Stuart. The package contained a photograph of himself that he had promised me, and a note, bright, genial, merry, like himself. That picture is hanging on my wall now. On the back is written by a hand long crumbled into dust, "To her who in being a devoted wife did not forget to be a true patriot." The eyes smile down upon us as I lift my little granddaughter up to kiss my gallant cavalier's lips, and as she lisps his name my heart leaps to the memory of his dauntless life and death.

He was shot one beautiful May morning in 1864 while trying to prevent Sheridan's approach to Richmond. It was at Yellow Tavern—a dismantled old tavern not many miles from the Confederate capital—that he fell, and Colonel Venable, who was serving with him at the time and near him when he fell, helped, if I remember aright, to shroud him. When he told me what he could of General Stuart's last hours, he said:

"There was a little Catholic medal around his neck, Nell. Did you give him that? We left it on him."

And so passes from this poor history my beloved and loyal friend, my cavalry hero and good comrade. Virginia holds his dust sacred, and in history he sits at the Round Table of all true-souled and gentle knights.

CHAPTER 21

Rescued by the Foe

MILICENT'S ARREST IN WASHINGTON AS RELATED BY HERSELF.

I passed May and a part of the summer of 1863 in fruitless efforts to get a pass to Virginia. This was when the Civil War was at its whitest heat, and I was in the city of Baltimore, where a word was construed into treason, and messages and letters were contrived to and from the South only by means of strategy. One by one my plans failed. Then came the battle of Gettysburg, and as I heard of our reverses I felt an almost helpless lethargy stealing over me—as if I should never see Nell or mother again. How long the war would last, and what would be the end of it none could tell. Nell and mother were in a besieged country, and the blockade between us seemed an impassable wall. The long silence was becoming unbearable as I slowly realized that it might become the silence of death and I not know.

At last came news which I thought affected them, and which startled me into instant energy.

One morning my friend, Miss Barnett, a beautiful girl, rushed into my room, and, throwing herself on the floor beside me, began telling me with sobs and tears that my brother-in-law, Major Grey, or his brother Dick, was a prisoner in the Old Capitol at Washington. She begged me to go at once and see what I could do. If I could not find some way of helping the prisoner to freedom, I could at least add to his comfort in prison.

"You could at least show him that he was remembered," she said. "You could take some little delicacies which would be grateful to a prisoner. I will help you to get them up."

Poor Isabelle! It was one of the tragedies of the war. She was too wretched to attempt any concealment.

"You see, if I had any right to go myself I would not ask you to go for me. If I were even engaged to him—but I am not. You see, it couldn't be. But, O Millie! I wish there wasn't any war that I might be my love's betrothed and go to him!"

For a minute her proposition daunted me. To rush into Washington, a Southern woman, alone and unprotected; to be surrounded on all sides by the government officials and spies whose business it was to watch and report every careless word and act of any one who was known to be interested in the South or in Southerners—the undertaking seemed desperate. But there were Isabelle's tearful eyes, and there was the fear that Nell's husband might be the prisoner. I determined to make the trip at all hazards.

Together we made purchases of what we considered the most tempting delicacies to take to an invalid or prisoner. There were cheeses, crackers, oranges, lemons, jellies; and we did not forget to add to our stock wine, whisky, pipes, and tobacco. Isabelle herself sent a box of fine cigars, a costly gift, for the war with the Southern States affected the price of tobacco.

The next morning I started off by myself to Washington in fear and trembling. Taking a hack there, and trusting to a kind Providence for guidance and protection, I drove first to the office of the provost marshal for a permit. On entering his office, to my consternation I recognized in him the judge-advocate under whose protection our truce boat had gone to Richmond not many months before with the distinct understanding that her passengers were not to return from Dixie while the war lasted. But it was too late to retreat. Rallying all my courage and self-control I greeted him as a stranger, asking whether or not I was addressing Judge Turner. Answered in the affirmative, I requested permission to visit the prisoners in the Old Capitol.

While I was talking he looked up and a glance almost of recognition lighted his face. It was succeeded by a more scrutinizing regard as I stood in perfectly assumed unconsciousness before him. Bowing, he asked me to be seated, and to repeat my petition. Others were waiting their turn, and his answer was prompt:

"Certainly, madam. You can see the two prisoners mentioned, or anyone you wish, and take with you what you please."

An easy job certainly!

My heart grew light; I arose to go, thanking the judge cordially.

He said: "One moment, madam."

I went back, and he handed me a pen, ink, and slip of paper, saying:

"Just sign this, please. It is of no consequence at all—a mere matter of form—only you cannot see your friends without it."

There spread out before me was the ironclad oath!

Without a moment's hesitation I replied:

"The oath, Judge Turner! Am I to sign that? I cannot! and never will!"

He smiled apologetically and said:

"It is of no consequence—only a little form that we have to insist on. Sign it, and you can go to your friends."

"If it is of no consequence to your side, provost, why should it be of so much to mine that I cannot see my friends without it?"

He smiled, and still held the pen out to me.

"No! never!" I said.

"Then I cannot help you. I am sorry. You must apply at military headquarters."

He kindly directed me to the same. I hurried down the steps, jumped into my hack, and drove quickly to the War Department. Here I made my request again and again met with the same polite consent backed with the oath. Again I refused and turned to go, when one of the officers kindly suggested:

"Make application to the officer at the Old Capitol. He may permit you to see the prisoners without oath, though I fear not."

As there was not much time left before my train would start for Baltimore, I urged my driver to do his best, and we sped on in haste until we stopped before the gloomy, formidable-looking prison of the Old Capitol. With the permission of the guard I entered. The officer in command received me with kindness and courtesy, and with his consent I was about to ascend the stairs when he extended his hand, saying:

"The oath, if you please. I presume you took it at the War Department, and have your pass."

Again I was foiled. This was my last chance. There was no use pleading, and I was in despair. I leaned on a chair to rest a moment before leaving the room, defeated. I had not a word to say, and I did not say a word. I suppose my deep dejection touched him. I was about to go when he said with great kindness:

"Wait here near these steps. I will send up an order, and if he is there, he can come to the railing and you can speak to him, and send him anything you wish. But you can not go up."

An orderly ascended with the message, and I waited at the steps, watching anxiously for Dan or Dick to appear at the railing. I did not have many minutes to wait. The orderly returned with the reply that Lieutenant—not Major—Grey had been exchanged that very morning, and was now on his way home. Happy for Nell and Isabelle and myself, I poured out my thanks to the officer in command for helping me to such good news, and asked his permission to send the large basket of good things I had brought to the other prisoners. He gave it, and I saw the orderly again mount the stairs, burdened this time with good wishes and my still more substantial and acceptable offering. As I went out, passing again through the prison gates, my driver whispered in the most excited manner:

"Lady! lady! do take care! The prisoners are all at the windows, and if you look up or speak to them we will both be arrested instantly."

I seated myself quickly, and then, in spite of all fears and warnings, glanced up, to see the windows filled with faces, and hands and handkerchiefs waving to me inside the bars. As we dashed forward, I leaned out of the window waving my handkerchief in vigorous response. In the excitement, the enthusiasm of the moment, I lost all sense of fear or danger—my whole heart was with those desolate, homesick Confederates behind the bars. Fortunately the driver was frightened out of his wits and drove like mad, or we should never have gotten to the train in time.

I had been fortunate enough to find in my driver a strong, if secret, sympathizer with the South. As I bade him goodbye, and thanked him for the care and promptness with which he had carried me about, and for his unheeded warning as well, he said:

"Oh, lady, lady, you ran a great risk when you waved that handkerchief! I saw it and drove as fast as I could to get you away from there. It is a wonder we were not arrested."

I stepped on the car, and was taking my seat, when a hand lightly touched my shoulder from behind, and I heard myself arrested by a name that was not mine. Behind me stood a sergeant in the United States uniform, who informed me that I was his prisoner.

I tried to shrink away from him.

"That is not my name," I said.

Still he kept that light grip on my shoulder. I felt sick. The day had been a long one of exercise and excitement. I had eaten nothing since my early breakfast of a cracker and a cup of coffee, and I was physically weak. The terror of the situation, the full foolhardiness of my undertaking flashed upon me. Alone in Washington, not a friend near, and under arrest! For an instant everything whirled around me, and I fell back against the breast of the sergeant; but as instantly I pulled myself together and stood erect.

"You are mistaken," I said quietly, "I am not the person you have mentioned."

And I threw back my heavy mourning veil and looked my captor full in the face.

"Ain't you? It's widow's weeds this time!"

These words were spoken sarcastically by a man in civilian dress who was with the sergeant—a detective, I suppose.

"I am Mrs. Milicent Duncan Norman, of Baltimore," I said firmly. "You can telegraph to No.—Charles Street and see. You will please remove your hand," I continued. "If necessary I will go with you, but I am not the person you wish to arrest. You are making a mistake."

I turned my face full to the light, and stood, calm and composed, though my knees were trembling under me, and I felt as if I should faint. I saw Bobby at home waiting for me!

"I must stay over if you insist," I repeated, "but I hope you will permit me to convince you of your mistake. It would be extremely inconvenient to me to be detained here. I left Baltimore this morning, and my little boy has been without me all day. He will cry himself sick if I don't get home tonight."

In spite of all I could do my lips quivered.

"I am sorry, madam," said my sergeant, more respectfully than he had hitherto spoken, "but you will have to come with me. If it is as you say, you can telegraph and satisfy the authorities very quickly."

My arrest had attracted some attention. I saw that people in the car were gathering around me, and I saw curiosity in some faces, sympathy in some, but among all those faces none that I knew. This was my first visit to Washington, and there was not a soul to identify me. There was nothing to do but to go and telegraph—if they would let me. I would have to miss my train. Bobby was watching from the window for me this very minute—Bobby would cry all night. I told the sergeant that I would go, and tried to follow him, and then everything grew dark around me, my head whirled, and I dropped across the seat nearest me.

I could not have been unconscious more than a second. The kind gentleman over whose seat I had fallen had caught me, and was slapping my face with a wet handkerchief, and assuring the sergeant that he knew by my face that I was perfectly harmless and ought not to be arrested, that he would bet anything on it, when a new passenger hurriedly entered the car and brushed squarely up against us.

The sergeant was saying: "We must hurry," and offering me his arm very courteously. "You will feel better when you get out in the air. And you will perhaps come out all right, and be able to go on tomorrow."

The newcomer looked over the sergeant's shoulder and saw me.

"Milicent!" he said, and clasped my hands.

It was a dear friend whom I had known in my girlhood days as Captain Warren.

"What is all this?" he asked quickly of the sergeant.

The sergeant was staggered, the little man in civilian's clothes cringed, the old man who had offered to bet on me was in the majority.

"We must get out of this, commodore," said the sergeant quickly, "the car is moving."

The commodore got out with us, lifted me bodily off the train, and then, as we stood together, while the sergeant explained, supported me with his arm. I was too weak and ill to hear their talk. I think I was very nearly in a faint while I stood, or tried to stand upright beside him.

He told me afterward that I had been arrested by mistake for some famous political spy in petticoats. He answered for me, made himself responsible in every way, lifted me into a carriage, and told the driver where to take us. I was too nearly dead to listen to what he said. As the carriage whirled along I tried to sit up, to lift my head, but every time I attempted it I grew blind and sick.

"I would not try to sit up just yet, Mrs. Norman," he said very kindly. "In a few minutes, perhaps, you can do so without risk, but I'd be very quiet now. In a little while I will hand you over to my wife—she is a wonderful nurse."

"My little boy is looking out of the window for me, waiting for me; he has been by himself all day," I sobbed.

"Ah! I am so sorry you have had this annoyance and detention. I wish I had boarded the car earlier; you should have gone on if I had. I was outside talking with some friends, and I did not jump on the train until she was about to move off, but I can telegraph to your friends, and you can go on tomorrow."

The ride in the open air had revived me, and I found now that I could sit up without fainting.

"*You* were going to Baltimore tonight," I said. "I am putting you to so much trouble."

"None at all. And if you were"—with a tremor in his voice—"I should be glad of it. *Can* you sit up? Ah! I am so glad you are better. When I first took you into this carriage I was afraid I would have to stop with you at the first doctor's office. We are nearly home now."

"You are very good," I said, still too weak not to speak with tears in my voice.

"I am fortunate—but too much at your expense, I am afraid. You forget how large my debt is. I shall never forget the old days in Norfolk and the kindness that was shown me by you and yours. I owe you a great deal, Mrs. Norman, as yourself and as your father's daughter. I shall never forget his charming hospitality. I am sorry you can't go on to Baltimore, but I am glad of my opportunity."

"That is a nice way to put it, commodore."

"A true way to put it, Mrs. Norman. Please don't be too sorry. Where is Nell?—Mrs. Grey, I suppose I should say. I can't think of the saucy little fairy who used to sit on my knee as a madam."

"I don't know just where Nell is, or how. The fortunes of war have separated me from her, and mother as well."

"And you are alone, without kindred, in Baltimore?"

"Yes, except my baby. I wish you could see Bobby—he is so sweet!"

"He must be."

"He has Nell's eyes and her golden curls—you remember?"

"Too well!"

"And her saucy sweet ways—wilful and almost bad—if he were not so sweet and true. But I tire you. Mothers who talk about their babies bore people. I make many good resolves not to talk Bobby, and, break every one."

"You could never tire me. I am charmed to hear about your boy. Maybe you can find him a little sweetheart in my house. Here we are."

He lifted me out of the carriage and led me into the house.

"This is an old friend of mine, dear," he said to his wife. "She is sick and in trouble, and I have brought her to you. Her father's home used to be my home in Norfolk. Mrs. Norman is Miss Duncan that was."

She had heard of me. He began to explain how he had met me, but she interrupted.

"I will come back and hear," she said, "when I have made Mrs. Norman comfortable. She looks worn-out. I must take her to her room and see what I can do to make her more at ease." While she was talking she had me in a chair, holding my hand, and giving me a glass of wine.

Commodore Warren took my Baltimore address, and went out saying he would send the telegrams at once—a special one to Bobby all by himself.

Then Mrs. Warren saw me to my room. As we passed through hallways and up the stairs, our feet sank into soft, thick carpets that gave back no sound. Through an open doorway I caught a glimpse of her own exquisite chamber and of a cosy nursery where children's gowns were laid out for the night. Everywhere around me were evidences of wealth, luxury, and refinement.

After a little rest I felt better.

As I went down to dinner I heard the street door open, and Commodore Warren's voice in the hall.

Then children's voices:

"Papa! papa!"

He was taking his children in his arms and kissing them, and I heard the glad murmur of his wife's welcome.

Together they took me in to their table, and showered upon me courtesies and loving-kindness. Such a delightful dining-room it was—such lovely appointments and such perfect serving! and such charming hosts they made! The children are beautiful and well trained. They were brought into the parlour after dinner, and made great friends with me. You know children always like me, Nell. This trio took possession of me. They hovered around me, leaned against me, climbed into my lap, and the youngest went to sleep in my arms, her soft golden head nestled under my chin. We decided that she is to be Bobby's sweetheart. Their parents were afraid that I was not strong enough for such demonstrations, but I begged that they would not interrupt the little people, whose caresses really did me a world of good. But the commodore called the nurse when the baby dropped to sleep, and she took it to the nursery, the other children following her. By this time I was quite myself. A telegram had come from Isabelle, saying she was with Bobby and that Bobby was comforted.

Commodore and Mrs. Warren suggested that we should go to the opera. It was rather late to start, but the carriage would take us in a few minutes, and we should not miss more than the first act. A great singer was to be heard, and the commodore remembered that I was fond of music. When I objected on the score that I was not in opera dress and that my wardrobe was in Baltimore, they explained that they kept a private box, and that I could hear without being distinctly visible—if I was not too fatigued to think of going.

"Oh, no!" I said. "You know I love opera, and, thanks to you both, I am entirely rested and comfortable about Bobby."

Mrs. Warren ran upstairs to dress while the carriage was being made ready. As for me, there was nothing to do but to put on my bonnet and cloak, so I sat still, and Commodore Warren drew up a chair in front of the sofa where I sat.

"This is like old times," he said.

I tried to keep them back, but somehow I felt the tears starting to my eyes.

He got up and walked to the other end of the room, and brought a book of drawings of queer places and people he had seen in his journeys around the world. While he was showing them to me he remarked:

"I've a box somewhere of curious toys picked up in various parts of the world at different times, and I think Master Bobby would be interested in them. We'll get Mrs. Warren to look it up, and I'll ask you to be kind enough to take it to him with my compliments. It may—in a measure—recompense him for his mother's absence tonight."

"Bobby will be delighted—if he is not robbing your children."

"My children," he laughed, "have a surfeit of toys from the four corners of the earth. They have almost lost appreciation of such things. By the way, has Nell"—he caught himself with a laugh—"Mrs. Grey, I should say, any little ones of her own?"

"Bobby is the only baby in the family; but he is enough to go around."

"I remember with profound gratitude the many expressions I used to receive of Nell's regard in those old days, and seeing you brings them back. Oh, forgive me—I know there have been many changes."

"Don't apologize," I said, smiling; "I am always glad to have old days and old friends recalled. Usually it does not shake me even to talk about father—it's a pleasure to think people remember him. In the first part of this evening I had not quite recovered—from my arrest. But Richard is himself again now. I haven't forgotten how to be happy, and I'm going to enjoy this opera." And I did enjoy it.

Mrs. Warren took me to my train in her carriage; and there he met us to say goodbye to me, and to tell me that he would see that I had a pass to Norfolk in a day or two. They both saw me comfortably seated, and after farewells were said and he had seen his wife to her carriage he stepped back on the cars with a handful of flowers for me.

"Is there nothing," he asked, "nothing that I can do for you? If you are ever in any trouble when I can help you, won't you let me know?"

I bowed my head.

"And Bobby—if there is ever anything I can do for your child, you will let me know?"

"Goodbye," he said, "it is good to meet old friends and find that neither time nor war changes them. Goodbye—we shall see you again some day."

Isabelle was very happy when I told her that Dick was safe, and now that it was over she regretted having sent me into such dangers and tribulations.

"I ought to have gone," she said. "I could have taken the oath, you see, if they had asked me. And then, well, papa is known there, but—I couldn't ask papa to help Dick. He wouldn't have done anything for him."

Chapter 22

With Dan at Charlottesville

MILICENT ALWAYS CAME AS A SOUL COMES.

The day after we got the batch of letters the door opened softly, and there she stood, holding Bobby by the hand. She had come so quietly that we did not know it until she stood in our midst. But Bobby was a veritable piece of flesh and blood. As soon as he saw it was grandma and auntie, he made a bound for us, and overwhelmed us with his noisy and affectionate greetings, while his mother submitted to being loved and kissed, and in her quiet way loved and kissed back again. Then she told us how she had come from Norfolk to Petersburg. It was a long, dreary trip.

"I went on a flag-of-truce train to Suffolk. Dr. Wright's family were on the train, and I spent the night with them. Bobby burned his throat at supper by swallowing tea too hot for him, and he did not rest well in the early part of the night and slept late the next day, and I was very anxious about him. This, and the difficulty in getting a conveyance, kept me at Dr. Wright's until the afternoon. By that time I had secured a mule-cart to take me to Ivor Station, on the Norfolk and Petersburg Railroad. Ivor, you; know, is not more than twenty-five miles from Suffolk by the direct route, but the route we had to take for safety, as far as the Yankees and mud were concerned, was longer, and our one mule went slowly.

"The first afternoon we travelled till late in the night. Bobby would insist on driving the mule, and the driver humoured him. In spite of the pain in his throat, he stood up against my knee and held the lines until, poor little tired fellow! he went to sleep holding them. I drew him on to my lap, covered him up, and we went on, the old negro, old mule, and baby all asleep. At last we stopped at a farmhouse to feed the mule. The woman who lived there asked me in. I laid Bobby down on her bed, dropped across it, and in five minutes was asleep myself. I don't know how many other people slept in that bed that night, but I know that the old woman, Bobby, and I slept in it. When I woke up it was several hours after daylight. Our breakfast the next morning was a typical Confederate breakfast. My hostess gave me a drink made of parched wheat and corn which had been ground, a glass of milk, and some corn bread and bacon, and I enjoyed the meal and paid her cheerfully.

"We reached Ivor late that afternoon, my driver got his fee and departed, and Bobby and I were left to wait for the train. But we were not the only persons at the station; two other women were waiting at Ivor. If those two women could have had their way there would never have been another sunset on this earth. Their two sons were to be shot at sundown—they were watching for the sun to go down. Up and down, up and down, they walked in front of a tent where their sons under military guard awaited execution, and as they walked their eyes, swift and haggard, shifted from tent to sky and back again from sky to tent. As my train moved out of the station I glanced back.

They were walking with feverish haste, and the sun hung low in the heavens."

"Hush, hush!" I cried, "I can't stand another word—I shall dream of those women all night. Tell me how you got here at last!"

"When I reached Pocahontas I meant to go to Jarrett's, and stop until I could find out where you were, but while I was looking around for a carriage who should I come upon but John, our old hackman. He told me that you were both out here at Uncle William's, and I made him drive me out."

Soon after my sister's arrival we moved into town and boarded at Miss Anne Walker's, an old historic house then facing Washington Street, which runs east and west, paralleling the railroad at Jarrett's Hotel—or rather where Jarrett's used to stand—an ugly old hotel in the heart of the town. It was beside this railroad that I ran bareheaded along Washington Street some months later to get out of the way of the Yankee cannon. I was at Miss Anne's when Dan gave me leave to visit him at Charlottesville. His headquarters was a small cottage in sight of the university and of my window. He came home every night—home was a student's room in the university—and very often I went with him in the morning to his cottage.

One morning as I sat in the cottage, turning a pair of Dan's old trousers, the door opened, and a fine-looking cavalry officer entered. Surprised to find a lady in occupation, he lifted his hat and started to withdraw. Then he hesitated, regarding me in a confused, doubtful fashion. Whereupon I in my turn began to stare at him.

"Isn't this John—John Mason?" I asked suddenly.

"That is my name," with a sweeping bow. "And are you not my old friend, Miss Nellie Duncan, of Norfolk?"

"Yes," I answered smiling, "but you know I have a third name now."

"Of course. Unpleasant facts are always hard to remember. I heard of your marriage, certainly, but for the moment the remembrance of it escaped me. You are here with the major?"

The last time I had seen John was on that day which closed the chapter of my happy girlhood in Norfolk. He had been with me when the telegram came telling us that father could not live, and from that day to this I had never seen him until he surprised me patching Dan's old trousers in the cottage at Charlottesville.

He took the chair opposite, and began talking about the work I was doing and the evidence it bore to my being a good wife. But so far from being pleased I was very much mortified, for the old trousers were in a dreadful state of wear and tear, and he was resplendent in a new uniform. But after a while we dropped the trousers, and got on the subject of Norfolk and old times, and had quite a pleasant chat till my husband came in and he and John turned their attention to business.

I was seeing more of my husband than at any previous or later period of the war, and having altogether a delightful time. One of the things I enjoyed most were our horseback rides.

Dan had two horses for his own use—Tom Hodges, his old army horse, and Nellie Grey, a fine new mare that he had christened for me. When his horse was shot under him in that charge which has been mentioned before, the people of his native town had sent him Nellie Grey in its stead. Nellie was a beautiful creature, docile but very spirited, and I was not often trusted to ride her unless Dan himself was along. Tom Hodges was not so handsome, but he was a horse of decorous ideas and steadfast principles.

I remember well my first ride on Nellie Grey. I had the reputation of being an excellent horsewoman, and Dan wanted to show me off. He was inordinately proud of me, to my great delight, but I could have dispensed with the form his vanity took on that day.

As we rode in an easy canter down University Avenue he gave Nellie Grey a cut, without my knowledge, that sent her off like the wind in a regular cavalry gallop.

Well, I kept my seat—somehow—and I brought her to her senses and a standstill, and then I looked back to see Dan beaming with pride and pleasure.

"What is the matter with this horse?" I asked. "She's a fool!"

Then Dan told me of that secret cut.

"I knew just what she would do," he said "and I knew what you'd do. I wanted to show the boys over there what pluck my wife's got."

"Dan," I said solemnly, "it's not Nellie Grey that's the fool."

I was breathless and vexed, and I had to use the strongest language at my command to express my opinion of Nellie Grey, but it wasn't strong enough to express my feelings toward Dan! I simply had to look my thoughts!

"You see, wifie," he went on apologetically, "you did look so pretty and plucky that you ought to have seen yourself."

Sam had gone home on a furlough, and in his place Dan had a very magnificent body-servant named Napoleon Bonaparte, and an under boy named Solomon. Napoleon Bonaparte brushed the major's boots, and Solomon brushed Napoleon's. Napoleon Bonaparte was a bright *mulatto*, Solomon was as black as tar. It was Napoleon Bonaparte's business to supply my room with wood, but this task he delegated to Solomon. Whatever menial work the major ordered Napoleon Bonaparte to do, Napoleon turned over to Solomon. "Solomon," he said, "was nothin' but a free nigger nohow." It came to pass finally that Solomon, ostensibly hired to one master, in reality served two.

Of course, Napoleon Bonaparte feathered his own nest and worked things so that the major was really paying two men to do the work of one. When the major could not ride with me, he sent Napoleon Bonaparte to act as groom. This Napoleon Bonaparte esteemed an honour, and he only appointed Solomon in his stead when he himself was in demand as equerry for the major. Napoleon always elected to follow the major in such case, as that was higher employment in his eyes than riding behind me. One morning I stood waiting in my habit a long time for the horses. At last when they appeared Solomon came on a sorry mount, leading Tom Hodges. The procession moved at a snail's pace, and Solomon looked dreadfully glum.

"What makes you so late?" I asked impatiently.

"Dunno 'zackly, marm. Evvybody in de camp got de debbul in

'em. Major, he got de debbul in him! 'Poleon Bonaparte, he got de debbul in *him*. An' evvybody got de debbul in 'em!"

"There seem to have been a great many devils in camp. Wasn't there one to spare for you, Solomon?"

"Nor'm, I ain't had no debbul in me—me an' Tom Hodges. We's been de onliest peaceable people in camp. Ef I hadn't er kep' de peace, me an' 'Poleon Bonaparte would ha' fit, sho!"

"I should think you would like to fight Napoleon—I should, if I were you."

"Nor'm, I don' b'lieve in no fightin'—'cep'in' 'tis ter fit de Yankees. I'm er peaceable man, I is."

I told Dan what a bad report Solomon had made out against him.

He laughed. "Solomon has the grumps this morning. He seemed to have quite a time with your namesake, as well as with the rest of us. Napoleon Bonaparte sent him to rub Nellie Grey down and saddle her for me. The mare threw her head up and jerked him about a little, and we could hear him saying: 'Whoa! Nellie Grey, whoa! You got de debbul in *you* too! Who-a, Nellie Grey!' Between the two of them I am having rather a hard time lately," said Dan. "Solomon blames 'Poleon Bonaparte directly for all the hard times he has, and me indirectly. If something isn't done as it should be, and I take Napoleon to task, he lays it thick and hard on Solomon. Solomon did have a time of it at camp this morning. You see, 'Poleon Bonaparte is very particular about the way the horses are kept, but he makes Solomon do all the rubbing down, and Solomon doesn't understand how to manage horses and is a little afraid of them. 'Poleon Bonaparte found fault with his job this morning, and made him rub Nellie Grey down twice. It naturally occurred to Nellie that so much rubbing meant an opportunity for playing. Black Solomon really was the good angel at camp, for before he and Nellie Grey got us to laughing, swearing had been thick enough to cut with a knife. I had turned loose on 'Poleon, and 'Poleon had turned loose on Solomon."

"Dan, what *makes* you keep them both?"

"Keep them both! I don't. I don't want either of them, but I can't get rid of them."

"Make Napoleon do his work and send Solomon off."

"Make! Nell, how you talk! And 'Poleon's got just as much right to hire a nigger as I have to own one."

And during our stay in Charlottesville Dan's servants gave him "more trouble," he said, "than fighting the Yankees." But it was a very happy time in my life.

The late springtime of '64 found me again in Petersburg.

More vacant chairs, more broken hearts, more suffering, and starvation nearer at hand was what I found there. Milicent was spending her time in nursing the sick and wounded in the hospital, and winning from them the name that has clung to her ever since. There are old white-haired men in the South who still call her "Madonna."

Chapter 23

"Into the Jaws of Death"

One lovely morning mother sat at an upper window shelling peas for dinner. The window commanded a view of the Petersburg heights and beyond. Presently she stopped shelling peas, and gazed intently out of the window.

"What is that on the heights, Nellie?" she asked, and then, "What men are those running about on the hill beyond?"

I came to the window and looked out. The hills looked blue.

With a sinking heart I got the field-glass and turned it southeast. The hills swarmed with soldiers in Federal uniforms! Men in gray were galloping up to the reservoir and unlimbering guns. We heard the roar of cannon, the rattle of musketry. The heavens were filled with fire and smoke. Men in blue were vanishing as they came; they thought Reservoir Hill a fort. That was the ninth of June, when 125 old men and boys saved the town by holding Kautz's command, 1,800 strong, at bay on the Jerusalem Plank Road as long as they could and long enough to give Graham's and Studivant's batteries and Dearing's cavalry time to rush to the front. The Ninth of June is Petersburg's Memorial Day, her day of pride and sorrow.

A few days after—mother was shelling peas again—whiz! whack! a shell sung through the air, striking in Bolling Square. Whiz! whack! came another, and struck Mrs. Dunlop's house two doors from us. Mrs. DeVoss, our neighbour on one side, and Mrs. Williams and her two daughters who lived on the other, ran in, pale with terror, and clamoured to go down into our cellar. We were like frightened sheep. I half laugh, half cry now with vexation to think how calmly and stubbornly mother sat shelling peas in that window. She was bent on finishing her peas before she moved. Finally we induced her to go with us, and we all went down into the cellar. There we huddled together for the rest of the day, and until late into the night, not knowing what went on above or outside, little Bobby asleep in his mother's lap, and the rest of us too frightened to sleep. At last, when we had heard no guns for a long time, we crept upstairs and lay down on our beds and tried to sleep. The next morning the shelling began again. Shells flew all around us. One struck in the yard next to ours; another horrid, smoking thing dropped in our own yard. We decided that it was time to abandon the house.

As the firing came from the south and the east, and the Appomattox was on the north of the city, we could only turn to the west. Any other direction and we would have run toward the guns or into the river. With no more rhyme or reason than this in our course we started up Washington Street, running west, but without regard to the order of our going.

Crossing the railroad at Jarrett's Hotel, I saw a Confederate soldier whom I recognized as an old playmate and friend of Norfolk days. We stopped each other.

"Where did you come from, Harry?"

"Where are you running to, Nell?"

"Why, we were at Miss Anne Walker's and the shells were bursting in our yard, and we are getting out of the way."

Zip! a shell passed over my head and burst a few yards away. I didn't wait to say goodbye, but ran along Washington Street for my life. At last we got to Mr. Venable's house, which was out of the range of the guns, and there we stopped with others. Many people had passed us on our way, and we had passed many people, all running through Washington Street for dear life. Everybody seemed to be running; in Mr. Venable's house quite a crowd was gathered. His family were from home, but their friends filled the house. We watched from doors and windows, and talked of our friends who had fallen, of the Ninth of June, and of how Fort Hell and Fort Damnation got their names.

We spoke of a friend who had kissed wife and children goodbye, and gone out that fateful Ninth with the militia up the Jerusalem Plank Road to Fort Hell. Later in the day a wagon had come lumbering up to the door, blood dripping from it as it jolted along. In it lay the husband and father, literally shot to pieces. His little boy walked weeping behind it. His widow had shrouded him with her own hands, and trimmed his bier herself with the fragrant June flowers that were growing in her yard—flowers which he had loved and helped to tend. She had a house full of little ones around her. She had never known how to work, and now she was going about finding tasks to do, bearing up bravely and strengthening her children, she who had been as dependent upon her husband for love and tenderness as his children were upon her.

As the day waned we saw people hurrying past the Venable home bearing the wounded. I remember one poor fellow who was lying on a stretcher that was borne by his friends. He seemed to be shot almost to pieces. Graycoats were passing now, marching into the city.

As we sat at supper that night—a large party it was at that hospitable board—a servant brought a message to the three of us. A gentleman—a soldier—wished to see us. I went into the hall, and there was Walter Taylor. I don't think I was ever so glad to see anybody in my life. Walter was not only "Walter," but he was General Lee's adjutant, and the very sight of him meant help to us. What did mother, Millie, and I do but throw our arms around his neck and kiss him like crazy women.

"I can't stop a minute," he said. "I heard you were here, and felt that I must come out to see how you were getting along. But I *must* go straight back to my command. Let me know if I can do anything for you."

"Walter, where is Dan?"

"I don't know, Nell, but I think he will be here tonight—if he is not here already."

We felt like clinging to Walter and holding him back. I for one had lost my nerve. I was sick of war, sick of the butchery, the anguish, the running hither and thither, the fear. Soon after supper my husband came in. I was tremblingly glad to see him again, to touch his warm living body, to see that he was not maimed and mutilated—yet it hung over me all the time that he must go away in a few minutes—to come back, or be brought back—how? I kept my hand on him all the time he sat beside me. Every time he moved I trembled, feeling that it was a move to go.

"What are you doing out here?" he asked; "I thought you were at Miss Anne's and went there for you."

"We left there."

"What for?"

"The shells were flying all around us, and we were afraid, and ran out here, I tell you."

"Afraid? Why, Nell, you weren't afraid?"

"Yes, I am— I'm terrified."

"A soldier's wife—a regular campaigner!"

"I can't help it. I'm scared."

"After all you've been through, like the brave girl you are, to break down like a coward!"

"I can't help what you call me, I'm scared—I'm scared to death."

"Nell, I'm ashamed of you."

"I can't help it, Dan; I'm scared."

"What would General Stuart say if he could know?"

"I don't care what he would think. I'm terrified. I'm going to run from those shells as long as there is a place to run to. I'm not going to stand still and let a shell strike me to please anybody. I'm for getting away from town. If I had my way we'd take to the woods this night, and let the Yankees have it."

"They'd mighty soon find us in the woods."

"Then I'd move on. They can have everywhere they come to now, as far as I am concerned."

Dan looked aghast. I was completely demoralized. Knowing he must go, I summoned all my strength and braced myself for the parting, but though Dan was sorry for me, my effort to be brave was so comical that he had to laugh. By morning the range of the guns was changed, shells were flying all over the city, and our present quarters were not exempt. *Zip! zip! crack! bang!* the nasty things went everywhere.

We piled ourselves, pell-mell, helter-skelter into the first ambulance we could get and started out Washington Street again as fast as ever we could get the driver to urge his horses.

Everybody was racing out Washington Street, still running west. Pell-mell, helter-skelter, they ran, any way to get out of the range of the horrid, *whizzing, singing, zipping* bombs. We met Mr. McIlvaine driving toward town, that is, in the direction from which we were running.

He hailed us.

"Where are you going?"

"We don't know where we are going. We are not going anywhere that we know of."

"Go to my house. My family are away, but I can make you welcome. Quite a number of people are out there now."

We found this to be the literal truth. All the floors were covered with mattresses—if you rolled off your own mattress you rolled on to some one else's, for they were laid so thick that they touched. But things might always be worse.

Mr. McIlvaine had an excellent cook. She made delicious rolls and wonderful muffins and wafers, and as far as skill went our provisions were turned into delicious food. There was quite a colony—seven women besides ourselves—and we told Mr. McIlvaine that we could not expect him to feed us all, that we were thankful enough for shelter and to have our cooking done, and that we would all throw in and buy provisions. So we made a common fund, and sent for such things as could be had by Mr. McIlvaine whenever he went into town.

My husband came out to see me quite often during the weeks that followed, and Colonel Taylor and many of our military friends remembered us by dropping in to tea and spending an evening with us when they could. There was a piano in the parlour, and our evenings were often gay with singing, music, and dancing. There was but one servant on the place as I remember—the cook I have spoken of, and whom I remember vividly and affectionately for the good things to eat she set before us. To cook for us, however, was about all she could do. We had but few clothes with us, and when these got soiled there was no washerwoman to be had, so when Sue Williams said she was going to wash her clothes herself we all got up our washings, and went down into the back yard with her.

We found some tubs and drew our water, and made up some fire under a pot, as we had seen the negroes do. I can see Sue now, drawing water and lifting buckets back and forth from the well. We tied some clothes up in a sheet and put them into the pot to boil; then we put some other clothes in a tub and began to wash; meanwhile we had to keep up the fire under the pot. It was dinner hour by the time we got thus far. The weather was very hot and we were dreadfully tired, and we hadn't got any clothes on the line yet. We stopped to swallow our dinner, and went at it again. The sun was going down when we had a pile of clothes washed, rinsed, and wrung, ready for the line. We didn't know what to do about it. There didn't seem to be any precedent that we had ever known for hanging clothes out at sundown.

On the other hand, if we didn't spread them out they would mildew—we had heard of such things. If they had to be spread out, certainly there was no better place to spread them than on the line. So at sunset we hung out our clothes to dry. There were handkerchiefs on the line and a petticoat apiece. The rest of the clothes were in the pot and the tub, and they are there now for aught I know to the contrary. I don't know what became of them, but I know we went into the house and went to bed with the backache and every other sort of ache. I have never in all my life worked so hard as I worked that day trying to wash my clothes out; and the next day the clothes on the line looked yellow for all the labor that was put upon them. I have never known why they looked yellow—not for lack of work, for we had rubbed holes in some of them. We did not undertake to iron them for fear we should make them look still worse, but wore them rough dry.

Early one morning we waked suddenly, and sprang to our feet and reached for each other's trembling hands. There had been a sudden and terrific noise. The earth was shaking. That awful thunder! that horrible quaking of the earth! as if its very bowels were being rent asunder! What was it? We tried to whisper to each other through the darkness of our rooms, but our tongues were dry and palsied with fear. We feared to draw the curtains of our windows, we dared not move. That was the morning of the 30th of July, the morning when the Crater was made—when an entire regiment was blown into the air, and when into the pit left behind them Federals and Confederates marched over each other, and fought all day like tigers in a hole. If you ever go to the quaint old town of Petersburg, you can drive out the old Jerusalem Plank Road to Forts Hell and Damnation, and you can turn out of it to a large hole in the earth which is called the Crater. The last time I was at the Crater it was lined with grass; some sassafras bushes grew on the sides; down in the hollow was a peach-tree in blossom, a mocking-bird sang in it, and a rabbit hopped away as I looked down.

Soon after the explosion occurred, we saw from our windows that the McIlvaine place was swarming with soldiers who were throwing up earthworks everywhere. They were our own soldiers, of course, and we applied for an ambulance and got one, and went back in it to Miss Anne's in town.

I shall never forget how that deserted house felt when we three women and little Bobby entered it. The dust was on everything and there was a musty smell about everywhere. That night Millie had high fever. Such a wretched night as it was! no servants, no conveniences, little or no food; Millie in a raging fever, little sleepy Bobby crying for his mother and his supper; the shock of the Crater still upon us, danger underneath, overhead, everywhere. The next morning Millie's fever was lower, and she seemed better.

"We must get her away from here, or she will die," mother said.

But how? We could hear nothing of Dan, and didn't know where to find him. Mother sent a note to General Mahone by a passing soldier asking for a pass to Richmond. Her reply was an ambulance and a driver who brought a note from the general, saying that we would be taken outside of the city to the nearest point to where our trains from Richmond were allowed to come. We got Millie into the ambulance and were taken to the Dunlops', a beautiful place on the Richmond Railroad. Here we waited for a train which did not come. Night came on; still we waited, but no train. We sent into the house and asked for lodgings. Answer came that the house was full, and no more people could be taken in. Millie's fever continued to rise. We sent again, saying how ill she was, and begging for shelter for the night. The same answer was returned, and there we were out on the lawn, our shawls spread on two trunks and Millie lying on them, and looking as if every breath would be her last.

"Do you know where Colonel Walter Taylor is stationed?" I asked our driver.

"Yes, ma'am. I know exactly where he is. His camp is about a mile from here."

"How could I get a note to him?"

"I will go with it. I'll take one of the horses out of the ambulance."

I scratched off:

Dear Walter: We are out in the woods near Dunlop's without any shelter, and Millie is very ill. Can you help us?
    Affectionately,

                                     Nell.

The driver took the note and Walter came back with him.

"I don't know what to do, Nell," he said. "There is no train to Richmond till noon tomorrow, but you can't stay out here."

He went himself to the house, but without effect.

"I will send you a tent and a doctor," he said. "That is the best I can do for you. I wish I could stay here with you all and help take care of Millie tonight, but I must go back at once."

The tent came and with it Dr. Newton, and Millie was made as comfortable as was possible on the trunks.

An old negress who was passing saw our strait and brought us her pillow in a clean pillow-case, and we put that under Millie's head. We gave "aunty" some tea that we had with us, and she took it to her cabin and drew us a cup or two over her fire, and we got Millie to swallow a little of it. We had picked Bobby up off the grass, and dropped him on a pile of bags in a corner of the tent.

At one time that night we thought Millie would die—the doctor himself was doubtful if she could live till morning. When morning came she was alive, and that was all. Dr. Newton sent for a stretcher and had her lifted on it into the train. That was a terrible journey; there were many delays, and we thought we should never get to Richmond, but we were there at last. We went into the waiting-room at the station and sent for Major Grey's brother. Fortunately, he was quickly found, and took us to the house at which he boarded and where there was a vacant room. The city was crowded, and on such short notice it was the best he could do, but it was a stifling little place.

The room was small, its only window opened on a little dark hallway, there was an objectionable closet attached to the room, and the close, unwholesome air made me sick and faint as we opened the door. We laid Millie on the bed. Suddenly she gasped, moaned something that sounded like "I am dying!" and seemed to be dead.

"Air!" cried mother hopelessly, "she needs air."

But there was no window for Dick to throw up.

He picked her up in his arms, ran down the steps with her, and into the open street. The ladies in the house .all came out to us, offering help and sympathy, and with us got Millie into the parlour, where we laid her on a lounge, and where two physicians worked over her for hours before they were sure she would recover entirely from the attack. They said it was heart failure. That evening we carried her on a stretcher to the Spotswood Hotel. She was ill for two weeks. Then Bobby was ill for five. Our funds ran out. What moneys we had were in the Yankee lines and inaccessible, and Millie determined to put her education and accomplishments to use. She set herself to work to find something to do, and a lady from Staunton who happened to meet us at this time, learning that she wanted work, offered her a position in a young ladies' school. So Millie and little Bobby went to Staunton.

Chapter 24

By the Skin of Our Teeth

Not long after they left, mother and I came in from a round of calls one day to find a telegram awaiting me:

Dan wounded, but not dangerously. Come.

Gus.

I hurried into my room and changed my dress—to be careful of wearing apparel had become a pressing necessity—while mother went out to see about trains. We found there was no Petersburg train till next day; there might be one at seven in the morning. I was up at daybreak, got a cup of tea and a biscuit, looked at mother as she lay asleep, and with my satchel and little lunch basket in my hand went to the depot. There were crowds of soldiers there and a train about to start, but no woman was to go on it—it was for soldiers only. I went from one person who seemed to be in authority to another, seeking permission to go, but received the same answer everywhere—only soldiers were allowed on the train.

"But," I said at last, "I am an officer's wife, and he is wounded." I broke down with the words, and in spite of my efforts to keep them back my eyes filled with tears. It was what I should have done in the beginning. I at once got permission. I went into the car, took my seat at the extreme end and shrunk into the smallest space possible. The car was packed with soldiers and I was the only woman on board. When we were about half-way a young lieutenant who occupied part of the seat in front of me said:

"Madam, if I can be of any assistance to you, please command me. I suppose you know that our train stops within three miles of Petersburg."

"I did not know," I said, "and I do not know what to expect, or what I shall do, or where I shall find my husband, although I suppose I shall be met."

"If not," he said, "I am at your service."

No one was waiting for me at the depot; but the lieutenant secured an ambulance, got in it with me, and directed the driver to take us to Petersburg. We soon met Gus, Dan's cousin, coming to meet me in a buggy. While I was getting out of the ambulance into the buggy I was plying Gus with questions about Dan. "Dan is at our house," Gus told me. "His wound is a very ugly one, but the doctors say that he'll get well. At first we thought he wouldn't. He is shot through the thigh, and will be laid up for some time—that's what he's kicking about now."

Our most direct route to Mansfield, where Dan was, lay through Petersburg, but we could not follow that route. The Yankees were everywhere about the city, Gus said, so we went through the outer edge of Ettricks, skirting the city proper. When we reached Mansfield my husband on crutches met me at the door. He looked pale and weak, but he was very cheery and tried to joke.

"He ought not to have got up, Nell," whispered Grandmamma Grey. "He thought it would shock you to find him in bed—that is why he got up."

Of course I immediately put him under orders. He returned to bed meekly enough, and from that time I did all I could, and it was all I could do, to keep him still until his wound healed. We read and sang and played on the banjo and had a good time. But as soon as he was able to hobble he would go to camp every day and sit around. General Lee's headquarters were about a mile and a half from our house. Colonel Taylor and a number of old friends were there, and Dan could talk fight if he couldn't fight. At last he insisted that he was ready to join his division, and we set out to reach it in an ambulance drawn by three mules.

When we came to Hatchers Run we found that creek very much swollen and the bridge not visible, but there were fresh tracks showing where a wagon had lately gone over.

"That shows well enough where the bridge is," said Dan, pointing to where the wagon had left a track close to the water's edge and visible for a short way under the water.

"Follow that track," he commanded our driver, who was three-quarters of a man, being too young for a whole man and too old for a lad, "the mules will find the bridge. They are the most sure-footed animals in the world. Just let them have their heads as soon as they get in the water."

Jerry obeyed instructions. Sure enough, the mules got along well enough. That is, for a short distance. Then, splash! down they went under the water! We could just see their noses and their great ears wiggling above the surface as they struck out into a gallant swim for the opposite shore. Splash! we went in after them, and mules and ambulance were swimming and floating together. Jerry was terrified, and began to pray so hard that I got to laughing. All we could see of the mules were six ears sticking out of the water and wiggling for dear life, while our ambulance swam along like a gondola.

But things changed suddenly. Our ambulance was lifted slightly, came down with a jolt, and wouldn't. budge! The mules strained forward, but to no good. The ambulance wouldn't stir, and their harness held them back.

"The ambulance has caught on some part of the bridge," said Dan.

We were in a serious dilemma. The road was one in much use, and we pinned our hopes to some passer-by, but as we waited minutes seemed hours. No one came. Perhaps the wagon that had preceded us had given warning that the bridge was wrecked. We sat in the ambulance and waited, not knowing what to do, not seeing what we could do. By some saplings which stood in the water we measured the rise of the tide, and we measured its rise in the ambulance by my trunk—I was getting wet to my knees. Finally I sat on top of my trunk and drew my feet up after me. The situation was serious enough, and Dan began to look very anxious—Hatchers Run was always regarded as a dangerous stream in flood time. Still, no sign of anyone coming. The rain continued to fall and the water to rise.

"At this rate we are sitting here to drown," Dan said. "There's but one way out of it that I can see. From what I know of the situation of our army there must be an encampment near here. Jerry, climb out of this ambulance over the backs of these hind mules till you get to that leader. Get on him, cut him loose, and swim out of this. Ride until you find an encampment and bring us help."

But Jerry didn't look at it that way.

"I'm skeered ter fool 'long dat ar mule. I ain't nuvver fooled 'long er mule in de water. I kaint have no notion of de way he mought do wid me. You kaint 'pend on mules, Mars Dan, ter do jes lak you want 'em ter on dry land, much less in de water. Arter I git out dar, cut dat ar mule loose, an' git on him, he mought take out an' kyar me somewhar I didn't wanter go. I mought nuvver git ter no camp, nor nowhar, Mars Dan, ef I go ter foolin' 'long er dat mule out dar in de water."

The major caught his shoulders, and turned his face to the stream. "Have you watched that water rising out there for nothing?" he asked sternly. "We are sure to be drowned if you don't do as I tell you—all of us."

Between certain death and uncertain death Jerry chose the latter, crawled over the hind mules, got on the leader and rode him off. He took this note with him:

> Nearest Encampment of any Division, C. S. A.:
> I am in the middle of Hatchers Run in an ambulance with my wife. The stream is rising rapidly and ambulance filling with water. Send immediate relief.
>
> Daniel V. Grey,
Adjutant of the Thirteenth

After the boy was gone there we sat and waited while the water rose. I got very cold and Dan, who was yet weak from his wound and confinement, got chilled and stiff. After more than an hour of waiting we heard from the woods on the other side a noise as of men running, and then there came rushing out of the woods toward us thirteen men of mighty girth and stature. They were Georgia mountaineers who had been sent to our rescue. When they came to the water they didn't like the look and feel of it, and evidently didn't want to get in it.

"What is we uns to do?" they called across.

"Something to get us out of this," Dan hallooed back, "and be quick about it, or we shall drown."

"How is we uns to git to you uns?"

"Get in the water and swim here."

They talked among themselves, but none of them seemed disposed to do this.

"Men!" called my husband, "I am hardly well of a wound, I am stiff and weak. I can not save my wife, who is up to the waist in water. Will you stand there and see a woman drown?"

They seemed ashamed, but none of them made the move to go in. Then the largest of them all—he seemed a mighty giant-stepped forth and took command.

"You say thar's a lady in that ambulance?"

"Yes, my wife."

"Wall, I'm blowed! An' she ain't a-hollerin' and a-cryin'?"

"Do you hear her?" asked Dan irritably. "She's braver than some men I know. But you can count on it that she is wet and cold. We are nearly frozen!"

"Wall, I'm blowed! An' she's right out thar in the middle er that run, an' she ain't a-hollerin' and a-cryin'! Tell you uns what I'll do. I'll swim out there and bring her back on my back. An' then I'll swim back agin an' bring you on my back."

"I can't!" I said. "I'm cold enough to die now, and I can't get in that water. I'll die if I do."

The giant gave orders. The men hung back. Then we heard him roaring like a bull of Bashan.

"Git into that ar water, evvy man of you uns, an' swim fur that ar ambulance! I was put in comman' er this here expuddition, an' I means ter comman' it. 'Bey orders, you uns is got ter, or you uns'll git reported to headquarters ez I'm a sinner. Git in that thar water. Furrard! Swim!"

How well I remember the great, goodnatured giant as he swam around our ambulance, bobbing up and down, and taking in our bearings!

"You see, cap," he said, "all the bridge is washed away but the sleepers, an' that's what you uns is hung on. Unhitch them mules," to some of his men.

"Now, cap, soon's them mules is loose we uns'll lif' the ambulance off er this, an' pull you uns to shore. Jes you uns make yourse'fs easy, and we uns'll git you uns out er this."

The mules unhitched were led to shore, and then the men pulled the ambulance safely to land. I don't remember what became of the thirteen mighty men. Nor do I recall clearly the rest of that cold ride when I shivered in my clothes, but I remember getting to a house where I was seated in a great chair close to a blazing fire of hickory logs, and I remember that when I went to get out my nightdress I found all the clothes in my trunk wet, and that when I went to bed I felt as if I were going to be ill, and that I rested badly. But the next morning I was up and on my way again. Again we came to a swollen stream. This time we could see the bridge, and it wobbled about. Dan thought it was safe to drive over. But not I!

Just then some gentlemen came up behind us and insisted that I was right. So I got out of the ambulance and was helped across on some logs or beams or something which stretched across the stream underneath the bridge, and may have been a part of it, but whatever they were I thought them more secure than an ambulance and mules and an uncertain bridge. I made Dan cross this way, too, though he said it wasn't best for his leg, and made all sorts of complaints about it. The ambulance was obliged to cross on the bridge, and the devoted Jerry drove it, quarrelling and complaining and praying all the way. We had not gone much farther before, lo! here was Stony Creek, swollen to bursting, rushing and furious, and again a hidden bridge.

"I nuvver seed so much high water befo' in all my life," said Jerry, thoroughly disgusted, "nor so dang'ous. Water behin' an' befo'. We all is in a bad way."

There was a wagoner on the bank who said the bridge was all right and but slightly under water. I protested, but Dan made Jerry drive in. I wanted to turn back. But Dan argued that there was as bad behind us, and that he must get to camp by the time he was due, and after a little the mules found their footing and kept it, though the water swished and whirled over the bridge. We saw a man and a horse swept down the stream—I thought they might have been swept by the current off the very bridge we were crossing. The current was too strong for the horse; he could do nothing against it, and had given up. As they passed under a tree the man reached up, caught a sweeping branch and swung himself up in the tree; the horse was drowned before our eyes before we got across the bridge.

We left the man in the tree, but promised to send him help. There was a house two miles from the creek, and to this we drove. It was full of people; the parlour was full, the halls were full, and the kitchen and the bedrooms were full of men, women, and children. It reminded me of a country funeral where people are piled up in the halls, on the steps, and everywhere a person can stand or sit. Soldiers were always passing to and fro in those days and stopping for the night at any convenient wayside place, and as for not taking a soldier in— well, public opinion made it hot for the man who would not shelter a wayfaring soldier and share the last crust with him. The house held a large number of soldiers that night, and in addition a water-bound wedding-party. On this side the creek was the groom; on the other side the bride. The groom had on his good clothes—good clothes were a rarity then— but he looked most woebegone.

We told the people in the house about the man in the tree; and every man in the house went down to see about him.

They called out to him saying they would throw him ropes and pull him in, but when they tried to throw the ropes out to him they found that he could not be reached in that way. The tree was too far from the shore. It was after midnight when they gave up trying to reach him with ropes. Then they told him to keep his courage up till morning, and they made a great bonfire on the banks, and some of them stood by it and talked to him all night. First one party and then another would go out and stand by the bonfire, and keep it up, and talk to him. The relieved party would come to the house and warm themselves and go back again. Nobody slept that night. There was nowhere for anybody to lie down. When morning came the creek had fallen and they pulled the nearly frozen man to land.

The next day found us at our destination, Hicksford.

Chapter 25

The Beginning of the End

While I was at Hicksford I stayed at General Chambliss's. I was very happy there. Dan's camp was not far off, and he came to see me very often and every morning sent his horses to me. In my rides I used frequently to take the general's little son, Willie, along as my escort, and one morning, when several miles distant from home and with our horses' heads turned homeward, who should ride out from a bend in the road and come toward us but two full-fledged Yankees in blue uniform and armed to the teeth. My heart went down into the bottom of my horse's heels, and I suppose Willie's heart behaved the same way. We did not speak, we hardly breathed, and we were careful not to quicken our pace as we and our enemies drew nearer and nearer, and passed in that lonely road a yard between our horses and theirs.

We did not turn back; we crept along the road to the bend, until our horses' tails got well around the bend. Then Willie and I gave each other a look, and took out at a wild run for home. We went straight as arrows, and over everything in our way. I had all I could do that day to stick on Nellie Grey, who went as if she knew Yankees were behind— only in her mind it must have been the whole of Grant's army. Dan laughed our "narrow escape" to scorn, and said the two Yankees were probably Confederates in good Yankee clothes they had confiscated. At this time Confederates would put on anything they found to wear, from a woman's petticoat to a Yankee uniform, but Dan never could convince us that those two Yankees were not Yankees.

After this I rebelled less against going out, as I sometimes had to do, in "Miss Sally's kerridge." This was an old family carriage, a great coach of state with the driver's perch very high. The driver, an old family negro as venerable and shaky in appearance as the carriage, attached due importance to his office. He thought no piece of furniture on the place of such value as "Miss Sally's kerridge." He cared for the horses as if they had been babies. This part of the country had not been so heavily taxed as some others in the support of the two armies, and a little more corn than was usual could be had. Uncle Rube was sure that his horses got the best of what was going, and also that everything a currycomb could do for them was theirs. He himself when prepared for his post as charioteer wore a suit of clothes which must have been in the Chambliss family for several generations, and an old beaver hat, honourable with age and illustrious usage. When we were taken abroad in "Miss Sally's kerridge," we were always duly impressed by Uncle Rube with the honour done us. On the occasion of a grand review which took place not far from General Chambliss's residence, I, with three other ladies, went in the "kerridge." The roads were awful—in those days roads were always awful. Troops were travelling backward and forward, artillery was being dragged over them, heavy wagons were cutting ruts, and there always seemed to be so much rain.

Uncle Rube quarrelled all the way going and coming. He sat on his high perch, and guided his horses carefully along, picking the best places in the road for "Miss Sally's kerridge," and talking at us.

"It's jes gwine to ruin Miss Sally's kerridge takin' it out on sech roads as dese hyer.... Nuf to ruin er ox-kyart, dese hyer roads is, much mo' er fin' kerridge.... Well, 'tain' no use fur me ter say nothin'.... Jest well keep my mouf shut.... Monstratin' don' do er bit er good. ...When dey git it in dar haids dey's gwine, dey's gwine, don't kyeer what happens.... Ain't gwine heah nothin', dey ain't, not ontwell dey gits Miss Sally's kerridge broke up.... *I* say folks orter go ter ride when de roads is good, and stay at home when de roads is bad.... An' lemme take kyeer uv de kerridge."

With these intermittent mutterings and frank expressions of displeasure Uncle Rube entertained us until we got to the review stand.

To crown his disgust we were late in starting back home, and at dark he was leaning forward from his lofty altitude, peering into the road ahead and seeking vainly "de bes' place ter drive Miss Sally's kerridge along." He said "dar warn't no bes' place," and was in despair of ever getting that valuable vehicle home in safety. At last the crash came! Down went one carriage wheel into a mud-hole! It stuck there, and we were rooted for the time being. However, I think Uncle Rube would have got us out but for some untimely assistance. Bob Lee, the youngest of the Lees, and Bob Mason (the son of the ex-United

States Minister to France, whose home was near General Chambliss's) came riding by. They stopped and shook hands with us through the carriage window, and asserted their gallant intention of getting us out of our mud-hole. They tried to lead the horses forward, to pull and push "the kerridge" out, but in vain. Then Bob, to Uncle Rube's utter amazement and indignation, made him get down, while he, Bob, mounted the box. Uncle Rube stood on the roadside, the picture of chagrin and despair.

"Dar ain't no tellin' what's gwi' happen now!" he exclaimed. "Mars Bob don' know how ter manage dem horses no mo'n nothin'. Don', Mars Bob! Mars Bob! don' whoop 'em! Law-aw-dy!"

Bob had gathered the lines in one hand and with the other was laying the whip on Rube's pets. The horses, utterly unused to the whip, plunged like mad. There was an ominous sound!—our axle was broken, and we were helplessly stuck in the mud.

"Dar now!" wailed Uncle Rube. "What I tole you? I said Miss Sally's kerridge gwi' git ruint! and now it's done been did. It's clean ruint, Miss Sally's kerridge is. I tole Mars Bob dem horses don't know nothin' 'bout a whoop. Dey ain't nuvver bin 'quainted wid er whoop. I bin er-sayin' an' er-sayin' all erlong dat de kerridge gwi' git broke, an' it's done been did. O Lawdy!"

Our young rescuers borrowed a cart from a farmer near by and got us home in it. I have forgotten how Uncle Rube managed, if I ever knew. But I shall never forget the scene when several hours later we all sat around the fire in the sitting-room, chatting over our adventures, and Uncle Rube, hat in hand, came to the door and made report to his mistress of the family misfortune. His eyes were big as saucers. He laid the blame thick and heavy on "Mars Bob's "shoulders, exonerating his horses with great care.

"Dey's sensubble horses ef anybody jes got de sense ter manage 'em, dey is."

And then Miss Sally, in spite of her efforts to preserve a gravity befitting the calamity, broke down like the "kerridge" and laughed hysterically.

There was plenty to eat at General Chambliss's. I always remember that fact when it was a fact, because it was beginning to be so pleasant and unusual to have enough to eat. Hicksford hadn't been raided, and there were still chickens on the roost, bees in the hive, turkeys up the trees, partridges in the woods, and corn in the barns. The barn, by the way, was new, and the soldiers gave a ball in it. We all went and had a most delightful evening. I well remember that I went in "Miss Sally's kerridge," and that General Rooney Lee and I led off the ball together. I remember, too, that we had a fine supper: turkeys, chicken-salad, barbecued mutton, roast pig with an apple in his mouth, pound-cake, silver-cake, cheese-cake or transparent pudding, "floating island" or "tipsy squire;" plenty of bread, milk, sure enough coffee—everything and enough of it. We danced till morning and leaving our gallant entertainers in the gray dawn, went off to sleep nearly all day.

The next ball was in an old farmhouse where some of our cavalry were quartered. We had another good supper—everything good to eat and plenty of it—like the first. There were no chairs or furniture of any kind, as I remember, but there were benches ranged around the barn for us to sit on when resting during the pauses of the dance. After a dance with him General Rooney Lee led me back to the room where the banquet was spread to taste something especially nice which he liked and which I had not touched—eating a good thing when you could get it was a delightful and serious duty in those days. There was quite a circle around us, and we were all nibbling, laughing, chatting away as if there were no such things as war and death in the land, when a courier in muddy boots strode across the room to the general, saluted, spoke a few words, and the general walked aside with him. The music was enticing, and while the general was engaged with the courier I went back with some one else to the ballroom and took my place in the lancers. We were clasping hands and bowing ourselves through the grand chain when the dance was interrupted. The army was to march.

There was great confusion, hurried handshaking, sometimes no hand-shaking at all, no time for goodbyes. The soldiers could not stand on the order of their going. I do not remember how I came to the farmhouse, but I know that my husband bundled me unceremoniously into a cart with some people I hardly knew, and sent me home, telling me to pack my trunk but not to be disappointed if he could not take me with him. I did not lie down at all. I packed my trunk as soon as I got home, then sat down and waited, and before long my husband came for me in an ambulance. His courier, Lieutenant Wumble, was with him, and the ambulance was driven by an Irishman named Miles. The horses were tied to the back of the ambulance, and frequently my husband and Lieutenant Wumble rode ahead reconnoitring. It began to rain. "What made you always start in the rain?" I have been asked by friends to whom I was relating my campaigns. What I want to know is, what made it always rain when I started? Let me but step into an ambulance and immediately it began to rain. My movements had to be regulated by the movements of the army, not by the weather, though really the weather seemed to regulate itself by mine.

We found the roads worse as we advanced. The farther we went the deeper was the mud. Mud came up to the hubs of our wheels; the mules could hardly pull their feet up out of the miry mass in some places. At last we found ourselves regularly "stuck in the mud." There was no pushing or pulling the ambulance farther. It was nearly dark, but fortunately we were near a farmhouse, and at the side of the road where we got stuck was a stile made by blocks of unequal heights set on either side of a plank fence. These blocks were simply sections of the round body of a tree which had been sawed up. On the opposite side of the stile a pathway led to the house. The mud-hole in which our ambulance was embedded was about ten yards from the stile.

My husband insisted that I be carried bodily to the stile, and Lieutenant Wumble, who was one of the most gallant fellows in the world, took it as a matter of course that he must carry me. He urged that he had been brought along to be useful and that Dan had never recovered entirely from his wound. But Dan hooted at the idea! He was very much obliged to the lieutenant, but really he was used to this sort of thing, and understood lifting ladies about much better than Wumble. It was not altogether brute strength, but some science that was required. So Dan stepped out of the ambulance on to the side of the mud-hole, where of course the ground was not so muddy as in the centre where we were stuck, but where it was rather slippery, nevertheless. Balancing himself nicely, he took me out, but just as he poised me on his arm with scientific ease and grace he slipped and fell backward, sprawling in the mud, and I went over his head, sprawling, too.

Whereupon Lieutenant Wumble, laughing, came to pick me up, saying as he did so:

"I told you that you ought to let me carry you. Just lie there, major, and I'll come back for you as soon as I set your wife down. Keep quiet, major," as Dan swore at the mud and slipped again, "and I'll pick you up and get you along all right."

As Dan dragged himself up he was a perfect mud man, and he had left the print of himself in the mud behind him. They took us in at the farmhouse, and sent men to help the driver prize the ambulance out of the hole. They scraped the mud off me, and a coloured woman washed my clothes and hung them by the fire, so they might be dry by morning. Of course, this process put me in bed at once. Our supper was poor and the bed uncomfortable, but it was the best our hosts could do.

After an uncomfortable night we started off again toward Dinwiddie Court-house, which was to be our next stopping-place. As we journeyed on we knew that we were getting into most dangerous quarters. The nearer we drew to Petersburg the nearer we were to the tangle of Federal and Confederate lines; the nearer to skirmishers and scouts from both armies. The night got blacker and blacker—you could not see your hand before you—and the blacker it grew the more frightened old Miles became. Out of the darkness where, invisible, he sat astride the invisible mule he drove, he poured an unceasing stream of complaint.

"Arrah! the divil a bit can Oi see where Oi'm goin'. It's so dark ye couldn't see a light if there was any. The mules, intilligint crathurs they are, maybe they know where they be goin'. It's more than the loikes of me does. But what Oi've got agin a mule is that they don't know an honest Amerikin in gray clothes—or mixed rags it is now—from a nasty, thavin' Yankee."

If we were "silent for a few minutes, then Miles spoke out for company's sake, or asked unnecessary questions perhaps to find out if we were there, and that the Yankees hadn't spirited us away.

"These woods are full of Yankees," he said. "It's chock-full of them, it is. An' it's so dark, it is, they could just come out here an' kill us all, they could, an' we'd never know it."

"Shut your mouth up, you fool!" said my husband, who knew that the woods were full of Yankees. "If we can't see them they can't see us, and how are they to know but we are Yankees unless you tell them, you blathering idiot?"

"The divil a bit Oi'll be tellin' 'em, the nasty blue thaves. Thrust Miles O'Flannigan for thet. But they could just come out o' them woods, they could, an' take us all prisoners an' we'd never know it. An' the driver's the fust man they'd git, sure."

At last Dan got out, mounted his horse, and rode in front of the ambulance.

"Now," said he to Miles, "follow me, and if you open your d—— mouth again, I'll blow your brains out."

Lieutenant Wumble brought up the rear, riding behind the ambulance with a cocked pistol. And so we rode through the Egyptian darkness of the night, and the now more than Egyptian silence. Miles's mouth was effectually closed. He followed Dan, whom he could not see, by the sound of his horse's tread, and as he was careful to keep as close to him as possible we made better progress.

We had been in the darkness so long that none of us knew our whereabouts. Presently we heard the low, deep mutterings of thunder. It came nearer and grew louder rapidly. Suddenly the sky seemed rent! There came a sheet of white lightning and with it an awful crash which made my heart stand still. A tree a few feet from us had been struck. The lightning had shown us that we were only a few miles from the Court-house. I have never known such a storm as the one through which we travelled that night. One peal of thunder did not die away before another began. One instant we were in thick darkness—a darkness that could be *felt*—the next, ourselves, the woods, the road, were bathed in a fierce white light. Between the Yankees and the storm that night I think Miles would have become a gibbering idiot but for the equalizing influence of Dan's pistol.

"No trouble for the Yankees to rickonize us—ugh!" the rest of the sentence would be lost in the darkness, but I knew that Miles was feeling the salutary muzzle of Dan's pistol against some part of his face.

By the time we entered the village the storm had abated. We drove to the hotel. It was crowded, packed with soldiers; no room for us, nor food either, and nine o'clock at night!

"Two miles the other side of town there is a place of entertainment where you can be accommodated, I think," the hotel proprietor told Dan.

"I don't go any farther tonight with my wife," Dan said resolutely.

"It's not mesilf as wants to be travelling any farther aither," Miles put in. "It's divil a bit of a pleasure ride Oi'm havin'."

He was promptly silenced, and was made to drive us around to the various places in the village that had been mentioned; and in spite of the discouragements received, he added his earnest solicitations to ours that we might be lodged for the night. But in spite of our own pleas and Miles's eloquence, midnight found us out at the two-miles place. I don't know how long it had taken us to make those two miles. We had toiled over muddy roads, through fierce extremes of light and darkness, and amid deafening thunder, for the storm had come on again with renewed fury and was at its height when we stopped at the house to which we had been directed. In response to my husband's knock an old man came to the door—the meanest old man I have ever seen before or since. He said we couldn't come in, there wasn't standing room in the house, the house was full of soldiers. My husband said he *would* come in—that he had a lady with him. I think he would have shot that old man then and there rather than have carried me farther. But the old man said if he had a lady with him all the more reason why he should not come in; the soldiers were drinking, and he whispered to Dan, and I saw Dan give in. He told Dan that he had a cousin in the village who would house us, and he directed us how to get to this cousin's house, so we turned and drove back to the village we had just left. We made better time on our return, as we were better directed and took a shorter route, found the house to which we had been sent, and were taken in.

It was a strange old house, built in colonial days, with the veranda that ran all around it supported by tall Corinthian columns. We woke the owner up—an old man, who came down to the door shivering, candle in hand, and led us through a latticed room, then into another room and up a narrow flight of stairs with sharp turns to a bedroom with dormer windows and ancient furniture. We were welcome to our lodgings, he said, but he had nothing to eat in the house—we would be welcome to it if he had. He looked gaunt and hungry himself.

We had no fire. He left us his candle and went down in the dark himself and we got to bed as quickly as possible. Lieutenant Wumble, who was downstairs looking after Miles and the horses and the mules, got himself stowed away somewhere.

Next morning my husband was ill; but the old man's wife gave him some of her remedies, and with the help of a little money from me got something for us all to eat. About noon Dan insisted that he was able to travel, and that he must reach his command that day.

When we arrived at Petersburg my husband put me on the train for Richmond and bade me goodbye. It was the last time I saw him before the surrender.

CHAPTER 26

How We Lived in the Last Days of the Confederacy

Though the last act of our heroic tragedy was already beginning I was so far from suspecting it that I joined mother at the Arlington, prepared to make a joke of hardships and wring every possible drop of pleasure out of a winter in Richmond, varied, as I fondly imagined, by frequent if brief visits from Dan.

The Arlington was kept on something like the European plan, not from choice of landlady or guests but from grim necessity. Feeding a houseful of people was too arduous and uncertain an undertaking in those days for a woman to assume. Mrs. Fry, before our arrival in July, had informed her boarders that they could continue to rent their rooms from her, but that they must provide their own meals. We paid her $25 a month for our room—the price of a house in good times and in good money. During my absence in Mansfield, Hicksford, and other places, mother, to reduce expenses, had rented half of her room and bed to Delia McArthur, of Petersburg. I now rented a little bed from Mrs. Fry for myself, and set it up in the same room.

We had become so poor and had so little to cook that we did most of our cooking ourselves over the grate, each woman often cooking her own little rations. There was an old negress living in the back yard who cooked for any or all of us when we had something that could not be prepared by ourselves over the grate. Sometimes we got hold of a roast, or we would buy two quarts of flour, a little dab of lard, and a few pinches of salt and treat ourselves to a loaf of bread, which the old negress cooked for us, charging ten dollars for the baking. But as a rule the grate was all sufficient. We boiled rice or dried apples or beans or peas in our stew-pan, and we had a frying-pan if there was anything to fry.

Across the hall from us Miss Mary Pagett, of Petersburg, had a room to herself. She worked in one of the departments, and in order that she might have her meals in time she went into partnership with us. Every morning she would put in with our rations whatever she happened to have for that day, and mother would cook it and have it ready when she came. Downstairs under our room Mr. and Mrs. Sampson, their daughters Nan and Beth, and their son Don, all of Petersburg and old neighbours and friends of ours, lived, slept, cooked, and ate in two rooms, a big and a little one. They lived as we did, cooking over their grates.

Sometimes we all put what we had together and ate in company. When any of us secured at any time some eatable out of the common, if it was enough to go around we invited the others into breakfast, dinner, or tea, as the case might be. It must be understood that from the meal called "tea," the beverage from which the meal is named was nearly always omitted. Our fare was never very sumptuous—often it was painfully scanty. Sometimes we would all get so hungry that we would put together all the money we could rake and scrape and buy a bit of roast or something else substantial and have a feast.

We all bought coal in common. Mother's, mine, and Delia's portion of the coal was a ton, and we had to keep it in our room—there was no other place to store it. We had a box in our room which held a ton, and the coal was brought upstairs and dumped into that box. I can see those darkies now, puffing and blowing, as they brought that coal up those many steps. And how we had to scuffle around to pay them! For some jobs we paid in trade—only we had very little to trade off. How that room held all its contents I can't make out.

Dan sent me provisions by the quantity when he could get any and get them through to me. He would send a bag of potatoes or peas, and he never sent less than a firkin of butter—delicious butter from Orange County. The bags of peas, rice, and potatoes were disposed around the room, and around the hearth were arranged our pots, pans, kettles, and cooking utensils generally. When we bought wood that was put under the beds. In addition to all our useful and ornamental articles we had our three selves and our trunks; such clothing as we possessed had to be hung up for better keeping—and this was a time when it behooved us to cherish clothes tenderly. Then there was our laundrying, which was done in that room by ourselves.

And we had company! Certainly we seemed to have demonstrated the truth of the adage, "*Ole Virginny never tire.*" We had company, and we had company to eat with us, and enjoyed it.

Sometimes our guests were boys from camp who dropped in and took stewed apples or boiled peas, as the case might be. If we were particularly fortunate we offered a cup of tea sweetened with sugar. The soldier who dropped in always got a part—and the best part—of what we had. If things were scant we had smiles to make up for the lack of our larder, and to hide its bareness.

How we were pinched that winter! how often we were hungry! and how anxious and miserable we were! And yet what fun we had! The boys laughed at our crowded room and we laughed with them. After we bought our wood it was Robert E. Lee's adjutant who first observed the ends sticking out from under the bed; he was heartily amused and greatly impressed with the versatility of our resources.

"I confidently expect to come here some day and find a pig tied to the leg of the bed, and a brood or two of poultry utilizing waste space," said Colonel Taylor.

He wasn't so far out of the way, for we did get hold of a lean chicken once some way or other, and we tied it to the foot of the bed, and tried to fatten it with boiled peas.

We devised many small ways for making a little money. We knit gloves and socks and sold them, and Miss Beth Sampson had some old pieces of ante-bellum silk that she made into neckties and sold for what she could get. For the rest, when we had no money, we went without those things which it took money to buy. With money a bit of meat now and then, a taste of sorghum, and even the rare luxury of a cup of tea sweetened with sugar, was possible. Without money, we had to depend upon the bags of peas, dried apples, or rice.

"If I ever keep house," said Miss Mary one day when we were getting supper ready, "there are three things which shall never come into it, rice, dried apples, and peas."

Mother was at the bureau slicing bread, Delia McArthur was setting the table, I was getting butter out of the firkin and making it into prints, and Miss Mary with gloves on—whenever she had anything to do she always put gloves on—was peeling and slicing tomatoes.

"I never want to hear of rice, dried apples, or peas again!" came from all sides of the room.

"If this war is ever at an end," sighed poor mother, "I hope I may sit down and eat at a decent table again. And I fervently hope that nobody will ever set a dish of rice, peas, or dried apples before me! If they do, I shall get up and leave the table."

"Me too," I piped. "Even if I didn't hate the things I should feel sensitive on the subject and take the offering of such a dish to me as a personal reflection."

One day we agreed to have a feast. The Sampsons were to bring their contributions, Miss Mary and Delia McArthur to put in theirs as usual, and mother and I to contribute our share, of course. Each of us had the privilege of inviting a friend to tea. Our room was chosen as the common supper-room because it had fewer things in it and was less crowded than the Sampsons'. The Sampsons, in addition to their coal-box, wood-pile, bags and barrels of provisions, had one more bed than we had, and also a piano. We had our tea-party and, guests and all, we had a merry time.

I never remember having more fun in my life than at the Arlington, where sometimes we were hungry, and while the country, up to our doors, bristled with bayonets, and the air we breathed shook with the thunder of guns.

For hungry and shabby as we were, crowded into our one room with bags of rice and peas, firkins of butter, a ton of coal, a small wood-pile, cooking utensils, and all of our personal property, we were not in despair. Our faith in Lee and his ragged, freezing, starving army amounted to a superstition. We cooked our rice and peas and dried apples, and hoped and prayed. By this time our bags took up little room. We had had a bag of potatoes, but it was nearly empty, there were only a few handfuls of dried apples left—and I must say that even in the face of starvation I was glad of that!—and there was a very small quantity of rice in our larder. We had more peas than anything else.

I had not heard from my husband for more than a week—indeed, there seems to have been in Richmond at this time a singular ignorance concerning our reverses around Petersburg. There were hunger and nakedness and death and pestilence and fire and sword everywhere, and we, fugitives from shot and shell, knew it well, but, somehow, we laughed and sang and played on the piano—and never believed in actual defeat and subjugation.

Sunday morning, the second of April, as President Davis sat in his pew at St. Paul's Church, a slip of paper was brought to him. He read it, quietly arose, and left the church.

General Lee advised the evacuation of Richmond by eight o'clock that night. That was what rumour told us at the Arlington. At first we did not believe it, but as that spring day wore on we were convinced.

The Sabbath calm was changed to bustle and confusion—almost into riot. The streets were full of people hurrying in all directions, but chiefly in the direction of the Danville depot. Men, women, and children jostled each other in their haste to reach this spot. Loaded vehicles of every description rattled over the pavements.

During the day proclamation was made that all who wished could come to the Commissary Department and get anything they wanted in the way of provisions—without pay. I for one, in spite of my loathing for dried apples and peas, and a lively objection to starvation, would not entertain the thought at first. But the situation was serious. We discussed it in council, sitting around our room on beds, chairs, trunks, and the floor. We could not foresee the straits to which we might be brought. We considered that the evacuation of Richmond implied we knew not what. Unless we provided now by laying in some stores we might actually starve. Besides, Mrs. Sampson said she was just *bound* to have a whole barrel of flour, and she was going for it. That declaration wound up the conference.

Mother said she would go with Mrs. Sampson, and I must needs go, I thought, to protect mother. We put on our bonnets—home-made straw trimmed with chicken feathers—and started. Such a crowd as we found ourselves in! such a starveling mob! I got frightened and sick, and mother and Mrs. Sampson were daunted. We had not gone many squares before we changed our course, and went to Mrs. Taylor's (Colonel Walter Taylor's mother) and I ran up the steps and asked her to lend us Bob, her youngest son, who was at home then, for our escort.

She and Bob explained regretfully that he could not serve us. Walter was to be married that day, and Bob had his hands full at home.

"Married?" I cried in astonishment. I had known of his engagement, and that he expected to be married as soon as possible, but marrying at this crisis was incredible.

"Yes," said Bob. "I took the despatch to Betty while she was at church this morning. He told her to be ready and he would come to Richmond this afternoon for the ceremony. You see, General Lee is going to move the army west, and nobody knows for how long it will be gone, nor what will happen, and if Betty is married to Walter she can go to him if he gets hurt."

Of course, as Bob had to make all the necessary arrangements for the event his escort at the present moment was out of the question.

Somehow Mrs. Sampson managed to get her barrel of flour and

have it brought to her room, but we didn't get anything.

That afternoon as I sat at my window I saw Walter ride up to the Crenshaws', where Betty was staying. He remained in the house just long enough for the ceremony to be performed, came out, sprang on his horse, and rode away rapidly.

President Davis and his Cabinet left Richmond that afternoon in a special train. Everybody who could go was going. We had no money to go with, though we did not know where we would have gone if the money had been forthcoming.

As darkness came upon the city confusion and disorder increased. People were running about everywhere with plunder and provisions. Barrels and boxes were rolled and tumbled about the streets as they had been all day. Barrels of liquor were broken open and the gutters ran with whisky and molasses. There were plenty of straggling soldiers about who had too much whisky, rough women had it plentifully, and many negroes were drunk. The air was filled with yells, curses, cries of distress, and horrid songs. No one in the house slept. We moved about between each other's rooms, talked in whispers, and tried to nerve ourselves for whatever might come. A greater part of the night I sat at my window.

In the pale dawn I saw a light shoot up from Shockoe Warehouse. Presently soldiers came running down the streets. Some carried balls of tar; some carried torches. As they ran they fired the balls of tar and pitched them onto the roofs of prominent houses and into the windows of public buildings and churches. I saw balls pitched on the roof of General R. E. Lee's home. As the day grew lighter I saw a Confederate soldier on horseback pause almost under my window. He wheeled and fired behind him; rode a short distance, wheeled and fired again; and so on, wheeling and firing as he went until he was out of sight.

Coming up the street from that end toward which his fire had been directed and from which he had come, rode a body of men in blue uniforms. It was not a very large body, they rode slowly, and passed just beneath my window. Exactly at eight o'clock the Confederate flag that fluttered above the Capitol came down and the Stars and Stripes were run up. We knew what that meant! The song "On to Richmond!" was ended—Richmond was in the hands of the Federals. We covered our faces and cried aloud. All through the house was the sound of sobbing. It was as the house of mourning, the house of death.

Soon the streets were full of Federal troops, marching quietly along. The beautiful sunlight flashed back everywhere from Yankee bayonets. I saw negroes run out into the street and falling on their knees before the invaders hail them as their deliverers, embracing the knees of the horses, and almost preventing the troops from moving forward. It had been hard living and poor fare in Richmond for negroes as well as whites; and the negroes at this time believed the immediate blessings of freedom greater than they would or could be.

The saddest moment of my life was when I saw that Southern Cross dragged down and the Stars and Stripes run up above the Capitol. I am glad the Stars and Stripes are waving there now. But I am true to my old flag too, and as I tell this my heart turns sick with the supreme anguish of the moment when I saw it torn down from the height where valour had kept it waving for so long and at such cost.

Was it for this, I thought, that Jackson had fallen? for this that my brave, laughing Stuart was dead—dead and lying in his grave in Hollywood under the very shadow of that flag floating from the Capitol, in hearing of these bands playing triumphant airs as they marched through the streets of Richmond, in hearing of those shouts of victory? O my chevalier! I had to thank God that the kindly sod hid you from all those sights and sounds so bitter to me then. I looked toward Hollywood with streaming eyes and thanked God for your sake. Was it to this end we had fought and starved and gone naked and cold? to this end that the wives and children of many a dear and gallant friend were husbandless and fatherless? to this end that our homes were in ruins, our State devastated? to this end that Lee and his footsore veterans were seeking the covert of the mountains?

Chapter 27

Under the Stars and Stripes

The Arlington is one-half of a double house, a veranda without division serving for both halves. Just before noon up rode a regiment of Yankees and quartered themselves next door. We could hear them moving about and talking, and rattling their sabres. But I must add that they were very quiet and orderly. There was no unnecessary noise. They all went out again, on duty, I suppose, leaving their baggage and servants behind them. They did not molest or disturb us in any way. After a while we heard a rap on the door, and on opening it three men entered. They were fully armed, and had come, as they said, to search the house for rebels. The one who undertook to search our rooms came quite in and closed the door while his companions went below. He was very drunk. Anxious to get rid of him quickly I helped him in his search.

He touched my arm and whispered: "Sis, I'm good Secesh as you—but don't say nothin' about it."

"You'd better look thoroughly," I insisted, pretending not to hear him.

Going to the bed I threw the mattress over so he could see that no one was concealed beneath. He followed and touched my arm again.

"Good Secesh as you is, sis. I ain't agwine to look into nothin', sis."

"There's nothing for you to find," I informed him, as I pulled a bureau drawer open for his inspection.

He waved it away with scorn. "I," he repeated, touching his breast, "am good Secesh. Don't want to see nothin'. Don't you say nothin'—I'm good Secesh as you is, sis."

I led the way into the next room to be searched, he following, asseverating in tipsy whispers, "Good Secesh as you is, sis," every few minutes.

We found little Ruf Pagett cleaning his gun.

"Better hide that, sonny," said our friend, glancing around. "That other fellow out there, *he'll* take it from you. But *I* won't take it from you. I won't take nothin'. I'm good Secesh as you is, bud. Hide your gun, bud."

Downstairs our friends were having a harder time. The men who went through their rooms searched everywhere, and tumbled their things around outrageously. I could hear Mrs. Sampson quarrelling. They went away, but returned to search again. She said she wouldn't stand it—she would report them. She saw General Weitzel and made her complaint, and he told her that the men were stragglers and had no authority for what they had done. If they could be found they would be punished. Before this time the fire had been brought under control. Houses not a square from us had been in flames. What saved us was an open space between us and the nearest house which had been on fire, and wet blankets. Mrs. Fry's son had had wet blankets spread over our roof for protection, and we had also kept wet blankets hung in our windows. At one time, however, cinders and smoke had blown into my room till the air was stifling and the danger great.

A niece of my husband's, a beautiful girl of eighteen, who had been ill with typhoid fever, had to be carried out of a burning house that night and laid on a cot in the street. She died in the street and I heard of other sick persons who died from the terror and exposure of that time.

As night came on many people were wandering about without shelter, amid blackened ruins. In the Square numbers were huddled for the night under improvised shelter or without any protection at all. But profound quiet reigned—the quiet of desolation as well as of order. The city had been put under martial law as soon as the Federals took possession; order and quiet had been quickly established and were well preserved. Our next-door neighbours were so quiet that with only a wall between we sometimes forgot their presence.

I must tell of one person who did not weep because the Yankees had come. That was a little girl in the house who clapped her hands and danced all around.

"The Yankees have come! the Yankees have come!" she shouted, "and now we'll get something to eat. I'm going to have pickles and molasses and oranges and cheese and nuts and candy until I have a fit and die."

She soon made acquaintances next door. The soldiers or their servants gave her what she asked for. She stuffed herself with what they gave her, and that night she had a fit and died, as she had said in jest she would, poor little soul!

That afternoon there was a funeral from the house, and all day there were burials going on in Hollywood.

Early on the morning of the third, when Miss Mary Pagett threw open her blinds, she beheld the gallery under her window lined with sleeping Yankees. When Delia McArthur and I went out for a walk we came upon Federal soldiers asleep on the sidewalks and everywhere there was a place for weary men to drop down and rest. In all this time of horror I don't think anything was much harder than making up our minds to "draw rations from the Yankees." We said we *would* not do it—we *could* not do it!

But as hunger gained upon us and starvation stared us in the face Mrs. Sampson rose up in her might!

"I'll take anything I can get out of the Yankees!" she exclaimed. "They haven't had any delicacy of feeling in taking everything we've got! I'm going for rations!"

So Mrs. Sampson nerved herself up to the point where she took quite a pleasure and pride in her mission. But not so with the rest of us. It was a bitter pill, hard, hard to swallow. Mother, to whose lot some species of martyrdom was always falling, elected to go with Mrs. Sampson. So forth sallied these old Virginia matrons to "draw rations from the Yankees." However, once on our way to humiliation we began to console ourselves with thoughts of the loaves and fishes. We would have enough to eat—sugar and tea and other delights! Presently mother and Mrs. Sampson returned, each with a dried codfish! There was disappointment and there was laughter.

As each stately matron came marching in, holding her codfish at arm's length before her, Delia McArthur and I fell into each other's arms laughing. Besides the codfish, they had each a piece of fat, strong bacon about the size of a handkerchief folded once, and perhaps an inch thick. Now, we had had no meat for a great while, and we were completely worn out with dried apples and peas, so we immediately set about cooking our bacon. Having such a great dainty and rare luxury, we felt ourselves in a position to invite company to dinner. Mrs. Sampson invited half of the household to dine with her, and we invited the other half. Soon there was a great sputtering and a delicious smell issuing from the Sampsons' apartments and from ours.

Mother sliced the meat into the pan, and I sat on the floor and held it over the fire, while Delia spread the table. There was a pot on, which had to be stirred now and then. I, who always had a fertile brain in culinary matters, suggested that the potatoes—I neglected to state that a handful of potatoes had been dealt out with our rations—should be sliced very thin and dropped into the pan with the meat; and this done I fried them quite brown, taking much pains and pride in the achievement. Mother dished up the peas and set them on the table before our guests; and I passed around the fried meat and potatoes in the frying-pan, from which the company, with much grace and delicacy, helped themselves. Oh, how delicious it was!

As for the codfish, we had immediately hung that out of the window. The passer-by in the street below could behold it, dangling from its string, a melancholy and fragrant codfish. From Mrs. Sampson's window just below ours hung another melancholy codfish just like the one above it. We paid the old negress to do things for us with codfish—but not a whole codfish at a time. We cut off pieces of it, and so made good bargains, and one codfish go as far as possible. We had by this time got to a place where economy was not only a virtue but a necessity of the direst sort.

The last time I was in Richmond I took my children by the Arlington and pointed out to them the window from which our codfish hung.

And now Betty Taylor—Walter's bride—and I began planning to run through the Yankee lines together and join our husbands.

We did not think even then, you see, that the war was over. Our faith was still crediting superhuman powers to Lee and his skeleton army. Then there was President Davis's proclamation issued from Danville, wherein we found encouragement for hope. Then came the blow. We heard that Lee had surrendered. Lee surrendered! that couldn't be true! But even while we were refusing to believe it General Lee, accompanied, as I remember, by one or two members of his staff, rode up to his door. He bared his weary gray head to the people who gathered around him with greetings and passed into his house.

Hope was dead at last. But other things, precious and imperishable, remained to us and to our children—the things that make for loyalty and courage and endurance—an invincible faith—the enduring record of heroic example. Lee had surrendered, but Lee was still himself and our own—a heritage to be handed down by Americans to America when sectional distinctions have been swallowed up in the strength of a Union great enough to honour every son, whatever his creed, who has lived and died for "conscience' sake."

Sitting in my window that sorrowful day I saw three officers in gray uniforms galloping rapidly along Main Street. I recognized familiar figures in them all before they came as far as the Arlington. One turned out of Main Street, riding home to his wife, as I knew, before they reached the window; another did the same.

The third came galloping past.

I thrust my head out of the window. .

"Walter!" I called.

He looked up.

"Hello, Nell!" he cried, waving his hat around his head and galloping on.

He was on his way to his bride from whom he had parted at the altar.

But even at this supreme moment of their lives he and Betty were good enough to remember me, and in a few hours after I hailed him from the window Walter called.

"Where is Dan?" was my first question.

"I don't know, Nell," he answered. "But I know he's alive and well and will be along in a few days."

That was all the comfort I got from any friends returning from the field.

A little later there was a grand review of Federal troops in Richmond, and I remember how well-clad and sleek they were and how new and glittering were their arms. Good boots, good hats, a whole suit of clothes to every man—a long, bright, prosperous-looking procession. On the sidewalk a poor Confederate in rags and bootless, stood looking wistfully on.

The next day I heard that General Rooney Lee had arrived, and I went to see him. I was shown up to his mother's room, and she told me that he had not come, but was hourly expected. When I called the next day I met him and Miss Mildred Lee in the door. They were going out, but the general stepped back with me into the hall.

"I came to see if you could tell me anything about Dan, general."

"Mrs. Grey," he said, "you know Dan as well as I do. He isn't whipped yet. I told him it was all foolishness, and that the war was over, but he wouldn't surrender with me, and is going through to Johnston's army. But he will have to come back, and he will be here soon, I think. Johnston's army has surrendered."

"You think then that nothing has happened to him, general?"

"Oh, no. I am sure of that."

General Lee dropped his voice.

"Mrs. Grey, it may be several days before Dan gets in. In the meanwhile let me supply your wants as best I can. You should not mind applying to me or accepting assistance from me."

"I appreciate your kindness more than I can tell you, general, but I don't really need anything."

"If you should stand in need of money or assistance of any kind before Dan gets in, let me know, won't you?"

"Indeed I will, dear general."

We all three walked down Franklin Street together until Miss Mildred, who was going to see some friends on Grace Street, had to turn. After the two had just turned the corner I heard the general say:

"Wait for a minute, Mildred."

He slipped back, put his hand in his pocket, and took out a thin roll of bills, a very thin roll.

"Mrs. Grey," he said, "here is all the money I have in the world, ten dollars in greenbacks. Take half of it—I wish you would—it wouldn't inconvenience me at all. I will make some more soon, and then I will divide with you again until Dan comes home."

I could hardly speak for tears. At that moment I was richer than my general. I had at home in gold and greenbacks more money than General Lee.

"God bless you, general!" I managed to say. "But really I don't need it. If I do really and truly I will come to you for it."

Franklin Street wasn't a good place to cry in, so I hurried home.

Still the days that passed did not bring me Dan. I became thoroughly miserable. I sat in my window and watched and was cross if anybody spoke to me.

One day a servant brought up a message:

"Er gent'man in de parlour to see yer, missy."

"What sort of a 'gent'man' is it?" I asked tartly. There was but one man in the world I wanted to see or hear about just then.

"He ain't lak our people, missy. He's furrin—French or suppin nuther. He say how he usen ter know yer in Petersburg. An' how you lent 'im some—er—music—er suppin lak dat. An' he got—er—errah—suppin—I clar fo' de Lord, missy, I dunno what 'tis—but he got suppin "

"Oh, I know," I said. "He's that old French music-teacher, and he's brought back that old music I lent him in the year one. Go tell him that I don't want it; he can have it."

Jake departed only to return in a more perplexed frame of mind and state of speech.

"He say how 'tain't no music he's got fur yer. He say—he do say, missy—but de Lord knows I dunno what he say!—but anyway be bleeged to see yer."

I got up and went down to the parlour in desperation.

Sure enough, it was the little French music-teacher, and he began apologies, acknowledgments and what not in his dreadful English.

"*Madame*, I haf no mooseek to you—not at all. I haf one message of you to ze majaire. If you not b'lief me," he fumbled in his pocket and brought out a dirty bit of paper, "look at ze cart—vat sail I call him? ze lettaire. If *madame* vill look—I beg ze pardon of *madame*"

I snatched the paper out of his hand. And then—I couldn't make it out. Written in the first place with an indifferent pencil on a worn bit of the poor paper of that day and carried in the little Frenchman's very ragged and grimy pocket, the scrawl was illegible. It had never been more than a line of some five or six words. While I was trying to make it out the little Frenchman explained that it was merely a line introducing himself as the bearer of a message.

What that message was I never did hear, though the little Frenchman did his best to deliver and I to receive it. I got enough out of him, however, to know that Dan was well and on his way to Richmond. I also understood that he was not far from Richmond now, but what was detaining him I could not make out, though the little Frenchman, with many apologies, conveyed the hint to me that it was a delicate matter. After he was gone I wondered why I was so stupid as not to get the little man's address so that I could send some friends who understood French after him. From what he had said I had inferred that my husband would be with me the following day. I watched in a fever of impatience, but two days passed and no Dan.

The third night as I laid my aching head on the pillow I said: "Mother, if he don't come tomorrow, the next day I start out to look for him."

Do you know how it is to feel in your sleep that some one is looking at you? This is the sort of sensation that aroused me the next morning, and I opened my eyes in the early dawn to find my husband standing by the bed with clasped hands looking down at me.

Ah, we were happy—we were happy! Ragged, defeated, broken,

we but had each other and that was enough.

But there is a ludicrous side that I must tell you. I must explain how Dan was dressed. He wore a pair of threadbare gray trousers patched with blue; they were much too short for him, and there were holes which were not patched at all; he had no socks on, but wore a ragged shoe of one size on one foot, and on the other a boot of another size and ragged too; he had on a blue jacket much too small for him—it was conspicuously too short, and there was a wide margin between where it ended and his trousers began, and he had on a calico shirt that looked like pink peppermint candy. Set back on his head was an old hat, shot nearly all to pieces—you could look through the holes, and it had tags hanging around where the brim had been. He was a perfect old ragman except for the very new pink shirt.

"My dear Dan," I said, "what a perfect fright you are! What a dreadful ragtag and bobtail!"

"Why, Nell," he said, "I thought these very good clothes. What's missing, my dear? My suit is very complete; whole trousers, jacket, new shirt, hat on my head, even down to something on both feet. Last week I didn't have any shirt, nor any jacket to speak of, and my trousers weren't patched and I didn't have anything on my feet. One reason I took so long to get here was because I was trying to get a few clothes together—I wasn't dressed to my taste, you see. It took much time and labour to collect all this wearing apparel. I got first one piece and then another, until I am as you see me, fit to enter Richmond. Somebody stole my trousers one morning—I was in an awful plight. That was the time the little Frenchman passed and I sent you a message. Did he tell you that I'd get home as soon as I got another pair of trousers if somebody didn't steal my jacket by that time?"

I was laughing and crying all the time he was talking. When I pulled off boot and shoe I found that he had spoken the truth in jest when he said he had been walking barefoot nearly all the way. His feet were sore. I had some good shoes for him, and I got out an old civilian suit that he had worn before the war. It didn't fit him now and looked antiquated, but he donned it with great satisfaction.

Then we went out shopping. It was shopping in a city of ruins. As we walked along the streets there were smoking pits on each side of us. Here and there the remnants of what had been a store enabled us to purchase shoes at one place and the materials for two white shirts at another, and to our great joy we found a hat for which he paid two dollars, United States money.

We had nothing on which to begin life over again, but we were young and strong, and began it cheerily enough. We are prosperous now, our heads are nearly white; little grandchildren cluster about us and listen with interest to grandpapa's and grandmamma's tales of the days when they "fought and bled and died together." They can't understand how such nice people as the Yankees and ourselves ever could have fought each other. "It doesn't seem reasonable," says Nellie the third, who is engaged to a gentleman from Boston, where we sent her to cultivate her musical talents, but where she applied herself to other matters, "it doesn't seem reasonable, grandmamma, when you could just as easily have settled it all comfortably without any fighting. How glad I am I wasn't living then! How thankful I am that 'Old Glory'" floats alike over North and South, now!"

And so am I, my darling, so am I!

But for us—for Dan and me—we could almost as easily give up each other as those terrible, beloved days. They are the very fibre of us.

www.ingramcontent.com/pod-product-compliance
Lightning Source LLC
Chambersburg PA
CBHW031306150426
43191CB00005B/97